# POLICE ETHICS



*Police Ethics: The Corruption of Noble Cause*, Fifth Edition, provides an analysis of corruption in law enforcement organizations. The authors argue that the noble cause—a commitment to "doing something about bad people"—is a central "ends-based" police ethic. This fundamental principle of police ethics can paradoxically open the way to community polarization and increased violence, however, when officers violate the law on behalf of personally held moral values. This book is about the power that police use to do their work and how it can lead police officers to abuse their positions at the individual and organizational levels. It provides students of policing with a realistic understanding of the kinds of problems they will confront in the practice of police work.

This new edition offers police administrators direction for developing agency-wide corruption prevention strategies through an application of the Model of Circumstantial Corruptibility. In response to recent issues affecting the relationship between police departments and minority communities, like the Black Lives Matter organization and the death of George Floyd, this new edition provides workable solutions. Finally, this edition contains a discussion on what might be an emerging trend in American policing the authors call the over-politicization of the policing function.

**Jeffrey D. Dailey** is Professor in the Department of Security Studies and Criminal Justice at Angelo State University. He received his Masters of Science degree in Criminal Justice from Eastern Kentucky University and Ph.D. in Criminal Justice from Sam Houston State University. He has authored several books on the topics of intelligence, homeland security and border security.

**Brian L. Withrow** is Professor at Texas State University, San Marcos. Prior to his scholarly career, Brian worked for the Texas Department of Public Safety. He started this part of his career in 1981 as State Trooper in a rural part of the Texas Panhandle, rising to the rank of Training Officer, Inspector, and Bureau Commander. Withrow earned his Bachelor of Arts degree in Criminal Justice from Stephen F. Austin State University, his Master of Public Administration from Southwest Texas State University, and his Ph.D. in Criminal Justice from Sam Houston State University.

**Michael A. Caldero** was a former police officer who presented seminars on the subject of police ethics to police commanders across the United States. He taught in the Department of Administration of Criminal Justice at Bellevue College.

# POLICE ETHICS

## THE CORRUPTION OF NOBLE CAUSE

FIFTH EDITION

JEFFREY D. DAILEY

BRIAN L. WITHROW

MICHAEL A. CALDERO

Routledge
Taylor & Francis Group
NEW YORK AND LONDON

Designed cover image: Alfred Georg Sonsalla via Getty Images

Fifth edition published 2026
by Routledge
605 Third Avenue, New York, NY 10158

and by Routledge
4 Park Square, Milton Park, Abingdon, Oxon, OX14 4RN

*Routledge is an imprint of the Taylor & Francis Group, an informa business*



[First edition published by Routledge 2006]
[Fourth edition published by Routledge 2018]

ISBN: 978-1-041-04120-7 (hbk)
ISBN: 978-1-041-04089-7 (pbk)
ISBN: 978-1-003-62691-6 (ebk)

DOI: 10.4324/9781003626916

Typeset in Sabon
by Apex CoVantage, LLC

For Sam
For Buck
For Jeffrey Allen

# Table of Contents

Preface ix

Introduction 1

Part 1
Value-Based Decision-Making
and the Ethics of Noble Cause 11

Chapter 1
Value-Based Decision-Making: Understanding
the Ethics of Noble Cause 15

Chapter 2
Values, Hiring, and Early Organizational Experiences 53

Chapter 3
Values and Administrative Dilemmas 75

Chapter 4
The Social Psychology of Cops' Values 95

Part 2
Noble-Cause Corruption 117

Chapter 5
From Economic to Noble-Cause Corruption 119

Chapter 6
Stress, Organizational Accountability, and the Noble Cause 151

Chapter 7
Ethics and the Means-Ends Dilemma 175

Chapter 8
Police Culture, Ends Orientation, and Noble-Cause Corruption 203

Part 3
Ethics and Police in a Time of Change 239

Chapter 9
Policing Citizens, Policing Communities: Toward an Ethic of Negotiated Order 243

Chapter 10
The Stakes 277

Chapter 11
Recommendations 301

Chapter 12
Conclusion: The Noble Cause 325

Bibliography 331

Name Index 349

Subject Index 353

# Preface

On Friday, October 9, 1981, I stood with all of my academy classmates, raised my right hand, and took an oath.

> I, Brian Withrow, do solemnly swear, that I will faithfully execute the duties of the office of State Trooper of the State of Texas, and will to the best of my ability preserve, protect, and defend the Constitution and laws of the United States and of this state, so help me God.

A few days later, I was at my first duty assignment—Childress, a small town in the Texas Panhandle. It took about 50 minutes to move everything I owned into my rented duplex. Just as I was thinking about a trip to the grocery store, my sergeant arrived and invited me to supper at his house. Probably the most enduring value among Troopers in the Texas Department of Public Safety is that we looked after each other.

The next day, I woke up at 5:00 A.M., polished my boots, ironed my uniform, cleaned my service revolver, and treated the leather on my new Sam Browne belt. At 7:00 A.M., I left my house and drove to the area office on the outskirts of town. My commute was ten minutes. When I arrived, my sergeant was waiting for me. We completed some paperwork. He introduced me to some of the other Troopers and the Police Communicators. Then we went to town for a round of introductions to various public officials—judges, clerks, elected officials, the local police chief, the county sheriff, the school superintendent, businessmen, bankers, pastors, and everyone in that small town that might have anything at all to do with my work.

Just before noon, he asked me, *How much money do you have in your wallet right now?* I retrieved my wallet from my back pocket, counted the bills, and reported to him, *$42.00. Good*, he said. *Let's go eat lunch.* At that moment, I remembered that in my morning nervousness, I had overlooked eating breakfast. I was famished.

We drove to a little diner on the outskirts of town. My sergeant explained, *The reason I asked you how much money you had is because you really cannot predict how much it will cost to eat lunch at this place. When the owner is happy with us, he encourages us to eat here by giving us half-priced meals. He thinks the marked patrol cars parked in front of the diner deter would be robbers and other riff-raff. If he is angry with us, he charges us full price. One of the other troopers issued the owner's son a speeding ticket last week, so I do not know whether or not he is still mad at us. So I wanted to be sure you had enough cash to pay your bill.* This was before the days of debit cards or automatic cash machines, and I didn't even have a checking account at the local bank. I was glad he asked.

On the way into the diner, I thought of my dad, who was a Dallas police officer. I recalled that he occasionally talked about free coffee, half-priced meals, and the occasional bottle of whiskey at Christmas from local liquor stores. He disliked this practice. In his words, *It offends me that these guys think they can "rent" private security services from us for half the price of a cup of coffee.*

When the bill for lunch arrived at our table, it was evident that the owner had forgiven my colleague. It was exactly half-price. At that moment, I chose to leave enough cash at the table to cover the full price of my meal plus a gratuity. The sergeant commented, *You left too much money*. Cautiously, I explained that I had decided not to participate in the half-price game. *It just doesn't feel right*, I explained. He smiled and said, *I understand. I do the same thing.*

A conscience is present in every human being. It is the origin of that little feeling we get when something just does not "feel" right. The challenge to behaving ethically is to teach ourselves to listen to our conscience and, through reason, respond to it appropriately.

One way of doing this is to treat the conscience like a muscle. Generally, the more a muscle is used, the more efficient it becomes. This is also true in how we are able to listen and then respond to feelings that come from our conscience. So it would seem reasonable to spend some time teaching ourselves to listen to our conscience and making preliminary decisions *before* we are confronted with an ethical question. This is how an ethical conscience is formed.

Something about accepting a half-priced meal caused my conscience to question the diner owner's motivation. I did not deserve it. And my time and attention as a State Trooper had already been purchased by the taxpayers. So realizing a personal gain in providing additional private security for an obscure diner on the edge of small town in the Texas panhandle, no matter how brief, just didn't feel right. So I made the decision to never accept free or reduced priced meals, goods, or services offered because of my official capacity.

The same sort of mental calisthenics is useful in preparing for other potential ethical issues. Although this may require one to write an occasional fictional script or even daydream. For example, one day, a colleague told me about a traffic stop wherein the violator handed him his driver's license with a folded $20.00 bill underneath it—a clear attempt at bribery. Thinking through how I might respond to this, I came to the conclusion that I would simply hand the $20.00 bill back to the violator and tell him that it was "stuck" under his driver's license. Or if I am feeling ornery, I may give it back to the violator folded into the speeding ticket.

As we progress further into our careers, ethical dilemmas tend to get more complicated. *How would I respond to a potential vendor who wants to take me to an expensive restaurant or offers me free tickets to a game? What if my partner suggests overcharging a suspect in order to increase the probability of him pleading out to a lesser charge? What if an employee of mine informs me of a coworker's addiction to illegal drugs? What if I overhear a colleague tell an offensive racist joke?*

My experience teaches me that regardless of the seriousness of the ethical dilemma, my conscience is capable of generating an uncomfortable feeling. My task is to listen to this feeling and then to develop a reasoned response to satisfy this nagging feeling.

*Brian L. Withrow, Ph.D.*
*Texas State University*
San Marcos, Texas

# Introduction

Officers stroll into the room and take seats. In the back of the room, there are the usual coffee dispensers for decaf and regular, Styrofoam cups, a plate of bagels and sweet rolls, and a tray of fruit with too much rind left on the cantaloupe. Today, the command staff is attending a lecture on police ethics, and the speaker, Michael A. Caldero, is from a northwestern city. The chief walks in, chats briefly with a couple of the officers, and takes a seat in the back of the room. In the minds of the officers is a single sentiment. Who in the heck is this person telling me about police ethics?

That's what the audience thinks when Mike begins his presentation on police ethics. This sentiment is expressed in several ways.

- What does education have to contribute to police work?
- Forget everything you learned in a book. Here's how we do it on the street.
- An outsider can never understand police work.
- Why do I have to waste my time listening to this crap?
- His experience is with another agency. We don't work that way here.

Mike has heard it all. When they don't say it, they are thinking it. No one wants to hear a discussion on ethics. Ethics is learned in the streets. It's about victims and the assholes who prey on them. Mike organizes his materials and prepares to begin. He has talked to commanders before. They're accustomed to leaving a lot unsaid.

He begins. *Why are you people here today?*

A commander responds. "Same reason you are."

Mike laughs at this comment. It's the laugh of a cop. It's a half-second late. Like he's heard something hidden in what you said that even you don't know.

DOI: 10.4324/9781003626916-1

We put the question to you, reader. Why are you reading this book?

Chances are that if you're reading this book, it's because you have to, so you might as well grin and bear it. You can bet that your instructor will test you on the material!

More importantly, we have something to say. Something that we think is important. Something we believe in. Our message is vigilance. The danger here, though, is not from predatory offenders or dangerous, unknown circumstances. The question central to our inquiry is this: How well do you know yourself?

This is a different kind of book on police ethics. We provide very little discussion of ethical dilemmas such as accepting free gifts and the like and then only as a secondary issue. If you're a police officer, you have department policies that clearly state what you are permitted to do and what is illegal or inappropriate. Whether or not you accept gratuities, you know when you are doing right or wrong by your department. In this book, we have our sights set on a different kind of ethical issue, one less clear but more important.

This book aims squarely at noble-cause corruption. What do we mean by noble-cause corruption? It is corruption committed in the name of good ends, corruption that happens when police officers care too much about their work. It is corruption committed in order to get the bad guys off the streets, to protect the innocent and the children from the predators that inflict pain and suffering on them. It is the corruption of police power, when officers do bad things because they believe that the outcomes will be good.

Some readers will no doubt feel betrayed by our approach to ethics. At times, we will seem too quick to criticize the police, to make them out to be bad guys. Without a doubt, we are raising moral questions about the behavior of police officers who see themselves as warriors against evil, the guardians of the thin blue line between order and disorder. Noble-cause corruption is a difficult topic to write about because we are committed to the police and because we also carry the beliefs that drive the noble cause. Yet in today's world of intricate social and legal complexity, we recognize that there has to be a limit on the zeal police show for their work. All too often, as you will see in this book, there is not.

The time for discussing the ethics of police power is long overdue. It is a neglected topic, though a few researchers are beginning to acknowledge its importance in today's world (Carter, 1999; Barker and Carter, 1999; Kraska and Kappeler, 1997). We live in a country where the authority of the police to intervene in the affairs of the citizenry is on the ascent. Traditional due process restrictions on police authority are being relaxed. Citizens and politicians sometimes encourage illegal police behavior to "do something about crime." And increasingly, local police are seen to be the first line of defense in terrorism prevention and the first responders to terrorist incidents. With these changes, opportunities for noble-cause corruption are increasing. Consider the following four examples.

The first example is drug interdiction activity, where we encounter such tactics as "drug-courier profiles." Routine automobile stops aimed at the interception of drug couriers are conducted in many states, and permitted by the Supreme Court, without the prior requirement of probable cause for stopping the vehicle. A "profile" based on a vehicle's and occupant's similarity to known drug-courier activity can provide the basis for a stop, and cars that are profiled are routinely searched in some states. Profiles, however, create easy opportunities for what has been called race-profiling—stopping vehicles based on the race or ethnicity of their occupants. Cops know, for example, that they can stop Latinos in old, beat-up cars in farming areas and sharply increase the production of statistics for license, registration, and insurance violations. Some observers call the practice of profiling "DWM"—driving while minority. Given the nature of profile stops, it is extremely difficult to determine whether race-profiling occurs, thus increasing opportunities for noble-cause corruption.

Second, the courts are relaxing the circumstances under which confessions are admissible. Under *Arizona v. Fulminante*, the Supreme Court provided a basis for permitting coerced confessions under certain circumstances. What is the impact of such decisions on the police? In this decision are the seeds of noble-cause corruption. As Skolnick and Fyfe (1993:65) observe, "If courts allow the police to deceive suspects for the good end of convicting criminals, can we really expect the police to be truthful when offering testimony?"

Third, we witness the expansion of police authority in various versions of "community policing." Some reformers argue that police should be able to intervene even when a law has not been broken, on behalf of community civility (Wilson and Kelling, 1982; Kelling, 1987; see also Klockars, 1985). It is argued that the police have become too concerned with the rights of individuals and detached from the needs of local communities. Police, it is suggested, need the authority to intervene in ordinary problems of public order on behalf of their local communities. Bums need to be rousted out of parks. Skateboarders create fear and need to be controlled. In short, the police should have the authority to do something about problems that do not involve the breaking of the law, but are disruptive to local ideas of public order.

Fourth, under expanded counter-terrorism protocols in many cities, police are re-engaging in the surveillance of citizens in public gatherings. This surveillance has been encouraged by the federal government, who has used expanded counter-terrorism laws under the 1996 anti-terrorism law and the 2001 USA PATRIOT Act to deal with a widespread concern about terrorism following the terrorist attacks on the Pentagon and World Trade Center, commonly known as 9/11. The police, working with other governmental agents at the local and federal level, can help "connect the dots," a phrase popularized following 9/11 which referred to the need to increase the flow of information across governmental units in order to identify potential terrorist threats. However, many citizen's groups have expressed the concern that expanded police powers will be used to surveille, track, and harass political dissidents rather than actual terrorists. Police, they contend, will use their expanded authority to suppress legitimate political dissent, a critical element in the preservation of democracy. The use of counter-terror authority to suppress political dissent or to track citizens engaged in legal organizing activities would be a form of noble-cause corruption.

In the United States today, police power is an awaking leviathan. The power of the police to intervene in citizen's lives stems directly from the courts, whose legal opinions are in turn driven by public opinion favorable to stern justice. It is a power that can be used for good or evil. It has enormous power to corrupt.

To understand how police can be corrupted by their work, we need to first recognize that they strongly believe in the "core" activity of their work: doing something about crime. Sometimes the public thinks of the police as automatons in blue, without feelings, dispensing law. This is called the "just the facts, ma'am" approach to police work. The police, however, believe in their work, and they carry it out passionately. They care about getting bad guys off the streets. They are morally committed to their work. Their morality is based in traditional and straightforward beliefs in right and wrong, good and evil. For the police, good and evil is a concrete notion practiced in the day-to-day work of policing. The police see themselves on the side of angels. And they deal with bad guys and assholes, who they firmly believe are associates of the non-angelic crowd. But it is precisely this—the nature of "good and evil" and who decides which is which—that is up for grabs in the current era.

This book is about the power that police use. It examines how power can remove criminals but also corrupt police at individual and organizational levels. This book is intended to provide students of policing with a realistic understanding of the kinds of corruption that can envelop police officers. We recommend that students and recruits carefully consider what we have to say; the problems we describe are in their future, and they must be prepared for it if they wish to undertake a career in police work or other justice careers. This book is also designed to be an exercise in ethical tuning-up to street officers, a call from us to them to act from an ethically alert frame of mind.

This book is also for police commanders. Importantly, we argue throughout that the focus of ethics in police organizations should not begin at street level; properly applied, it begins at the level of administration and command, where leaders teach by example. Here, we apply an old adage: "I teach and you forget. I behave and you learn. I involve and you understand." Commanders teach best by involving officers in the decision-making process and through the example they set in making decisions. Without these elements, all the ethics training in the world is worthless.

There are many public voices, including respectable citizens and legislators, who should know better yet encourage the police to be tougher than the bad guys, to step over the line if that's what it takes to do something about crime, to do what it takes to win the war on crime. We're here to steer recruits and students interested in a policing career away from stepping over that line. We're here to provide a different view, maybe not so simple in its good-guy/bad-guy imagery, but a view more consistent with the kind of work that the police do. Our ethics come from the way the police and the public share similar dreams, struggle through ordinary problems, and seek peace and happiness in their daily lives. We believe in the noble cause, but we believe that noble-cause corruption breaks the bond that links the police to those they are sworn to protect.

When police reformers talk about corruption, they are mostly concerned with the illegal use of police authority or power for economic gain. A review of the many police ethics books shows that, with a few important exceptions, they seem to be more concerned with grafting and illegal economic gain—a free cup of coffee, for example—than with violence and corruption in the name of law and order. There are several good reasons for this. Economic corruption is more tangible; it is easier to identify. Economic corruption has historically been the most important corruption problem faced by the police. On the other hand, in recent years, noble-cause corruption has been of increasing importance. And it is more difficult to talk about and treat. An illegal search of an offender to find drugs is much more difficult to explain, and putting someone in jail for a weekend for COC—contempt of cop—is intangible. These latter types are noble-cause corruption, more difficult to deal with because they are closely aligned with the morality of the police; they serve purposes that the police tend to support. But they are far-reaching in their consequences. When they occur, the damage to the person impugned by a police officer may be substantial—a beating, jail, or prison time and a criminal record—hopes for a return to a normal life damaged beyond repair. The department becomes vulnerable to liability. And perhaps most importantly, the legitimacy of the police is undermined.

It is more politically expedient to talk about economic corruption than noble-cause corruption. Economic corruption is usually explained in terms of criminal acts and described in terms of a slippery slope—small crimes (for example, taking a bribe from a motorist) provide the justification for more serious ones, such as shaking down a drug dealer for cash. When we look at economic corruption, we can explain everything in terms of "rotten apples" (an aphorism for bad cops), and we don't have to ask the deeper, harder questions about the nature of police work. Even when many officers in the same agency are involved in economic crime, we think about their criminality in terms of economic temptations and their impact on individual weaknesses. It is the explanation that departments most frequently use to explain corruption problems.

Noble-cause corruption is different. When we look for explanations of noble-cause corruption, we have to look for an explanation for crime in the nature of police work and the kinds of people who are drawn to policing. We begin to recognize how our values themselves contribute to our corruption—how we become that which we most dislike. When an officer makes a questionable arrest, or when an asshole is thumped, the police are acting out of strongly held moral beliefs. Both of these are noble-cause corruption—corruption in the name of the moral rightness of good ends. Ethics aimed at economic crime will not help us understand these kinds of corruption. Noble-cause corruption is about how we can be corrupted while we are carrying out our most highly held beliefs. In a dark way, it is our strongest desire to protect the innocent from the cruel that sometimes carry the seeds of our own undoing.

We believe that the noble cause is something of which the police can be proud. The noble cause enables police to celebrate their special craft, to find meaning in the day-to-day activity of their work. Without the noble cause, police work would lose its meaning, and police officers would lose their sense of humanity, their concern for the innocent, and their dislike of bad people. This makes it difficult to write about the noble cause corrupted, about how our own values can corrupt us.

Where do we draw the line between where we act on behalf of the noble cause and where we encounter noble-cause corruption? The line is fuzzy, indistinct. It is a gray line, worked out in the day-to-day world of police work. There is not an absolute rule an officer can memorize from his or her department's standard operating procedure or some school's academic textbook to distinguish this line. Noble-cause corruption is not in any department's code of ethics; indeed, noble-cause corruption can be a consequence of the interpretation of a department's ethics, as Mike A. Caldero observed in the prologue.

Although the line may be fuzzy and indistinct, there are real consequences for the corruption of the noble cause. For an individual officer, it is paid in terms of stress, sleepless nights, and the possibility of lawsuits, criminal charges, unpleasant media attention, alienation from the public and from former friends, friction with supervisors, increasing difficulty in gaining promotion, and maybe a visit from the internal affairs officer. A few officers will commit noble-cause corruption and be unable to reconcile it to their sworn obligations to uphold the law. These officers will suffer a great deal of job-related stress. Sometimes the price is a retirement spent justifying what they did. For managers, it is stark disbelief, a denial followed by loss of esteem and frustration. For departments, the cost is a loss of legitimacy in the eyes of the public, an inability to get witness and victim testimony because ordinary people are afraid of the police, a change of executive leadership, corruption scandal in the headlines, and civil litigation. For all of us, it is a threat to the democratic values we cherish.

We're not asking police officers to believe in their work any less. To paraphrase Skolnick and Bayley (1986), we think that the answer for police officers—for us all, for that matter, certainly the public no less than the police—lies in understanding the petty problems and frustrations that can overwhelm people. It is in the ordinary struggles of everyday life that the battle between good and evil is fought with the greatest intensity; it is a struggle that we all share.

We're not going to provide absolutes. If you are a police officer or recruit, we can't tell you that you'll never encounter situations in which ends outweigh means. What we're telling you is to be very, very careful. There are many people out there—prosecutors, the public, legislators, even colleagues—who will make it easy to justify corrupting the noble cause. They will lead you down the garden path. They won't tell you what you are getting into. Or if they do, it'll be like a footnote in a book, the kind of footnotes you never paid attention to in school. You thought ethics was about accepting a free cup of coffee. If you read this book, you'll know what you're walking into. Forewarned is forearmed. Now you're warned.

## Purpose of this Book

We have written this book in accordance with the admonition: that instead of being ethically disinterested "fence-pole sitters," as academics tend to be, we benefit from examining police problems in the light of basic moral principles and from a moral point of view. If we want to live by principles of personal responsibility, a moral foundation and ethical sense may well be the only road that will get us there.

The purpose of this book is to provide a way of thinking about police ethical dilemmas and for police officers to think ethically about their work. It is a product of our understanding of the police, what they do, and why they do it. In the text, we challenge contemporary ways of thinking about the police on a variety of issues. Sometimes we are intentionally provocative.

The narrative in this book is developed from an ethics presentation Dr. Michael A. Caldero developed for police commanders. The presentation is a one-day event, a condensation of the information presented here. Our tone is a blend of academic and conversational styles, emphasizing key points of the presentation. Quotes from Dr. Caldero are italicized. Some of the quotes are not from a specific presentation but emerged from discussions and emphasize core presentational issues. The narrative is expanded by additional material intended to clarify particular points of emphasis.

This book is about who police officers are and who they should be. For those of you that are or will soon be police officers, it's about your moral self. It's about how to think about the communities where police do their work. And it's a way to think about how communities should be policed in the face of the profound changes our country is encountering in the early twenty-first century.

This book is intended for three audiences: students interested in criminal justice and policing issues, police recruits, and police commanders.

The primary focus of the narrative is a command group, but the book is written in a way to reach each audience. The issues presented in the book are useful for studying ethical issues in policing and for understanding the everyday world street officers inhabit and in which they work. Sections in the book are also written for police managers and commanders. Too often, in the ranks of management, commanders forget about the constant temptations of the street. When things go sour (and here's a rule of thumb: they either just have or are about to), it's always a surprise for managers. It shouldn't be. We explain why.

We think that general criminal justice students will also have much to gain from this book. It provides a perspective on police work not often discussed openly in the classroom. Today, too many college instructors take sides; they either know nothing about real police work and distrust police altogether, or they are cheerleaders for the police regardless of what the police do. This book aims at an ethical balance between these two viewpoints.

The narrative of the book flows back and forth between its twin audiences of college students and police officers. This is intentional. Many students who read the book will become police officers and will be informed by the discussions. And many police officers who read the book are, or will become, students.

What can we hope to accomplish by ethics education and training? Ethics training enables us to think about why we make the decisions we do. But ethics training, to be useful, has to be about more than lofty, academic thinking about why we act the way we do. Ethics has to be practical—that is, be useful in the kind of decisions we make in our daily work routines. When confronted with a routine situation, an officer has to decide the right way to act and avoid doing the wrong thing. A practical ethical standard is the standard we bring to bear when deciding what is right and what is wrong. This book also helps think through the consequences of noble-cause corruption. It is unfair to hold police officers responsible for their behavior if they are uninformed as to its consequences. This book, we believe, helps make those consequences clear.

Our view, stated simply, is that police work is too "ends" focused. Our police sense of identity is bound up in the achievement of law and order. We tend to believe that there are ends so noble, so right, that sometimes it's okay to bend the rules a bit. Sometimes we end up bending the rules a lot.

We argue for a means-oriented ethic of negotiated order that will prepare police for America's future. The United States is in the midst of profound demographic changes, in rural as well as urban areas. The population of the United States is radically diversifying its ethnicity and racial character, and growth is creating crime and disorder pressures in traditionally rural areas. The reality we confront in the United States is a polyglot of ethnic, religious, racial, age, and income groups. Citizens seem to be increasingly enclaved by minority status, by income, and by age. Policing's future, in order to adapt to the needs of the twenty-first century, requires a refocusing from moral ends to negotiated ends. Order is not to be asserted but negotiated.

At the end of the twentieth century, the police were responding to changes in the urban and rural American landscape by implementing practices under the umbrella of community policing. At the end of the first decade of the twenty-first century, many scholars and professionals alike have pronounced the death of community policing. What role changes are in store for the police? Broad changes sweep across the landscape. We are a decade into a war on terror, and the police are broadly affected by this conflict. Departments have adopted counter-terrorism into their missions, and many officers are either veterans who are returning from Iraq and Afghanistan or are closely related to veterans. Yet the terror mission for police is yet to be articulated; it lacks focus and direction. One area, adapted from the counter-terror discourse, is called "intelligence-led policing." Intelligence-led policing is a blend of counter-terror practices and problem-oriented policing, with an emphasis on tactical intelligence, real-time crime management, and intelligence gathering. COMPSTAT is widely popular among police agencies, with its emphasis on law enforcement facilitated by mapping technologies. It remains to be seen if COMPSTAT will live up to its promise of reducing crime through focused law enforcement, though at the current time, it seems promising.

All of these changes, however, are leading the police away from a community negotiator role and toward "hard law enforcement," as conceived by and anchored in state notions of public safety. It is unclear that the broad mandate of the police under community policing, with its focus on community protection through police-community reciprocity, and by implication the close partnerships of citizens and police, will survive. In the current era, we witness few of the hoped-for fruits of community policing in minority neighborhoods. To the contrary, extraordinarily high arrest rates have decimated some African and Latino communities, and generations of young languish in jails and prisons for nonviolent offenses. When one looks at contemporary arrest and incarceration rates, combined with continued high levels of drug use and poverty levels in minority neighborhoods, one could easily conclude that the community policing movement, as a strategic effort to enhance minority community quality of life through propositive police-citizen relations, was a complete and utter failure.

The United States continues to diversify along religious, ethnic, and racial lines. To respond to the dramatic internationalization of American society, we need police to be more than hard-edged law enforcers. They will need to be negotiators of public order. Skills at negotiating order will be the tools police use to enable people to get along. Ends-oriented thinking cannot get them there. Means-oriented thinking, we believe, can.

## Overview of Book

The book is organized into three parts. Part 1 frames the central idea of the book. It is that police officers are value-based decision-makers. The core value is a commitment to the noble cause. The noble cause is allied with two other values—a commitment to the problems faced by victims and a willingness to place themselves in harm's way for strangers. These values are powerful and admirable elements of police work, and they provide the core elements of value-based decision-making. But they also foster a psychology that can justify noble-cause corruption. We present a review of the literature on the police that has dealt with noble cause and its corruption. Part 1 concludes with an analysis and discussion of research carried out on police values.

Part 2 presents noble-cause corruption as a form of what ethicists call a means-ends dilemma. Herbert Packer's justice model is used to describe how the justice system creates pressure to de-emphasize police concerns over the due process laws and administrative guidelines and emphasizes criminal justice "ends," such as the accumulation of arrest statistics. The corruption of noble cause, we argue, is at the core of many entrenched police problems. Where noble-cause corruption is widespread, police culture acts as a shield to protect officers from oversight. The consequences of noble-cause corruption include insularity, secrecy, and loss of legitimacy. Many elements in this section are particularly aimed at commanders. We encourage commanders to recognize how traditional police hiring and training practices unintentionally contribute to noble-cause corruption. A balanced orientation to police work that recognizes the importance of both ends and means, we suggest, provides an alternative ethic that can protect officers and agencies against the corruptive effects of the noble cause. We suggest that it is the "golden apples," sometimes the best officers in the department, those most committed to their work, who are the most vulnerable to noble-cause corruption.

Part 3 considers ethical dilemmas we think the police will face in the twenty-first century. Through various examples, we try to show how community policing fits with a means-oriented ethical outlook. Through an analysis of demographic patterns and population changes in the twenty-first century, we construct a role for the police in terms of the "negotiation of order." By this we mean that the responsibilities of the police will increasingly be to help different and often conflicting groups coexist in a society increasingly divided along status, religious, racial, and ethnic lines. An ends-oriented ethic, we argue, will be ineffective and out-of-touch, contributing to growing internal strife and a breakdown of internal security. By viewing their work in terms of a means-orientation to the coproduction of community order, police can help us deal with the profound social changes that even now are occurring. This part concludes with a discussion of recommendations for departments interested in addressing noble-cause issues.

# Part 1

# Value-Based Decision-Making and the Ethics of Noble Cause

The police are essential to democracy. By ensuring that no person is above the law, the police protect citizens from victimization. Through the enforcement of the law, police ensure that no individual or group violently asserts its will over the public order. In the United States, we tend to take the police for granted. Yet, over the past 50 years, we have witnessed the collapse of the Soviet Union and the destabilization of many countries in the Middle East and Africa. Many nation-states have failed, or are barely surviving, with collapsed internal security controls.

Democratic countries walk a fine line between the anarchy and civil violence of collapsed states and the suppressive citizen controls exerted by highly authoritarian regimes. It is through the commitment of the police to the citizenry, their capacity to control crime, and their ability to act according to the rules they enforce—that they also are not above the law—that democracy survives.

The rules for enforcing the law and the rules for protecting citizens' rights can conflict with each other. Police are expected to stop, detain, sometimes seize, and if necessary, injure or kill citizens when they are engaged in wrongful behavior. There are many complex rules of process, both in terms of law and in terms of department policy, that surround each of these expectations. These rules are expected to conform with criminal and civil law in issues of due process. And there is a great deal of confusion and lack of agreement when it comes to holding police accountable for these rules.

Consider, for example, an illegal search of a suspect in order to find out if he or she is carrying drugs. Is an illegal search wrong? How about when an informant calls the police to tell them they know of a suspect who has drugs in his or her house? Should the police use the informant's information and raid the house? And what if the informant is himself a police officer who believes that the suspect is a drug dealer, wants to look

DOI: 10.4324/9781003626916-2

around the house, and then "stiffs in a call" as if he were a citizen. Is that alright? And what if the police officer crashes the door, the suspect defends himself with a weapon and is killed, and there are no drugs in the house, only a homeowner defending his or her property? Is that alright?

All of the activities described earlier are acts committed on behalf of a good end—getting bad guys off the streets. Some of them are also illegal. They represent noble-cause corruption—when an officer breaks the law in order to achieve a good end.

Over the past 100 years, the police have been transformed in important ways. Economic corruption has diminished dramatically. The quality of police professionalism has increased. And the police have become much keener in the ways of public order maintenance as we move toward a multicultural society. The police are committed to doing good, to finding and arresting bad people, to the assistance of victims, and to protecting communities; in short, they have become professional in ways that many police reformers sought throughout the twentieth century.

Yet their commitment to what we call the noble cause carries a special peril. Crime control sometimes seems to require behavior that is not particularly legal. For example, officers might "testilie," which refers to giving false information as sworn testimony, in order to take a felon off the streets who has an extensive violent rap sheet and whom the officer believes to be a community danger. This is the sort of behavior that we call noble-cause corruption.

The topic of noble-cause corruption, like the examples earlier, frequently involves behavior that cannot be easily defined as good or bad. Sometimes trying to define what is wrong with it is like grasping at smoke. If an officer conducts a search in an inappropriate place, in the process uncovers information about a serious crime, and then does not mention that the search was, at that moment, illegal, is she a "golden apple" or a "rotten apple"—a good cop or a bad cop? How about when the officer adds drugs to a search warrant to justify a detailed search, even though the officer does not have any probable cause that drugs will be found but has probable cause on other, larger items—a car for example—and wants to fish around a bit? It is sometimes difficult to tell what is right or wrong behavior, particularly when an officer is committed to a good outcome. It is easy to overlook small procedural details of the law in the service of good ends. Yet noble-cause corruption goes to the heart of democratic process in the United States. Noble-cause corruption represents the authority of the sovereign to intercede with impunity into the affairs of the citizenry, and there is no democracy in that.

Chapter 1 provides background on the noble cause. The opening chapter argues that the proper understanding of police morality and ethics begins by understanding that they are value-based decision-makers. This means that they are strongly affected by the values and beliefs that characterized their upbringing, and they bring these value dispositions to their work. The central elements of value-based decision-making are the noble cause and two of its important occupational elements, described as the "smell of the victim's blood" and "the tower." The central theme of this book—the responsibility of command in noble-cause corruption—is discussed using examples from diverse sources, including Abu Ghraib. The chapter concludes with a discussion of the literature that has developed elements of value-based decision-making and the noble cause.

Chapter 2 considers the hiring process. We argue that in most departments, the process is a collection of complicated procedures that converge on a simple purpose—hiring officers that have a particular set of values. Hiring, we argue, is a values-based process aimed at ensuring that recruits carry values sympathetic to the noble cause. Early organizational experiences refine and redirect the way in which officers enact their beliefs in the noble cause.

Chapter 3 looks at administrative dilemmas related to the noble cause. This chapter presents a perspective on the profound difficulties encountered when we hold public servants accountable for their behavior. Three accountability dilemmas are presented. The chapter concludes that there is a limit on the extent to which accountability is a reachable goal.

Chapter 4 assesses efforts to measure police values. It argues that police values are not learned on the job but are fully in place when officers are hired. The psychology of emotion is presented to describe the powerful pull the noble cause has on individuals. This chapter concludes with a re-consideration of police morality and discretion, arguing that discretion among the police is highly overrated. Given our knowledge of police values, it argues, how can we not know how they will act?

# Value-Based Decision-Making: Understanding the Ethics of Noble Cause

1

## Key Terms

"The Asshole"
bounded rationality
perspective
informal organization
culture
"Dirty Harry" problem
just means
maturity
means-ends conflicts
Abu Ghraib
noble cause
passion
Stanford Prison Experiment
power of self
the tower
value-based decision-making
negative concept of police culture
British Broadcasting Company (BBC) Prison Study

## Introduction

This chapter explores the ethical complexities of policing through the lens of value-based decision-making, emphasizing the centrality of the noble cause—the moral imperative to protect the innocent and remove wrongdoers. Drawing on real-world and experimental examples, including the Stanford Prison Experiment, the British Broadcasting Company Prison Study, and the abuses at Abu Ghraib, the chapter illustrates how culture, leadership, and situational pressures can shape officer behavior.

A police officer is the willful embodiment of the state's morality. An officer's actions are the morality of the state made kinetic, making sure that bad people (those that have broken existing laws, or have been accused of doing so) are dealt with, public order is asserted, and laws are enforced. The power carried by a police officer defines the limits of

DOI: 10.4324/9781003626916-3

individual freedom in a most immediate sense: the authority of the state to seize someone's body or to initiate a process that can end in situational justice, jail or prison, and in rare cases, death. To do their work, police place their lives on the line for strangers, arrest criminal suspects, cite or arrest misdemeanants, (sometimes) distribute rough justice for troublemakers, and deal with victims who may be traumatized or grotesquely wounded.

To do their work, officers enact the morality of the state, represented facially by the existing laws on the books. They must have a clear and straightforward notion of what behavior is right (legal) or wrong, based on whether or not the exhibited behavior conforms to existing law, and what kind of a person is good or bad. Every decision they make about the conduct of their work is value-based, enacting the broader moral standards of the state in the way in which they control their beats. They are, in fact and deed, value-based decision-makers, and their work is moral work through and through.

The (perceived) morality of the state is codified in its system of laws. This code is invigorated and enlivened by many groups who encourage the harsh treatment of people they believe are bad. Legislators argue about whether the courts are too lenient. Citizens repeatedly call to complain about neighbors who create public disorder. Business people rail against local panhandlers who do their work in front of their store and chase off customers. Prosecutors are resolutely focused on the conviction of suspects. Judges are selected for their toughness toward those convicted of crimes. "Mothers Against Drunk Driving" is one of many citizen groups who advocate the punishment of particular types of criminal behavior. Schools want resource officers to protect kids from bullies. And police organizations push for increased criminal penalties that, it is widely believed, will dissuade individuals from committing crime (based on the theoretical deterrent effect of increased penalties for specific crimes).

The ethical dilemma faced by many police officers is in adapting the powers they are endowed with by the state to the way in which they carry out the state's justice. One of the most common moral dilemmas faced by officers is whether or not to bend some of the rules limiting their behavior in order to deal with people they believe are criminals or troublemakers. Officers indeed have a great deal of power, power they can use to really hurt people, by asserting rough or situational justice, but far greater power by starting the legal process that will put them (the perceived "bad people") in jail or prison. Many officers, and the reader may be among them, have seen colleagues engage in legally questionable behavior and that some prosecutors, superiors, and judges wink and look the other way. Officers may pressure suspects to find out what they are up to so that they will not cause problems on their beat. Indeed, many officers see a cruel world in which good citizens are routinely victimized and a court system that is unresponsive and believe they have few alternatives other than to enact their own particular brand of extralegal justice. This view is reinforced by the commitments officers have to their beats. Many of them are convinced that if they don't control it, no one will, and that they must sometimes set the laws and policies designed to control their behavior aside in order to do something about bad people. Police power should be used for the good of citizens and the community, even if laws or policies must be sometimes bent to do so.

Most ethics books will tell an officer to turn off that power—that police are creatures of the law and that due process and administrative protocols are rules that must always be followed. Police, according to this view, are supposed to be dispassionate law enforcers, robots in blue, enforcing the law equally and without bias or predisposition. We don't buy it. We have a different perspective. We don't tell police to turn it off; it can't be done. We counsel instead that it be used wisely.

We have a different way of thinking about ethics. We call it value-based decision-making. The values carried by police officers determine their decisions to intervene in the lives of citizens, what they do when they intervene, and the way in which they bring interventions to a conclusion. And the most important values that mobilize officers are embodied in the noble cause. The noble cause is, for most officers, the touchstone from which value-based decision-making occurs. Indeed, values are the cornerstone of the work police do; they dispense justice by controlling people. So we'll start this chapter with a discussion of value-based decision-making and what it means to police work.

## Value-Based Decision-Making

The presentation is in a converted meeting room, and 10 tables have been set up for Mike Caldero's presentation. Approximately 30 commanders and mid-level supervisors are present.

Mike looks at each officer, a quick scan, brief pause on each one. Contact. He begins. *What do you think of bureaucracies?*

"We work in a bureaucracy."

*Oh, I know you work in a bureaucracy. I spent my whole life in the bureaucracy. I was a police officer for a long time. Now I teach, which means that I'm still in a bureaucracy.* (A few officers smile). *But what do you think of bureaucracies? Are they efficient? Are they effective? Let me put it this way. When you need to get something done, does the bureaucracy help you get it done?*

Many officers in the room chuckle. One officer is not amused. He responds: "We are the bureaucracy."

OK, Mike thinks, here we go. *Exactly. And you use the bureaucracy to get work done. It provides a set of rules and procedures that enable the different parts of the organization to work together. Isn't that right?* This is a clear challenge for so early in the presentation. But understanding the noble cause requires challenges, and it's good to get some of them out of the way up front.

How well do you all work together? Do your different shifts work closely with each other? Your line officers, how well do they get along with you? How about promotions? Do your officers feel good about the work they do? How about standard operating procedures? Any complaints?

Mike gets stony looks from some of the officers. A captain responds. "We get along fine with our line officers. We don't have those kind of problems here."

OK, I'll take that. What if I were to get a group of your line officers together and asked them? What would they say?

A lieutenant looks at the captain, and then says "There are always some officers that complain. Some of them don't understand that being a police officer requires a lot of work. Self-responsibility." He is stating a mantra Mike has heard in every department "Officers today don't seem to understand the self-responsibility that officers used to have. There are some who just don't want to do any work."

Oh boy, aren't there some complainers! There are always some officers who can't be satisfied, who complain about everything. You know, I find that in every department. What do they complain about? Any sergeants in here? Sergeant, what do they complain about?

"Well, sometimes they complain about promotions."

How about brass? Administrators? You guys do community policing—do they complain about that? How about you sergeant, do you think they complain about the way they are evaluated?

"Well, sometimes, sure, all of that. Some are just complainers." The sergeant shifts uncomfortably in his seat. But he is favoured and will gain promotion quickly in this organization. He has some protection from saying bold words—as long as he knows when to stop. The sergeant continues "I know who I can count on to get work done."

Mike smiles for the first time. *Thank you. Yes, that's exactly right. You are the bureaucracy and they don't trust you. They complain about you. And you complain about them. And you think that, except for a few, they lack the kind of self-responsibility that cops used to have. You can tell me if I'm getting it wrong.* No one says anything.

I'm not saying this because I disrespect your department. I wouldn't be here if I weren't on your side. But I'm here today to show you how I make sense out of this, and I'm here to tell you that this is more than grousing about administrators. I bet a lot of you, maybe all of you, complained about administrators when you were starting out.

A captain responds "Yea, and we replaced them." This comment breaks the ice, everyone laughs.

*They—or you, 15 years ago—they and you are complaining about the bureaucracy. The complaint is about the way bureaucracy works, the formal rules and complicated standard operating procedures that list every screw-up in the past 100 years, the way in which it interferes with their ability to do real police work, the way it's used sometimes to punish people who are really committed to police work.* Mike pauses. *You are very stressful to them, you know.* He lets the comment hang in the air for a moment. *We'll talk more about that later. We'll talk a lot about that. What I am saying now is that they complain because they believe in police work. Just like you. Here's why.*

*Police work, in its heart, isn't about bureaucracy, even if it's organized that way. Police work is about values. This is where we begin. Real police line officer work is value-based decision-making. Police officers use the bureaucracy, just like they use the law, as tools to carry out value-based decision-making. This is the central and most important lesson today: that all of the decisions your officers make, on the street, doing their job, are value-based.* Mike writes the phrase "value-based decision-makers" in large letters on a whiteboard in the back of the room. Underneath, he writes:

VALUE-BASED DECISION-MAKING
Organization = means (tools)
Law = means (tools)
Morality = ends (contribute to society, make the public safe, protect and serve

A captain responds "What are you talking about?" Mike smiles again. If they had said nothing he would be in trouble. But they are talking, which means that they are engaged and interested. If they are critical and challenging, well, that means that they are good cops. They don't take what they hear for granted.

Mike shifts the direction of his discussion, coming in from a different angle. *Captain, why did you become a police officer?*

The captain responds "To retire before I was 50." Many in the room laugh. It is widely believed by police officers that they will not live long after retirement. "No, I'll tell you. I worked on my father's farm, it was hard work. Sometimes a Sheriff's deputy would come around. Once he helped us get rid of some kids that were breaking into a shed and vandalizing our property. He introduced me to the Sheriff, and I was really impressed. I told him "'One day I'm going to be a police officer like you.' And I am very proud to have ended up a police officer."

I bet I would get a story like that from all of you. And I bet I would get a story like that from your line officers as well. Some came from cop families. Some from military backgrounds. Some came from small cities and towns and saw police work as the way out. Some are the survivors of rough neighborhoods. They became police officers because they believe in it. Oh, sure, for some it was the only good work that they could get without a college degree. But that is not the whole picture. It's about a commitment to doing something meaningful with your life. That means helping citizens, dealing with the worst sorts of people to protect and serve. It's about values, from the start. You became police officers because you believed in the importance of those values. I want someone to tell me I'm wrong.

You joined a bureaucracy so that you could act out those values, and your officers use the law on the street to act those values out.

Get a room full of police officers together and ask them why they wanted to become cops. It doesn't matter if they're from New Mexico or Alabama. It doesn't matter if they're senior staff or probationary officers. If you think that they'll say that it was for the money, police work is not for you. The answer is the same everywhere, variations on a theme of personal commitment. "I believed in it." "I wanted to contribute to society." "I wanted to do something important with my life." Their reasons reflect a commitment to contribute to society in some meaningful way. It is an occupational predisposition that unites police officers.

Mike continues. *When I think of police, I think of people for whom values are very important. They do police work because these values are important to them. Hiring decisions are organized around these important values, and the daily work of police work is about these important values. But once I begin thinking in terms of values, I have to ask myself where these values come from. They come from their backgrounds. And this shows how important their cultural background is in understanding what the police are all about.*

## *Values and Culture*

Values don't emerge whole-cloth from police training and police work. To understand the occupational predispositions of the police, one begins by looking at their family backgrounds. Police officers bring to their work a set of cultural predispositions, and police work has only a minor effect on these predispositions (Crank, 2004a; Caldero, 1997; Zhao et al., 1998). Police work, like all forms of work in Western culture, can be described as an occupational culture made up of values imported from the broader environment from which officers are hired. These imported values are distilled and focused in particular occupational settings.

The notion of culture is quite different from "rational" notions of human behavior, according to which people logically select from among various courses of action to decide the best way to act. It means that we have **bounded rationality:** we act rationally, but we do so only in a limited fashion, after we take into consideration our cultural heritage. That cultural heritage includes what we might call "givens," ways of acting intended to produce predictable kinds of reactions in other people, ways of thinking through problems, ways of thinking about right and wrong, and a wide variety of gestures and nonverbal communication skills very early in life. These come to be taken for granted. Our rationality is bounded by these "givens," and they are very hard to change.

The notion of bounded rationality applies to police officers just like it applies to everyone else. Imagine a police officer responding to a call and finding a comatose, badly beaten 6-year-old child; present also is a father's brother who beat the child while baby-sitting because he thought the child was not minding and needed to be taught a lesson. Most of us have a cultural predisposition that suggests that a 6-year-old child is not responsible for his or her actions, and we reverse that notion for adults. This incident occurs within fundamental beliefs about the right way to treat a child, the kind of person who did such an act, and what the person who did it deserves. A police officer, and indeed most people, are incapable of seeing a beaten child and deciding that the child had it coming. That is a morally unacceptable way of thinking. Neither will an officer respond as an "automaton in blue," without emotions, simply recording information in order to conduct a required investigation. The feelings the officer feels are determined by their cultural heritage.

## What Is Police Culture?

### *What Does It Mean to Be "Cultural"?*

Central to Mike's discussion is the notion that police are profoundly cultural. But what does it mean to be "profoundly cultural"? In this section, we will look at some definitions of culture and return to Mike's comment.

Early definitions of police culture were stated in terms of the **"informal organization."** By informal was meant that, in order to accomplish day-to-day tasks, police officers developed cliques of communication, both vertically and horizontally. Groups of individuals who made up these cliques developed informal rules for getting along. In this sense, organizational culture represented a functional social and semi-professional adaptation to what was seen as a hierarchical, inefficient bureaucracy.

Later definitions of culture often focused on unpleasant or unpopular elements of police behavior and developed what we call the **negative concept of police culture.** These definitions, popular in the media, tended to look at examples of police wrongdoing and seek local organizational culture as an explanation. Waddington (1999) argued that a negative concept of police culture worked because of the condemnatory potential it afforded critics of the police. The police, from this notion of culture, could be blamed for all the ills of the criminal justice system. From this perspective culture was not so much a theory as an accusation. Reiner (1992:287) in Waddington (1999), studying this tradition in academic research, noted that police culture was to blame for "its in-group isolation and solidarity on the one hand, and racist components on the other; its authoritarian conservatism; and its suspicion and cynicism, especially towards the law and legal procedures."

Reviewing perspectives on police culture, Crank (2004b) argued that one's view of culture depended on one's standpoint. He expanded this notion by presenting six different standpoints on police culture, each tied to particular groups with an interest in the police. He argued that a police standpoint had emerged that viewed culture in positive ways. He identified ten ways that culture benefited the police, among which are the following four:

1. Culture enables police recruits to learn about police work.
2. Culture fosters a sense of responsibility for responsibility for the protection for one's community, acted out in terms of responsibility for one's beat.
3. Culture provides a core occupational identity to assist officers during periods of personal grief and professional tragedy.
4. Culture provides a set of stories and occupational gambits that enable adaptation to an unpredictable working environment.

In a broad review of notions of **culture,** Crank (2004a) also took an anthropological notion of culture and applied it to the police. In that conception, he noted five aspects:

> First, it is that people have ways of thinking about problems that make sense out of their lives (See Manning, 1989). Sensibility means that if a person does such and such, some specific thing is likely to occur. Sensibility includes a sense of morality, which identifies good and bad, or provides ways of recognizing good and bad. For the police, a commitment to the social good, described in this book as the noble cause, represents this sensibility. Sensibility also includes "common sense" or "sixth sense policing" such as the ability to identify potential lawbreakers from their appearance.
>
> Second, it includes behaviors that are learned as right ways of acting. Training provides a basic repertoire of responses for a variety of circumstances. TO [training officer] training extends and specifies this training to a particular beat. Officers through their experiences pass on tips and informal practices that fill out expected behaviors on the street.
>
> Third, culture has material elements. This means that culture is characterized by tool making and tool using. Among the tools widely shared by police officers, and which carries a great deal of value, are the weaponry carried by officers. Weapons, a central theme of police work, are familiar to most police officers from when they were children learning to hunt from their parents. Another material element that has had a large effect on policing is the patrol car, which has transformed the occupation from an urban-centered community activity to a (non-community-centered) city-wide area patrol.
>
> Fourth, culture carries a "social structural" component. This means that people surround themselves with acceptable ways to organize their

> lives. Examples include the way in which the organizational structure of shift work leads to a social and professional structure organized around a beat-shift unit. The smallest unit of social structure, heralded from the days of the two person patrol car, was the partnership and strong loyalties between two officers assigned together. Police officers who begin and end a shift at a particular time develop informal relationships, share information and discuss events, making this the smallest unit of social structure. Since some information is transmitted across shifts, all those assigned to a sector are a larger unit of social structure. Much like the military, men and women assigned to the same shift tend to not only work together, but socialize together, along with their families.
>
> Fifth, culture is always in the process of being created and modified. For example, flashlights were designed for illumination, yet the weight of batteries made them useful as surrogate batons. Officers developed informal rules and techniques for their use, even though most training programs do not train for their use as weapons. New stories infuse cultures with different ways of thinking, though these different ways tend to be organized around a common (and approved, by the group) identity as a beat officer.

This broad and multifaceted definition of culture means that police bring in a variety of predispositions that include behaviors they have learned at home and at school, their sense of morals and their ways of thinking about right human relations, a variety of tool-using skills (for example, weapons and computer skills), and speaking and other kinds of communications skills. These elements of culture are modified and molded to the specific needs of the occupation.

Which of these ways of thinking about police culture best captures Mike's sentiment? His concept of police culture seems closest to the first part of Crank's five-part definition, that culture is the sensibility out of which police view the world around them. Central to that sensibility is the moral sense they bring to their task. To say the police are profoundly cultural does not, however, somehow distinguish the police from other people. It is the nature of being human, by this perspective, to seek meaning in the world. Indeed, one of the central questions of philosophy is why we seek meaning in a universe that seems to have none. It is culture that equalizes us, even while making us incomprehensively different.

The search for meaning, and the effort to live our lives according to some meaningful principle, is irresistible. We lose that meaning, and life loses purpose. For the occupation of policing, that meaning—the purpose of occupational life—is tied up in the morality of the noble cause. Perhaps the most significant legacy of the police professionalism movement, police are hired today with a belief in what they do and why it is important. Without the noble cause, police work—and the cultural setting fostered by it—would be quite different.

## *From Culture to Value-Based Decision-Making*

The idea that police are value-based decision-makers makes sense when one thinks of the police as culture carriers. Cultural ways of thinking and doing things are expressed in an officer's upbringing, his or her belief of what's correct, the appropriate way to maintain a family, how children should be treated, and a sense of the abuse of innocence. The police bureaucracy is the social structural aspect of culture the officer has at her disposal to carry out what she believes in—the protection of innocents, doing something good for society. In this example, we see what Mike means when he says that police work is **"value-based decision-making."** The values officers have come from their cultural setting. They are sharpened and fine-tuned in their training for police work and the experiences they encounter. The organization provides a broad set of remedies, both in terms of arrest, in terms of non-arrest practices, and sometimes in terms of street justice, to carry out those values.

Without values, police work would be meaningless. Indeed, without values, human society would itself be impossible. It is in the values humans carry, in the feelings they have about others, and in the lessons they learn about good and bad, right and wrong, that life becomes meaningful. It is through those values that police are like everyone else. By understanding the cultural roots of value-based decision-making, we begin to understand how much the police are like the rest of us. And we also begin to place police bureaucracy in its appropriate role. It is the structural mechanism by which police achieve culturally desired goals.

> Mike continues. *I want you to go with me now. Let's say that police are value-based decision-makers. The next question is "what are the values that are important for understanding the police?"* Mike turns to the whiteboard and writes the following on it:
>
> Noble cause (commitment to get bad guys off the streets)
> Smell of the victim's blood (sensitivity to victim harm)
> The Tower (willingness to put life on line for strangers)
>
> *These three are all interrelated values. They are cop values. They are the fine tuning of the reasons someone becomes a police officer. Many people in society share these values with the police, but among the police, they carry a special intensity. They make police work meaningful. And they are the reason a cop will break the law or violate policy in order to do what he or she thinks is the right thing to do. The most important value is what I call the noble cause, the commitment to do something to make the world a better place to live. Right here.* Mike taps the top line on the whiteboard. *This value comes from the kind of backgrounds police officers have. It motivates them to become police officers. And it stays with them through their careers. Oh, sometimes they become cynical about their ability to do good, surrounded by the bad there is in the world. But even their cynicism cannot be understood without starting at the beginning—the noble cause.*

## The Noble Cause

What is the noble cause? The **noble cause** is a moral commitment to make the world a safer place to live. Put simply, it is getting bad guys off the street. Police are trained and armed to protect the innocent and think about that goal in terms of "keeping the scum off the streets." It is not simply a verbal commitment, recited at graduation at the local Peace Officer Standards and Training (POST) academy. Nor is it something police have to learn. It's something to which they are morally committed. Those who don't feel it are not destined for police work and will be quickly liberated from the hazards of a career in blue.

Baker (1985) sums it like this:

> "I know it sounds corny as hell, but I really thought I could help people. I wanted to do some good in the world, you know?" That's what every cop answers when asked why he became a police officer. He'll probably say it with a laugh or a touch of bitterness. That doesn't mean it isn't true. He just isn't a rookie any longer.
>
> (Baker, 1985:1)

The noble cause is not simply a theory of police work. It is practical and immediate. It's about an officer's conduct in day-to-day police work. The noble cause is the tie to the fundamentally moral nature of police work. It motivates an officer's behavior with citizens and mobilizes a great deal of police solidarity. Police, in this way, truly are creatures of the law: properly understood, this means that both the police and the law embody the moral commitments of the society from which they come. Two aspects of the noble cause help explain why police feel it so strongly—the smell of the victim's blood and the tower.

### *The Smell of the Victim's Blood*

Cops are acutely aware of victims. This is an aspect of policing that many reformers overlook. Yet it is one of the central components of the noble cause.

Mike looks across his audience, trying to find the words to explain the emotions that underlay the noble cause. *Cops can smell the blood of victims.*

The first time Mike refers to the smell of a victim's blood, it puts off listeners. But he explains. Victims motivate cops in a way no other cause does. Police are resolutely focused on the consequences of crime for victims. It's an aspect of our democratic heritage that is deeply ingrained in the sympathies of contemporary police. Guyot (1991) describes how police work forges a bond between police officers and victims.

> The relationship that can develop between an individual victim and an individual responding officer is a personal tie between one who is

> suffering and one who understands suffering. The officer's calm helps the victim to recover some measure of calm; the officer's concern gives emotional and psychological support.
>
> (Guyot, 1991:133)

The commitment of police to victims may seem a bit odd to outsiders. Yet it mobilizes and personifies much of how the police feel about the public they serve. See Box 1.1.

Box 1.1

**Victims and the Noble Cause**

Consider a deputy in Nampa, Idaho, who patrols and lives in an area that is a Hispanic labor camp. The camp is home to two groups of Latinos. The first group is made up of families whose roots extend to the highlands of Central Mexico and who were invited to farm in Idaho during the Second World War labor shortage and subsequently settled in. The deputy was born to a family from this group. The second group is represented by contemporary migrants who work in Idaho during the summer and return to Texas during the winter, a tougher crowd that is characterized by young men whose work separates them from their spouses regularly.

The deputy is particularly concerned about the children in the labor camp because they are often unattended and play out of doors. He is profoundly concerned that one of the children will be kidnapped by a stranger. He worries that the parents don't sense the potential danger to them.

An outside observer might notice that the chances that one of the children will be kidnapped by a stranger is somewhere between minuscule and nonexistent—that if a child were kidnapped, it is most likely that the kidnapper would be an estranged spouse. That observer, however, would be displaying his or her ignorance of the passion police carry for victims. To understand the police, one has to recognize that the fear and concern carried by this officer is unrelenting; it goes with the emotional territory and is central to the noble cause.

The phrase "smell of the victim's blood" is an intensely visceral image of police work. An occupation of the "street," police officers sometimes have to deal with the consequences of physical damage to humans. They know the limitations of flesh under physical assault from knife, baseball bat, and bullet. One of the original authors of this book recalls an officer showing him photos taken during an investigation. At first image, it looked like a woman, somewhat of a mess, in a bikini. After the eyes adapted to the picture, it was apparent that what would have been a bikini was actually the areas of her body that had been brutally cut away with a knife in a violent murder. The "smell of the victim's blood," in such instances, is more than a metaphor. It is occupationally acquired knowledge, emotionally and unalterably tied to the noble cause.

Delattre (1996:273) captures some of the commitment to victims in his discussion of the child abuse death of 6-year-old Eliza Izquierdo in New York City. New York police detective Nancy Farrell led the investigation into Eliza's death. Expressing her pain, Farrell stated, "I'm very angry that this was allowed to happen in the greatest city in the world, and nothing in my job makes me angrier. I've been wanting to hug and kiss every child that walks past me because of how I've spent the past few days."

When we think of police brutality, we sometimes imagine it as the unreasoned, vicious power of the state acted out against an individual citizen. Part of the reason we haven't learned how to control it is because we have failed to understand how it can be rooted in the way in which police relate to victims—protecting the public, doing something meaningful for other people. What reformers have failed to realize is how this kind of police violence is deeply rooted in our democratic traditions.

To overlook this dimension of violence is to fail to understand the roots of much of what is called brutality. If we fail to recognize that police smell the victim's blood, we have no hope to control the use of violence by police officers. The victim's blood mobilizes them. The more we want our street officers to reflect a democratic ethos, to be committed to the poor and care about the downtrodden, the more we open the door for noble-cause violence.

## *The Tower*

> Mike continues. *Imagine that there's a shooter. He's in a tower. It's at a university campus. The shooter has several rifles, and he has already killed 12 students. What are you going to do?*

Ask a room full of officers what they'd do, and they'll tell you. Take him out. Call for back-up. Bring in a sniper. In all of their responses, the underlying theme is the same. They will run toward the tower.

Now ask them what a sane person would do. They'll think a minute. Then someone will say, "They'll run away from the tower." They'll chuckle, recognizing the obvious difference between themselves and ordinary citizens. Ask them what a lawyer would do. Someone says, "Look for clients." They chuckle again. But they understand now. They are talking to a brother, someone who knows what the noble cause is. It's at the core of their being. The true nature of police work, they believe, is in the service of the noble cause.

The **tower** is a metaphor with substance. It means that the police are willing to place their lives on the line for strangers. It carries other themes of police work with it, an attraction to excitement, a willingness to immerse oneself in unpredictable situations, and a belief that they can survive substantial danger. All of these themes come together in the hypothetical tower situation. The officers in the tower situation act out the noble cause. They are contributing to society by putting their lives on the line. They take chances. It could go wrong; they could be killed. But that is part of the police mythology as well. If they are killed, they will be mourned and celebrated by their kind.

> Mike looks across his audience. *When a police officer is killed, what happens? Think about it for a minute. Do citizens discover the event by reading about it in the obituaries? No. They hear about it on the news, no matter who the police officer is. There's a parade. Do doctors get a parade? No, not even if they're excellent doctors. But police officers do. They do so because they risk their lives for strangers. The police run toward the shooter; they risk their lives for the sane person who runs away from the shooter. When they are killed, they are mourned publicly. More than any civilian occupation, police are embedded in the moral fabric of the nation. Their life is dedicated to the noble cause, the protection of the innocent, in service to mankind. It is a standard that is for most officers higher than the law. It is why being a police person is not simply a job, it is a calling. It is why police run toward the tower.*

## *The Core of Value-Based Decision-Making: The Noble Cause, the Victim, and the Tower*

The noble cause, smell of the victim's blood, and the tower are the core elements of value-based decision-making. They represent values that are imported from broader American life and accentuated in police work.

Consider the noble cause, with its focus on good ends. The intense, consuming focus of the police on morally good ends is not a cultural aberration, somehow making the police different from the rest of us. It's an ordinary trait, American as apple pie. We "want the bottom line." We believe it is a question of "moral fiber" to "not let anything get in our way." We have our "eyes on the prize." It's important to "give our all." We think we should "have it your way, baby." "Don't look back." "Winning isn't everything—it's the only thing." "The race isn't run until you reach the finish line." "It ain't over till it's over." "Never say die." "Go the distance." It's a "run for the roses." "Perseverance wins the day." You've got to have "true grit." And on, and on. The focus on the moral rightness of success in whatever we do is ingrained in us from birth. Sociologists describe it as a subcultural trait, imported from the broader cultural milieu and intensified in police work. Put plain, it's bred in the bone.

Concern with victims represents a similar subcultural pattern. A concern with victims is as American as cheering for the underdog, hoping that even an ordinary citizen can have a chance at success. The bully that brings about pain or suffering is punished in kind; it is the just and ordinary ending to many a story and movie line. The storming of the tower represents the ultimate conclusion—that no one shall stand above the law. The tower is a parable as corny as a WWII movie: Good shall prevail, whatever the cost. Yet it is a parable acted out by the police and for which the public celebrates them as heroes and gives them parades when they are killed in the line of duty.

## *The Moral Environment of Value-Based Decision-Making*

MIKE. *Let's talk about the moral environment of the department. There's a moral environment here. Some people call it culture. Some people call it—well, all kinds of things.*

His audience laughs lightly.

MIKE: *I am talking about how your officers learn to be good police officers in your department. Here I'm not about how recruits were before they were hired. You hired them. They believe. Now you point the gun. I want to talk about how you point the gun. How you pull the trigger. I want to talk about an experiment that really told us a lot about people in authority positions.*

One officer responds. "Our laboratory is the real world." This is a way of saying that most social science doesn't have much respect among police.

Mike nods his head up and down. "*It's a tough lab, too. I'm with you on that. But this one was important, because it showed us something about what it means to be human. It's called the Stanford Prison Experiment. And it is important for how you think about what you are doing with your recruits.*" He had their attention now.

## *The Stanford Prison Experiment*

The 1971 Stanford Prison Experiment was designed by Philip Zimbardo, a psychology professor at Stanford University, to measure the effect of situational factors on individuals. Originally funded by the Office of Naval Research to study antisocial behavior, the planned two-week exercise was meant to measure the psychological effect of being assigned the "role" of either prison guard or prisoner. After undergoing some basic interviews and exams to assess their psychological capability to withstand the two-week experiment, 24 student volunteers were selected and, based on a coin toss, assigned as either a full-time prisoner or a guard. Nine of the 12 volunteer "guards" were given one of three 8-hour shifts, guarding nine full-time prisoners. Six of the 24 were alternates. Incarcerated in "cells" converted from offices in the basement of the Stanford Psychology building, three guards in each shift were assigned to watch nine prisoners, three per cell. The students were paid $15 per day to participate.

The student volunteers, in an effort to make the experiment as "real" as possible, were "arrested" by local police, at their homes, without warning, and then taken to the "police station" to be "booked," similar to an actual arrest by the police. The first four picked up were told they were being arrested for felony burglary, the next four for armed robbery. After being booked, they were taken to the detention cell at the station and then transported, blindfolded, to the basement of the Stanford Psychology building, where they were stripped and "deloused," in an effort to further immerse them in the prison culture. They were then lined up and given a smock and a skull cap (to simulate having their heads shaved), assigned an arbitrary number, and then told the prison rules (which included only using their numbers, in communicating with other prisoners, or the guards). The procedure was designed in part to humiliate the prisoners and further remove their individualism.

The degradation was furthered by the type of "uniform" given to the student inmates, which was a smock, purposefully similar to a dress, worn without any underclothes, and with a number sewn on each garment, front and back. In addition to the smock, each "inmate" also had a chain wrapped around his right leg, with a padlock, to constantly remind him of the oppressiveness of his environment. At night, if he moved, the chain would wake him, to be a 24-hour reminder. The skull cap was another example of an attempt at degradation, as it was made from women's nylon stockings.

The student volunteer "guards" were given no specific instructions, other than to maintain "law and order" in the institution. They were free to come up with their own rules and procedures for establishing respect from the inmate volunteers, under the supervision of the prison "warden," who was actually Zimbardo, participating in the experiment. In an orientation meeting, the guards were instructed not to use any violence against the prisoners, not to allow any escapes, and to try and create a sense of "powerlessness" among the volunteer inmates.

Similar to the volunteer inmates, the guards were dressed the same: khaki uniforms (bought at an Army-Navy surplus store), whistles around their necks, night sticks (borrowed from the local police), and mirrored sunglasses (an idea borrowed from the movie *Cool Hand Luke*, which Zimbardo had seen). The sunglasses were worn to provide anonymity to the guards by hiding their eyes and emotions. They also provided a psychological sense of "distance" between the guards and inmates.

At 2:30 A.M., the first of many "counts" took place, in the corridor outside the three cells within the makeshift prison. The idea of counts, taken from prisons, is ostensibly to verify that all inmates are accounted for, but it was also used to provide not only an opportunity for interaction or confrontation between guard and inmate but also allow the guards an opportunity to establish "order" within the environment. It also required the inmates to respond to orders given by the guards and use their new (forced) identity, their prison number.

Zimbardo studied not only the inmate volunteers but also the guards, unknown to them. The roles forced upon the students not only required them to adopt new mannerisms but also allowed them the opportunity to express themselves in a power-laden role (as guards). The student inmates were also forced into a new environment, where they had to submit to forced physical activity (push-ups, jumping jacks), as well as responding to commands, multiple times, reciting numbers (their given prison numbers), backwards, forwards, in song, etc. This was a new experience, either degrading (as inmates) or inherently power-laden (as guards). Some of the individuals in the latter category reveled in the new opportunity, coming up with unique ways to humiliate their former student peers. Zimbardo (2008) noted that the "counts" transformed over time from a simple way to verify that all inmates were accounted for into opportunities for the guards to reinforce their control and complete authority over the inmates.

Although the first day of the experiment passed without any major incidents, the morning of the second day brought problems. Tired from a lack of sleep from multiple and extended long counts the previous night, the student inmates were awakened at 6 A.M. and ordered to sing their prison numbers, then the rules. Then the guards told them new rules regarding their bunks and gave them three minutes to make them "neat and orderly." This was not done to the satisfaction of the guards, and an altercation ensued between an inmate and one of the guards. The inmates became increasingly tired of the authoritative control of the guards and the restrictions, including the lack of eyeglasses, medications, and books, confiscated by the guards. Surprisingly, although they had the ability to simply leave the experiment, no one had, at that point.

The guards decided it had become necessary to increase the number of mindless tasks given to the inmates, so they instituted a morning work period, ordering the inmates to scrub the walls and floors. They then removed the blankets from cells 1 and 2 (cell 3 inmates were "good") and dragged them through the underbrush until they were covered with stickers, which further angered the inmates. The antagonism escalated and resulted in the cell 1 inmates barricading themselves in by placing their cots against the door. The guards called in the reserves and used fire extinguishers to force the inmates away from the door. In retaliation, the guards removed all inmates, stripped them, and placed the leaders into "solitary confinement" (a storage room at the end of the hallway).

The guards then decided to use psychological tactics, setting up a "privilege cell," among the three cells. Assigning the least aggressive inmates to the "special" cell, they were given their uniforms, beds, and allowed to wash and brush their teeth. After half a day of using the "privilege cell," some of the "good" inmates were replaced with "bad" prisoners, which confused the inmates. The inmate leaders came to the conclusion that the prisoners which were moved into the privilege cell were informers, which resulted in creating distrust among the inmates.

The prison "rebellion" created more solidarity among the guards. They began to believe that the inmates were an organized group, "out to get them," as opposed to a collection of students trying to earn some extra money by participating in a unique experiment (Zimbardo, 2008).

After approximately four days, Zimbardo asked a Catholic priest to come in and speak with the inmates. The Catholic priest told each one that if they wanted to leave, they had to ask their parents to contact an attorney. Some of them did so, and the parents then called Zimbardo. He called a lawyer, who spoke with some of the students. Although the attorney was aware of the experiment, he asked each student the same legal questions. At this point, Zimbardo decided to end the prison experiment, after six days, based on the fact that some of the student inmates were becoming increasingly withdrawn and behaving pathologically, and some of the guards were behaving sadistically.

> The Stanford Prison Experiment began as a simple demonstration of the effects that a composite of situational variables has on the behavior of individuals role-playing prisoners and guards in a simulated prison environment. For this exploratory investigation, we were not testing specific hypotheses but rather assessing the extent to which the external features of an institutional setting could override the internal dispositions of the actors in that environment. Good dispositions were pitted against a bad situation.
>
> (Zimbardo, 2008:195)

The experiment was set up to see which was stronger, the "good dispositions" of the college students or the psychological pressure of the situation applied to the individuals. And the situation won.

The striking feature of the experiment, for both prisoners and guards, was the extent to which they adapted to roles completely inconsistent with the college experience. The most common interpretation is how good people can be led—quite easily under some circumstances—to do cruel things to each other. Our humanity may be more easily shorn away than we would like to think. One of the implications is that the most ordinary people can do the most evil things. As Hanna Arendt observed, the Nazi commander Adolf Eichmann was a thoroughly ordinary man, guilty of banal evils.

The Stanford Prison Experiment has been heavily criticized for the way Philip Zimbardo, the lead researcher, allegedly manipulated the situation and his findings. The experiment's premise, that situational factors can lead individuals to adopt oppressive behaviors was heavily influenced by Zimbardo's own biases and instructions to the guards, as well as his dual role as both the researcher and the "warden" of the simulated prison. According to McLeod (2025), Zimbardo became emotionally invested in the experiment and delayed halting it, which some see as a direct conflict of interest and a lapse in objectivity. The guards were instructed by Zimbardo that although no physical violence was permitted, they were to exert power and maintain order to make the "prisoners" feel like they were in a real prison. The design of the experiment, with its clear roles and expectation of a certain outcome, could have led the participants to act in ways that they thought were expected, as opposed to acting naturally. Based on what they were told by the "warden" Zimbardo, the student "guards" could have believed the only way to achieve the experiment's goal was to act in an abusive manner toward the student "inmates."

> One officer comments: "You can't maintain decorum in a prison without controlling the inmates."
>
> MIKE: *They weren't inmates. They were students.*
>
> ANOTHER OFFICER: "We see inmates who are not guilty of the charges they were put in jail for. They might be covering up for someone else. They might be hiding another crime. They might be innocent. If we show special favor it will only cause trouble. They have to do their time, like everyone else."
>
> Mike responds, *That's good. I've seen that too.*
>
> Another officer presses the point. "And the guards weren't real guards. It was a bunch of kids who were untrained, and who didn't know what they were doing. We are trained professionals. We know what works, and we know what the law says. That's what we're all about. We're not college kids."
>
> MIKE: *I'll take that. You are not college kids. You know exactly what you are doing.* What did that mean? The audience sat back, waiting.
>
> MIKE: How do your recruits think about their work? Is it all paperwork? Administrative protocols? Weapons training? The law? There's more stuff, about how to think like a cop. They get it from their TOs, from other officers, from the organization. There's a lot of cop training that goes into how to think like a cop. How about TOs? Don't they show them how to make an arrest so as to minimize the resistance? Deal with force in a practical way? See if they can be trusted to back up another officer? The point is this—your recruits are totally vulnerable to what their TO wants them to do. Moreover, they already believe in police work. Do you want your recruits to get the wrong lessons about how to use coercion from the TO?
>
> Our TOs are well trained.
>
> Mike does a double-take. *Oh are they? I just heard you say that people who are in prison have to do their time, whether or not they are guilty. That maintaining decorum—what a nice word for thumping someone—is more important than someone's innocence. Are you guys TOs? Do*

*you think like that? When I look at the tapes of the Rodney Kind beating, there were 5 TOs standing around. Were they well trained? What message were they sending to the trainees?*

The room was quiet.

I'm not here to criticize your TOs. I know it's a tough business to role model a recruit. But why is the TO, for example in the Rodney King case, role modeling recruits like that? Why does the TO think it is right? He or she is getting it from somewhere. Those 5 TOs in the King case. They didn't get their attitudes from the air. They got it from somewhere. You know where. You.

How many times do you think higher administrators look the other way, encourage TOs to make sure recruits understand they have to get arrests, get away with that kind of abuse, then celebrate the arrests they are getting? TOs carry the message, but they didn't write it. And I'm here to tell you, they can't change it, not by themselves. In the end, it's not about them. They're like line officers—easy to blame.

A captain challenges this. "Are you saying there is something wrong with the hiring process? With the way we hire and train recruits? I have oversight of TOs in my sector and I make sure they are trained. I frankly think we do a pretty good job in screening new recruits, in training, and also in training our TOs."

How do you explain to someone that they're part of the problem, when they cannot see it and absolutely believe in the rightness of their work? It's like calling the air they breathe poisonous. Well, that's why he was brought here.

"I'm glad to hear that. Hiring practices are important. Training is important. But most organizations 'train and walk away.' This may work with firearms training, accident investigation, and first aid. But most of what police officers do depends upon a very dynamic, emotional, physical, and psychological process that MUST be 'modeled and nurtured' not 'trained and blamed.' How do you train officers for the impact of their actions upon the legitimacy of the legal process?"

CAPTAIN: "OK, what do you mean, legitimacy?"

MIKE: *Oh, we'll talk a lot about that today. But first, let's do an experiment. Pretend you are about to testify in court against one of your officers who has committed a noble-cause violation and now you are going to demonstrate how that mentality has not become a functional aspect of your organizational culture. You must show that you have devices in place to prevent or deter such practices. Please articulate for us the aspects of your hiring, evaluation, promotion, policy and ethics, and training that formally and informally address this issue on an ongoing basis. OK, go ahead.*

The room is silent.

The role of the top cannot be overestimated. What happens when the top is silent?

Let's talk about Abu Ghraib. What happened at Abu Ghraib? We've all heard about the charges of torture and seen the pictures on television. I want to talk about the soldiers responsible for providing the staffing for the prison. Weren't they already taken from among the best? Don't we have the best military in the world? Do you think we accidentally staffed the prison with some bad soldiers? A bunch of rotten apples? That's what the government would like us to believe.

## A Lesson from Abu Ghraib

**Abu Ghraib** is a notorious prison complex taken over by U.S. troops during the occupation of Iraq. It came to worldwide attention with the delivery, by Spc. Joseph Darby to the Army's Criminal Investigation Command, of vicious images of detainee abuse and torture, captured by 279 photos and 19 videos in 2004. It has emerged as a worldwide symbol of torture and abuse. For enemies of the United States, Abu Ghraib stands for torture carried out under U.S. authority. Many scholars on terrorism argue that the events at Abu Ghraib have provided terrorists with an immensely powerful recruiting tool—visual, photographic evidence of torture by the U.S. One particularly graphic act of terrorism—the video-recorded beheading of Nick Berg—has been directly attributed to the actions of American troops at Abu Ghraib.

Accusations of U.S. torture burst on the U.S. news media with a Seymour Hersh article in the *New Yorker* in 2004 (Hersh, 2004). In a series of accusations supported with photographs, Hersh presented the case that the U.S. was systematically torturing prisoners at the facility. Subsequent investigations have associated American troops with 19 deaths through torture at Abu Ghraib and related institutions (Miles, 2006).[1] In his article, Hersh cited the brutality noted in the military's own Taguba report (2004):

> Breaking chemical lights and pouring the phosphoric liquid on detainees; pouring cold water on naked detainees; beating detainees with a broom handle and a chair; threatening male detainees with rape; allowing a military police guard to stitch the wound of a detainee who was injured after being slammed against the wall in his cell; sodomizing a detainee with a chemical light and perhaps a broom stick, and using military working dogs to frighten and intimidate detainees with threats of attack, and in one instance actually biting a detainee.

The most damning testimony came from extensive photographs taken of detainees being harshly mistreated. Ultimately, 12 soldiers were convicted of charges, including dereliction of duty, conspiracy to maltreat detainees, failing to protect detainees from abuse, cruelty, maltreatment of detainees, assault, indecency, adultery, obstruction of justice, and committing an indecent act.

As a topic of discussion in a police department, Abu Ghraib cuts into uncomfortable turf. Many cops have family relatives who served in Iraq. Many new recruits have served in one of the current wars in Iraq and Afghanistan, and some low- to mid-level officers were in the first Iraq war. Officers see homeless veterans who are coping with mental distress, alcohol and drug abuse, and fragmented lives. Some of them are entering the criminal justice system from the wrong side—as convicted felons (see Carroll, 2007).

> Mike is interested in the soldiers who were convicted of charges related to the mistreatment of prisoners at Abu Ghraib. *You know, when I read about Lynndie England, Charles Graner, Jeremy Sivitz, Sabrina Harman, Carlos Cardona, and Megan Ambuhl, I feel bad for them.*[2]

The soldiers to whom Mike refers were members of the 372nd military police company. The 372nd reserve unit was called to active duty in February 2003 and reported to Fort Lee, VA. They were initially deployed to Kuwait and then moved to the city of Al Hillah, Iraq. Their first mission was to integrate themselves into the Iraqi police and run a police academy. They also worked with marines in securing the region around Al Hillah. The 372nd received its second mission in October 2003—to assist in detainee operations in the largest detention center in Iraq and rebuild local police stations, courts, and schools near Abu Ghraib, Iraq. Their third mission was to provide escort for civilian and military convoys carrying supplies for the U.S. and Coalition forces. In 2004, the unit returned to Leesburg, where they underwent demobilization processes. It is the second mission that has made some of their members, including those listed earlier, infamous.

The 372nd, assigned to Abu Ghraib, faced an impossible task—running a prison without training, without adequate facilities, with a confused command structure, under constant bombardment from outside, and in which the prisoner-staff ratio was approximately six times greater than what U.S. prisons mandate. From the beginning, Abu Ghraib was arguably out of control. Consider the following description:

> For U.S. military police officers in Baghdad, the Abu Ghraib prison was particularly hellish. Insurgents were firing mortar shells and rocket-propelled grenades over the walls. The prisoners were prone to riot. There was no PX, no mess hall, no recreation facilities to escape the heat and dust. About 450 MPs were supervising close to 7,000 inmates, many of them crowded into cells, many more kept in tents hastily arranged on dirt fields within the razor-wired walls of the compound. Around the perimeter, GIs kept wary eyes on Iraqi guards of questionable loyalty.
>
> (Higham et al., 2004)

The supervisory ratio was 1 in 18. In civilian prisons, the ratio is 1 in 3. Moreover, the 372nd had scant experience in prisons. Except for two, none of them has any experience as prison guards, and no one had administrative experience. The 372nd was put in charge of wings 1A and 1B of the prison, where the most important detainees were handled. Their relationship with the military interrogators from intelligence was unclear. Some of those later convicted said that they were under pressure to facilitate interrogations:

> "In Wing 1A we were told that they had different rules," Davis, a college dropout from New Jersey, told investigators. He said intelligence officers frequently said things such as "loosen this guy up" and "make sure he has a bad night." Davis said he was told: "Good job. They're breaking down real fast."
>
> (Higham et al., 2004)

Karpinski, the commanding general responsible for Abu Ghraib, said later that military intelligence gave the MPs "ideas" that led to the abuse. She herself was later implicated. The Taguba Report recommended the following charges be brought against command officers:

> In March (2005), he recommended that Karpinski (reservist general in charge of the 800th Military Police Brigade, with primary oversight responsibility for Abu Ghraib) and Phillabaum (Officer in charge of the prison and reservist who commanded the 320 Military Police Battalion) be relieved of their commands and given reprimands for various command failures. He recommended the same for Col. Thomas M. Pappas, commander of the 205th Military Intelligence Brigade and his liaison officer, Lt. Col. Steven L. Jordan. Reese, the commander of the 372nd soldiers, should also be relieved and reprimanded.
>
> (Higham et al., 2004)

However, the brunt of military prosecution has focused on the soldiers of the 372nd. They have been widely portrayed in the media as out-of-control "sexual sadists." The media, their commanders, and the American public have shown little sympathy for these soldiers.

> MIKE CONTINUED: *They did what they thought was right with the tools they had. And boy did they get hung out for it. Who covers your ass when you make a mistake?*
>
> That comment generated uncomfortable silence. Mike knew he was on dangerous ground; a lot of loyalties could emerge darkly here. Well, some points are more uncomfortable than others.
>
> ONE OFFICER WAS CLEARLY PUT OFF BY THE DISCUSSION. *They deserved to be prosecuted. They broke the law. I have no sympathy for them. My sister was a veteran and she never did that shit. Nobody told them to abuse those prisoners.*
>
> MIKE TURNED AROUND SHARPLY, EYES FLASHING. *Nobody told them NOT to abuse them. That's the point. Read all the records. Did they have*

*training to tell them what they shouldn't do in human rights situations? Where's the training? Did they have commanding officers tell them what not to do? Where were the commanding officers during this? Off drinking tea in Baghdad? Did they have the intelligence officers tell them what not to do? Did they even have a copy of the Geneva Convention? No, no, no, and no.*[3] *That's the point. They're in a war. They're committed to doing something about the bad guys, and by God they're going to do it. They're going to kick ass. But there's no moral leadership. There's no training, at least not the right kind. There's no direction except to get results. How do they know what's right? Where does that knowledge come from?*

*What are their commanders saying? Aren't they talking about how evil the enemy is? How we won't respect Geneva conventions? How the gloves are off? How they'll gnaw through the fuel lines on a plane? How we have to find out when the next terrorist attack will be? Isn't that message coming to them, in one form or another, every day? And isn't it coming from the top of the command? What is the message? How can they not . . . how can they not do the meanest, vilest things imaginable? It's what is expected of them. As long as they don't get caught.*

Then Mike puts it out there. *Sound familiar?* He lets it hang in the air and gets a glass of water.

## *The Command Message in Doing Nothing*

Mike picks up the thread of discussion. He is somber, to the point. *You're in a war too, though it's a different kind. You're bringing in new officers to help fight the good fight. How do they know what's right? They're already committed to the good end. You don't want your recruits to end up like the soldiers at Abu Ghraib—doing all the wrong things for the right reasons, and then hung out to dry. Make sure they learn the right lessons and do the right things.*

*What are the lessons? The important lessons—about what it means to be a good cop, to work in a democracy, to respect people, to act within the law, those lessons come from you. It's all up to you. You all have to be moral leaders. If you give hints that it's OK to break the law, sometimes, if the cause is right, then they will do that. If you look the other way, they will think that it's all OK. They will find ways to develop techniques to get around search and seizure; they will thank you for it. If you provide little suggestions for giving bogus testimony they will be grateful. They will be whatever you want them to be. You aim them, and you pull the trigger. If you do nothing, you tell them that everything they do is OK.* He turns his attention to the captain who previously justified oversight of TOs in terms of training. *You, captain, it's about you, not them. Do you know what your TOs are really doing? How could you not know? They do what you want them to do.*

A review of the Stanford Experiment suggests the substantial problems with group behavior, under stress, when leadership lacks the right kind of training. The leadership of both the guard and prisoner groups emerged internally, as the groups adapted to the role expectations they thought were appropriate. One can see that one of the graduate students in charge of the guard group tended to "go native." This shift likely affected the experiment in unpredictable ways.

> Gordon (a friend of Zimbardo's) asked me a very simple question: "Say, what's the independent variable in this study?" To my surprise, I got really angry at him. Here I had a prison break on my hands. The security of my men and the stability of my prison were at stake, and now, I had to deal with this bleeding-heart, liberal, academic, effete dingdong who was concerned about the independent variable! It wasn't until much later that I realized how far into my prison role I was at that point—that I was thinking like a prison superintendent rather than a research psychologist.
>
> (Zimbardo, 2008)

Zimbardo was acting, not like a prison warden as he states in the quote earlier but like he thought a prison warden would act. That is part of the central issue here. They are taking on roles—including the staff—when they do not actually know how to do them.

> MIKE: *Let me talk about another experiment, one that gives us something to work with. It is called the British Broadcasting Company Prison experiment. It tells us about the importance of leadership in stressful prison settings.*

In a **British Broadcasting Company (BBC) Prison Study** intended as a follow-up to the Stanford Experiment, Haslam and Reicher revisited the Stanford experiment and came to different findings (see Reicher and Haslam, 2006). Group culture and leadership, they found, affected the tendencies of groups to become more authoritarian. When stress increases on group members, the result can be increasing support for authoritarian leadership. Group effectiveness, the authors suggested, tended to provide some protection against authoritarianism.

> Perhaps the most surprising finding from the BBC Prison Study was its demonstration of the way in which our participants, who started off holding democratic views and opposing inequality, gradually became more authoritarian as their groups failed to function effectively and the overall system fell into chaos. In such situations, the notion of a strong leader who would forcibly—even brutally—impose and maintain order became, if not actually attractive, at least less unattractive.
>
> (Haslam and Reicher, 2008)

Leadership was also a key variable:

> In the BBC study, participants as a whole may have become relatively more authoritarian, but it still needed active leadership to exploit this and to make the case for a new tough regime. The role of leaders becomes particularly pernicious when they suggest that "our problems"

come about because of the threats posed by a rebellious outgroup. In this way they can begin to take the groups with which we already identify and develop norms of hostility against outsiders.

(Haslam and Reicher, 2008)

MIKE: *Your department leaders, and that's you, are important. You're the most important part of this moral experiment we call a police department, because you set the moral standard. You are there to be emulated—it's the most important thing you can be for your officers. To be seen acting the way you want them to act.*

That's the lesson of the BBC experiment. Leaders can really screw things up. (A couple of officers quietly laugh.) And misuse of authority is about leadership.

You're the leaders. You can make sure your officers are aimed in the right direction and that if you have to pull the trigger, the aim is true. You want to help citizens? Help victims? Then be a good leader. All you have to remember is that you are a leader anyway. You are the role model, like it or not. You're always giving messages, especially when you say or do nothing. Doing nothing always, always means "OK, I support you. I just don't want to know about it." Well, it doesn't always work out that way. Remember Abu Ghraib. Remember King. You never know when there will be a visual record. That's some deterrent, huh? So be worthy of emulation, and be who you want them to be. Remember that and you're three-fourths of the way there.

## *Value-Based Decision-Making and the Means-Ends Dilemma*

A central issue in value-based decision-making is especially pertinent to police work. It is that the noble cause, the commitment to doing something about bad people, creates a tension between the means and ends of policing. The means of policing are organizational policy, criminal law, due process protections, and POST training that legitimizes particular police practices. The ends of policing are moral; they are doing something about bad guys, and they are embodied in the noble cause, in taking out the tower shooter, and in protecting the innocent. The means-ends dilemma occurs when officers think that they have to choose between the means of policing—acting legally according to due process ideas or following departmental procedure—and the ends, which involve the protection of victims and innocents by removing dangerous people from society. The following three documents discuss the means-ends dilemma faced by the police.

## Van Maanen and "The Asshole"

Van Maanen's brilliant essay titled **"The Asshole"** (1978a) is a study into value-based decision-making. Under what circumstances, he asked, do police officers find themselves in confrontations with troublemakers, and why do police sometimes end those confrontations violently? To answer this question requires that we examine the moral roots of police work.

Van Maanen noted that the moral mandate felt by police as their responsibility at the societal level, protecting people and preserving order, is transformed at the street level into controlling assigned territory and the people in it. Challenges to police control of their territories are sometimes corrected with acts of street justice—violence or rude treatment carried out against citizens. Under what conditions, he asks, is street justice acted out? He argued that street violence was more likely to occur when police officers thought that they were dealing with assholes.

Who are assholes? According to Van Maanen, assholes were not necessarily lawbreakers. They were citizens who challenged police efforts to control police-citizen interactions and, by implication, a threat to an officer's responsibility to control their assigned beat. Consider the example provided by Van Maanen (1978a:228).

> POLICEMAN TO MOTORIST STOPPED FOR SPEEDING: "May I see your driver's license, please?"
>
> MOTORIST: "Why the hell are you picking on me and not somewhere else looking for some real criminals?"
>
> POLICEMAN: "Cause you're an asshole, that's why . . . but I didn't know that until you opened your mouth."

The term asshole takes on significance only if you understand the way in which police morality is wedded to their occupationally defined sense of territory. Anyone who disputes the police right to control their territory is likely to receive a rude pronouncement to the contrary.

What values are the police using to decide who is or is not an asshole? Assholes are those who aggressively challenge the police officer's sense of the right way to conduct their beat. That "sense of the right way" is a value-based decision in the rightness of the way they do police work, and when encountering what Van Maanen called "assholes," they go through a concrete process that makes a moral decision about the rightness (or wrongness) of the use of "rough justice" to deal with a particular kind of person. Officers are, at each step, making a value-based decision.

## Delattre and the Noble Cause

Delattre (1996:190–213) was one of the few writers to specifically use and discuss the ethical implications of the term "noble cause." Delattre wrote that the way we think about our own worth is in terms of the "causes" that we take on. We are frequently judged and often judge ourselves, he observed, by whether our goals are admirable or despicable. Commitment to a noble cause can lead us to believe that some ends are so important that any means to achieve them is acceptable.

Noble-cause commitment troubled Delattre. Ends in themselves, Delattre warned, were insufficient to justify all behaviors needed to achieve them. Delattre quoted Camus (1974:5):

> There are means that cannot be excused.

In other words, no matter how noble the end, and no matter how worthwhile the goal, some ways of acting are unacceptable to reach that goal. The question that confronts police officers when they are committed to a good end is where and how to draw the line between acceptable and unacceptable behavior to reach the noble end.

When Camus made the statement earlier, he was trying to convince a young friend that the need for justice outweighs the greatness of country. He was talking to a young friend who had become a Nazi and was subordinating all his values to a Nazi cause that was soon to sweep across Europe. The German people carried a great bitterness for the way the Versailles treaty had subjugated their homeland after World War I, and the Nazi movement represented for many young Germans the resurgence of homeland independence and patriotism. To his young friend, the highest value was patriotism. Justice, according to Camus, was a higher standard—a means that was more important than the brutal ends sought by the Nazi movement.

A belief in justice, Delattre stated, was why American traditions have embodied the principle of fair play into the high law of the land, the Constitution. He argued that means embodied in legal due process—conforming to the dictates of the law—must be carefully weighed against any end, no matter how right the end seems at the time. We call this perspective **"just means,"** by which we mean the ethical concern that means used to achieve ends should conform to broad considerations of human values, particularly as those values are embodied in legal and administrative due process. His recommendations for managing the noble cause are presented in Box 1.2.

Box 1.2

**Delattre: Managing Noble Cause**

Delattre framed noble-cause corruption as follows: In law enforcement, are illegal actions that violate the rights of citizens ever morally right or excusable? Is there such a thing as excusable police wrongdoing? The answer is difficult, not clear. Yet from Delattre's thoughtful musings, a few important principles come through:

1. Lower-ranking personnel should never have the authority to make such decisions. The decision is so inherently grave and so important that only a commander should make it. The decision

Box 1.2, *Continued*

to use illegal means should never be left to the discretion of line or even middle management personnel in a police organization.

2. If a commander were to initiate the use of the third degree or other illegal police tactic to acquire information in order to deal with a compelling circumstance, he or she should immediately order an inquiry into the incident, to avoid the stigma of cover-up. He should avail himself of constitutional protections, and at the same time resign immediately from his position "to make clear that no one who has violated the standards of a position of authority should continue in it."

(Delattre, 1996:213)

The reader is invited to read Delattre's excellent discussion of noble-cause corruption; it discusses with clarity the many ethical problems associated with noble-cause corruption. It is particularly useful to commanders who may have to make such decisions or who have the courage to deal with noble-cause problems faced by their lower-ranking officers.

## Carl Klockars and the "Dirty Harry" Problem

Carl Klockars (1983) presented the noble-cause dilemma in terms of what is widely called the **Dirty Harry problem** (see also Klockars, 1985). When should an officer commit a dirty act to achieve a good end? Klockars (1983:429) presented a thought experiment. He described a then-popular movie titled *Dirty Harry*. Klockars described the following scene:

> A 14-year-old girl has been kidnapped and is being held by a psychopathic killer. The killer, "Scorpio," who has already struck twice, demands $200,000 ransom to release the girl, who is buried with just enough oxygen to keep her alive for a few hours.
>
> "Dirty Harry" gets the job of delivering the ransom money. Scorpio reneges on the deal and lets the girl die. Scorpio escapes, but Harry tracks him down. He confronts Scorpio on the 50-yard line of a football field. Harry shoots him in the leg while Scorpio is trying to surrender.
>
> As the camera draws back from the scene, Harry stands on Scorpio's bullet-mangled leg to torture a confession of the girl's location from him.

In the incident, there is a good end, an effort to save the life of an innocent victim of kidnapping. There is also a bad means, extorting a confession using third-degree torture tactics. There is also the connection between the end and the means—as Klockars (1991) noted, a means that can be justified if "what must be known, and, importantly, known before the act is committed, is that it will result in the achievement of the good end."

Klockars presented a compelling argument that the "Dirty Harry" problem is at the core of the police role. He identified four elements of police culture that predispose police to believe that they are dealing with guilty people, even in the absence of evidence, and thus justify the corruption of noble cause (see Box 1.3).

Box 1.3

**Klockars: Elements of Police Culture That Predispose Guilt**

*The operative assumption of guilt.* The police tend to assume guilt as a working premise of their craft. Officers believe that any questionable or furtive behavior they witness is evidence of some concealed offense.

*The worst of all possible guilt.* Police, Klockars observed, are obliged not only to make an operative assumption of guilt but also to think that the person is dangerously guilty: "the premise that the one who has the most to hide will try hardest to hide it is a reasonable assumption for interrogation" (1983:435). Consequently, it is imperative that police rapidly find out the underlying truth. This perspective justifies the use of the third degree.

*The great guilty place assumption.* Police are exposed to highly selective samples of their environment. Places are criminogenic, and the wise policeman sees danger where there might be none apparent to less suspicious eyes. *The not guilty (this time) assumption.* When a random stop of a motorist proves unwarranted, a vehicle search finds nothing, or an interrogation fails, police do not conclude that the person is thereby innocent. Most people have committed numerous crimes for which they have not been caught. Sometimes a little additional pressure will bring out an undisclosed truth that is being hidden by a seemingly innocent citizen.

Police officers, according to Klockars, tend to think that they are dealing with people who are factually guilty, even if they can't prove it in the current instance. Police think that they must use tricky means to find the guilt that people have. Bad guys know the ins and outs of the law and must be tricked or forced into telling the truth. Legal restrictions on police behavior consequently have a backfiring effect, intensifying the need for officers to use dirty means to uncover wrongdoing.

Dirty Harry problems can arise wherever restrictions are placed on police methods and are particularly likely to do so when police themselves perceive that those restrictions are undesirable, unreasonable, or unfair. The presumption of guilt can extend beyond illegal behavior. Our concern is that the police, convinced of the guilt of a suspect, may fabricate evidence in order to convince a jury of what officers already "know." This concern is demonstrated in Box 1.4 later.

Box 1.4

**Police Perjury in Homicide Cases**

The presumption of guilt is a pervasive characteristic of police work and can result in perjury on the witness stand to convince a jury of guilt. Because the stakes are high, one would think that cases of murder are the most carefully handled by the criminal justice system. However, homicide cases tend to be highly visible and emotionally charged. Consider the following three examples.

**Case #1.** On February 5, 1999, Anthony Porter was released from prison. He was held 16 years on death row. He had been scheduled to be executed the previous February, but his lawyers won a stay of execution. Subsequently, the main prosecution witness stated that he had been pressured by the police to implicate Mr. Porter. Another man has since admitted to the murders, and a corroborating witness has been found.

**Case #2.** Betty Tyson was, at one time, New York's longest-serving female inmate, in prison for 25 years for murdering a white, middle-aged businessman. Witnesses had placed Tyson at the scene, and she also confessed. She received a 25-to-life sentence for the murder. However, a reporter would later find that much of the case was falsified. The "confession" occurred following a severe beating she received at the hands of the police. One of the witnesses stated that "Detective Mahoney had actually put a revolver to his head and forced him to lie on the witness stand." And, in another document, one of the witnesses had stated that he had never seen Ms. Tyson at the murder scene, the opposite of what he stated at her trial. On May 25, 25 years after her arrest, a prosecutor announced that Ms. Tyson was free and would not be retried.

**Case #3.** This case is, in some ways, the most troubling because it displays collusion between the police and prosecutors in the prosecution of an innocent person. Two men were convicted of murdering and raping a 10-year-old girl in Illinois. A law professor at Northwestern University subsequently assigned the case to his students. Their research led to substantial evidence that the individuals who had been convicted did not commit the crime, and they were subsequently freed. Another individual has since confessed to the murder, and an investigator admitted he had falsely testified about evidence central to the case.

These cases are troubling. Many advocates of capital punishment contend that, with the substantial safeguards available for defendants, mistakes are rarely made. Yet this logic does not account for the noble cause, the tendency of the police to presume guilt, and sympathies for the victims, and the evidence suggests otherwise. Since Illinois has reinstated its death penalty, 11 individuals have been convicted, but ten have been found to have been wrongly convicted and have been freed. It may be that, because of their emotionally charged atmosphere and presumptions of defendants' guilt, death penalty cases are the most likely, rather than the least likely, to result in mistakes.

If Klockars was right, if the Dirty Harry problem is a dilemma frequently confronted by police officers, how should it be resolved? Is it acceptable for police officers to set aside legal means for good means?

His answer is frequently misunderstood by readers. On the one hand, he seems to be supporting the use of dirty means for good ends. Observe the following frequently cited quote in his article: "I know I would want him (Dirty Harry Calahan) to do what he did, and what is more, I would want anyone who policed for me to be prepared to do so as well" (Klockars, 1983:429). Yet, as Pollock (1998:189) observed, Klockars was making a more subtle point: "we all are guilty in a sense by expecting certain ones among us to do the 'dirty work' and then condemning them for their actions." In other words, when police commit legal wrongs, when they ignore the Constitution, use excessive force, or lie to convict a bad person, they are doing exactly what we want them to do. We just don't want to know that they're doing it. Klockars' conclusion, however, was that police who use dirty means to achieve good ends must be punished.

Klockars was aware that the punishment of police shifts the burden of using dirty ends to the public. "We recognize," he observed, "that we create a Dirty Harry problem for ourselves and for those we urge to effect such punishments." He concluded that:

> it is, in fact, only when his wrongful acts are punished that he will come to see them as wrongful and will appreciate the genuine moral—rather than technical or occupational—choice he makes in resorting to them. (1983:429)

It is a fitting end, one which teaches once again that the danger in Dirty Harry problems is never in their resolution but in thinking that one has found a resolution with which one can truly live in peace.

The strength of Klockars model is threefold. First, he shows that the actual occurrence of good ends can never be known for certain. We cannot predict outcomes. Our faith in good ends is sustained by hope, not fact. Obviously, the person Dirty Harry tried to save died. Second, the Dirty Harry problem reveals the way police officers think about their work settings, that is, as places of unknown dangers and dangerous people. Third, though it may not have been his intent, Klockars showed how the public is implicated in the pressures for police to use dirty means to achieve good ends.

## *Muir: The Tension between Means and Ends*

Muir (1977) argued that all police officers face a fundamental conflict. No matter what you do, he cautioned new police recruits, you will find yourself in situations from which you cannot escape without corrupting yourselves.

The corrupting situations he was talking about were **means-ends conflicts.** There were situations that police officers find themselves in, he cautioned, that presented a profound moral dilemma. If officers are committed to achieving good outcomes, they will, at some point in their careers, encounter situations in which the good ends cannot be achieved by legal ends. On the one hand, if they break the law to pursue those outcomes, they will have corrupted themselves by breaking the law that they are sworn to uphold. There is no way, Muir argued, to avoid being corrupted in one way or another. For example, officers have sometimes perjured their testimony in spite of a lack of compelling legal evidence because they were convinced of the suspect's guilt. Muir called this way of thinking **passion** and police officers that thought this way "enforcers." Passionate officers were those so committed to good ends that they ignored just means.

On the other hand, if officers failed to pursue those ends that they knew were right, if they became too obsessed with the rules of the game, they corrupted themselves by abandoning that in which they believed. He called this view **perspective** and labeled cops that thought this way "reciprocators." Officers with too much perspective were so committed to just means that they lost their sense of noble ends.

Inevitably, officers encountered circumstances with means-ends conflicts. When they did, the dilemma was complete. If officers didn't use those bad ends, they corrupted themselves by refusing to get outcomes that they knew were morally right. If they did, they corrupted themselves, only in a different way, by violating the law they were sworn to uphold. Muir's advice? He presented the argument originally stated by Weber in an earlier time. He had two recommendations.

1. If you are uncomfortable with moral dilemmas, you probably don't belong in police work.
2. If you are committed to a career as a police officer and are willing to brave its ethical dangers, be prepared to temper your passion with perspective.

Police had to be prepared for situations where force might be used and had to learn to act even when all choices were difficult. Officers that balanced perspective and passion were what Muir called "professionals." The ability to balance the two perspectives revealed maturity in police decision-making (see Box 1.5).

Box 1.5

**Power and Wickedness**

Are there ways to prevent the person in power from becoming wicked? In his essay "Politics as a Vocation," the German social theorist Max Weber (1864–1920) probed the question. He framed the problem of personality and power as follows: "He who lets himself in for politics, that is, for power and force as a means, contracts with diabolical powers and for his action it is not true that good can follow only from good and evil from evil, but that often the opposite is true. Anyone who fails to see this is, indeed, a political infant."

The secret to avoiding corruption by coercive power—i.e., wickedness, banality, or cowardice—was to combine passion with perspective. Once again, to resort to Weber's language, the "good politician" was defined by an ability to forge together "warm passion and a cool sense of proportion . . . in one and the same soul."

Source: Adapted from William Ker Muir, Jr. (1977). *Police: Streetcorner Politicians*, pp. 49–50.

## *Muir Reconsidered*

Both authors of this book have lectured on Muir's ideas of passion and perspective every year to policing students. It's a great lecture—interesting to police officers, non-police students, and instructors alike. Yet Muir's intent is often misunderstood by students. What instructors want to convey is that the use of coercive force is ethically complex, that a police officer should not act hastily in the use of force even when force is legally authorized. But this is not what students hear.

Our experience as educators is that students hear their instructor telling them that, if they believe strongly enough, it's okay to break the law to get the bad guys. This may sound very old-fashioned. Yet we have experienced it repeatedly in classes. Because students are preparing for a career in the field of law enforcement, they tend to identify with someone called an enforcer. And—make no mistake—they are passionate about enforcement. In discussions on Muir's ideas of police ethics, they "hear" their instructor justifying noble-cause corruption. It's the worst lesson they could learn.

We will reconsider Muir's message for two reasons: (1) we believe that there is a need to communicate more clearly what Muir intended, and (2) Muir adapted his ideas on force from Max Weber (1981), but Muir and Weber's audience were different in ways fundamental for thinking about police authority and use of force.

First, Muir's ideas have, we think, been widely misunderstood. Muir nowhere suggested that illegal means were appropriate for the achievement of good ends. What Muir sought to convey in his discussion of Weber's political model of ethical decision-making was this:

1. Why coercion is necessary for legitimate police work. Muir does not discuss illegal coercion. He is trying to explain the necessity for police use-of-force in a democratic society.
2. Why legal coercion should be balanced with perspective, by which is meant the capacity to understand the way in which tragedy is interwoven with action. An enforcer is not someone who uses illegal force. It is someone who too rapidly uses legal force to solve problems when other strategies might be more effective.

An officer who sometimes feels compelled to use so-called dirty means to achieve good ends—and by dirty means, we mean illegal means, such as testilying (testifying under oath, usually at trial, but lying in order to convict a perceived bad guy), manipulating evidence, using unnecessary force, or the like—is acting in a way inconsistent with Muir's notion of a mature officer. It is not even close to Muir's idea of an enforcer, who Muir described as a person who can't integrate his or her use of violence into a broader moral point-of-view.

Second, Muir used Max Weber's (1981) political model to develop his ideas of police morality. However, there are limitations in the extent to which Weber's political model can be used as a scale to measure police morality. Weber's speech was directed to future politicians, individuals who would be legislating law. Politicians make the law. Police do not. There are many of us who sometimes wonder if this is an unfortunate turn of affairs. But it is how things are and how they will remain. Muir recognized the limited applicability of Weber's message to the police and, consequently, narrowly defined the notion of passion in terms of *acted or threatened physical coercion*. There is no suggestion in Muir's work that police had the authority to violate the law on behalf of good ends.

Muir is not seeking to discover a way to permit illegal violence. To the contrary, he is looking for a counterbalance, a morality to limit the corrosive effects of legal coercive power, or what we would call the use of violence in pursuit of the noble cause. Perspective is for him that counterbalance.

What is the ethical lesson provided by Muir to which we should attend? Police officers have three ways to get people to do what they want them to do. The first is the ability to trade something of value to get someone to go along. The second is truth. Sometimes people will act, not because they are coerced but because they are convinced of the rightness of the action. These ways are what Muir (1977:48) calls the "power of the purse and the word." Third is coercion—the threat or application of force.

The dilemma Muir described was whether or not police should use coercive means when such means seem to be the most reasonable way to solve a particular problem. It was about the process of adapting oneself to the use of force in order to achieve compliance, yet recognizing that other means might be more suitable. **Maturity** was in the ability to balance the use of force with power of the purse and the word and to integrate the three into a moral perspective that reconciled the use of force with a perspective of the human dilemma that tempered temptations to use force unnecessarily.

## *The Power of Self*

There is a dimension of Weberian power not discussed by Muir. It represents a powerful ethic central to many of the world's religions. It also provides a basis for thinking about the responsibility of authority in a democracy. We call it the power of self. And we believe that it is an important part of police work, a part frequently overlooked in police training.

The **power of self** is the power to show others correct behavior through example, to pass values on to others because one acts as a representative of the best of those values. It is different from the power of the word, which can be camouflaged in deception. It is different from the power of the purse, which can represent no value at all. And it is different from force, which is the enactment of the will of a sovereign over his or her minions. The power of self is that which we expect from our leaders—to lead through example as well as talent, to provide a role model appropriate for the rest of us to follow.

The power of self, we believe, is an important police contribution to a democratic environment. The morals and ethics we expect of our leaders are the ethics we also expect from each other. These are ethics acted out by all of us in our everyday lives, striving to do better than we can sometimes, but as well as we must. We look to the police, as we look to other public servants, as models for what we should be. We recognize the moral role carried by the police in society, and we expect them to behave in a way that reflects a democratic ethic—fair play, honesty, perseverance.

The power of self is the power of the police to lead through example, to encourage people to treat each other fairly because police behavior is fair. It is the power to encourage peaceful resolutions to problems because they maintain public order through peaceful means. It is the power to approach conflicts not from the perspective of asserting some vague idea of public order but to seek a negotiated end to disorder. It is the power to work with the policed, particularly the poor, to help them resolve the petty problems that overwhelm their daily lives but are rarely seen and not understood by well-heeled legislators and policymakers.

We believe that the power of self is an important though neglected power that the police have. Moreover, the power of the self will have to be developed in order for the police to successfully deal with the profound demographic and social changes that will characterize the twenty-first century. The power of self—to lead by example and to act on behalf of the policed—are important and overlooked dimensions of the police today. The power of self is one way that the police temper the tendency to act too passionately on behalf of the noble cause. It does not solve all problems, and it is not law enforcement behavior. It is another aspect of the justice work carried out by the police, contributing to society through community action activities.

The power of self is a tempering of the noble cause, in which the police contribute to society through their active commitments to the work they accomplished in local communities. It is not behavior acted out behind the blue curtain, and it is not secretive. It begins with commanders and is passed on to line officers. It is the capacity to lead by example.

We see the power of self acted out every day by individual police officers. When police take on responsibility for mentoring youth, they are acting out of the power of self, leading through example. When they work with community groups to solve problems faced by those groups, they are acting out of the power of self.

One of the authors served with an organization sponsored by a sheriff's office for many years on a youth foundation, acting to place troubled youth in after-school programs. The sheriff, Vaughn Killeen, was displaying the strongest aspects of the power of self, publicly organizing the funding and organization of the foundation. Acting as the director, he attended the meetings, and he worked with people in the public and private sector to emphasize the importance of the program.

A social scientist would look at the program sponsored by the Sheriffs Youth Foundation and think about its evaluation. An evaluation would focus on program integrity: Was it implemented the way it should have been implemented? And they will look at outcomes: Did the program make a difference? These are rational considerations.

A police officer, and indeed leadership across the municipal spectrum, will consider a different dimension of the program. Is it trying to do good for young people, and are its supporters and workers committed to doing good? These people, in other words, look at the moral aspect of the program and then think about that morality in terms of the community's children. This is where the power of self is important. Killeen demonstrated his commitment, to advocate for the program, to approach other community leaders, and to use his reputation to try to make the program work. This the power of self-leadership by example, by being "out there" in the public eye so that others can see what you do and take hope and heart from it.

## Notes

1 Miles (2006:71–72) noted that 19 prisoners are known to have died of beatings, asphyxiation, or being suspended by American soldiers or intelligence officials. These men died at Asadabad, Bagram, and Gardez in Afghanistan and at Abu Ghraib, Camp Bucca, Camp Whitehorse, Basra, Mosul, Tikrit, and another unidentified facility in Iraq. . . . It undoubtedly fails to include some homicides of ghost prisoners, such as Al-Jamadi, . . . people who were secretly imprisoned by U.S. intelligence agencies.

2 All were prosecuted for crimes stemming from Abu Ghraib, and all were convicted.

3 Harold Brown (2004) submitted the testimony for the Final Report of the Independent Panel to Review Department of Defense Detention Operations in which he observed:

> the number and mix of detainees went far beyond what had been planned for. And the respective responsibilities, authorities and modes of cooperation for MP and MI units were poorly defined. Separately, the policy failure at all levels to assure a clear and stable set of rules for treatment and interrogation further opened the door to abuse. The problems were compounded by inadequate training, confused command arrangements and, at Abu Ghraib, personal deficiencies at command levels up to and including the brigade level. Hindsight always finds it too easy to assign blame. Nevertheless, varying degrees of responsibility for failure to provide adequate resources to support the custodial and intelligence requirements throughout the theater, and for the confusion about permissible interrogation techniques, extend all the way up the chain of command, to include the Joint Chiefs of Staff and the Office of the Secretary of Defense.

# 2

# Values, Hiring, and Early Organizational Experiences

## Key Terms

Black Swans
value-based hiring
latent content
value-predisposition perspective
value-neutral perspective
culture of policing
manifest content
pre-hiring procedures
value-neutral model of discretion
values-learned-on-the-job perspective
value transmission

## Introduction

This chapter explores the ethical foundations of police hiring and early organizational socialization. Contrary to the value-neutral perspective, which assumes pre-hiring procedures are impartial and objective, the chapter argues that policing is inherently a value-based profession. Through rigorous screening, departments engage in value-based hiring, selecting candidates already aligned with the noble cause—a moral commitment to justice that can supersede legal constraints. This value predisposition perspective challenges the values-learned-on-the-job model, asserting that recruits enter the force with pre-existing moral frameworks. The culture of policing, shaped by conservative backgrounds, facilitates value transmission from society to the profession.

> Mike scans his audience and smiles. *You're hiring cops. That means that you're hiring authorized representatives of a moral standard.*

DOI: 10.4324/9781003626916-4

Ethics in criminal justice is one of the most popular topics in current teaching curriculums today. It is increasingly difficult to receive a two- or four-year degree in criminal justice without having a class in ethics. Introductory textbooks on the police today typically will have a chapter on police ethics. An increasing number of textbooks are devoted to ethics.

There is an up-side and a down-side to ethics education. The up-side is that academicians and professional trainers are beginning to recognize the extent to which police work has strong moral and ethical elements and that values are important in police officer decision-making. The down-side is that much ethics education and training does not occur at the level of the ethics problems faced by officers and tends to make them out to be morally inadequate. It carries the implication that their moral identity is incomplete and that training or education can fill in the moral "gaps." The same message is stated repeatedly: shame on officers who take advantage of graft, free coffee, and free meals. Shame on officers who break the law. Shame on officers who hit citizens. Those are all prime examples of what is known in the media as bad cops.

Our position, however, is that recruits tend to be exceptionally ethical. They are chosen through rigorous hiring standards designed to make sure that they are ethical. Individuals who express the wrong kind of morality (that is, considered to be "out-of-line" with existing ethics of the local police culture) are weeded out during the probationary period. In the early years of employment, an officer's pre-existing morality is finely tuned to match the ethics of local police cultures.

In this chapter, we are going to first discuss the ethical bases of hiring. Officers, we contend, are screened by a value-based process that seeks to identify those committed to the noble cause. Second, we describe how early training selectively highlights particular experiences and values as ethically meaningful. Early organizational experiences reinforce their noble-cause commitment in a context of officer loyalty. Third, we discuss how the police organizations provide an environment supportive of value-based decision-making. The police organization, an "upside-down bureaucracy" from the point of view of public decision-making, enables officers to make value-based decisions in the routine course of daily activities.

## Pre-Hiring Procedures

What does it take to become a police officer? Of those who seek a career in policing, only certain ones will make the grade. How are officers selected? **Pre-hiring procedures** assess the qualifications of recruits for police work. The elaborate pre-hiring screening procedures, described typically as in Box 2.1, have been viewed by observers of the police as value neutral (Roberg et al., 2000, Reynolds, 2015). Value-neutral hiring is consistent with the view that police officers should not carry or act out predispositions about social rights and wrongs.

Box 2.1

**Pre-Hiring Procedures**

***Application.*** Applicants must submit an application. The application, listing background and personal characteristics, is the first stage of candidate evaluation. Candidates are expected to conform to certain criteria. The applicant's age is typically restricted to a range of 21 and 35. Height requirements, a traditional hiring criterion, are increasingly challenged in departments for being discriminatory to women and Asian Americans. Some departments have residency requirements.

A criminal record does not automatically disqualify a person for a police position. Many departments will also accept candidates who have used drugs, such as marijuana, but only if it was very infrequent, it was youthful, and if a certain quantity of time—three to five years for most departments—has elapsed. Some departments require that candidates are nonsmokers.

***Knowledge Testing.*** Many departments use some sort of standardized intelligence tests to evaluate the intellectual capabilities of candidates. Some departments have moved to make these tests more skills based and job related. Departments want smart officers but not officers who question procedures.

***Physical Agility Testing.*** Physical testing has traditionally focused on tests of physical strength—push-ups, weightlifting, chin-ups, and running distance and speed. There is little evidence that these tests have adversely affected either women or minorities, but they screen out candidates who are in poor physical condition or overweight.

***Background Check.*** This is an attempt to assess the character and suitability of candidates. Investigators want to know if the personal history given by the applicant on the application form is truthful. Of particular interest is past experience and lifestyle.

***Polygraph.*** This checks the accuracy of background information and looks for inappropriate behavior. As important as the polygraph is the pre-polygraph screening, when candidates are advised about the questions to be asked. It is during the pre-polygraph period that examiners find out a large quantity of information about the candidate.

***Psychological Testing.*** Testing assesses emotional stability and maturity. A common testing bank is called the Minnesota Multiphasic Personality Inventory. The California Psychological Inventory is also widely used. Both are called inventories because they test for a wide variety of psychological traits.

***Oral Interview.*** Candidates are measured on communications skills, confidence, interpersonal style, decision-making skills, and demeanor. Questions may include, "Why do you want to become a police officer?" Candidates may make decisions about what to do in hypothetical situations.

Source: Adapted from R. Roberg, J. Crank, and J. Kuykendall (2000). *Police and Society.* Los Angeles: Roxbury.

According to the **value-neutral perspective,** officers are not screened for their value predispositions, except for general factors of honesty, psychological stability, and evidence of criminal history. Many departments, for example, use the Minnesota Multiphasic Personality Inventory (MMPI), a test that looks at several dimensions of psychological identity, to assess the overall stability of a person, within accepted psychological limits. The argument in favor of these complex procedures is straightforward: a thorough screening and testing process ensures that only the most highly qualified candidates will be hired as police officers. The thoroughness of these procedures matches the public expectations of what police should be. The disadvantage of using the MMPI and similar psychological exams is that they are designed to "weed out" or identify those individuals who are far above the norm, in terms of general psychological "normality," or what is accepted as normal, in terms of neuroses.

Hiring, however, is not value-neutral. Elaborate screening protocols ensure that only a particular "type" of person will be hired. This type is squeaky clean (at least for the years immediately preceding the application), has limited tolerance for wrongdoing, and already carries a commitment to the noble cause.

If background checks are so thorough, then why has accountability been an ever-present problem in police departments? Does police work, given its tremendous opportunities for graft and abuse, simply encounter the limits of human virtue? In part, yes. Police work provides temptations in the absence of supervision. Do we unwittingly hire a type of officer who is more, not less, prone to some kinds of corruption? In part, yes. The corruption faced here, though, is not simply limited to economic corruption. It is more complicated. It is a corruption of democratic values to ensure that bad people do not get away with lawbreaking. Today, officers sometimes act on the belief that the noble cause is a standard higher than the law.

To understand the way in which this kind of corruption can occur, we first need to discuss the way in which hiring and screening are value-based process.

## Hiring Is a Value-Based Process

Mike asks the commanders about hiring protocols used in their agency: *With so many hiring procedures, what are you looking for? Why are there so many procedures? Who is it that you are afraid of hiring?*

Administrators will often comment that the different ways of gathering information tend to overlap. In the group Mike is talking to today, answers ranged widely. They're looking for indicators of past or potential problems. They want to know about criminal record. Lifestyle problems, including above-average debt. Drug use, including alcohol. Ability to handle stress.

> Mike continues. *Suppose a candidate comes to the oral interview. He's got a perfect background, checks out, passes the polygraph. But he shows up with hair down to the middle of his back, a peace symbol earring, and a hemp tie. Would he get the job?*
>
> No one answers.
>
> Mike singles out one of the officers. *Would he get the job?*
>
> "Well, maybe" the officer responds. The room is quiet for a moment. Then everyone bursts into laughter. Maybe is a good answer when "yes" is unthinkable and "no" is inappropriate.
>
> *Would you hire him?* He asks another officer.
>
> "Maybe."

The point Mike is making is this. Hiring is value-based. In **value-based hiring**, we hire police officers for their values, we check them out relentlessly to make sure that their values are in order, and then we double-check our decision to hire them with value-based tests during their probationary period. How do they handle their first arrest? Will they back up another cop without hesitation? These are value judgments. The judgments police make and for which they are screened during recruitment and probation are based more in values than in knowledge of the law. Recruits are tested to see if considerations of loyalty and commitment to the noble cause will override personal safety considerations.

Officers are screened out who don't perform adequately in legal history, physical strength and agility, psychological suitability, and weapons training and skills. But these are threshold requirements, necessary conditions to becoming a police officer. They are not sufficient conditions. Values are the glue that unites the elements of the hiring process.

## Screening for Values versus Job-Learned Values

Our **value-based perspective on hiring** differs sharply from most discussions about the police. As we noted previously, when officers are hired, their moral commitments are already in place. Hiring procedures are designed to screen out those who don't have the right way of thinking about police work, who lack the "right stuff"—loyalty and commitment to the noble cause.

This is not a fashionable way to look at values of police officers. The most popular academic view is that a "police perspective" is learned on the job, in the doing of police work. Academics are fond of asking the question, "Why are police different from everyone else?" Of course, the question is biased with its presumption that police are different. But police also see themselves differently, as special members of a select and inwardly focused group (Van Maanen, 1978b; Bouza, 1990). It is a bias shared by the police and non-police alike.

The question "Why are police different?" has two answers that have been popular in different times. The first is that differences come from the nature of the work that police do, from values learned on the job. This perspective is the most popular in the current era. The second is that a particular type of person is attracted to policing. This perspective was popular in the 1960s but has lost market value. Yet it is our perspective.

The **values-learned-on-the-job perspective** is that officers come from diverse backgrounds and represent many different groups and belief systems in society. Pre-service training and assignment to a training officer are a socialization and educational process that teach someone how to think like a police officer. They learn what it means to be committed to the service of police work. In the first few years, police undergo a socialization process that prepares them mentally and physically for a career in policing.

The values-learned-on-the-job perspective is not a way of thinking about the police that we share. We argued in Chapter 1 that important values associated with police work and with the noble cause are already in place at the time of hiring. Training teaches recruits how to apply those values to a police work setting. Prospective police candidates are individuals who already hold a positive reservoir of sentiment for the police. They tend to share the police moral sensibility, dividing the world into good guys and bad guys. They feel good when bad guys are hurt, and they want to be one of the good guys. They already have in place a clear sense of moral justice. They have friends (or relatives, or both) who are police. Long before they have taken their first examination for a position in a police department, they are committed to the noble cause. They already understand policing, by spending many hours talking to officers, and they know, or think they know, what makes a "good" cop.

Our view, called a **value-predisposition perspective,** is that officers are hired with their values in place, and these values are selectively highlighted and finely tuned during academy and on-the-job training. This perspective is as follows: A person who aspires to become a police officer selects policing from a variety of employment options that he or she is thinking about. Fine-tuning of his or her values, focused on organizational loyalties and local justice practices, occurs during early organizational experiences. This process happens quickly, in the first year or two. Within a relatively short period of time, a fully framed "police" way of looking at the world is formed. The primary formative influences are the academy (Harris, 1973), the field training officer (Van Maanen, 1978a), the police culture (Manning, 1997), the danger and isolation of police work (Skolnick, 1994), internal pressures for the production of arrests (Manning and Redlinger, 1977), and sometimes darker elements of the police socialization process, such as corruption (Kappeler et al., 1994), to name but a few.

Police officers tend to be drawn from a **culture of policing** (Crank, 2004a). This means that police officers come from backgrounds already sympathetic to the police. Their backgrounds include police families, small towns, military personnel, and other similar groups. These groups form a culture of policing because they carry values similar to police, particularly conservative values about the desirability of order in human relations.

Groups that comprise the culture of policing have many elements in common. Economically, they tend to be blue-collar working-class. They are often politically conservative in orientation, though they are slightly less likely to be Democrats than Republicans. Their values are old-fashioned; they do not see the world in terms of competing values and situational ethics. They believe that being American is, at its most basic, about moral fiber. And for young people, police work is a way to participate in an important endeavor, to contribute to and maintain the traditions of American society. Police work is perceived by many as one of the primary occupations through which they join the ranks of the middle class in the United States.

Values are carried from broader society to police work by a process called **value transmission.** Pollock (1998:7) provides a way to think about the process of value transmission from early upbringing to the working police environment. Morality, she observed, "is used to speak of the total person, or the sum of a person's actions in every sphere of life." Ethics, on the other hand, "is used for certain behaviors relating to a profession." Morals, we suggest, represent the values that a person is taught during their upbringing and are learned from parents, schools, and other important social institutions. Police ethics represent the way those moral values are channeled into specific occupational experiences. Recruits undergo a transition that shapes their moral sense into something which allows individuals to make specific ethical decisions (Fitch, 2014). According to Klaver (2014), "Formal socialization processes, ethics training, coaching and support, recognition and reward of behaviors that support organizational values, and insuring the proper fit of individuals to the organization and its environment are all mechanisms that support this objective" (2014:21, cited in Fitch, 2014). The underlying ethic that mobilizes police behavior is the noble cause.

New recruits are value-based decision-makers, and they are already committed to the noble cause. They believe in it. It's not something they learn from some dark police subculture. It's not as if a recruit in a POST ethics class watches the instructor draw a stick figure of a suspect with a frowny face behind bars, slaps his forehead, and exclaims "Oh! Now I get it!" The noble cause is an interior psychological map of the beliefs and morals developed during their upbringing. Every time they turn on the tube and see a report of a 10-year-old girl that has been kidnapped, the fires of the noble cause are stoked. Each time they hear that some killer has been granted a stay of execution, their blood boils. An abstract ethics discussion will be irrelevant to them, and meaningless, both personally and professionally.

## Early Organizational Experiences

Early organizational experiences focus the way officers act out their values. In this section, we discuss the influence of early organizational experiences on recruits, particularly focusing on the training officers. We also look at discretion from a value-based perspective.

> MIKE: *Your idealistic young officers are going to go to training. Much of their training is about how to apply the noble cause to specific situations. By the time you are through training them, they will all be thinking just like you want them to think. Do you know what you're teaching them to think? In this section we'll see what they learn from their trainers.*
>
> A commander responds. "We don't teach them about the noble cause." Mike stops for a moment and then raises his index finger in the air. *Right. You don't. You take it for granted. You don't want officers who aren't committed to doing something about bad people. Do you?*
>
> He smiles. *It's so obvious that we don't look for it. The commitment to the noble cause. It's like the air we breathe. It's the touchstone that makes everything else work. So when we train, we are always training from the touchstone, the noble cause.*

Pre-service training provides the setting in which an officer's predispositions are molded to fit particular local cultural characteristics. The general "type" who is hired as a police officer becomes a specific "type" participating in local organizational culture. Officers quickly become aware of the rites and rituals of their organization and, in a relatively short period of time, complete the process of socialization into their department (Van Maanen, 1978b).

Many people have suggested that pre-service training contributes substantially to the process of local socialization. Van Maanen (1978b) suggested that this occurs primarily through war stories: it is through the telling of war stories that recruits learn the history and traditions of the department. He also suggested that stress training, in group cohorts, reinforces the view that officers can only trust other officers. Yet many of the lessons learned in training are widely associated with some of the less pleasant elements of police culture such as secrecy and violations of due process. And stress training is nowhere as widespread as it was when Van Maanen carried out his work. How can local socialization to police culture occur today in a contemporary environment designed to teach about the law, necessary police skills, and participation in routine organizational processes?

## Ford: Values and Pre-Service Training

Ford (2003) suggested a mechanism by which elements of police culture are taught in today's training processes. War stories were "a narrative presented to an academy class or during field training that describes a particular incident or circumstance" (2003:89). War stories carry two kinds of content. Their **manifest content** is the "front page" message or the "overt message of the story." The latent content was the "message beneath the message." These are hidden or covert messages that are conveyed in the manifest message.

Ford (2003) did not claim that the covert messages were always intentional or purposeful; rather, the trainer may be giving a message he or she doesn't realize is being given. For example, Ford described a story of the stop of a black motorist.

> The officer asks to see the driver's license and registration. The driver advises that his license is located in the car trunk in his wallet. The officer looks in the trunk to get the wallet; while the officer reaches into the trunk, the driver who is alongside the officer slams the trunk and the fight is on.
> (Ford, 2003:91)

The manifest content of the story is that suspects should be at a safe distance during a search. Noteworthy was the identification of the suspect's race. When suspects were white, war stories never identified the race of the suspect. When minority protagonists were identified, Ford noted, the stories were more detailed; they taught technique and warned from what quarter an officer might be attacked. In this way, messages that were politically or socially incorrect, such as race-based messages like the one earlier, were likely to be conveyed as latent content.

Ford analyzed 269 stories. Of these, 58 percent had street skills as their primary message, followed by tales of danger or uncertainty (21 percent). Other stories included pro-citizen and anti-citizen views; anti-citizen views were roughly twice as prevalent as pro-citizen stories. Many stories also focused on the police organization. About one-half of these were favorable to the police organization, and the other one-half were critical. Many stories also had a secondary manifest content. These were stories in which a message was clear but was more subtle. Ford notes with regard to these that "primary story lines underestimate the count of stories with sexist, racist, or ethnic content." These stories accounted for 12 percent of the secondary content.

**Latent content** analysis produced quite a different set of findings. Ford found that 83 percent of the stories reinforced local subcultural values, while only 2 percent were critical of local subculture. He also noted that 14 percent of the stories "supported ethical values," while 48 percent were neutral and 38 percent were anti-ethical. Most of these were critical of community policing. Most stories had a latent value that was legally neutral. Four percent of the stories supported the law, while 11 percent, slightly less than three times as many, supported views that were against the law. These typically involved "testilying" (giving false testimony), use of force, and illegal searches. Regarding the organization, 18 percent were organizationally positive, while 25 percent, about one-third more, were organizationally critical. A few were "Black Swans" (see Box 2.2).

Box 2.2

**Buerger (1998): War Stories and Black Swans**

Occasionally, the recollections into past incidents are illuminative, providing practical insight into both situational assessment and tactical response. More frequently, they are **Black Swan** anecdotes that contradict the primary message of the instruction, whether intentionally or inadvertently; the latter usually occurs when the speaker, presenting in "good faith" mode but with no personal investment in the material, fails to recognize that the anecdote undermines the primary purpose of the lesson.

Buerger cites the following anonymous quotation from a West Coast police academy:

> [trainers] . . . were just spouting the official [agency] line on everything, all the while strongly suggesting that it was all bullshit and that we would learn the real stuff out on the street—"ya know, we can't tell you to slap the shit out of those punk gang-bangers back in the alley here, but don't worry about that, you'll learn soon enough."
>
> "What we teach here," they often said, "is the official bullshit to cover our butts legally, not the real deal."
>
> (1998:44–45)

Source: Michael Buerger (1998). "Police Training as a Pentecost." *Police Quarterly*, 1–1:31.

How did training recruits respond to these stories? Of the 89 officers interviewed, all but two said that war stories were important to their training. As Van Maanen noted in 1978(b), recruits view war stories as an important part of their training regimen and as something more than just the opportunity to tell stories in the absence of formal training. Indeed, as Ford emphasized, stories *are* training. They provide recipes and ways of thinking about specific kinds of encounters and types of individuals.

Ford allows us to understand how pre-service training is a mechanism for the rapid socialization of new officers into local cultures. Through the manifest content of stories, officers learn about dealing with danger and the development of street-wise skills. However, through the secondary content, and through latent content, officers are exposed to local cultural values; put differently, they are learning how to be actors in their local organizational cultures. The group of recruits studied by Ford had listened to 269 stories during their training. By the end, they had been exposed to a great deal of local culture. Storytelling, through the delivery of manifest and latent content, is the mechanism for rapid socialization among a group of individuals who seek such socialization.

## *Values and Getting PC*

If a police officer approaches a citizen and suspects that the citizen may have committed a crime or is about to commit a crime, the officer has a legal tool at her disposal. That tool is a legal standard called "reasonable suspicion." According to this standard, a police officer may approach, ascertain the identity of a person, conduct a brief field interrogation, and conduct a pat-down search of an individual, primarily to look for weapons, if the officer thinks a person has committed or is about to commit a crime. The reasonable suspicion standard, established in *Terry v. Ohio, 392 U.S. 1 (1968)*, permits police to investigate the possibility of criminal activity at a level lower than the standard required for arrest, which is probable cause.

Probable cause means that a set of facts and circumstances would induce a reasonably intelligent and prudent person to believe that a particular person had committed a specific crime. This is required for a seizure, the legal term for arrest.

A vehicular stop is a seizure under the law. It is a seizure because a person's freedom of movement is restricted. Hence, the standard for a vehicular stop is probable cause. This raises a question. What happens when officers are suspicious of a vehicle or its driver but lack those facts that satisfy the probable-cause standard? This is one of Mike Caldero's favorite topics.

> What do you do when you are following a vehicle and let's say you suspect the person is carrying drugs. You want to take a closer look. What do you do?
>
> "We develop probable cause. It's in our training."
>
> It's in your training.
>
> "We're taught to use all our senses. We're taught what we can look for how to follow a vehicle, to look for nervousness in the driver, a plate that doesn't match the car, all the things that justify a seizure. We have been through a lot of drug interdiction training and we learn a lot of signs to look for. And we learn how to write up the case to justify the stop. Paperwork is a lot of what training is all about."
>
> How do you do this writing exercise in training?
>
> "Well, one way we do it is by taking a scenario and writing down what we do that justifies each stage of the investigation associated with the stop."
>
> So you record all the information in a way that it stands up under close legal scrutiny.
>
> "Exactly. That's exactly what we do."
>
> So that paper record that you create enables you to translate the stop that came from your suspicion into a bona fide probable cause legal stop. How is that not noble-cause corruption?

This stops the officer for a moment. He responds, "We keep track of the facts of the case."

This is not what you've been saying. What you've been saying is that you develop a written document that legally justifies your stop. Isn't that what you've been saying?

"That's what we do."

That's noble-cause corruption! Think about it. You are suspicious. You want to make a stop. So you start using your imagination—as you are taught to do, using all your senses—to try to make this into probable cause to justify a seizure. How—how is that not noble-cause corruption?

"What are we supposed to do? We could be following someone that we know is carrying drugs. Why shouldn't we be able to stop a car like we stop individuals? We have no alternative but to develop probable cause."

A trainer in the back of the room looks down and shakes his head. For him, the point has come home.

Mike stops for a moment, and then looks directly at the officer. Thank you. *Thank you for saying that. That kind of honesty is what we need here today. Yes, what you say is exactly right. It's about the noble cause, stopping someone you think may be up to no good, and you use the law to carry out the noble cause, to make the stop. You have shifted the way you think about the vehicular stop. You are not doing "just the facts" policing. Your question has become "how do I find a way to get a seizure?" Value-based decision-making. You are making a moral decision and looking for ways to convert it into a legal story line.*

Trainers inadvertently contribute to this way of thinking. They too often do not mention the need to document facts. They tend to focus more on "building the case." They focus on "developing," which a rookie officer can hear as "use your imagination."

Let's look at another dimension of this stop. Suppose that a patrol officer stops someone that she believes is carrying drugs. She recognizes the occupants. She thinks they're up to no good. She follows them, they get nervous after a while, and they decide to stop. That's PC. She tells them to stand behind the car and open the trunk. Legal standing is on her side, right? She has probable cause so far. She tells them to open the trunk or she will get a warrant, and that will make things worse. She searches the trunk, empty, and then looks around inside the vehicle. She opens a box in the backseat and finds several unlicensed weapons, including two M82A1 sniper rifles. She also finds a white powdery substance in a small bag that she suspects is cocaine. Illegal search. But this guy was up to no good and she's got an arrest that makes her feel good. Later, a tape from her vehicle is reviewed by the patrol sergeant. It clearly shows the illegal search. The sergeant has to decide whether to erase the tape or to turn it over to the Chief. If you were the Patrol Sergeant, what would you do with the tape?

Officers look straight ahead.

What would you do with the tape?

"I bet I could get a grand from CNN for it," responds one officer. Others laugh.

Mike points at another officer. *What would you do with the tape?*

"What tape?" A few officers chuckle.

Tough question, isn't it? Who in here is willing to rat on another officer? You see, we have three instances in this example where the law was used on behalf of the noble cause. The first was the stop. The second was the search. The first was legal, but if you look at the underlying morality, it was all noble cause. The second took the noble cause a step further, into noble-cause corruption. And no one in here is willing to say it's wrong. Everyone is side-stepping the issue. That's the third instance.

You see how value-based decision-making runs through all decisions? It's the air you breathe. We have four decisions in this example that involve value-based decision-making. We also have several instances of noble-cause corruption, which tended to be about whether the officer would be caught.

Mike finishes on this topic. *What you need to realize is that this value-based way of thinking about getting PC underlies a great deal of what the police do. It is used in stops and it is used in searches. It is especially prevalent in "consent searches." And it is at the heart of so-called racial profiling. We will have a great deal to say about racial profiling this afternoon.*

## *Values and the Training Officer*

One of the ethical dilemmas noted by many observers of the police is the powerful influence the training officer has on new recruits. The training officer introduces recruits to the craft of policing. However, training officers sometimes undercut all administrative efforts to control line-level behavior.

Training officers (TOs) are another one of Mike Caldero's favorite topics.

What person has the most influence on your new recruits?

The answer, of course, is the training officer.

Your recruits are going to be with the officer for maybe six months. They're going to role model that young recruit down to the last doughnut. If that TO you've got out there that is taking him to the doughnut shop is not the individual you want him to emulate, then it's your screw-up, not theirs.

Let's think about this for a minute. Mike is talking to command-level police managers. They've heard all this ethics talk before. They know that some officers are not molded from the "right stuff." They believe that a few bad apples always slip through the screening process. But they haven't been told that it's their fault. How can this **be?**

From their earliest training in POST, officers have been taught to avoid any illegal conduct. They are taught to avoid such activities even if other officers around them do not avoid it. They are expected to resist the activity and to report it. Even the appearance of unprofessional behavior is unacceptable. They've been drilled in ethical conduct. They've been scolded for looking cross-eyed at a free hot meal. They may have studied the Law Enforcement Code of Ethics, the California Highway Patrol Statement of Professional Values, and all 51 standards of the eight canons of ethics of the Code of Professional Conduct and Responsibility for Peace Officers (see Miller, 1995). Then they're turned loose to their TO, who wants to know if they're loyal and if they will back up other officers. They are told by their TO to forget everything they learned in training: "Here's how we do it in the field." And they know that the TO can make or break their careers.

Mixed signals? What recruits are being told in their "formal" ethical training or education is to report any inappropriate or illegal behavior. They're provided an elaborate, complicated set of written standards to guide their behavior. And if your training officer or other members of your squad do something wrong, stop them and report the incident to their superiors.

Mike mimics a sergeant cynically telling an officer what will happen to him if he turns on his TO or fellow officers.

> Yea, that'll work. How are you going to explain that to the orals board on your next job interview?

## *Van Maanen and Early Organizational Experiences*

How influential is the TO? Van Maanen's (1978b) research provides us with an understanding of the influence of the TO in training new recruits. New recruits, he suggested, are the most vulnerable to organization pressures. During the probationary period, an officer has no job protection and can be terminated for failing to satisfy the expectations of his or her TO. Van Maanen put it this way:

> It is during the breaking-in period that the organization may be thought to be the most persuasive, for the person has few guidelines to direct his behavior and has little, if any, organizational support for his "vulnerable selves" which may be the object of influence.
>
> (Van Maanen, 1978b:293–294)

The most important influence on a recruit, Van Maanen observed, was the field training officer.

> It is commonplace for the rookie to never make a move without first checking with his TO. By watching, listening, and mimicking, the neophyte policeman learns how to deal with the objects of his occupation—the traffic violator, the hippie, the drunk, the brass, and the criminal justice complex itself. . . . A whole folklore of tales, myths, and legends surrounding the department is communicated to the recruit by his fellow officers—conspicuously by his TO. Through these anecdotes—dealing largely with mistakes or "flubs" made by policemen—the recruit begins to adopt the perspectives of his more experienced officers . . . he learns to be protected from his own mistakes, he must protect others.
>
> (Van Maanen, 1978b:301)

And we think that we can provide ethics training in college or in training and recruits can overcome this kind of organizational influence?

> Mike describes to his audience a training film used in a department in California. *A cadet is riding along. A routine stop is made. Of course, it's a minority person. They tell him to get out of the car. And sure enough, they get into a fight. Another car shows up. And then there are five cops fighting. Mob mentality has taken over. They're beating him into the ground. The cadet is expected to push everybody away and turn right around, get all of their names, and report the incident. Can you imagine that happening in your favorite city?*

Every officer out on the street knows that if they turn on another cop, their life is going to take an unpleasant turn. This is not unique to cops. Our research on whistleblowing shows that whistleblowers (i.e., people who seek recourse to organizational problems by reporting those problems outside the chain-of-command or to authorities outside the organization)—the media for example—suffer a variety of professional indignities (see Box 2.3). Moreover, they rarely recover their jobs or their professional reputations. In police work, a whistleblower will

Box 2.3

**Retaliation**

Consider the following description of a retaliation, reported by Pollock (1998):

> A typical example of retaliation is reported in a San Diego newspaper concerning an officer in the San Diego police department who arrested a sergeant for driving while intoxicated. Even though the officer previously averaged fewer than two complaints a year during his 11 years at the police department, after he arrested the sergeant, he received nine complaints resulting in a total of 68 days of suspension.

Box 2.3, *continued*

> He also experienced the following: he encountered hang-up calls on his unlisted home telephone, his belongings were stolen, his car was towed away from the police parking lot twice, officers refused to sit next to him, and officers did not respond to his calls for back-up. . . . The sergeant who was arrested for drunken driving was released before being taken to a magistrate, contrary to departmental policy, and received no disciplinary actions.

Source: Casey, R. (1996). "Cop Wins One Million in Whistleblower Appeal." *The Ethics Roll Call*, *4*: 6.

be ostracized by his or her fellow officers and, if the whistleblower is a recruit, is unlikely to receive regular employment. As one observer of the training film described by Mike Caldero observed, "He [the recruit expected to report the wrongdoing] has got a sidearm. He might as well take it out and pull the trigger, because he's just committed suicide on the job." Now let's see that training film again.

Managers understand line officer morality, even if they no longer have a practical sense of the "street." They were selected from the same moral cloth. TOs fine-tune recruits so that they don't embarrass the department, and managers guard against blunders that threaten departmental legitimacy or create liability problems. Managers, nevertheless, can't resist trying to control line personnel. They are patriarchal, like those they hire, and take a view of their line officers as untrained children who need discipline to act right. Of course, failure is inevitable. Characteristics of police organizations mitigate against effective oversight of discretion. These characteristics are discussed in the next section.

## The Myth of Police Discretion

After a break, Mike expands the discussion of value-based decision-making to the topic of discretion. His theme is that police discretion is, in part, an illusion of how we think about modern bureaucracies. So-called "discretionary" police behavior, he argues, is value-based and predictable.

> Okay. Imagine this. There's a car full of fat white men in $1,000 suits. The driver's license of the driver is expired. Now, in your mind, imagine slamming these guys on the hood of the car, palms down. Kicking their feet apart. Screaming at them. Can that image, that CONCEPT even enter your mind? It's not even possible. The image doesn't work.
>
> Now imagine doing this to a car full of black teenagers with baseball hats on backwards.

> The audience laughs quietly. Mike laughs too, nodding his head up and down.
>
> See. Now that works, doesn't it? You can imagine that. Now you understand that your officers are making value-based decisions about their work. They're not making discretionary decisions. The issue for many police officers is not what they do. It's whether they're caught.

The notion that police make discretionary judgments in the conduct of their work, particularly with regard to the decision to arrest, emerged in the 1960s. A discretionary perception of police work represented a sharp break from the then-popular perception of "just the facts" decision-making, where police decisions flowed from rational, non-valued judgments of the facts. The ABF survey (noted in Box 2.4) unleashed a torrent of research on the discretionary nature of criminal justice decision-making (Walker, 1993). Today, police are commonly believed to exercise wide discretion in many aspects of their work that cannot be brought under administrative control. Indeed, a central tenet of the community policing movement is that police officers should have wide discretion to act upon their judgments of situational dynamics in police-citizen encounters.

Box 2.4

**Discretion and the American Bar Foundation**

In 1996, Kleinig observed that "in the American Bar Foundation (ABF) survey of 1956, it was discovered that at each stage of an individual's encounter with the criminal justice system the outcome was determined by a decision that was essentially 'discretionary' in character." This finding was controversial because it suggested that the most important police decisions, those involving the immediate freedom of a suspect, were being made outside formal administrative and legal protocols (Kleinig, 1996:1).

We contend that values predispose behavior across the decision-making process, not only in the invocation of a criminal sanction of arrest. When an officer uses force to gain compliance, the officer is, by the general definition, making a discretionary judgment. The decision to use force may be legal, but the officer is applying his or her judgment to the level of force displayed by a suspect and making an additional judgment about the appropriate force response. Or when an officer makes a decision about when to intervene in a suspicious circumstance, the officer is making a discretionary decision.

## Values and Discretion

The administrative response to discretion is to try to bring it under organizational control and regulate it. Policies, rules, and regulations provide a managerial basis for attempting to control behavior. Administrators operate under what might be called a **"value-neutral" model of police discretion.** This means that discretionary judgments of line officers are viewed as a sort of unregulated, uncontrolled form of decision-making that, with correct policy, can be controlled by the organization (Cohen, 1996). Officers, armed with the appropriate policies, will not use discretion unwisely but will thoughtfully apply discretion to make good decisions. They become good street bureaucrats.

This "value-neutral" model of administrative control over discretion comes up short. The value-neutral model presumes (1) that police have wide discretion, and (2) the use of discretion will tend toward uncoordinated decision-making that can be corrected with proper training and thoughtful policy. The model, however, doesn't adequately consider the values that motivate police officers (see Box 2.5). It utterly fails to recognize that officers are making morally important, value-based decisions on the use of discretion. If the values that underwrite the decisions are known, then the "unpredictable" nature of police discretion disappears. The administrative problem is consequently framed as follows:

> Mike argues that if someone's values are known, their behavior can be predicted, and the issue of discretion disappears. He compares the police to the military.
>
> In order to get people to do something you want them to do, especially if it's risky, you have to underpin their behavior with a value system. If you can do that, you can predict what their behavior is going to be, in a given situation, at least within reasonable limits.
>
> You can't get people to fight wars if they don't believe in the reasons for fighting. If you understand that, you have already explained away most decisions that are called discretionary.
>
> Think about the "war on crime" mentality. We underpin anti-drug police tactics with a simple morality. Good, bad. Good cop. Bad drug user. One value system against another. We hire for this. When an officer starts work, he's already thinking this way. It's not discretion he doesn't understand. He's making moral decisions, and his morally good ends determine his means. He has to learn how to avoid getting caught.
>
> This is why all this literature about the rational use of discretion is nonsense. We can assert that police officers have little or no discretion. They are selected for their values. You hire them from this value set, you train them to focus on officer safety, thus even further removing them from the policed. You train them for quick, "in your face" decisions. Make a decision, move on to the next. Instant solution-makers.

You arm them, give them a car. You've aimed the weapon and cocked the hammer. You know how they think and what they're going to do. Where's the discretion? How can you NOT know what they're going to do?

Box 2.5

**The Paradox of Moral Decision-Making in an Administrative Setting**

The proper question facing administrators is not how to coordinate uncontrolled decision-making but how to bring value-based decision-making under the umbrella of administrative and lawful influence. Their moral paradox is that the more they appeal to line morality, the more likely they are to lose control to pre-existing noble-cause commitments. And the more they appeal to administrative responsibilities, the more likely they are to alienate line officers behind the "blue curtain."

The police task is often described by outside observers as highly flexible and vulnerable to many discretionary outcomes and cannot be brought under the control of administration or the law. That means that outsiders, examining what police do, would conclude that a wide range of outcomes are possible, even reasonable, for the kinds of encounters in which police find themselves.

Police officers, however, don't use discretion from a value-neutral perspective. They are hired with a sense of "noble-cause" morality already fully in place. As soon as they begin patrol work, their values influence and are refined by the decisions they make about suspects, assholes, and victims, about when and where to intervene, about who is a good guy and a bad guy, and about loyalty to their colleagues. Their decisions about appropriate means are based on terminal or ends values, and knowledge of those ends values enable an insightful observer to predict police behavior in any given police-citizen encounter. And the central end value is the noble cause—getting the bad guys off the streets.

## Value-Based Decision-Making and the Limits of Ethics Reform

This chapter has developed three closely related themes. The first is that police recruits undergo a recruitment process designed to winnow out those who fail to carry appropriate values. Second, early socialization experiences reinforce those values. Third, historical and organizational features of the police organization and its upside-down nature enable street officers to enact their values in discretionary encounters. This has implications for ethics training.

Most contemporary ethics education and training occur in classes either in colleges or in POST academy training. Ethics instruction ceases after pre-service training. Organizational accountability—the enforcement of its ethical standards—shifts to oversight vis-à-vis the enforcement of standard operating procedures (SOP) and internal affairs. The organization backs up SOP with threats of punishment for violators and may have undercover officers in the field testing the corruptibility of traffic officers and detectives. This is how ethics are trained and enforced. This is not, however, how ethics are learned.

Ethics are learned and imprinted at home. Ethics upbringing is emotionally imprinted through somatic markers and is fully in place when someone is seeking employment. Ethics are passed on from the stories told and the behavior of family members or relatives who were, or are, cops. Once on the job, the application of one's ethics is reinforced and honed in a variety of settings. They are embedded in stories told during training. Ethics are learned from the TO and from the older, more seasoned street officers, who become a rookie's police family and siblings. Ethics are passed on by the behavior of commanding officers (Klaver, 2014). This is especially important because, if commanding officers are not around when it counts, out on the street, they cannot be a guide for ethical behavior.

When officers are introduced to local police culture, they learn practical rules-of-thumb for maintaining harmony with other cops and for dealing with routine police problems. They learn to trust only other officers, to take charge of their assigned territories, to keep a low profile and avoid making waves, to always back up another officer, and how to use force. (Van Maanen, 1978b; Reuss-Ianni, 1983; Shearing and Ericson, 1991; Manning, 1997; Crank, 2004a). Their commitment to the noble cause is enclosed in a culture that will protect them from accountability, particularly by organizational management.

Recruits are hired because they satisfy minimum criteria of intelligence and physical health and because they carry particular values about society and the role of police in it. They are then introduced to a working environment that encourages value-based decision-making. These values are reinforced during the training process. Ethics training that is counterproductive to those values is ineffective and is considered to be silly and a waste of time.

Ethics, to be taken seriously, has to be consistent with local cultural values, not run counter to them. The temptations of police work, the "seductions" of the unknown, the desire to be a prince of the street, of being tougher than the tough guys, must be acknowledged in efforts to deal with police ethics. These things link closely to police activity and morality; they are not inconsistent with it. Telling a cop not to accept a "free cup of coffee" just doesn't capture the wild, self-affirming energy of smashing a scumbag that just stole an old lady's purse. Besides, what cop's going to turn on another cop for "street-cleaning"? If ethics training doesn't recognize noble-cause corruption and how closely it's tied with values carried by line officers, then it's doomed to irrelevance.

Ethics should help an officer be a good cop. By good, we mean that ethics has to be consistent with other moral elements of the police craft, particularly the use of coercive force. Ethics cannot exist as a vaporous, universal set of beliefs taught at training and subsequently abandoned. If it is expressed as an abstract set of beliefs about rightness and wrongness, then it is useless. However, if it is a way to think about policing that actually makes police work more effective, and it is believed in and carried by commanders and trainers alike, it can infuse the organization with vitality and strength.

# Values and Administrative Dilemmas

# 3

## Key Terms

central ethical dilemma
internal ethics
Accountability Dilemma 1
external accountability mechanisms
formal ethical codes
internal accountability mechanisms
Accountability Dilemma 2
upside-down bureaucracies
Pascal's wager
police accountability
scandal cycle
stealth driving
task environment

## Introduction

This chapter examines the paradoxes of police accountability within the framework of value-based decision-making. At the heart of the discussion lies the central ethical dilemma: How can police organizations ensure accountability without undermining the moral autonomy that drives officers to pursue the noble cause? The chapter introduces two key challenges—**Accountability Dilemma 1**, where efforts to control unpredictability through bureaucratic oversight intensify secrecy among line officers, and **Accountability Dilemma 2**, where attempts to instill internal ethics clash with officers' pre-existing moral convictions, leading to resistance against managerial control. Police departments, described as **upside-down bureaucracies**, invert traditional organizational hierarchies by placing discretionary power in the hands of street-level officers rather

DOI: 10.4324/9781003626916-5

than top executives. This structure complicates the implementation of **formal ethical codes** and **external accountability mechanisms**, such as internal affairs, citizen review boards, and civil litigation.

Mahatma Gandhi said, "There go my people: I must rush to catch up with them, for I am their leader." The quote can be interpreted various ways; one possibility might be as a description of administrators' efforts to control the behavior of street-level officers. Police chiefs provide both administrative and moral leadership for their departments. A chief, to survive and flourish as the head of his or her organization, must acquire the loyalty of the rank and file (Bordua and Reiss, 1986; Klaver, 2014). He or she is expected to be the undisputed moral leader on issues of departmental responsibility and the ethical behavior of the officers, as well as to provide managerial leadership on administrative and command tasks. Yet the reasons for which chiefs were hired are often intimately tied to the reasons for which they will be ultimately removed—an inability to control line officers' behavior. In spite of a variety of efforts to control line-level behavior over the past century, accountability problems persist. Executives often find that they are a step behind what their officers are doing on the streets.

This chapter focuses on dilemmas of administrative accountability. By accountability, we mean efforts to control the behavior of line officers. This chapter is somewhat abstract because issues of accountability are difficult to resolve. We argue that accountability is paradoxical, in that efforts to hold police officers accountable tend to backfire and undermine the very goals they seek—controlling police behavior. Both the nature of the police craft and the command structure of organizations limit efforts to hold officers accountable for their actions. Two kinds of accountability procedures are discussed, oversight mechanisms and personal morality. The chapter closes with a discussion of reasons for focusing on ethics as an accountability mechanism.

> Mike begins his presentation to the commanders. *You manage an organization that is about doing law enforcement, but is also about controlling your lower-ranking officers. What you need to understand is that these two goals, law enforcement and controlling line officers, can conflict with each other. I'm going to show you why the values that your officers carry, the same values that you hire them for and in which you take personal pride, get in the way of your efforts to control them.*

## Scandal and Accountability Cycles

We live in a country where personal responsibility is highly valued. We believe that people should be held accountable for their behavior. We want the police to hold citizens accountable when they step over the line and engage in criminal conduct. And we hold the police to a higher standard. We not only expect them to enforce the laws of the land but also want them to commit to and exhibit a strict standard of ethical conduct. They not only have to act legally but they are also expected to stand above any hint of moral and legal impropriety, including any possible perception of unethical behavior.

Unfortunately, like the rest of us, the police do not always act legally, and illegal police behavior is always of interest to the media. Television and the internet are sometimes filled with accounts of police scandal. And it always seems to come as a surprise to police departments to which the scandal is linked, directly or indirectly. It is possible to examine almost all instances of police misconduct and find that other officers in the departments where they worked expressed surprise and denial, followed by outrage if the charges were sustained.

Police departments sometimes seem to be caught in **scandal cycles.** Some officers are accused of scandalous behavior, administrators and city councils hold hearings, the city acts to rid itself of corruption, and then departments pass through a "professionalizing" period under the guidance of a new chief. If a scandal is severe enough, and if there is sufficient clout among municipal leaders, the chief will be forced out of office. And a new chief will be selected with a new mandate: to sweep with a new broom, to clean up the graft, to control his or her officers. Like the character in Gandhi's opening quote, the chief (or sheriff) takes charge of a runaway organization. He or she will put new policies into place and institute command-level reviews that overhaul the image of the department. A few police officers will be branded as rotten apples and will be invited to participate in the department's early retirement program.

Within a short period of time, the department will begin making information publicly available about how things have changed. Newspapers will discuss how the new chief's policies have cleaned up the department, how arrests are up, and how the agency is coming down hard on real crime. And, like hail over a field of young corn, corruption of all types returns, to destroy the professional image of the department. There is new media coverage of a scandal. The cycle repeats itself.

**Police accountability** refers to efforts to control police behavior. Since the founding of modern policing in Britain, accountability has been a significant problem for police administrators. Since the turn of the twentieth century, it has been one of the central problems of policing in the United States (Walker, 1977; Gamez and Collins, 2014) (see Box 3.1). At the center of almost every police reform movement has been an effort to develop new strategies to hold the police accountable for their behavior (Fitch et al., 2014).

Box 3.1

**Police Reform and Controlling Police Officers**

The law enforcement strategy, as envisioned by early twentieth-century reformers, contained two elements. The first was a narrowing of the police function to law enforcement. The second was controlling officers. Kelling and Bratton describe this second function as follows:

> At first this assertion (the officer control function) seems strange—control of officers should be a means of improving police performance, not an end in itself. Yet, one has to put oneself in the position of the reformers. For them, political meddling, corruption, and abuse were so rampant in policing that it was impossible to direct effectively efforts to any desired goal; therefore, control was in the forefront of all their innovations. Concern for means overshadowed ends. Control became the strategy. Thus, it is no surprise that even as recently as the 1970s in New York City, patrol officers were constrained from making low-level drug arrests because administrators feared they would be corrupted.

Source: Kelling, G. and W.J. Bratton (1993). "Implementing Community Policing: The Administrative Problem." In *Perspectives on Policing*, Vol. 17. Washington, DC: National Institute of Justice. Washington, DC: US Department of Justice, p. 2.

Consider the works of the International Association of Chiefs of Police in 1893, the Wickersham Commission in 1931, the President's Commission on Law Enforcement and Administration of Justice in 1967, and the Christopher Commission in 1991. All these commissions were convened in part or in whole because the police were charged with corrupt practices, and the public—or at least important legislators—were outraged. All commissions submitted recommendations about how to improve problems. And police departments responded! Police agencies throughout the past century have intensified accountability procedures, added new agency units, created more paperwork, assigned new supervisory responsibilities, and in some cases, have permitted citizen oversight.

These changes, though well-intentioned, were largely ceremonial, which means that they changed the structure of the police organization. On the street, where the bullet hits the bone, organizational changes have had less of an effect. Police confront the same issues today that they did 100 years ago (see Box 3.2).

Box 3.2

**Police Commissions and Police Brutality: An Historical Overview**

The National Commission on Law Observance, also known as the Wickersham Commission, was established by President Hoover in 1929. In 1931, it published 14 volumes, two of which were about the police. One of these volumes focused on police lawlessness and identified widespread police abuses to obtain coerced confessions.

As the result of the commission findings, Hopkins (1931) wrote *Our Lawless Police*. Hopkins developed what he called a "war theory of crime control." He suggested that police believe they are waging a war on crime and that any means are justified to win that war. The police perceive themselves pressured by the public to get results, and the consequences of that pressure include a tendency to settle matters "in the streets," by applying "back-alley" or "curb-stone" justice. In effect, these officers believed that illegal behavior (police brutality) was necessary if law and order were to be maintained (Roberg and Kuykendall, 1993:164).

Subsequent commissions found evidence of police brutality. The President's Commission on Civil Rights, appointed by President Truman in 1947, expressed deep concern about police brutality. In 1961, the U.S. Civil Rights Commission stated that police brutality continued to be a serious problem throughout the United States (Wagner and Decker, 1997).

In 1967, the President's Commission on Law Enforcement and the Administration of Justice (also known as the Crime Commission) again noted problems of police brutality. The Crime Commission recommended a wide variety of controls over inappropriate and illegal police behavior, including emotional stability testing, judicial review, and the use of civil liability.

Have these commissions been successful in their advocacy of external and internal controls over police behavior? The answer is "yes and no." By "yes," we mean that external and internal oversight of police officers has expanded and has done so dramatically. For example, civil liability against the police is commonplace today, and many departments have video cameras installed in patrol vehicles in order to monitor police-citizen interactions during routine stops.

By "no," we mean that it is far less clear that these oversight mechanisms have had an impact on police behavior. As recently as 1991, the Independent Commission on the Los Angeles Police Department, also known as the Christopher Commission, observed significant problems of brutality and excessive force committed by Los Angeles police officers. Importantly, these problems were occurring in spite of the presence of a highly regarded internal review mechanism for police accountability. The Human Rights Watch (1998:27) observed that police brutality was "persistent" in the 14 major U.S. cities they evaluated and that both internal and external oversight mechanisms designed to deal with brutality were ineffective.

## Police and Accountability Procedures

Today, we have immersed the police in accountability procedures. Let's review the various ways that the police are held accountable for their behavior (Walker, 2005). There are **external accountability mechanisms** for police organizations: these include the Supreme Court decisions concerning due process, civil litigations against the police at the federal level, civil litigations against the police at the state level, criminal charges against the police at the state level, criminal charges against the police at the federal level, citizen review boards, ombudsmen, mayors and city councils, and of course, the newspapers and national press for major scandals. Within the organization, police organizations try to hold their officers accountable with **internal accountability mechanisms**, such as the chain of command, internal affairs, written standard operating procedures (as one police officer put it, written accounts of "100 years of departmental f___-ups"), video cameras mounted on the patrol car dash, dispatch notification when an officer leaves the patrol car, and citizen complaint files. Are you a police officer? Do you have the feeling someone is watching you? Today, police officers have to submit to random drug tests in their own department. This means that they have to pee in a cup and then give the cup to a technician. Degrading? You bet it is.

And no one is satisfied. American citizens are as concerned about protecting democratic rights against a standing militia—and that's what the police are—as they were 180 years ago when the first police department was founded in the United States (in Boston, in 1838). Perhaps this is a healthy attitude for Americans, existing as we do in a world where democracies are rare and notoriously unstable. But it makes the police one of the most scrutinized occupations in the United States. We continue to seek ways to control the police, to make sure that no wrong is done, to ensure that they conform to standards of public and private conduct the rest of us would heartily and righteously resist.

## Ethics as Accountability: Managerial Limitations

The primary work of police departments is carried out by street-level officers. Street-level officers conduct the work of the organization in its most practical sense; they make concrete decisions about how to deal with everyday human problems. They exercise wide latitude when deciding to intervene, how to intervene in citizen affairs, whether to make an arrest, what level of force to use, and how to exit situations. Very little of this latitude can be brought under administrative control for two reasons. First is unpredictability: officers are charged with uncovering that which many people do not want to reveal—criminal wrongdoing—and who will sometimes resist being seized if the wrongdoing is uncovered. Police consequently have to adjust their behavior to changing circumstances in which the outcome is neither known nor predictable. Second is discretion: the independence of officers in their day-to-day work and flexibility in deciding whether and how to enforce the criminal law enables officers to follow their moral predispositions to deal with crime and public-order problems (Wilson, 1968). Officers are, for the most part, out of direct administrative supervision when they are on patrol. And their encounters with citizens are initiated and concluded with discretionary decisions about whether and how to intervene and whether or not to invoke criminal sanctions.

The nature of line-level police work—its unpredictability and discretionary nature, coupled with the moral predispositions of police officers—create profound accountability problems. In this section, we're going to discuss the two types of efforts to control street accountability—through external oversight and through ethics training aimed at providing an appropriate moral sense.

In their efforts to control line officer behavior, administrators confront a **central ethical dilemma.** The dilemma is two-pronged. The first dilemma stems from the use of external oversight to control behavior. If administrative oversight mechanisms are used to control the behavior of street-level officers, then they will resist, disguise, or obscure their behavior under the secretive protection of line-level culture. In other words, efforts to control discretion through external control tend to backfire, bolstering secretive elements of police culture. The second dilemma stems from the use of internal, moral controls over behavior, and is enacted by efforts to hire the right kind of officer. If managers try to control behavior by hiring morally righteous officers, the morality of the officers they hire will undermine subsequent administrative efforts to control their behavior. In other words, psychological and moral controls are likely to limit accountability: officers will find ways to circumvent commands in order to carry out what they believe is right behavior and achieve what they believe is a good end.

Consider administrative, oversight-based accountability. Under administrative means of accountability (e.g., chain of command, internal review), the police organization uses written policies, which are codes of conduct. These policies are the department's standard operating procedure. Individual policies sometimes tell officers what to do and sometimes tell them what not to do. For example, policies identify the appropriate dress code for a police officer. However, policies also are written to tell police officers what not to do. Most typically, policies identify inappropriate behavior. Violations for inappropriate behavior may involve a mild, informal chastisement, verbal reprimand, removal from promotion eligibility for a fixed period of time, or suspension (see Box 3.3).

Box 3.3

**Stealth Driving and Departmental Policy**

Officer J was frustrated with his inability to catch prostitutes and crack dealers on his nighttime beat. He knew that they avoided the streets and conducted their work at night inside a large park next to a busy city street. He also knew that the park was unlit at night, except for lights around a central fountain, adding to opportunities for victimization. Small-time criminals, such as potential drug buyers and johns, were occasionally robbed and beaten upon entering and leaving the park. He was also concerned that children, playing in the park in the daytime, would prick their finger on a used syringe and contract AIDS. So he began the practice of stealth driving. He would turn off the lights of his squad car and, narrowly passing through the wrought iron gates at the entrance of the park, drive his vehicle through all its dark areas. He continued the practice for a couple of months. A complaint to the chief's office, however, abruptly changed his pattern of **stealth driving**. Concerns were voiced that the "stealth" patrol might accidentally run over a drunk or homeless person sleeping in the park. A formal policy was posted, and commanders announced at all shifts that officers were not to drive their automobiles through the parks. Officer J also was assigned responsibility for all "ride-alongs" as an informal punishment. However, he did not wholly abandon the practice of stealth driving but confined the driving to the principal sidewalks in the park where drunks were unlikely to sleep.

In the example provided in Box 3.3, we can see how the police organization develops a policy—in this instance forbidding stealth driving in the parks—to control the behavior of its line officers. It is an administrative solution to accountability. However, efforts at administrative control over what street officers do can create conflicts between line officers and administrators, as it did in the example of Officer J. In that example, a departmental policy was used to prohibit an officer from doing what he thought was good police work—stealth driving—to suppress criminal activity and protect children. And the policy did not work—at least, not as intended.

Police organizations also make use of **formal ethical codes,** which are formal, recognized standards that apply generally to conduct. The prologue to this book contained one such code, the Police Officers Code of Conduct. These ethical codes, together with the department's policies, represent an organization's ethical principles. Ethics, under an administrative model of accountability, are external to police officers, in the sense that they are administrative codes produced by police managers to inform officers about organizationally correct behavior. They are a standard that officers can use to learn about appropriate behavior. The moral psychology of an officer is of secondary importance—the department tells them what is right and wrong, by means of departmental rules and regulations (Fitch et al., 2014).

On the other hand, ethics can be internal. **Internal ethics** means that officers carry within themselves a sense of ethical or moral responsibility about what constitutes "correct" behavior. If officers are ethical and moral, they do not need external oversight. Their morality is greater than their commitment to the organization itself, coming from their moral conception of "goodness" and "badness." Indeed, a great deal of prehiring screening is devoted to insuring that officers think a particular way about police work and that police are committed to a particular way of looking at the world (Gamez and Collins, 2014). "Internal" ethics consequently seems to be a perfect solution to the problems created by external oversight.

The internal solution to ethical accountability hides a problem that is very difficult to solve. It is the problem of morally valued ends. If officers are committed to a moral way of viewing the world, then efforts by managers to control their behavior are profoundly limited. If police officers believe that policing is a just cause, policies that interfere with their work will be viewed as immoral. And police officers may circumvent the organizational rules in order to do what they believe is right. This is precisely what Officer J did in the scenario in Box 3.3.

The reader might ask, "Don't all officers, including line personnel, managers, and commanders, share a 'common' way of looking at police work, a similar sense of right and wrong?" The outward answer is yes, they do. At least that is the public face they present. Inside the organization the answer is very different. There are two important reasons why the ethics of line officers and managerial policies conflict with each other. The first reason is the unpredictable nature of police work and results in Accountability Dilemma 1, oversight problems. The second reason is the ethics that officers themselves individually carry—a commitment to the noble cause and a willingness to circumvent due process and administrative protocols to carry out the noble cause—getting bad guys off the streets, and which can result in Accountability Dilemma 2, a situation where enforcement efforts drive officers behind the secrecy of police culture.

***Accountability Dilemma 1: Unpredictability.*** Michael Harmon (1995) describes Accountability Dilemma 1:

> Even if managers were able to eliminate sources of unpredictability within their organizations, such actions would be incompatible with dealing sensibly in the face of the unpredictable environments they are committed to changing. This is because organizational success (that is, effectiveness in the broader sense of the word) requires continuous innovation, adjustment, and problem- and goal-redefinition that are directly at odds with controlling and making predictable subordinates' behavior in order to achieve predefined goals.
>
> (Harmon, 1995:183184)

What does **Accountability Dilemma 1** mean? Consider the normal daily routine work carried out by line officers. They are provided with an automobile (or other means of transportation) so that they can cover their assigned beat, and they are expected to move from situation to situation, resolving problems of all kinds. When wrongdoing is suspected, they investigate. Wrongdoers, however, do not normally admit illegal behavior to a police officer, and few people want to be arrested. Consequently, police seek to penetrate the reality presented to them in order to uncover hidden culpability. This work—trying to find hidden guilt—makes patrol-citizen interactions unpredictable.

Line officers are consequently presented with work that may be uncertain and is unforeseeable from one moment to the next (Manning, 1989). Their work is characterized by powerful cultural themes of unpredictability, the unknown, danger, and edge control (Crank, 2004a). What an officer is doing any one minute may provide no clue about what's going to happen the next. Chance encounters play a surprisingly high role in daily police work and can undermine police efforts to control behavior. Uncertainty is central to the street officer's working personality, as indicated in Box 3.4.

Box 3.4

**Survival on the Street**

Ever notice two police officers talking to each other on the street? They never look at each other. One is always looking behind the other. They very seldom look each other in the eye. It's a survival mechanism. They want to know what's coming up at them (Fletcher, 1990:12).

Police organizations, on the other hand, are bureaucracies, and bureaucracies do not deal very well with unpredictability. Bureaucracies like their organizational parts to be well-oiled, all functioning together. They work best when all the parts combine their efforts to achieve some clearly defined goal or goal cluster. Managers try to control unpredictability through bureaucratic procedures, by developing standard operating procedures, chain-of-command, internal affairs, written objectives, goals and standards, and policies (Fitch et al., 2014). The logic behind many of these complex bureaucratic procedures is to identify inappropriate behavior and to provide penalties for violations of appropriate behavior.

**Accountability Dilemma 1** states that, if managers were to be successful at eliminating unpredictability among line officers through the use of bureaucratic procedures—that is, if line officers rigidly followed bureaucratic protocols—they would be incapable of dealing with their day-to-day work environment. The work environment of the police involves dealing with people in unpredictable situations in which the "truth" is deliberately obscured and adapting to changing situational circumstances. If we were to make the police perfectly regimented, true automatons of bureaucracy, they would be perfectly unsuited for their work.

Managers, concerned over the control of line behavior, tend to elaborate and add to the body of policies already in place. Bureaucratic "accountability" consequently grows (in terms of the quantity of documents related to rules and procedures) but does not increase in effectiveness (often increasing managerial frustration with their line personnel as a consequence). Is the reader a manager? Does this sound familiar?

***Accountability Dilemma 2: Line Officer Morality.*** If bureaucracy is unable to adequately deal with line officer accountability, then how can we ensure that officers act right? An alternative in today's world is to instill a sense of order and morality through ethics training. If, the logic goes, a person has internal or "psychological" checks for inappropriate behavior, then there will be no need for external controls. By instilling ethics as an internal value system to guide their conduct, it is believed that individuals will act responsibly (Gamez and Collins, 2014). Their ethical training should serve as an accountability "anchor" for the moral responsibilities that they carry as a public servant.

**Accountability Dilemma 2** is the managerial effort to instill ethical values in officers who already carry strong values about police work and human nature. Ethics training does not occur on a moral "blank slate." Recruits already have strong moral commitments to the occupation of policing—that's why they became police officers. Through socialization processes, they fine-tune their crime-control focus to develop the tools and skills needed to control their assigned territories. In other words, police have an ethical way of looking at the world fully in place before they are hired, an ethic that is honed during pre-service training and assignment to a training officer. Police are morally predisposed to seek what they consider to be good ends. They are surrounded by audiences that encourage them to seek the morally good end. In short, they are moral creatures, acting in an uncertain world to bring about a noble end.

The issues Buerger describes in Box 3.5 are the pre-existing views of recruits about police work, the similarity of views regardless of personal racial or ethnic differences, views that stem from a familial background in policing, and an environment that celebrates a view of police work as law enforcement. These issues are central to understanding the ethical predispositions of police. Ethics training cannot act as if police are insufficiently ethical or that they are not yet ethical; they are indeed ethical but in ways that bewilder reformists.

Box 3.5

**The Ethical Predispositions of Recruits**

Far from being tabula rasa, candidates for police employment present themselves with (and perhaps because of) an already developed idea of what constitutes police work. Recruits expect to do "law enforcement," not "problem solving" or "community service." Some are "legacies" from police families, the second or third generation to enter policing: A *New York Times* study of recent New York City Police Department (NYCPD) academy class indicated that one-half of the white recruits, almost one-half of the black recruits, and one-third of the Hispanic recruits had a relative who was a current or former member of the NYCPD (Kilborn, 1994). Almost all will have had an exposure to media police work, whether reconstructions like *Top Cops* or the live-action displays of *Cops*. Many recruits already have an ingrained idea of what police work is supposed to be; among legacies, that conceptual framework and belief system will likely have been shaped by family members and friends whose viewpoints embody exactly the attitudes that reform training hopes to eradicate.

Source: Michael Buerger (1998). "Police Training as a Pentecost." *Police Quarterly*, 1–1:31.

The problem for ethics training is not that police are not ethical but that they are ethical in a way that can confound administrative efforts to control their behavior (Grandani, 2014). Street officers are committed to a noble end, and that commitment sometimes justifies violating administrative protocols and principles of due process. Consider, again, the example of stealth driving described in Box 3.3. An officer was engaged in behavior, stealth driving, aimed at encountering or suppressing criminal activity. Administrative protocols, in the form of a written policy, prohibited this activity. Informally, the officer ended up "eating the s___ end of the Sergeant's stick" by having to do the ride-along detail. He did not stop doing stealth driving, though he did confine the driving patterns to the principal sidewalks in the park. In short, the officer's commitment to the good ends of policing justified creative circumvention of administrative protocols, even in the face of departmental sanctions.

The final consequence of the enforcement of ethics and legal codes that are seen as inconsistent with the moral predispositions of officers, particularly the noble cause, is that they backfire, resulting in the formation or intensification of the "blue curtain." As Crank (2004a) noted, officers will develop ways to resist administrative protocols that are seen as inconsistent with their moral commitments to do something about troublemakers, criminals, and dangerous people. The consequence of this is that the greater the managerial efforts to stamp out value-based decision-making, the greater will be the development of sources of cultural resistance to managerial oversight.

## Chiefs and the Control of Line Behavior

### *Police Departments Are Upside-Down Bureaucracies*

> *Who,* Mike asks, *are the guys who make the discretionary decisions that reflect the nature of your police organization? Who are they?*

Line officers are the public representation of departmental activities and policies. They carry out the purposes of the department in view of the public. When the press writes about the police organization, they are usually writing about what some line officer did, not what the chief did. Yet this answer to Mike's question, seemingly clear as it is, reveals profound differences between business organizations and police work.

Consider large businesses. The role of the chief executive officer (CEO) is as the top decision-maker. The CEO makes decisions about the future of the organization. He or she delegates responsibilities. He or she makes decisions about product sales and distributions. He or she makes decisions about firing or retention of employees. He or she makes big dollars. And he or she retires, at some point, with a "parachute" of valuable stocks and bonds. A CEO exerts almost unlimited power over the conduct of the organization and can make or destroy it. His or her power is limited primarily by the organization's board of stockholders.

Police organizations are **upside-down bureaucracies** because they reverse the distribution of organizational authority in important ways. Chiefs have limited influence over the day-to-day affairs of street officers, even in today's bottom-line oriented business-mimicking world of public services. A chief certainly cannot hire and fire at will.

In a business, discretionary decisions that reflect the organization's values are the province of the CEO, at the top of the organization. In a municipal police organization, discretion that reflects the organization's values is acted out at the bottom of the organizational chart and is vested in the decisions made by line officers. It is the line officer, not the chief, who makes the decisions that reveal to the public the nature of the police organization. Police organizations reverse the organizational location of discretionary decision-making and, in this sense, are upside-down when compared to businesses. Why are police organizations like this? There are organizational and historical reasons for this.

The two organizational reasons have to do with the nature of the work that police officers do. First, the uncertainties of the task environment preclude tight administrative management. By **task environment** is meant the physical space in which a police officer does his or her work, usually an assigned beat. Police work is characterized by dealing with unpredictability in citizen encounters and by having to make decisions based on anticipated behavior of other people (Crank, 2004a; see also Harmon, 1995). Uncertainty is particularly important in police work because police officers occasionally deal with individuals who have something to hide and who will resist providing incriminating information. Much of the uncertainty that police encounter is intentionally produced by citizens and sometimes gives a dangerous edge to police efforts to uncover truth.

Secondly, the occupation of policing, unlike business, has few clear or "bottom-line" outputs that provide a measure of work activity. Some departments use informal quotas for arrests and traffic stops, but there is little beyond this for which officers are held accountable. As in other public sector organizations, police work is mostly about the well-being of citizens, not the marketability of an economic good. Third, police work is low-visibility decision-making. This means that officers do their work mostly out of sight of supervisors and usually involving only a few citizens. Consequently, it is difficult to bring line-level police activity completely under administrative control.

There are also historical reasons for the limited control chiefs have over lower-ranking officers. Limits on the power of police chiefs over line personnel can be traced to the early days of the International Association of Chiefs of Police (IACP). The position of the IACP paralleled the views of political progressives in that era (Walker, 1977). A component of the progressive platform was to further the political independence of municipal police organizations. Its platform, however, held two goals that worked at cross-purposes. These goals were (1) hiring independent-minded executives for the position of chief and (2) protecting line officers from arbitrary personnel policies.

Central to the platform of the IACP at the end of the nineteenth century was acquiring independence of the chief from local party machines. The IACP advocated the selection of chiefs from the ranks of the military and business. The position of chief under machine politics was largely ceremonial, with little real influence over the day-to-day activities of the organization.

The IACP believed that, by hiring business and military professionals, rather than political cronies, as chiefs, the powerful influence of local politics would be weakened and chiefs could assert control over their organizations. In retrospect, we see that this goal was partially achieved. Today, about one-half of all chiefs in municipal departments in the United States are selected from outside the organization, and large urban departments are more likely to hire outside chiefs.

Reformers thought that the powerful influence of political machinery over the police could be broken if officers were protected from arbitrary hiring and firing, that is, by ending the patronage system (Fogelson, 1977). The idea that police personnel should have employment protections was, however, controversial. Should line officers, reformers wondered, be provided with civil service protections? Civil service was a new governmental form in that era: it protected governmental employees from arbitrary hiring and firing and established job standards for work performance. Reformers saw it as a double-edged sword. If officers received civil service protections, they would be protected from arbitrary firing when an election swept in a new mayor. On the other hand, civil service protections would limit the ability of chiefs to hire, reward, or punish its officers.

Ultimately, the idea that officers should have civil service protections carried the day. However, a price was to be paid. Chiefs, though gaining a limited degree of independence of their organization from municipal politics, nevertheless had scant authority over their own officers. Their influence within their own organization was severely constrained by a powerful and protective personnel system. Even in the current era, many observers argue that civil service protections are so deeply entrenched in contemporary law that changing them is like "bending granite" (Guyot, 1979). For police commanders, this means that personnel decisions made during hiring will be around for a long time. If a mistake is made at hiring, it will be very difficult to undo later (Gamez and Collins, 2014).

> Mike continues. *Police departments are upside-down. The officers on the street—the lowest-ranking officer in the organization—makes the day-to-day decisions that demonstrate the values of the department. This guy got out of the academy yesterday. He's out there making decisions, writing traffic tickets, making arrests, risking his life and limb. Where's the chief? When the public looks at the organization, they see this guy. They don't see the chief.*
>
> *Where's the chief? The chief's probably out having lunch with the mayor somewhere. Worrying about his heart.* Mike points to the chief attending the meeting and chuckles. *How ya doin' chief?*

Chiefs tend to participate in their department's early retirement program. The average tenure of a police chief in the United States is about four years. Unless a chief voluntarily retires from office, an infrequent occurrence, they are fired. When a new one is hired, they are hired with a mandate to fix whatever went wrong and caused the previous chief to get fired (Crank and Langworthy, 1992). Often, they are hired to fix problems over which they have no control. They have to overcome resistance in the organization while implementing changes in a timely way. This is often impossible. As Ahern (1972) observed, a chief may spend the remainder of his or her career in an agency fixing the problems seen on the first day of employment. In most instances, the remainder of the career is brief.

A new chief is hired. The chief has a new broom to sweep, out with the old, in with the new. Maybe he or she is going to convert a department to community policing. Will his or her officers follow?

> Mike continues. *You can put a set of rules out there, but if I don't believe in them (he pats his heart) they're not doing you any good. Who governs policing? If I'm one of your officers, I do. What really governs policing? I'm making a case for morality, not law, which has a lot to say about an organization you call law enforcement.*

***Backfiring Effects of Control-Oriented Chiefs.*** Chiefs are not as influential in the affairs of street officer activity as we would like them to be and indeed as they themselves would like. A chief, concerned that he or she has control problems, may take a harsh, "no-nonsense" approach to line indiscretions. Yet this approach may backfire, intensifying resistance and further weakening control. Consequently, we do not believe that chiefs have much of an effect on the early organizational experiences of line officers.

MIKE: *Beware of chiefs who say "thou shalt change."*

By "thou shalt change," Mike is describing how crime control chiefs tend to approach their work. They believe in crime control, in the military style of command, and in the importance of discipline. Chief executives have sometimes viewed their responsibilities from a tough, no-nonsense perspective. This perspective is well-received by the public and street officers alike when it focuses on crime. However, the traditional, rigid leadership style creates control and management problems and is particularly inefficient for dealing with noble-cause dilemmas. If a police department has a noble-cause corruption problem at the line level, the traditional strategies that chiefs use—reliance on chain of command controls—are unlikely to have much of an impact. Indeed, they're likely to cause more problems than they will solve. Their impact is likely to generate resistance on the part of line officers, create increased tensions between line personnel and supervisors, and intensify the darker aspects of the police culture, those aspects that hide line behavior from external accountability.

The limitations of chiefs over their officers have been noted since 1968, when James Q. Wilson observed that professionalizing chiefs tended to face opposition from line officers, who viewed their work in terms of public-order problem-solving. This is no less true today. One of the most difficult problems facing chiefs may be the need to trust their officers, to be willing to face mistakes and encourage them to improve. A punitive approach to problem-solving will not help chiefs gain control. But it will alienate officers and ultimately lead to loss of control of the department.

You want to hold your officers accountable for their behavior, Mike concludes. When your chief says "thou shalt change," you've just lost control.

Mike concludes this section, returning to the whiteboard.

By thinking about the accountability dilemmas, we can see how the organization is actually a source of resistance to value-based decision-making.

Mike writes on the whiteboard:

DILEMMA 1: Managerial efforts to control unpredictability of line behavior increases line secrecy.

DILEMMA 2: Managerial efforts to enforce morality decreases effectiveness of managerial controls.

DILEMMA 3: Police departments are upside-down bureaucracies.

MIKE: *It all comes down to this:* (he writes on the whiteboard):

**VALUE-BASED DECISION-MAKING**
Organization ≠ means (tools)

# Police Are Value-Based Decision-Makers

MIKE: *This says that the organization is no longer the means to carry out the noble cause. Remember when we started out this morning, the organization was one of the means to carry out the good ends? Now we see that it really isn't. The organization is a problem. The answer, for your line-officers, is secrecy. It means that officers become secretive about doing what they believe is right. And it's your fault.*

Several commanders bristle over this. One responds, "Are you saying that we don't know what we're doing?"

Mike responds. *You know what you're doing. But at your rank, the organization is how you carry out the noble cause. You understand the organization. It is a tool you use to make plans, to budget, to develop strategy, to develop community contacts, and to build relations with other justice organizations. That is not the world your line officers see. They see commanders holding them back from promotions or punishing them for being too aggressive. I bet that when I talk to them tomorrow, they will tell me about how every small mistake they make is harshly punished.*

You understand your work very well. That's not the problem. The quality of command decision-making today, in your department and in others I have been to, is at the highest level I've ever seen it. But in all the departments I've been to, I also see that commanders need to understand their line officers better. They need to communicate better. And they need, most of all, to be good role models, which means that they need to be seen. I don't mean in their offices. I mean in the street, where it counts.

When we started out today, the organization and the law were the means, and morality, especially the noble cause, was the end. Now, the organization is no longer the means. It interferes with the ability to achieve the good ends. This means that traditional ways to control the organization don't work. They're based on outmoded notions of control that don't work for problems of noble-cause corruption. You need to develop new ways of thinking to deal with where your line officers are coming from. Second, it means that, when you begin to encounter problems of noble-cause corruption, you're not going to know it.

# Forewarned Is Forearmed: A Message for Line Officers

The preceding section has focused on command issues. However, though we see the primary issue of noble-cause corruption training as a command issue, this does not mean that line officers and recruits are not responsible for their behavior. Ethics is a feature of a department's style. For it to work, all have to participate, from the chief to the newest recruit.

We recognize that some police officers or college students who read this book will be suspicious about our concern over the noble cause—that they will view it as too against-the-grain of the daily work of the police. If this is you, think about Mike's words as a police version of **Pascal's wager.** Pascal offered that it was impossible to know with certainty the existence of God. However, the wise man won't take the chance and live a sinful life. If he gambles, and bets on the wrong side, he might suffer an eternity of brimstone and damnation.

You can consider letting ethical decision-making control your passions. There will be many opportunities to mess up; it goes with the territory. With so many people tracking you, it's impossible to do right all the time, and there will be times when you need your colleagues to stand by you. What does the wise police officer do? Box 3.6 might help you think about what you do.

Box 3.6

**Who's Watching?**

Let's look at two dimensions of police surveillance reported in the news. The first is a conference on suing the New York Police Department in October 1999 at Fordham Law School. Topics for the conference included "legal nooks and crannies of choke holds, vehicular pursuits, qualified immunity, reasonable suspicion, and deadly force" (Flynn, 2003). Speakers included lawyers who handled landmark cases against New York City.

The conference took place in New York, which is believed by many to be a particularly fertile place to litigate against the police. Federal prosecutors, for example, had recently stated that the department fostered brutality because it failed to discipline abusive officers.

The sponsors said that they were not sponsoring the conference only for the money. They noted the mailing list was monitored to make sure that notices were sent to the civil rights section of the American Lawyers Association, not the personal injury bar. However, trends in New York City show that suits against the police are steadily rising. Such suits are a "growth industry": in fiscal year 1998–1999, New York paid out $40 million to settle cases, 40 percent more than the previous year.

The police are not happy with the conference. The department said it was an example of lawyers running amuck and future ambulance chasers. However, the sponsors counter that it is a necessity in a city where bad policing is a problem. One of the participants noted that "I think a lot of what we are talking about today is that this seminar is even taking place is the climate we are living in" (Flynn, 2003).

Box 3.6, *continued*

> The second is the growth in the use of camcorders nationally. The Rodney King incident, in which Los Angeles police officers were covertly taped beating a motorist, was memorialized by a citizen with a private camcorder. Current estimates are that there are about 16 million camcorders in the United States (Walsh, 2003). Camcorders are put to a wide variety of uses. Among these are amateur news buffs (Luft, 1991). Luft noted:
>
>> Some of the amateurs who catch newsworthy events on tape do it more by accident than by design. George Holliday, who videotaped the beating of Rodney King, is an example. According to Holliday's lawyer, James Jordan, Holliday was in bed when he heard sirens and then a ruckus outside his home. He got up and videotaped the action from his balcony without realizing what was going on.
>
> Others, like Roger Harris of Orange, California, are news-video junkies who have police scanners in their homes and race to potential news events, hoping their footage will gain them fame or profit (Luft, 1991).
>
> Many news stations actively solicit amateur news products. They consider it an opportunity to improve many of the offerings available on local news, and the news media has increasingly blurred into entertainment. In this way, camcorder news and related industries have become a growth industry and a significant outlet for contemporary and sometimes national news and entertainment programming.

Source: Adapted from Flynn, 2003; Walsh, 2003; Luft, 1991.

> MIKE: *I've read a lot of police books. I've taught from those books and they all say the same thing. Thπy say that police work is low visibility, right? They say that police officers tend to work out of sight of administrators and singly or in pairs, with only a few citizens at a time. That's what they say, isn't it?*
>
> An officer nods, most sit quietly.
>
> They're all wrong. Police work is about as high visibility as it could be. You screw up? Someone is watching. Someone is always watching. You screw up, someone'll say "See, can't trust the cops." You don't want that.

If you think there's no brimstone and living hell for a police officer, you might be surprised. There are video cameras everywhere, waiting to put your face on national news. There are lawyers who specialize in cases against the police. And no matter how good at being bad you think you are, there's always the chance, the thin chance, that one day you'll wake up to the tap-tap-tapping of an internal affairs officer at your door. Believe me, these things will ruin your life. Do you know for certain that you aren't being watched? If you don't, here's a simple experiment. Find your name and address on the Internet. I'll bet you that I can do it in two minutes.

Take Pascal's wager. Bet wisely.

# The Social Psychology of Cops' Values

4

**Key Terms**

| | |
|---|---|
| hypothesis | terminal values |
| instrumental values | value systems |
| matched groups | values |
| somatic net | emulation |
| rational decision-making | somatic marker |
| representativeness | |

## Introduction

This chapter critically examines the formation and persistence of police values through a criminological lens, integrating psychological and sociological frameworks. Drawing on Antonio Damasio's somatic marker hypothesis, the authors argue that emotional conditioning—encoded in a "somatic net"—guides officers' moral and rational decision-making, often preconsciously. These emotional predispositions, formed early in life, influence perceptions of threat and criminality, contributing to biased discretionary practices. The chapter also revisits Milton Rokeach's value theory, distinguishing between terminal values (e.g., equality, family security) and instrumental values (e.g., obedience, responsibility), and applies matched groups methodology to assess the origins of police value systems. Findings from longitudinal and comparative studies suggest that occupational socialization has minimal impact on officers' values, which are instead imported from broader societal subgroups.

DOI: 10.4324/9781003626916-6

> MIKE: *I've suggested that the values your line officers have were in place before they were hired. Would you be surprised if I said that your local police culture had almost no impact on them, and that it didn't make any difference if they were men or women, or if they were black, green, yellow, or white, and that police officers' values probably haven't changed in the past 40 years?*

The commanders look at him in disbelief. They have been taught that the principal source of resistance to their command was police culture, or whatever word was used to describe line officers who acted on their own. They also know that the occupation of policing has changed a great deal in the past 40 years. And they have been told that a way to reform policing—make it more friendly to minorities and different ethnic groups they come into contact with in police work—is through the hiring of women and minority group members. Mike's observation contradicts these views.

This chapter is about the values police carry and where they acquire those values. Our perspective draws heavily from two sources. First, we discuss Damasio's theory of the emotional basis of decision-making. Central to his theory is that emotions are tied to events early in life, and these emotional ties provide guidance for subsequent decisions that people make. Through what he called somatic markers, emotions provide our "gut reactions" to the world around us and help account for positive sentiments, such as the noble cause, and negative sentiments, including racism and the like. This discussion is important to understanding how the noble cause can have a powerful hold on police and why most of the sentiments associated with police culture are actually formed well before a person enters police work.

The second review measures police values through the lens of Milton Rokeach's values survey. The purpose of this part of the chapter is to provide the results of measures of police values and assess what those values mean to reformers. A review of our research and pertinent findings reveal both patterns and sources of values carried by the police. Our discussion will draw heavily on the work of Rokeach in the early 1970s and follow-up research in the 1980s and early 1990s. At times, the discussion will be a bit technical, and we ask that readers bear with us. It is important, we think, that readers understand the nature of the research that was conducted.

## Part I: The Noble Cause and the Social Psychology of Emotions

The concept of the noble cause goes to the heart of the police. It dovetails with a law enforcement orientation but is something more than a rational, dispassionate invocation of the law or strict interpretation of the legal code. It is "in the blood" at a level that psychologists studying human emotion are only beginning to understand. This section argues that the noble cause is deeply embedded in an officers' emotional make-up. As noted in Gamez and Collins (2014), "[E]vidence suggests that ethics and morals are learned and reinforced throughout the course of a lifetime, with early formative years being particularly pivotal" (2014:41).

We believe that the noble cause carries powerful emotional currents and that those need to be understood in order to recognize its hold in those who carry it. To argue for an emotional basis for the noble cause seems to suggest that we are treating police officers as irrational and perhaps inferior to the citizens they serve. To the contrary, central to our outlook throughout this book is that police are quite like those they serve.

What we are arguing in this section is that the rational model of human decision-making is itself flawed. **Rational decision-making** means that we select from among the available alternatives, weighing the possible outcomes of each, the best and most reasonable. We argue that rationality is itself in the service of human emotions. The best decision, according to this perspective, often means the decision that is the most emotionally satisfying. But why should an emotional decision outweigh a seemingly rational decision?

To better understand people and the kinds of decisions they make, we need to understand the way in which their emotions work. Contemporary psychology today is beginning to rediscover the centrality of emotions in decision-making. "It appears that human reasoning, decision making, and behaviour are more often the product of emotion than logic" (Fitch et al., 2014:78). It is that psychology, and its implications for policing, that this section references. The centrality of emotions has several important consequences, which we will discuss:

1. Emotions significantly influence not only who the police choose as receivers of discretionary outcomes but also those who are viewed as dangerous and those whose rights should be circumvented.
2. The police view of the world should be understood as largely in place from early socialization processes, reinforced by emotional content—their gut reactions to different kinds of people. This suggests that their sense of the world, complete with emotional reactions, is not caused or created by a deviant, racist, and violent police organizational subculture. It is already in place when they are hired. It is characteristic of a broad swath of American culture.
3. Powerful emotional currents—the feelings of good and bad an officer feels when he or she acts on the noble cause, her or his reactions to kinds of people, and feelings about what is important in life—are tied to emotional states that are, for the most part, uncontrollable. "Evidence suggests that in many day-to-day decisions, the emotional brain (limbic system) reaches a conclusion long before the more logical neocortex has fully processed the information" (Goleman, 1994, quoted in Fitch et al., 2014). Much seemingly discretionary activity is explained by understanding these emotional predispositions.

Research has identified a number of areas in which police seem to react emotionally to events around them however (Bennett, 1984). Jerome Skolnick (1994) asserted that police officers' behavior patterns were predisposed by their view that certain groups in society are "symbolic assailants" and thus a potential source of violence and suspicion. Symbolic assailants, a growing body of literature on racial profiling suggests, may be identified by race. These emotions carry over into organizational processes. Sullivan (1989) and Reaves (2012) contended that the traditional police selection process favors applicants who are white males and have demonstrated a value system favorable to middle-class conformity. Consequently, most officers on the streets today are unable to identify with many members of the marginal groups in society. Later, we review Damasio's (1994) work on emotions and discuss its linkage to the noble cause.

## Emotion and Somatic Markers

Antonio Damasio, one of the world's leading researchers in neuroscience and head of the department of neurology at the University of Iowa College of Medicine, has produced the compelling "somatic marker" hypothesis that provides a framework for understanding the emotional roots of decision-making (Bechara and Damasio, 2005). This concept argues that emotions are an important factor in the process of decision-making despite the well-held views that "emotions cloud the mind" or that "cool heads will always prevail." The fundamental tenant of the somatic-marker hypothesis is that emotions play an important role in guiding decisions, especially in situations in which the outcome of one's choices, in terms of reward and punishment, are uncertain (Damasio, 1994).

The basic idea of a **"somatic marker"** is that when we act, the outcome of our actions leaves an emotional "marker" that tells us if we were rewarded or not. If we are rewarded for our actions, the marker is a positive emotional sentiment. The next time we encounter a similar situation, the mind simplifies our decision-making processes by reinstating the somatic marker. Emotionally, we feel that we are making the right decision. The somatic marker is unconscious, in that when confronted with a situation, our emotions automatically tell us what the best course is. Reinforced, it becomes a "gut" or immediate emotional reaction. Of course, the emotions don't actually know the best outcome; they are relying on a person's early life or initial experiences when markers were first placed. But somatic markers guarantee that the emotional response, true or not, "feels right" and that it feels like "truth."[1] The importance if this is (1) emotions guide and simplify complex reasoning processes, and (2) emotions are learned early on and constrain future choices a person makes.

Damasio (1994; see also Glimcher, 2003; Bechara, 2005) asserted that the reasoning system evolves as an extension of the automatic emotional system. Emotion consequently plays a variety of roles in the reasoning process.

> 1. Emotion may increase the extent to which we believe our actions have particular consequences or produce particular results. They "bias" our ability to see the full variety of outcomes.
> 2. Emotion assists with the process of balancing multiple facts that must be considered in order to reach a decision. The somatic markers insure that outcomes we have faced in the past will continue to stir an emotional reaction, and consequently we are able to emotionally juggle the relative favorability of different courses of action.
> 3. We give substantial legitimacy to "gut" feelings when we do not know outcomes. Those gut feelings are simply the mind finding a similar outcome, again at the unconscious level, associated with its somatic markers. In all three of these ways, emotion plays a key role in the decision-making process.
>
> (Damasio, 1994)

Emotions, via somatic markers, consequently are integral to human decision-making in the face of multiple or uncertain outcomes (Naqvi et al., 2006). Even when making an economic decision—which is considered by many to be the quintessential rational decision—people rely not only on "cold-hearted calculations of expected utility based upon explicit knowledge of outcomes but also more subtle and sometimes covert processes that depend critically upon emotions" (260). One cannot escape emotional decision-making.

## Emotion and Morality

Emotions similarly guide moral sentiments and actions. Greene et al. (2001) examined the neural systems that enable the making of moral decisions. They discovered that moral dilemmas activated a network of reasoning structures of the brain. These structures, including the ventromedial prefrontal cortex, are engaged in emotional decision-making. Moreover, activation is greater when the moral decision involves negative consequences for another person. That is, our moral sensibility is even more dependent on preconscious emotional states when other people are involved. These findings suggest that moral decisions, compared to non-moral decisions, "engage emotions, especially when one is required to consider the consequences of one's actions for another's well-being" (2001:263).

The sum of our somatic markers is a **somatic "net"** that guides the emotional psychology of our decision-making. When we deal with other people, we immediately—and preconsciously—engage this somatic net, forming immediate predispositions about the likely behavior of the person we are dealing with, who and what that person is, and how they are likely going to react to us.

In police work the classic example of such preconscious decision-making is Skolnick's "symbolic assailant," a person who, according to their characteristics, is likely to be a criminal or have criminal intent. What this perspective tells us is that the symbolic assailant cannot be understood only as a rational assessment of an individual's dangerousness but may represent a rapid-fire moral reaction as well. This is because somatic markers are involved in the assignation of a "symbolic assailant." And that suggests that the identity of a potential symbolic assailant is likely already in place early in life, in that some kinds of people were marked as "other" and morally suspect early in life. It becomes rather easy to add to this assignation "dangerous."

## Social Stereotypes

If the "somatic net" notion of cognitive/emotional development is correct, then three potentially important issues emerge for minority-police relationships.

1. Police may carry an emotional predisposition—a gut-level response—to minority group members, regardless of what that emotional predisposition is. It is a response possibly learned early in childhood, which may continue to exert a powerful influence in later occupational life.
2. Minority group members may also carry such predispositions that influence their emotional reactions to police. If, for example, someone was raised in a family in which a parent had been arrested and incarcerated, the emotional negativity of the somatic marker, particularly if reinforced with other negative interactions, would predispose police encounters with a great deal of potential hostility. Or, if the minority group members were stopped by the police, with or without probable cause, and submitted to searches, with or without consent, this may also "predispose" some emotional negativity toward future police encounters.
3. According to the "somatic net" notion, such hostility would be difficult to avoid; it would go against the emotional "grain" for both police and minorities who have "biasing" somatic markers. Powerful emotional currents could predispose both parties to a sharp distrust at the beginning of any encounter and could easily lead to a spiral of growing distrust and hostility, possibly ending in a violent confrontation.

Moral predispositions, because they are somatically marked, emerge at an early age. And they may tie racial characteristics to moral notions of good and bad. Dunham et al. (2008), for example, discovered that white preschoolers tended to categorize racially ambiguous angry faces as black rather than white; they did not make this connection with happy faces. Baron and Banaji (2006) found that fully developed racial bias emerged in children by the age of six and acted as filters through which they saw the world. These filters never subsided.

Consequently, broad stereotypes associating race with gut-level emotional responses form early in life. These responses include the linking of race to criminality. Richeson and Trawalter (2008) from Northwestern University demonstrated that cultural stereotypes that link young black males with crime, violence, and danger are so robust that they immediately prioritize treatment to blacks as a threat category equal to snakes and spiders.

They also discovered that white college students' visual attention was drawn more quickly to photographs of black versus white men, even though the images were flashed so quickly that participants did not consciously notice them. This heightened vigilance did not appear, however, when the men in the pictures were looking away from the camera. This reaction is noteworthy, they assert, because averted eye gaze is a signal of submission in humans and other animals and, as such, extinguishes explicit perceptions of threat.[2]

Stereotyping, reinforced by somatically marked "gut" reactions, is preconscious and can act against conscious preferences. People may hold values, attitudes, and beliefs about social groups that they may not be explicitly aware of. In other words, by the time someone thinks "That person is different. I should try to understand their differences," negative somatic markers may already be acting on them. These markers stereotype the person as "bad" or "dangerous" and predetermine the failure of efforts to understand or make sense of differences, even when one wants to.[3]

The power of the "somatic net" is particularly acute in gut-level, reflexive, or rapid-response situations. Reflexive actions and snap judgments from emotional associations can lead to catastrophic mistakes. Carpenter (2008), for example, suggested that blacks and whites tend to mistake harmless objects such as a cell phone or other personal device for a gun if a black face accompanies the object. This mistaken judgment or "weapon bias" is especially strong when people have to judge the situation very quickly (Carpenter, 2008). In an attempt to explain these perceptual differences, Dovidio and his colleagues (2004) analyzed the reaction of black and white college students to each other's verbal and nonverbal behavior during a series of recorded conversations. He found that blacks interpreted the nonverbal behavior of whites as "prejudice," even though the verbal interaction explicitly intended by the white participants was the opposite. This difference in perspective is viewed as an indication that blacks and whites can look at the same thing but, through their divergent somatic nets, see it sharply differently.

Consider the following incident. On February 4, 1999, while conducting a rape investigation, four New York City police officers approached a black male named Amadou Diallo at his apartment because he matched the description of the suspect. As the officers approached the suspect, they became so alarmed by his movements, they shot at him 41 times, striking him 19 times and causing his immediate death. The motion that triggered such an alarming response was later determined to be the simple attempt of Diallo to locate his wallet. Although the officers were subsequently charged with homicide, they were acquitted, after arguing they believed their lives were in danger. This incident, along with numerous others involving the police over-reaction to minority suspects, have been addressed in a growing body of research that indicates that emotional reactions, based on incorrect information, can easily contaminate our perceptions and behavior.

## Police Organizational Culture and the "Somatic Net"

On March 3, 1991, in Los Angeles, California, two California Highway Patrol officers, along with an estimated 27 other officers, pursued a speeding motorist in what is now known as the infamous "Rodney King" beating. The central issue for many was the seeming disproportionate magnitude of the police response to King's behavior. What could trigger such an emotional and violent police response to a seemingly routine vehicle pursuit? Studies have focused on several key factors of the event. First was the number of officers present during the traffic stop and subsequent beating. Second was the recollection of events and physical condition of the suspect from the officers' perspective. And third was the number of recorded radio messages following the beating that displayed racial bias on the part of some L.A. police officers.

Investigators have noted that between 21 and 27 officers from three training agencies, including one supervisor and four training officers, were present at the scene of the Rodney King incident (Baker and Wright, 1991; Christopher Commission, see Christopher, 1991). Scholars have interpreted this to be evidence of a deviant subculture. Skolnick and Fyfe (1993:13), for example, noted that "Two cops can go berserk, but twenty cops embody a subculture of policing." Investigations also discovered recorded radio transmissions from LAPD officers that openly expressed racial hostility. The Christopher Commission's review of these communications found the following:

> an appreciable number of disturbing and recurrent racial remarks. Some of the remarks describe minorities through animal analogies. . . . Often made in the context of discussing pursuits or beating suspects. The offensive remarks cover the spectrum of racial and ethnic minorities in the

> City. . . . The officers typing the MDT messages apparently had little concern that they would be disciplined for making such remarks.
> (Christopher, 1991:4–8)

Scholars interpreted these events as evidence of well-established organizational culture that emphasized and condoned violence (Kappeler et al., 1994). The question raised by organizational sociologists was whether there was a "dark" element of Los Angeles police culture, reinforced by informal norms and in-group socialization processes, that nurtured racial hostility to African Americans. We view this event differently.

One explanation for what allegedly transpired during the situation is that in order for this kind of violent over-reaction to occur, a "somatic net" has to already be in place that reacts emotionally to African Americans negatively and that associates them with crime and violence. Once someone so predisposed is in the presence of African Americans in a tense and distrustful situation, a predictable, if not likely, outcome is violence out of proportion to the precipitating incident itself.

The somatic net explanation has broad implications for police. It means that racial or ethnic bias in police departments is not explainable only in terms of behaviors learned on the job but initially emerges from family background and upbringing. However, this is a troubling conclusion. If police tend to reflect the views of broad constituencies in U.S. society, our interpretation suggests that racial bias, distrust, and hostility are far more prevalent in U.S. society than most people would acknowledge.

## Racial Corruption of the Noble Cause

People choose to be police officers, in part, from their altruistic desire to "help people" or "make a difference in society" (Meagher and Yentes, 1986). Such views are consistent with the social psychological research discussed earlier that somatic markers placed early in life can orient a person morally and ethically. As their career progresses, these officers often find themselves engaged in emotionally dense situations; they may risk their life for strangers, they may find that they have to protect the public welfare in the face of perceived danger, they will be charged with the duty to apprehend dangerous persons, and they are likely to relate to the physical and emotional suffering of crime victims. During the course of these incidents, they will more than likely experience fear, anger, remorse, and sympathy. Somatic markers guide them through these complicated sentiments, both consciously and unconsciously. Complicating this process even further, emotions are particularly relevant at times when immediate decisions must be made concerning the welfare of others, especially when morality is a primary consideration.

Officers' commitments to the noble cause—their "gut" reactions that tell them to act on behalf of the welfare of others—cannot consequently be understood only in terms a sense of duty to carry out the intent of law. Rather, both duty to law and noble cause stem from learned emotional reasoning already established in the somatic net. It should, therefore, be no surprise to police administrators and supervisors that their officers sometimes feel compelled to engage in the noble cause.

If officers also have in place racist somatic markers, then through implicit and explicit bias, they may view and treat society's minority outgroup members as more dangerous than in-group members. Hence, when officers have somatic markers that both find good in the noble cause AND bad in minority group members, then the noble cause may be acted out on behalf of citizens and at the same time reinforce racist differences.

The conflation of the noble cause and racism, we argue, is precisely what we see in the Rodney King beating. That the officers do not distinguish between racism and the noble cause is suggested by the consequences of their actions. They engaged in physical brutality, created racially discriminatory evidence in the form of transmission records, and were recorded by videotapes and formal complaints.

## Policy Implications of Emotional Decision-Making

> "I'm a man, so I can change, if I have to, I guess."
>
> Red Green

In a popular Canadian sitcom series, Red Green runs the "possum lodge." At the end of each show, the members of the lodge, all men, repeat the "Man's oath," quoted earlier. Its humorous purpose is to indicate their adaption to a world in which they have to take seriously what their wives ask of them. It reflects the innate distrust of change and the general unwillingness of people to undergo change. But it also reflects a capacity for change, desired or not, and it is to that capacity that we turn now.

There is a cultural adage that applies to police officers. It is that people are not only role-takers, they are also role makers. This means that we are not inevitably committed to the predispositions, values, and attitudes that marked our upbringing. As Red and the "possum lodge gang" noted, under the right leadership, and with the recognition that change is needed, people can adapt. In terms of the social psychological perspective we have discussed throughout this section, this means that the influence of the somatic net—our initial emotional responses to people, morality, and behaviors—does not also have to be the final determinant in our behavior. We can change, if the motivation is sufficient enough.

For people facing conflicts between their behavior and their role expectations, change means going against our sense of who we are—our core identity. It will always be difficult, and rarely sought. It will feel wrong. And it will take a long time for change to seem right. But somatic markers can be retooled. It is an issue of time and willingness to explore alternatives.

For policymakers, it means that training—the correct application of the noble cause and the avoidance of its corruption—is not simply a matter of a few hours' academy instruction on proper legal behavior or ethical conduct. Human emotion and implicit bias affect every aspect of who an officer is and how she or he acts. That means that all your officers—TOs, commanders, and all those with whom new officers come into contact—must be role models. Mike is fond of reminding commanders that a TO will role model a rookie down to the last donut. Only the TO is in a position to recognize issues associated with race, as they are practiced in police work, and it falls to the TO to provide alternatives. But TOs are also relatively new for police organizations. In the end, it falls to commanders and upper administration, and the chief. The identity of the organization is the identity they confer.

The responsibility of the chief and command staff is to lead through emulation, through the sorts of role models they are, through their willingness to lead by example. We will repeat frequently that it is emulation, not education and training, that best creates the ethical climate in an organization. **Emulation** can be defined as efforts to strive or to excel, by modeling, mimicking, imitating someone else's behavior. Line officers will talk about command presence, attitude, and whether anyone really gives a damn. Commanders must act ethically if they are to be emulated by line officers. And they must be seen. It is not a perfect solution, and the problem of racial bias runs deep in American society and in many American police departments. But quality of leadership is the best solution we have, and it is an art and craft that must be continually honed and developed so that those who follow will do so the way we want them to.

## Part II: Rokeach and the Value Survey

In 1971, Milton Rokeach and his colleagues (Rokeach et al., 1971) published a paper on value differences between the police and citizens, whom they called the "policed." Their work had two purposes. The first was to determine the extent to which the values carried by police officers matched values of other American citizens. The second was to evaluate whether police officers' values resulted from the nature of police work or if they were already in place when officers were hired. Rokeach and his colleagues' work, because it focuses on values, is important in understanding the powerful pull the noble cause has on the police. Box 4.1 describes Rokeach's views of the importance of values.

Box 4.1

**Rokeach and the Importance of Values**

Rokeach's research on values emerged from his efforts to identify the way in which citizens engaged in political decision-making (1973). Rokeach observed that values are central to human decision-making. A person's values, he argued, provided a standard for understanding their decisions and actions. This can occur in seven ways:

1. They lead us to take particular positions on social issues.
2. They predispose us to favor one particular or religious ideology over another.
3. They guide representations of self (the image we want to portray) to others.
4. They allow us to evaluate and judge, to heap praise and fix blame on ourselves and others.
5. We employ values in order to assess morality and competency.
6. Values are used to persuade and influence others, to tell us which beliefs, attitudes, values, and actions of others are worth challenging, protesting, and arguing about or worth trying to change.
7. Values . . . tell us how to rationalize . . . beliefs, attitudes, and actions that would otherwise be personally and socially unacceptable so that we will end up with personal feelings of morality and competence, both indispensable ingredients for . . . self-esteem.

Finally, values do not act independently of each other, but operate together as clusters. When individuals are confronted with decisions, they will actuate a cluster of values in deciding how to act. These value clusters undergird our major political orientation. Rokeach identified particular value clusters that uniquely identified communism, socialism, capitalism, and fascism.

Source: Adapted from Milton Rokeach (1973). *The Nature of Human Values*. New York, NY: The Free Press.

Rokeach suggested that values carried by individuals tended to be relatively few in number, and all individuals tended to carry similar values, though they varied in the degree and pattern. **Values** were defined as "an enduring belief that a specific mode of conduct or end-state of existence is personally or socially preferable to (its) opposite" (Rokeach, 1973:5). An example of a mode of conduct was "loyalty" and an end state was "equality."

Values, Rokeach et al. continued, were organized into value systems. He defined **value systems** as "an enduring organization of beliefs concerning preferable modes of conduct or end-states of existence" (Rokeach, 1973:5). In all behavior worth understanding and investigating, Rokeach contended, one could see the workings of human values and value systems.

The police, Rokeach et al. observed, maintain public-order, control people, and provide important services in needy circumstances. In all of these activities, police officers act in such a way to ensure that orderliness prevails. Consequently, we should expect that they will carry values that stress the "desirability of maintaining the status quo," particularly values of obedience and conformity to laws and norms of society (Rokeach et al., 1971:156). The authors suggested that police were likely to be drawn from politically conservative groups where such values were prized, and within those groups, recruitment would favor individuals with a high desire for police work.

The authors tested the following four hypothesis sets or ideas they had about important relationships concerning police values. A **hypothesis** is a statement of relationship between two variables (an element or factor which is likely to change). Hypothesis 1 on the next page, for example, states that the importance of a value carried by the police will be different from its importance among the policed. If we measure an end-state such as "equality," for example, and find that the scores of police officers are different than they are for the policed, then we have support for Hypothesis 1. The research hypotheses tested by Rokeach are listed in Box 4.2.

Box 4.2

**Rokeach: Research Hypotheses**

| | |
|---|---|
| Hypothesis 1. | Police have distinctively different values from other groups in American society |
| Hypothesis 2. | Police values are highly similar to the values of the groups from which they are recruited. |
| Hypothesis 3. | Police values also are determined by particular characteristics of their personality. |
| Hypothesis 4. | Police values are "fine-tuned" by their occupational work. |

To measure values, the authors used the "Rokeach Value Survey," a set of scales that provided information on 18 terminal and 18 instrumental values. **Terminal values** were defined as "preferred end-states." **Instrumental values** were defined as "preferred modes of behavior" (Rokeach et al., 1971:158). Put differently, terminal values represent ends that we think are meaningful, and instrumental values are the means or behaviors we think are acceptable.

A survey was distributed to 153 white male members of a mid-sized police department. Participating officers were given a list of values and asked to rank them from the most important to the least important. By comparing recruits to officers that had been in the police force for a long time, the authors assessed whether police work had any influence on their values. The same survey had previously been administered by the National Opinion Research Center to the general population. This provided a non-police sample of citizens whose values could be compared to Rokeach's sample of police officers.

When terminal (ends) values were investigated, the researchers found that the police held the following four values to be more important than did the general population: *an exciting life, a sense of accomplishment, family security*, and *mature love*. Five terminal values were less important to the police than to citizens generally: *a world at peace, a world of beauty, equality, national security*, and *social recognition*. These findings meant that the police placed a higher emphasis on personal than social values than did the public generally.

When instrumental values were examined, police consistently ranked higher than the public on the following values: *capable, honest, intellectual, logical, obedient, responsible*, and *self-control*. They consistently placed a lower value on *being broad-minded, cheerful, forgiving, helpful*, and *independent*. The authors observed:

> Together these differences suggest an image of the policeman as a person who sees himself performing his occupational functions in a professionally competent and responsible manner. . . . But this professional orientation . . . has a special quality to it. . . . The data also suggest that police place a relatively higher value on professional fulfillment that takes place within the framework of an authority-dominated and rule-oriented social organization that provides a framework for dealing with people in an impersonal manner and according to previously formulated bureaucratic rules.
>
> (Rokeach et al., 1971:163)

These findings provided support for the authors' Hypothesis 1:

> Rokeach Finding 1: The police, in their survey, had a different value system than the policed.

The second hypothesis the authors tested was this: Did differences in values emerge from the process of occupational socialization, or were they already in place when the officers were hired? This time, the authors compared the police to a sample of white males matched for income, education, politics, and general background. Matching is a common way for experimenters to measure whether two groups differ in some important way. **Matched groups** are those in which members of the police department are measured for important demographic characteristics, such as sex, political affiliation, age, and education. They then are matched with adult males that are similar on these important variables but are not police. Then the values are compared. The two groups were very similar in values, suggesting that the values carried by officers were similar to selected groups of other adult Americans.

> Rokeach Finding 2: The police carry values similar to particular groups in society.

Third, the authors found that within the matched groups, police "recruitment" is more likely to take place among those who place a relatively lower value on *freedom, equality, independence,* and *a world of beauty*, and a higher value on *obedience, self-control, a comfortable life*, and *pleasure*. From this, the authors determined that both social background and personality factors were important in understanding police recruitment.

> Rokeach Finding 3: Socialization to important police values occurs prior to, not after, a person becomes a police officer, and the police are recruited from among individuals in particular groups with predisposing personality values.

With regard to the fourth question, the authors asked if occupational socialization also affected police values. **Occupational socialization** is the process by which a recruit learns the values, beliefs, habits, and norms of the organization into which she or he is hired. If this were the case, then older officers should reveal values different from young recruits. The authors found that there wasn't a single difference between younger and older officers on any of the 36 values.

> Rokeach Finding 4: Occupational socialization has no impact on police officers' values.

## Rokeach Revisited: Caldero's Re-Analysis of Police Values

Rokeach's research on police values was published nearly 55 years ago, in 1971. At that time, the United States was in an epoch of social upheaval, marked by inner-city rioting over racial equality and student demonstrations against the Vietnam War. Since the work was published, the occupation of policing has undergone profound changes. Education is more important to the police than ever before. Academy training is substantially longer and is required universally for sworn officers. These changes might well have affected the values carried by police officers. Is it not reasonable to speculate that police values have changed in the face of these sweeping occupational changes? What would happen if we were to re-analyze the police today using the Rokeach method? Would their values be different?

One of the original authors of this book, Michael A. Caldero, replicated Rokeach's study on police officers in the northwestern city of Tacoma, Washington (Caldero, 1997). Caldero carried out a questionnaire survey of detectives, patrol officers, and sergeants, distributing questionnaires on the principal shifts. Of 166 questionnaires distributed, 128 were completed and returned, for a response rate of 77 percent. What he found might be unsettling to police reformers.

First, Caldero was interested in value stability. Were values held by police similar over time, or had they changed? He first looked at terminal or "ends" values and found that the values of the officers he studied were similar to the findings presented in the original Rokeach research. This finding suggested that little change had occurred in police values over time and place. He found, for example, that the value for *freedom* was unchanged from the Rokeach study. Recall that the police in Rokeach's survey rated *freedom* comparatively low, when compared to citizens. Caldero next looked at instrumental or "means" values. When he compared his data to the Rokeach data, he again found few significant differences. In other words:

> Caldero Finding 1: Officers' values were remarkably similar across the two studies. Officers in this study carry the same value system, with values held at virtually equivalent levels, as Rokeach's officers 30 years' previously.

Police recruitment practices have also changed over the intervening years. A greater number of police officers are selected from the ranks of minority members. Police agencies today are also more likely to hire more-educated officers. Do these changes in recruitment practices, Caldero wondered, result in substantive differences in values carried by police officers as well?

Caldero's sample included 16 officers who were minority group members as well as 110 Anglo-Americans. He found that there were no significant scoring differences between the minority and Anglo groups among any of the instrumental (means) values and that there were only three significant scoring differences among the terminal (ends) values—*equality, inner harmony*, and *sense of accomplishment*. And in terms of relative importance of the different ends values, minority group members rated equality tenth versus 12th for Anglos, still substantially lower than non-police citizens in the Rokeach data.

> Caldero Finding 2: Whether members of minority groups or white, police officers hold similar values.

Comparisons across levels of education also showed only minimal differences. Caldero compared officers' values across three categories of education: officers with only a high school education, with some college, and with a college degree. No terminal (ends) values showed significant differences. Only two of the 18 instrumental (means) values showed differences. Officers with only a high school education were more likely to rank *courageous* and *responsible* highest, with officers with some college ranking them the lowest. There was no systematic pattern to the differences.

> Caldero Finding 3: Education has little effect on the values held by police officers.

Finally, Caldero looked at length of police service. Instead of looking at age as a substitute for years of service as did Rokeach et al. (1971), Caldero directly examined the actual years of police work served by police officers in three categories: 1–5 years of service, 6–10 years of service, and 11 or more years of service. Like Rokeach and his colleagues, Dr. Caldero found that there was no indication of acquired values over time for the police in the survey. In other words, there was no support for the idea that the police socialization process in some way changed police officers' values.

> Caldero Finding 4: The police socialization process has no effect on police officers' values.

What do Caldero's and Rokeach's combined findings tell us about the police? To the extent that the police in the two surveys are representative, they tell us a lot. First, between 1971 and Caldero's research in 1997, the values of the police hadn't changed much but instead were remarkably constant. Second, they indicated that police values are imported from particular groups in broader society. Third, they suggest that neither minority group membership nor education had much of an effect on police officers' values. If reformers hope that the employment of more educated minority group members will change police values, they may be mistaken. Finally, once police officers are hired, their values don't change much. In other words, efforts to change the values of police officers after they are hired, by modifying the socialization or training process, are not likely to be fruitful.

## Corroborative Research

In 1998, Zhao, He, and Lovrich conducted an investigation into the attitudes and values of police officers in the Spokane, Washington Police Department. They also used the Rokeach values scales, and their findings were similar to those reported by Caldero, earlier. Spokane police officers' rankings on values orientations appeared to be unaffected by their length of employment, again casting doubt on the argument that police cultural or socialization influences change officers' values. They also observed that "police officers ranked value items quite similarly regardless of whether they had college degrees (or beyond) or reported no college experience," suggesting that education did not affect officers' values.

Zhao and his colleagues were particularly interested in the values carried by Spokane police women. The recent history of women, they observe, has been a struggle for gaining equal employment in public service (1998:31). They found:

> The value distribution . . . indicates that there are generally no significant differences between male and female officers with respect to their value orientations. Only one item, "happiness," out of 18 produces a difference which is statistically significant. (It was rated higher by the men than the women.) In fact, the rank order is remarkably similar for male and female officers in the Spokane Police Department.

Finally, the authors considered the overall ranking of important political values. They found that the ranking of the value of equality, the single strongest predictor of overall value orientation, was virtually identical in all three surveys (Spokane, Tacoma, and Rokeach et al.). In the Spokane survey, it was ranked 13th. In the Tacoma and original Rokeach surveys, it ranked 14th overall.

Only three Rokeach-based surveys are discussed in this chapter. They are the only three that we know of that have used the Rokeach value system and to which we have access to the data. An observer might comment that there are more than 17,000 police departments in the United States. Are these surveys representative? The issue of representativeness is important: **representativeness** asks whether the findings of our research accurately reflect the entire population of police organizations in the United States. Clearly, that only three surveys have been conducted is not an adequate basis for representativeness. Yet the evidence we have thus far collected strongly supports, for the departments studied, the argument that values carried by police officers are imported from selected segments of the American population and only change marginally after that.

In 2007, Crank, Flaherty, and Giacomazzi developed a preliminary assessment of deputy's commitments to the noble cause in a Western city. The authors expressed the concern that literature on the noble cause rested on research on Rokeach's measure described earlier, which is an indirect measure. It will be recalled that Rokeach's measure assesses ends states and means states shared among different groups. It did not directly measure willingness to set aside means in order to achieve sought ends related to crime control.

The authors asked the following questions: When the noble cause it described, what does it refer to? And is there a "noble cause" per se, or a variety of related themes that make up somewhat overlapping issues regarding ends-oriented beliefs?

The authors assessed a 12-item set of measures designed to assess different items that represented ends-oriented thinking. None of the items tapped illegal behavior or behavior that represented a violation of department policy. The intent of the assessment was to measure and assess the nature of the noble cause, not noble-cause corruption. The authors found three underlying dimensions in their research. One set of items assessed willingness to use deceptive means to entice other deputies to commit illegal activity. This finding suggested that noble cause commitments outweighed culture commitments to the protection of other deputies. A second dimension showed that deputies were willing to give reporters erroneous information in order to trick suspects. The third assessed the extent to which deputies would use deceptive information in order to build cases generally.

The authors also looked at each of the 12 items individually. They found, not surprisingly, that the extent to which deputies supported the item varied considerably across items. They reasoned that this finding suggested that the way in which officers understood the noble cause was likely a product of local organizational dynamics and cultural expectations. That is, meanings were always worked out in concrete encounters. This article could not speak to the moral predispositions of officers prior to police work or to training. However, in terms of on-the-job commitments, it suggested that the morality was more complex than could be understood as a single "point" morality. Put differently, to understand police practices associated with the noble cause, one needed to recognize that moral commitments to particular ends varied substantially across different kinds of circumstances.

## Reform and Values

Perhaps the best summary statement that describes the Spokane survey is that the authors' findings are remarkably similar to those reported by Caldero in Tacoma and earlier by Rokeach. Zhao and his colleagues (1998:32) observed this similarity: "the type of persons attracted to police work differs little today from what it has been when traditional styles of policing held sway."

These findings are stone soup for reformers who believe that police values can be changed through higher education, minority hiring, by hiring women, or by changing the police socialization process. If values carried by individual officers are in some way a problem, they are likely to remain a problem.

How, then, can value change among police officers be carried out? We begin by recognizing that change is occurring. It may not be the change reformers want, though. Officers are rapidly socialized into support for local cultural values tolerant to organizational secrecy and to noble-cause corruption.

We believe that change can occur in three ways. First, administrators who want to instill long-term, systemic change in officers' values will have to do it through the general hiring process. Moreover, and here's the significant complicating factor, they will have to hire people that are different from themselves. People have to be hired who have different values from the people that are hiring them, whose values administrators don't share and probably don't believe in. Unless this improbable task can be accomplished, one cannot have but pale hope for significant long-term change.

The second change is through ethics education. If the goal is not to change police values but to change how police apply their morality to their work setting (a more limited goal), then we can hope for successes without the need to profoundly overhaul agency hiring policies. As we will argue later, some types of community policing programs may provide conditions for subtle changes in some values (Wycoff and Skogan, 1994).

Ethics training, we think, if done right and applied practically to the work setting, can also affect how officers apply the values they have. We seek, in other words, the more reachable goal of incremental change. We are not trying to re-make the police here, and we certainly don't want a police officer who is emotionally unmoved by the morality of the noble cause. We are trying to instill in police the means to think through and understand a difficult ethical dilemma, the dilemma of noble-cause corruption. And we're trying to inform them about what they're getting into when they abandon means for ends.

Third, and to be discussed in more detail in the recommendations chapter, is through modeling behavior. Currently, recruits are being role modeled by TOs, other senior line officers, and to a lesser extent, sergeants. All this modeling needs to be examined. This similarly applies to commanders, who may be good models but may be so infrequently seen that their potential contribution is unnoticed.

We want officers who believe in their work. We don't want police departments to hire recruits who "flake off" orders from higher-ranking officers, or who don't believe that there is a place for law and order in democratic society. Yet, as all veteran police reformers know, change is difficult. When it comes to the police, one should approach significant reform with a certain temperament for fatalism. If one can be content with smaller changes, well, with patience, with a lot of patience and a flair for departmental politics, one might be surprised what can be accomplished.

## Notes

1 It is a wholesale reversal of Cartesian logic, in that emotions are not only closely tied to and inseparable from reasons but they actually are also the embodied foundation from which reasoning emerges.

2 Deep within our subconscious, all of us harbor biases that we consciously abhor. And the worst part is this: we act on them. "There is nothing more painful at this stage in my life, Jesse Jackson once told an audience, than to walk down the street and hear footsteps and start thinking about robbery—then look around and see somebody white and feel relieved" (Carpenter, 2008). These remarks made by a prominent black political activist reveal aspects of human nature none of us can escape, that without our consciousness nor consent, our minds form judgments and expectations that shade our reality.

3 Such implicit biases form stereotypical associations such as "black and danger" or "white and good" or "female and weak." We are most likely to conjure up implicit bias under conditions that precipitate self-interest, such as the need to increase the status of the group we belong to by devaluing or decreasing the status of outsiders (Nosek et al., 2007). For example, visual perceptions are especially susceptible to being distorted in favor of the group to which we belong. Studies have shown that people are more likely to remember faces of their own race rather than those of other races and to exaggerate differences between their group and others (Cunningham et al., 2004).

# Noble-Cause Corruption

# Part 2

This section is transitional. Part 1 focused on value-based decision-making. This section aims more directly at problems associated with noble cause and its corruption. We argue throughout that the corruption of noble cause has many consequences.

Chapter 5 discusses the history of economic corruption and police reform. We argue that the reform of economic corruption among the police has been somewhat successful and that economic corruption has declined throughout the twentieth century. Reform was accomplished in part by hiring police officers committed to their work, in part by the establishment of more rigorous hiring standards, and in part through more rigorous supervision of patrol and investigative activities. Yet this accomplishment has had an unintended consequence: officers are hired that are already committed to the noble cause, and they are vulnerable to noble-cause corruption. In many departments today, many police officers have traded economic corruption for noble-cause corruption.

Chapter 6 examines noble-cause corruption from the perspective of commanders. In this chapter, we look at how managers often fail to recognize noble-cause corruption and are caught by surprise when noble-cause problems emerge. We argue that noble-cause corruption has a variety of unanticipated consequences for police organizations that are often overlooked by managers. This looks at two of the primary organizational consequences of noble-cause corruption as well, legitimacy and liability issues.

Chapter 7 returns to the means-ends dilemma. It shows how the noble cause is a particular kind of ends-oriented problem and discusses some of the problems with an ends orientation generally. This chapter discusses at length the environment of street officers and the groups in that environment who tempt officers to commit noble-cause corruption.

DOI: 10.4324/9781003626916-7

Chapter 8 looks at the noble cause from the point of view of police cultures. An expanded notion of police culture is presented. Arguing that police departments can be characterized by the presence of management and line cultures, this chapter discusses the implications of a multicultural environment for managers and for line officers. This chapter concludes with a discussion of the many different forms that noble-cause corruption can take.

# From Economic to Noble-Cause Corruption

# 5

## Key Terms

- August Vollmer
- Rampart CRASH unit
- contingency
- grass-eaters
- golden apples
- the gospel of professionalism
- grafting subcultures
- the magic pencil
- Mama Rosa's test
- material-reward corruption
- moral career
- slippery-slope model of economic corruption
- slippery-slope model of noble-cause corruption
- exchange
- corruptible exchange
- corruptibility
- model of circumstantial corruptibility
- roles of the giver
- roles of the acceptor
- hierarchy of wickedness

## Introduction

This chapter explores the evolution of police corruption from material-reward corruption to noble-cause corruption, emphasizing the moral complexities embedded in modern law enforcement. Drawing on historical reform efforts led by August Vollmer and the gospel of professionalism, the text critiques the limitations of the traditional slippery-slope model of economic corruption. It introduces the slippery-slope model of noble-cause corruption, where officers, often golden apples—morally committed and high-performing—gradually rationalize unethical actions in pursuit of justice. Through examples like the Rampart CRASH

DOI: 10.4324/9781003626916-8

Unit, the chapter illustrates how noble-cause corruption can escalate into systemic abuses. The Model of Circumstantial Corruptibility reframes corruption as a dynamic interaction between the roles of the giver and the acceptor, emphasizing corruptible exchanges.

> Mike tells the assembled officers that police officers out on the street have a perspective that directly influences how they apply morality, and they use the law to enhance that application.
>
> Officers look at Mike like he's from Mars when he says that. They're trying to figure out if it's threatening or supportive. It's threatening.
>
> I spent six years in the L.A. County Sheriff's Office. I never saw individual-level corruption. Putting something that's not yours in your pocket. I never saw that, not once. A little brutality. That happens. Don't do that. I saw noble-cause corruption, all the time. Individual-level corruption, never.

Today, we teach ethics in virtually every criminal justice department and training academy in the United States. What do we teach them? Don't take free coffee; it's wrong. It's a slippery slope, we say; soon, you'll be shaking down restaurants for free meals. Next, you'll be selling narcotics. Review any textbook on corrupt behavior, and they inevitably start their discussion with the wrongs of taking gratuities. Our position is that officers need this kind of ethics instruction but that they also need to be made aware of a different kind of corruption not addressed within an "economic corruption" model—noble-cause corruption.

We'll begin this chapter by reviewing the idea of the "slippery slope" and the history of efforts to control economic corruption among the police in the United States. Then, we subject the slippery-slope idea to considerable criticism and present the Model of Circumstantial Corruptibility. This model addresses many of the shortcomings of the slippery-slope perspective and explains the dynamic nature of corruption. We'll close with a discussion of noble cause corruption and its relationship to economic corruption.

## Sherman: Individual-Level Corruption

The **slippery slope** is a metaphor for a police officer's pattern of involvement in corrupt activities. What is meant by the **slippery-slope model of economic corruption** is that the first illegal acts committed by a police officer are minor, easy to justify. It becomes easier, however, to commit more serious wrongful acts after a person has committed minor acts of corruption. An officer who is presented with a bribe to overlook a traffic violation, for example, will find it easier to justify the bribe if she or he has already accepted small perks or has helped a bar stay open late. The officer has learned how to rationalize illegal and inappropriate behavior and can justify further and more serious wrongdoing.

Slippery-slope corruption has been described as a process of "becoming bent" (Sherman, 1985). Not all officers become bent; it happens where, according to Sherman, grafting subcultures are already in place in police organizations—that is, where some officers are already involved in economic corruption. **Grafting subcultures** are groups or cohorts of officers that are already "bent" and that socialize new officers into corrupt activities. Sherman observed that officers go through a series of stages during the process of becoming "bent," or partially corrupted, and these stages when considered together constitute a **moral career.** The stages of corruption are presented in Box 5.1.

Box 5.1

**The Stages of a Corrupt Moral Career**

**Minor "perks."** An officer accepts free coffee and meals from restaurants on his or her beat.

**Bar closing.** An officer stays after closing and accepts free drinks to keep the bar open.

**Regulative crimes.** A motorist gives an officer $100 to overlook a traffic violation.

**Gambling crimes.** Regular payoffs are paid by a local gambling operation to permit its continued operation.

**Prostitution.** Payoffs are given to police from brothel operations, prostitutes, or pimps to permit continued activities.

**Narcotics.** Police become involved in the distribution and use of controlled substances.

Source: Lawrence Sherman (1985). "Becoming Bent: Moral Careers of Corrupt Policemen." In F.S. Elliston and M. Feldberg (eds.). *Moral Issues in Police Work.* Totowa, NJ: Rowman & Allanheld, 1985.

The stages in a moral career, Sherman noted, are not fixed and inevitable outcomes for officers already involved in lower levels of corruption. Each stage is qualified by a contingency. **Contingency** means that the subsequent stage is not inevitable, and an officer can decide not to proceed. At each stage, an officer makes a moral decision, and each one is accompanied by varying degrees of peer pressure. A recruit may decide at any stage not to continue down the slippery slope of a moral career. However, recruits must recognize that they will likely be shunned by other officers if they decide to make a decision to "go straight."

The slippery-slope metaphor is a powerful way to think about police corruption. It recognizes the importance of police peers in encouraging corruption and the role played by the secretive elements of police culture.

And there is no doubt that economic corruption has held a powerful pull over police officers in many American police departments. Finally, the slippery-slope argument resonates well in the moral environment of policing; it allows problems of corruption to be conceptualized in terms of personal responsibility and moral weakness. Individual officers make bad moral judgments and slide down the corrupt path. They made bad decisions, and the culpability is theirs personally. Blame is clear.

But what of corruption committed because officers are absolutely committed to the moral righteousness of their work? This kind of corruption occurs when officers set aside legal principles and organizational policy for the noble cause, the good end. This kind of corruption does not fit within a slippery-slope model of economic corruption. Officers are becoming corrupted for a good reason, not a bad one—to be more effective in the fight against crime.

Using a simplified historical discussion, we discuss a process by which we think that economic corruption has given way to noble cause corruption. It is our belief that noble-cause corruption is a more widespread and significant problem today than economic corruption in American police departments and that noble-cause corruption is increasing in United States police organizations today.

## Economic Corruption and Police Reform

Police corruption and reform have been intertwined issues in the history of policing in the United States. Grafting and extortion were principal forms of corruption at the beginning of the twentieth century (Walker, 1984), and doing something about them has been central to police reform. Economic corruption took many forms in the late 1800s. Payments of bribes across all levels of police departments enabled racketeering to flourish. Officers received graft from illicit activities, such as prostitution, gambling, and illegal liquor sales (Berman, 1987). Corruption flourished inside departments as well. Officers routinely purchased promotions and preferred assignments. Indeed, as Walker (1977) observed, police were the crime problem in this era.

Corruption was closely tied to local political machines. Officers were hired for their loyalties to a particular political party. In return, they were sometimes expected to assist in electioneering fraud, assuring that their party was re-elected to office. Party machines, often as intimately tied to local graft as were police, turned a blind eye to problems of police corruption.

The progressive movement emerged in the late 1800s to advocate municipal reform. The progressive goal was to instill efficiency and morality into local municipal governance and police agencies. Progressives took an active interest in police departments. Police were a primary source of jobs for local political machines (Fogelson, 1977). Progressive reformers sought to reduce political influence by making police agencies more independent of machine politics (White, 1986).

The International Association of Chiefs of Police (IACP), founded in 1893 as the voice of police professionalism, represented the influence of the progressives in police reform. One of the purposes of the IACP was to exert control over the behavior of line officers by removing the influence of party politics from the activities of police departmental employment policies (Fogelson, 1977). The professionalism movement set a reform agenda that included the establishment of hiring standards, hiring outside the local jurisdiction, recruiting chiefs from military and professional backgrounds, and instilling officers with a crime control mission (Walker, 1977).

The early days of the police professionalism movement marked an important beginning for police corruption reform in the United States. Yet, in spite of the efforts of the professionalism movement, reform occurred slowly, in fits and spurts. Consider the words of Fogelson (1977):

> Despite these (professionalizing) changes most departments had only a slightly greater capacity to curtail criminal activity in 1930 than in 1890. For one reason, many policemen were not inclined to deal with crime. As the sensational scandals that erupted in Chicago, Philadelphia, and New York in the late 1920s and early 1930s indicated, some officers preferred to work with the gangsters. A few grew well-to-do from their share of the proceeds. Others preferred to pass their time eating, sleeping, and drinking, talking with buddies or visiting friends, and doing everything possible to stay away from trouble.
>
> (Fogelson, 1977:118)

In the 1920s, **August Vollmer**, sometimes called the patriarch of police professionalism, was emerging as an advocate of police reform. Working with the International Association of Chiefs of Police, Vollmer and his colleagues began "spreading the **gospel of professionalism**" (Fogelson, 1977:155). Departments focused on excellence through hiring standards, and officers were expected to be committed to the public interest and believe in what the police had to offer society. Vollmer believed that officers should view police work as a moral commitment, not simply a job (see Box 5.2).

Box 5.2

**Vollmer and Professionalism**

My fancy pictures to me a new profession in which the very best manhood in our nation will be happy to serve in the future. Why should not the cream of the nation be perfectly willing to devote their lives to the cause of service providing that service is dignified, socialized, and professionalized. Surely the Army offers no such opportunity for contributing to the welfare of the nation.

Source: Carte, G. (1986). "August Vollmer and the Origins of Police Professionalism." In M. Pogrebin and R. Regoli (eds.) *Police Administrative Issues: Techniques and Functions*, pp. 3–9. Millwood, NY: Associated Faculty Press, page 5.

> *Vollmer*, Mike Caldero notes, *understood people. And he understood values. He knew that if police had a particular value system, they would use those values to enforce the law.*

Vollmer believed that the police could carry a commitment to crime control and yet remain value-neutral about social issues (Carte and Carte, 1975). Yet values about crime control are intricately connected to values about social conditions as well. Vollmer was right about the power of values, though he might have underestimated the extent to which they would mobilize street decision-making.

In no small measure due to Vollmer's reform efforts, the police professionalism movement had a large impact on police in the United States (Sykes, 1989). The influence of local municipal politics in the daily affairs of departments declined, and the practice of patronage, whereby officers were hired and fired based on their political affiliations, was sharply curtailed. The Vollmerian idea that officers should be committed to police work has increasingly characterized recruitment and hiring practices. Those hired to become professional police officers were those who believed in the importance of their work, who believed in service to their communities, and who were committed to a contribution of police to society.

What sort of officer did Vollmer have in mind? Two aspects of the Vollmerian vision of professional police officers are important to this discussion. First, Vollmer was a harsh critic of even minor forms of graft. He was reported to have said that any officer accepting so much as a free cup of coffee would be fired (Carte, 1986). Another element of his legacy is the idea that officers should be morally committed to the occupation of policing.

Consider the following statement that Vollmer, in Box 5.2, made in a letter to a friend: Vollmer sought an officer that was highly educated, committed to police work, and skilled in the latest technologies. This vision of police professionalism is grounded in the moral rightness of the fight against crime. It is a moral commitment of service to the country and to the welfare of the nation.

The Vollmerian vision of police work has had a powerful sway on reformers since Vollmer (Jefferson, 1987). It is a vision of police work that was carried by his influential students such as O.W. Wilson, who became a proponent of scientific police management, and Robert Parker, who later became chief of the Los Angeles police department. It is a vision that has changed police work.

By the 1960s, by most accounts, police corruption had substantially declined. As Fogelson (1977:245) noted, they were "fairly honest," or at worst, **"grass-eaters,"** the Knapp commission's term for officers that passively accepted graft but didn't actively hustle it. We believe that, at least in part, today's relatively lower levels of economic corruption stemmed from reformers' successes in establishing personnel procedures aimed at hiring police officers with integrity and commitment.

Today, we have achieved much of Vollmer's dream of professionalism among the police, though not always in quite the way he envisioned it and not as thoroughly as he had hoped. Since the beginnings of the twentieth century, police reformers have sought a curative for police corruption in officers committed to the ideals of policing. They sought an officer committed to a moral vision. And they have largely succeeded.

In the current age, American officers are morally committed to their work. They believe in enforcing the law. They do not like "bad guys" and take pride in a "good pinch." Central to their beliefs is Vollmer's vision; they believe they contribute to the welfare of the nation—that their work is morally important. And the law is the tool they use to carry out this moral vision. The conversion of police mission over this century—from a public sector job to a profound moral commitment—may have been the most important success of the police professionalism movement. And it is among the least recognized.

## The Magic Pencil: Re-Thinking the Bases of Police Corruption

The professionalism movement, though successful in many ways, had some outcomes that were not quite as intended (Fogelson, 1977). This includes its success in efforts to stamp out corruption. Except for narcotics, where it is almost impossible to avoid corruption because of its high value, easy availability, and lightweight portability, levels of economic corruption known at the beginnings of the twentieth century have sharply declined. But this success applies particularly to economic corruption.

Unfortunately, the door may have been opened for another kind of corruption: the corruption of belief from caring about police work too much. Noble-cause corruption.

Noble-cause corruption can take many different forms. For example, an officer might be tempted to provide some "street justice" to an uncooperative suspect. The magic pencil is more effective. Mike explains this to his audience.

> I can beat up someone, and they have some marks on them. Maybe a trip to the hospital. Or I can pull out my magic pencil. You guys know what the magic pencil is. I start writing, and he's got a year in jail. Haven't your officers had a class in creative writing? You know what I mean. If you don't, you've been away from patrol too long. Your officers know.

Mike plays a training film. It includes a section about the magic pencil. An officer, "Officer Smith," is describing his experiences on patrol. Box 5.3 describes the film.

Box 5.3

**The Magic Pencil**

To take the dirt bags to jail, I would do anything—illegal searches, illegal seizures, anything. Besides, I had the magic pencil. Oh yea. Fantasy on paper. So here I was, Mr. Honor Code, doing what I had to do. Except that one day, something happened that changed everything.

The film changes scene. Three officers are discussing what to do about a suspected drug dealer. One of the officers suggests that they stiff-in a call (call and report a crime as if a citizen had seen one. In this case, it is a fantasy crime, called in to justify a search of the residence). "You," he observes, "just got to reach out and touch someone." Another officer replies, "I'll copy the call."

The officer makes the call. "Yes, I'd like to report an emergency. There's been a guy selling drugs to kids all morning. He just sold them to a little girl. And he drug her inside the house. It's 619 South Sycamore. Please hurry."

Smith describes what happened. "I covered for him. We went in on a stiffed-in call. And as things sometimes happen, things turn to shit. An innocent bystander, a pregnant woman was killed. . . . I started thinking, 'Who's the asshole here?'"

The **magic pencil** is a form of noble-cause corruption, in which police officers write up an incident in a way that criminalizes a suspect. It is a powerful tool for punishment, and in the hands of a value-based decision-maker—and that's what the police are—it carries the weight of the United States of America's massive criminal justice system. It proves the maxim that the pen is mightier than the sword. See Box 5.4

Box 5.4

**The Magic Pencil and Police Authority**

Consider the comments of one of Fletcher's (1991) Chicago Police Department confidants:

You want to know what the best brutality is? Stop him, search him, read him his rights, pull out your pen, and smile. You got him. You won.

Source: Connie Fletcher (1991). *What Cops Know*, p. 283.

Today, we've traded economic corruption, or corruption from lack of commitment to police work, for noble-cause corruption, which emerges from an excess of commitment. Yet there are those who will continue to justify noble-cause corruption. "So what," a reader might say, "if an asshole spends an extra weekend in jail? It'll be good for him. Maybe he'll learn a little respect for the law."

Let's see. How can we teach this "asshole" some respect? Let's consider a case in Newark, New Jersey. Vincent Landano was charged and convicted for the 1976 murder of a police officer. In 1998, 21 years later, he was acquitted after being retried. How could this happen? In 1989, the judge, H. Lee Sarokin, became convinced that the state held undisclosed evidence on the murder. He then ordered federal marshals to raid the files of police officers and the prosecutor's office. Evidence uncovered in the raids included information that witnesses were pressured by the police to identify Landano as the gunman. In fact, Landano had been in another state when the crime occurred (Sachs, 1998). Did Landano's experience teach him to respect the law?

Noble-cause corruption is a principal way that public respect for the law is undermined. Mike concludes with a comment on the criminal trial of O.J. Simpson, tried for two counts of first-degree murder in 1996 in a highly publicized trial. The defense had argued that the Los Angeles Police Department, and particularly the lead detective Mark Furman, were not to be trusted in the collection of evidence and were motivated by racist concerns. The jury, after a short deliberation, acquitted Simpson of all charges in spite of compelling DNA evidence to the contrary.

> Mike discusses the Simpson case with the commanders. *Do you understand the jury decision? Do you really understand it? The problems with Furman? That's what happens when your department loses legitimacy with the public it serves. Nobody believes you. That's the problem with noble-cause corruption.*

## The Mama Rosa's Test

> Mike resumes his discussion of noble-cause corruption. *OK, here's a new recruit on patrol. He's all charged up to be one of the guys. Excited. He's out with his training officer and they end up eating at Mama Rosa's café. They are joined by other officers who have been eating there for years.*
>
> At the end of a long meal, all the officers prepare to leave and there is no money on the table. The rookie has his money in his hand and asks how much he should leave. The veteran officers tell the rookie to shut up and put his money away. It seems the cops have been eating free forever and the place has never been held up, unlike other restaurants in the neighborhood. Mama Rosa is very appreciative of this. The rookie insists that he wants to pay for the meal, but he is told to shut up and not jeopardize a good thing.
>
> Here's his test. If the rookie goes along, he is tainted. He loses his virginity. If he doesn't play ball at Mama Rosa's, he won't be trusted as a team player. If he does, the next step is to test him in the field. This

might include dropsy testimony, or backing up another officer in court who makes an honest mistake by supporting his partner's version of events. This is how it happens. A test at the restaurant, then a test in the field.

The **Mama Rosa's test** is a loyalty test with a cultural slant—it assesses the willingness of a rookie to go along with other officers when they are acting against the grain of departmental policy. The test shows us how a rookie is learning "what real policing is." It is similar to the slippery-slope image of economic corruption described earlier. But there are important differences.

1. First, the test is not intended to prepare the rookie for a "grafting subculture." It's a test of his loyalty to the group. Recall that Mama Rosa is appreciative of what the police do. There's no extortion involved. If Mama Rosa has not been burglarized, although the surrounding restaurants have been burglarized, then the police are preventing crime by eating at Mama Rosa's. They are doing a moral good.
2. The second test involves supporting another officer's version of events. Again, it's a loyalty test. Note that the second test has two components. The first is loyalty: Will the rookie go along when the stakes are raised? The second is the good end; officers are trying to do something about crime. That is, it involves a commitment to the noble cause. What the second test shows us is that police loyalty to each other and commitment to the noble cause are intertwined phenomena. It's part of the reason that police will protect each other with such passion. Their beliefs and their loyalty are linked together. The brotherhood (and sisterhood) is familial, a bond of loyalty and morality.

Because low-level corruption involves perks that are so closely tied to loyalty and to the noble cause, administrative efforts to paint low-level graft in terms of personal irresponsibility fall on deaf ears. For a street cop, a bad police officer is a cop that doesn't support another cop. When administrators tell them that being bad involves free coffee, they'll just chuckle and talk about how far administrators are removed from the real world.

## Golden Apples

Chiefs will explain away corruption problems as individual-level corruption. They will find fault with what they call "rotten apples," officers who are morally corrupt but somehow slipped through pre-employment screening. What's a rotten apple? A rotten apple is someone who's bad to the core, who is acting alone out of his or her own badness, who, left unchecked, will spread the rot to the rest of the department. It is a favorite explanation for departments dealing with corruption (Knapp Commission, 1972).

However, in the case of noble-cause corruption, officers who violate the law or department policy aren't rotten apples. To the contrary, they're dealing with crime in an efficient and effective way.

> MIKE EXPLAINS THE DILEMMA AS FOLLOWS: *If you believe in the moral rightness of good ends, that the noble cause is incorruptible—and remember, that's what you hired your officers for—these are your golden apples and you're one of them.*

What is a **golden apple?** A golden apple is an officer, intelligent, committed to the noble cause, and highly focused on efficiency and effectiveness. These officers may represent the "best" police officers in a graduating police academy, that is, those who score the highest on tests and who morally exhort their fellow officers. They are morally committed to their work, dedicated, and energetic. Golden apples believe in the morally right ends of police work. Yet sometimes the golden apples will be the officers that corrupt the noble cause, that break the laws and violate policy in order to "do something about crime and criminals." In some cases, they believe in their work too much and sacrifice all for the "good end."

> Mike addresses the chief, also present at the conference. *Chief, how well do you know your troops?* This is an unexpected question to ask a chief. The chief attends out of courtesy, to show he's supporting the conference. Mike continues.
>
> Look at how it would force us to address the problem differently if we faced it squarely. If you acknowledged that you had people working for you who were making moral decisions, acting in the name of the noble cause.

Instead of blaming a rotten apple, we begin to see how the department's policies and practices are implicated in the problems police departments face. The rotten apple argument is a form of denial.

## The Slippery Slope Revisited

We are going to present our idea of the **slippery-slope model of noble-cause corruption.** It differs from Sherman's slippery slope in subtle but important ways. His concept is germinal to our idea; ours, however, is designed to describe a process of noble-cause corruption. Box 5.5 presents the slippery slope of noble-cause corruption.

Box 5.5

**Slippery-Slope Model of Noble-Cause Corruption**

1. **"Forget everything you learned in training (school). I'll show you how we really do it out here."** This is what an officer often first hears from a TO. The statement is only superficially about the lack of utility of higher education. What it is actually about is loyalty and the importance of protecting the local group of officers with whom the officer works.
2. **Mama Rosa**. It looks like a free meal. This is not to test willingness to graft but whether an officer is going to be loyal to other officers in the squad. It also serves to put officers together out of the station house.
3. **Loyalty Back-up**. Here, an officer is tested to see if he or she will back up other officers. This is more involved because officers may have to "testily" (give false testimony), dropsy (remove drugs from a suspect during a pat-down and then discover them in plain sight on the ground), the shake (similar to dropsy, only conducted during vehicle stops), or stiffing-in a call. These are like NC actions, and may indeed be NC actions, but their purpose is to establish loyalty.
4. **Routine NC (Noble Cause) Actions Against Citizens**. Magic pencil skills. Increase penalties by shifting the crime upward. Protect fellow officers with fictitious charges. Construct probable cause. Illegal searches of vulnerable citizens.
5. **I Am the Law**. This is the belief that emerges over time, in which officers view what they do as the right thing to do. This is the practical outcome of the old adage "power corrupts and absolute power corrupts absolutely." A police officer does not have absolute power, but he or she has the backing of the legal system in almost all circumstances. Behavior can become violent, as with the Rampart CRASH unit.

The process of noble-cause corruption presented in Box 5.5 may vary from department to department. But the following elements tend to be repeated. New recruits are tested for their loyalty through a minor violation of policy. Officers who perform appropriately in this test are "stuck" to their colleagues both in loyalty and in secrecy. In subsequent tests, which are as likely to be opportunistic encounters as staged events, recruits are pulled more deeply into noble-cause corruption. This can include testilying and drug-related noble-cause corruption. These further reinforce secrecy.

As we discussed earlier, by the end of pre-service training, officers had already become committed to values supporting noble-cause corruption and secrecy. The noble-cause slippery slope simply acts out what officers are already psychologically prepared for. Intentional or not, officers in many departments are trained for and then socialized into noble-cause corruption. And the values underpinning noble-case corruption are so pervasive to organizations that there are very few checks on the slippery slope.

Sherman noted that stages of material corruption were characterized by a contingency, in which officers could decide not to continue. In noble-cause corruption, this contingency carries less moral force because officers are already committed to the noble cause and are prepared to do what they have to do to deal with wrongdoers.

Finally, we believe that noble-cause corruption and economic corruption are closely tied to each other. Once started, a police officer may move back and forth across the two lines. In the following section, we will explain this linkage.

## The Model of Circumstantial Corruptibility

Most research on police corruption reaches at least one of the following conclusions.

1. Culpability for corruption is primarily focused on the public official and/or the department.
2. The seriousness of corruption is defined by the value of the item or service exchanged between the giver and receiver.
3. Peer pressure, endemic within the police subculture, enhances and sustains corruption.
4. Serious corruption tends to begin with relatively minor gratuities and progresses to more serious violations of the public trust.

These conclusions are somewhat useful in describing how corruption typically starts and grows within a police organization. They offer plausible explanations of the process by which a police officer might initially engage in petty bribery and eventually progress into extreme forms of criminal behavior. However, for several reasons these findings neither fully explain the nature of corruption, specifically the acceptance of gratuities, nor provide adequate insight in to the function of corruptibility.

First, throughout the literature on police corruption, the focus of discussion (and blame) is almost exclusively on the public official (i.e., the police officer). Admittedly, the integrity of police officers should be of great concern to citizens in a free society. The police routinely exercise wide-ranging authority with limited supervision. Furthermore, the potential social and personal harm that can result from unregulated police authority is considerable. However, the author takes issue with the fact that the participation of the giver is noticeably absent in almost all discussions of police corruption and argues that the giver is an essential participant in police corruption.

Second, individuals in all human organizations are susceptible to peer pressure. Police officers are not essentially more or less susceptible to peer pressure than any other professionals. To blame peer pressure for the onset and continuation of corruption requires that we also accept the notion of corruption as a norm within and a pervasive feature of the police organization. Although there are several celebrated cases of systemic corruption in some of the nation's largest police organizations, there is no evidence suggesting corruption is endemic of and pervasive in *all* police organizations. Peer pressure may be important, but it is not a *sufficient* causal factor leading to corruption.

Third, the slippery-slope perspective somewhat limits our understanding of the dynamics of corruption. This perspective does not consider the possibility that an officer, predisposed to do so, could *begin* with higher levels of corruption. But more importantly, the slippery-slope argument does not consider the role of the giver in the process leading to higher forms of corruption. This explanation focuses entirely on the police officer's role. The model outlined later substantially expands the slippery-slope explanation of the dynamics of corruption by including givers of gratuities.

Fourth, in most discussions on police corruption, the value of the material object exchanged between an officer and an individual defines the relative level of corruption. The model presented later is not dependent upon the value of the item exchanged. In fact, the model proposes that the value of the material object exchanged is, for the most part, irrelevant to the level of social harm. In this regard, the model is consistent with Cohen (1986:25), who writes:

> If the value alone determined the seriousness of taking gratuities, we might end up with and equation of four hundred cups of coffee to the television set. . . . This suggests that it is not primarily the value of what is taken that will differentiate these cases as exploitive or not.

The previous research is useful for explaining the process of corruption. However, the common conclusions of this research substantially limit our ability to understand the essential nature and dynamics of corruption. The model outlined herein responds to these criticisms. This model, called a Model of Circumstantial Corruptibility, expands our understanding of corruption by responding to the following questions.

1. At what point does the exchange of a gift or service between a giver and a receiver constitute corruption?
2. What factors determine the relative harmfulness of corruption?

The model is closely related to Kania's (1988) perspective on the relationships between givers and the police. While Kania focuses on perceptions of givers and the police, the model presented herein focuses on actual roles (intent) adopted by givers and receivers. Furthermore, the model later provides more insight into managing corruption at the individual and administrative levels.

The following definitions are presented to assist the reader with the intended meanings of the terms and concepts essential to the model.

**Exchange**—the transfer of something of value from one person to another.

**Corruptible exchange**—the transfer of something of value from one person to another wherein the giver expects something in return for the item or service and the receiver, in violation of prior responsibilities, accepts the item or service as well as the terms of the exchange. The terms of the exchange may either be implicit or explicit.

**Corruption**—the merger of a giver offering a gift or service with the expectation of a return from the receiver and a receiver, in violation of prior responsibilities, willing to accept the gift of service as well as the terms of the exchange.

**Corruptibility**—the capacity for both the giver and receiver to achieve a particular level of corruption as defined by its potential harm to society.

## *The Essential Elements of the Model of Circumstantial Corruptibility*

The Model of Circumstantial Corruptibility proposes that the level of corruption (as defined by its relative harmfulness to society) attained by the participants of a corruptible exchange is influenced by two, and only two, elements—the role of the giver and the role of the receiver. In this section, the essential elements of the model are defined. In addition, the functionality of the model is discussed in detail.

## *The Role of the Giver*

The role of the giver is one of two essential elements or circumstances that determines the level of corruption. In every exchange, the giver assumes one of the following roles.

**Presenter**—offers a gift voluntarily without any expectation of a return from the receiver.

**Contributor**—furnishes something toward a result. In this role, the giver expects something in return for his contribution. However, in this role, there is some level of voluntariness present in the exchange.

**Complier**—acts in accordance with wishes, demands, or requirements. The giver's level of voluntariness begins to erode.

**Slave**—acts slavishly submissive in response to the demands of the receiver. The slave, unless he escapes or is abandoned, acts involuntarily and has little control over the exchange.

**Capitulator**—acts in total submission to the demands of the receiver.

The level of voluntariness the giver assumes during the exchange primarily determines the giver's role. When in the *presenter* role, the giver has the highest level of voluntariness. Conversely, while in the *capitulator* role, the giver responds involuntarily to the receiver.

## *The Role of the Receiver*

The role of the receiver is the other one of the two essential elements or circumstances that determines the level of corruptibility. In every exchange, the receiver assumes one of the following roles.

**Acceptor**—receives a gift humbly and without any residual feelings of reciprocity.

**Hopeful**—looks forward to with desire and reasonable confidence that the gift will come. May change behavior in anticipation of the gift.

**Expector**—looks forward to the gift and regards it as likely to happen. Will be annoyed by the absence of the gift.

**Demander**—asks for the gift with authority and claims more than is generally felt by others to be due.

**Conqueror**—assumes total control over the exchange and influence over the giver.

The receiver's role is primarily determined by the level of influence he or she exerts onto the giver during the exchange. While in the *acceptor* role, the receiver exerts no control over the exchange or the giver. Conversely, while in the *conqueror* role, the receiver exerts total control over the exchange as well as the giver.

## *The Function of the Model*

The function of the model is centered on the intersection of the giver and receiver, each assuming his or her own role, around an exchange. For example, when the giver assumes the role of the *presenter* and the receiver assumes the role of the *acceptor*, the result is a *giving* exchange. At this level, the giver voluntarily offers a gift without any expectation of a return from the receiver. The receiver, exerting no influence on the giver, accepts the gift. As long as the giver and receiver continue to assume these roles, corruption cannot occur. However, if the giver and receiver assume other roles, corruptibility progresses to higher levels of social harm along a *hierarchy of wickedness*. The levels on the hierarchy of wickedness are defined as follows.

**Giving**—the act of voluntarily offering something of value without any expectation of prior or future reciprocity to another person as a symbol of affection, respect, or appreciation.

**Bribery**—the act or practice of giving or taking something of value wherein the giver expects something in return for his gift and the receiver, in violation of prior responsibilities, agrees to conform his behavior to the desires of the giver.

**Exploitation**—the act or practice of unjustly or improperly using another person for one's own profit or advantage.

**Extortion**—the act or practice of obtaining something of value from a person through illegal use of power or intimidation.

**Plundering**—the act or practice of taking by force.

Each level in this hierarchy is associated with the intersection of certain roles assumed by the giver and receiver. The following figure illustrates the relationships between the roles of the giver and receiver and the levels on the hierarchy of wickedness.

The confusion of roles between givers and receivers is inevitable. For example, a merchant may genuinely offer a free cup of coffee to a police officer simply in appreciation of the officer's contribution to the overall safety of the community. The officer may incorrectly perceive that the gift "has strings attached" and refuse the gift. Role confusion, although possible, will be mitigated by several factors. First, police officers are particularly keen at recognizing behavioral clues that offer insight into an individual's motivation. In fact, an officer's survival depends on identifying and proactively responding to potentially threatening patterns of behavior. Second, behavior (and our perception of its motivation) occurs in a context. If the officer has visited the establishment frequently and never received any consideration, then a single cup of coffee would unlikely be considered a potential bribe. Conversely, if the establishment has a special cup reserved only for police officers, then it is reasonable to assume that the establishment is actively *recruiting* the presence of police officers within its property. Third, role renegotiation is a common occurrence in human interaction. Often, roles are renegotiated informally and nonverbally. This process is largely dependent upon who is in charge of the exchange. The directional arrows located along the curved lines in Figure 5.1 indicate who controls each level of an exchange. For example, in a *giving* exchange, both the giver and receiver have equal control of the

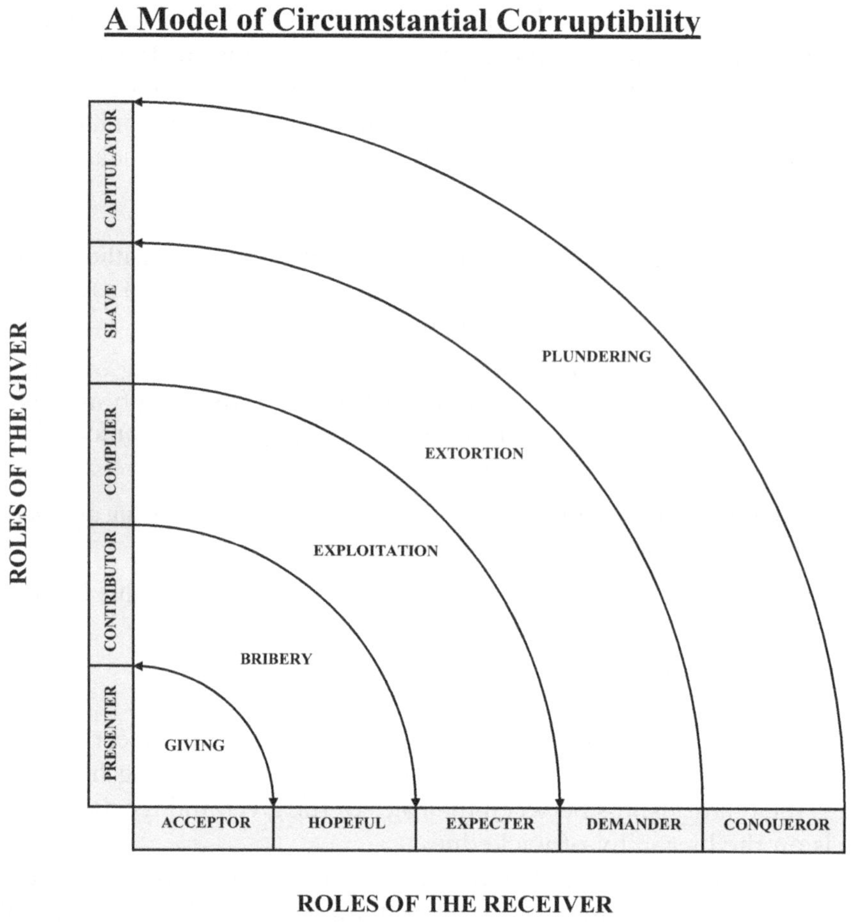


*Figure 5.1* A Model of Circumstantial Corruptibility

*Source*: Brian L. Withrow and Doug Dailey (1998), Bill Blackwood Law Enforcement Management Institute of Texas.

exchange. Givers may assume more control of an exchange and thereby progress into a contributor and ultimately a complier role. Receivers may exert control over an exchange by assuming a demander and, ultimately, a conqueror role.

## *Application of the Model*

The traditional academy approach for preparing officers to confront potential gratuity and corruption problems tends to focus on developing individual resistance skills. While at the academy, recruits are typically instructed how to "just say no" and politely refuse all gratuities or considerations offered to them. It is, however, difficult for an individual to refuse a bona fide gift. We are taught in our culture to be gracious and to "never look gift horses in the mouth." This often results in confusion on the part of the new officer on what is acceptable behavior. On one hand, the officer is taught to never accept a gratuity, and on the other, the officer is taught the value of maintaining close ties to the community. What better way to get to know a local merchant than to accept a gratis cup of coffee while discussing the merchant's safety and security needs? There is a very real possibility than an officer's refusal, no matter how polite, may alienate an officer with a merchant (Kania, 1988).

The application of our model at the street level relies primarily on awareness training. Police officers should be aware of the dynamics of corruption and the potential compromise of gratuity acceptance. But more importantly, these officers should understand how givers, typically merchants, can and do attempt to misappropriate the services of the police department through the manipulative and seemingly generous offering of relatively minor gratuities. Police officers are well trained for and capable of judging the intentions and motivations of other persons. In a very real sense, an officer's survival is dependent upon this skill. Indeed, many police officers have developed informal strategies for refusing gifts. Some officers insist on paying full price. Others will leave the difference between the amounts charged (i.e., half price) and the actual amount owed in the tip to the waitperson. In extreme cases, some officers simply avoid patronizing certain businesses that insist on offering gratuities.

At the administrative level, the issue of gratuities becomes more acute. Many departments attempt to regulate the acceptance of gratuities through a strict prohibition policy. Promulgation of such a strict policy is relatively easy. However, in most situations, compliance is next to impossible. Police officers typically work at considerable distance from routine supervision. Merchants that offer gratuities are not usually willing to report officers for violating strict prohibition policies. Why should they? More often than not, strict prohibition policies are only useful *after* an officer has been compromised and there is a need, pursuant to an official sanction, to tie the behavior to a violation of policy.

A few departments attempt to control corruption by imposing a dollar limit on gratuities. This policy is based on the notion that the value of the gratuity is directly proportional to its corruptibility. Instead, the change of behavior or role assumed by the receiver, e.g., the relative level of influence exerted by the receiver to insure the delivery of the gratuity, is a more important indicator of corruption than the value of the item or service exchanged. For this reason, the policy focus should be on an officer's or merchant's actual behavior. For example, frequent, or even chronic, patronage of one particular restaurant, especially by officers from far away beats, may indicate that the establishment is offering something more than good food and courteous service. It is wholly within the right of management to question the motivations of overly generous merchants.

Recognizing givers as a potential threat to the equity and fair accessibility of policing services provides administrators with another line of defense against possible corruption—the givers themselves. Limiting the number of on-duty police officers that may frequent a place of business at any one time is an important first step in responding to merchants that attempt to *commandeer* policing services through the offering of gratuities. Police leaders should not be discouraged from proactively contacting merchants that flagrantly offer gratuities in order to encourage officers to frequent their places of business. Ultimately, it is conceivable that a department may designate some places of business off limits to any officer not on official business, i.e., responding to a call for service.

One of the considerable accomplishments of the community era of policing has been the enlistment of private citizens, neighborhood groups, and business associations into the fight against crime. Many communities report substantial reductions in the fear of crime and even in the rate of crime due to creative police and community partnerships. Often, community groups and business associations are more than willing to support proven crime control or fear reduction strategies but not necessarily for altruistic reasons. For example, recognizing the value of bicycle patrol, a group of merchants representing the restaurant/entertainment district may offer new bicycles to the police department. Of course, these bicycles are to be used exclusively within the local entertainment district, especially on weekend nights. One national fast food chain even sets aside a booth in the dining area for local police officers. Some restaurants even reserve these booths with engraved signs including the officers' names and equip them with telephones, facsimile machines, and laptop hookups. These public gestures of support are potentially thinly veiled attempts to misallocate public policing services.

The administrative response to such gestures is relatively simple. If it is a gift, then there can be no expectation on the part of the giver as to how the gift is to be used by the receiver. If the merchants or neighborhood associations wish to donate bicycles to the police department, then they must be told that this equipment may be used in other areas of the city considered more in need of this type of enforcement strategy. Acknowledging when and what strings are attached should be a primary step in examining the potential for corruption.

## Noble-Cause Corruption and Material-Reward Corruption

Noble-cause corruption and material-reward corruption are fundamentally different, though related in practice. Tom Barker (1996:25) defined **material-reward corruption** as "whatever the officer receives through the misuse of his or her authority." By material gain, he meant "some tangible object, either cash, services, or goods that have cash value." Noble-cause corruption, on the other hand, is inspired by personally held values of morality rather than material reward. However, we think that there is a relationship between noble-cause corruption and material-reward corruption.

Police reformers have sought to make the police answerable to the law. When police are answerable to the law, they are creations of the law and are accountable to it. They do law enforcement. Consider Pomeroy's (1985:183) comments about police and the law:

> Men and women who are police officers have absolutely no identity or power as police officers outside the law (their jurisdiction). Police officers are creatures of law, their powers are described and limited by law, and if they operate outside the law, they become criminals just as everyone else and should be punished.

Noble-cause corruption carries with it a different way of thinking about the police relationship to the law from that described earlier. When officers believe that noble-cause corruption is justified, and they act on that justification, they are operating on a standard that places personal morality above the law. The police cease being enforcers of the law and become legislators of the law. Put simply, police act is if they are the law. What the police do is what the law is. Instead, the law becomes one of many tools officers use to act out a moral standard. Pomeroy warned us of the consequences of this possibility:

> If the police are, as a matter of conscious policy, allowed to use force that exceeds what the law allows, the physical freedom and safety of each one of us depend only on the fairness, the political philosophy, the goodwill, and the whim of the person or group that controls the police.
>
> (Pomeroy, 1985:185)

Pomeroy recognized the difference between the police as creatures of the law and police as the makers of law. If the police act on their moral predispositions in pursuit of good ends, then whatever they do must be itself good. In such an ethical environment, efforts to control the behavior of police are viewed as disloyal. If police are the law, what they do must be right. If they accept a free dinner in order to safeguard a restaurant, it is because society owes it to them. And if they mistreat suspects, it is because they are the law, and suspects get what they deserve. Noble-cause corruption thus becomes a gateway for material reward corruption. Where noble-cause corruption flourishes, material reward corruption cannot be far behind.

When police "become the law," disregard for the well-being of citizens can become a tempestuous problem. Yet the police cannot carry out their task with impunity. The federal government itself may decide to take over a local police department that it thinks is out of control.

The following section titled "The Perfect Storm" describes in detail an example of "we are the law" policing, its connection to the noble cause, and its consequences.

## The Perfect Storm

MIKE: *Have any of you seen the movie The Perfect Storm?*

ONE OF THE OFFICERS REPLIES: "I saw it. Outstanding movie. George Clooney. It was about three different storms that came together to create one great monster of a storm."

That's it. Why did they call it the perfect storm?

OFFICER: "As I recall, it was a true story. The three storms came together in such a way as to make the worst storm possible. Each of the storms added to the intensity of the others. They called it the storm of the century. There was no way anything caught in it could survive."

Yes, that's it. The perfect storm. The crew of a fishing boat went to the Outer Banks, and then headed out even further, to a dangerous area known as the Flemish Cap because they couldn't find fish in the Banks. That's where the storm got them. Now I'm going to tell you about the police version of the perfect storm. It's called Rampart.

The problems surrounding the Rampart police station in Los Angeles are said to be the worst police scandal in the history of Los Angeles. The station is situated on the edge of downtown Los Angeles, in an area characterized by a great deal of gang activity. The area is densely populated, with a mix of Latinos and Korean immigrants, up to 30 gangs, and many drug addicts.

To deal with the gang problem, the LAPD established the Community Resources against Street Hoodlums (CRASH) unit. The officers in the **Rampart CRASH unit** were given wide latitude to deal with gangs, including anti-gang injunctions that permitted aggressive police tactics against suspected gang members. During the 1990s, the CRASH unit developed a style, called the "CRASH way," which was highly confrontational, and by many accounts highly successful. As Cohen (2000) noted, the area had 170 murders a year in the 1960s. In 1999, it had only 33.

Through this success, rumors circulated that CRASH was not only playing hardball; it was playing dirty as well. Gang members complained of being set up, having drugs and guns planted on them, drugs stolen by cops, being recruited to sell drugs, and violent beatings and shootings by the police. It was even suggested that the unit might be associated with the unsolved murder of rap star Christopher Wallace, a.k.a. "Notorious B.I.G."

In May of 1998, LAPD Chief Bernard Parks established an internal investigative force, which came to be known as the Rampart Corruption Task Force. This task force focused primarily on the prosecution of Rafael Pérez. In December, Pérez was tried on charges of possession of cocaine with intent to sell, grand theft, and forgery (Frontline, 2004). After deliberation, the jury deadlocked. The prosecution prepared for a second trial, with 11 additional charges related to suspicious cocaine transfers. On September 8, 1999, Pérez cut a deal with prosecutors. In exchange for a five-year sentence, he told a story. It was the story of CRASH, a police unit that operated beyond the constraints of the law, who carried out their task focused only on the good end: do something about gang bangers. They went beyond the boundaries of the law and enjoyed immense success for a while. Then everything that could have gone wrong went wrong. It was the perfect storm.

Pérez described a police unit that behaved as if it were above the law. According to Glover and Lait (2000a), Pérez indicated:

> an organized criminal subculture thrived inside the Los Angeles Police Department, where a secret fraternity of anti-gang officers and supervisors committed crimes and celebrated shootings by awarding plaques to officers who wounded and killed people.
>
> (Glover and Lait, 2000a:1)

Officers involved in the subculture included "more than 30 current and former Rampart Division CRASH officers who were 'in the loop,' including at least three sergeants. (They) conspired to put innocent people in jail and to cover up unjustified shootings and beatings." By February 2000, more than 70 LAPD officers were under investigation either for committing crimes or for knowing about them and helping cover them up. In one incident, Pérez claimed to have witnessed the following:

> An officer placed a gun on a dying suspect and listened to a supervisor delay an ambulance so that the officers could concoct a story to justify their shooting of the unarmed 21-year-old man.
>
> (Glover and Lait, 2000a:2)

In another, he described officers as secretively approaching and firing on two New Year's Eve celebrants who were firing weapons into the air and who posed no direct threat to the police. Moreover, many also planted evidence.

Corruption was pervasive across CRASH. Pérez stated:

> I'm going to make a very broad statement. And you're not going to like it. I would say that 90 percent of the officers who work CRASH, and not just the Rampart CRASH, falsify a lot of information. They put cases on people.
>
> (Glover and Lait, 2000a:2)

## *Socialization to CRASH*

Particular officers were selected for participation in CRASH and then underwent socialization after selection. According to Glover and Lait, Pérez described this process as follows:

> "an officer learns very quickly that he is expected to fall in with the rest of his colleagues. In fact, even to join the unit, a person has to be personally 'sponsored' or voted in by the other officers."
>
> "We have a round table and we discuss this person," Pérez said. "We talk to people who he's worked with and find out what kind of person he is." Once he is in the unit, all eyes are on the newcomer as the rest of the group determines whether he is trustworthy to be "in the loop," Pérez said.
>
> Pérez added that the CRASH cops who were regarded by colleagues as "solid" or "stand-up" guys were not the ones who were by-the-book officers. Rather, he said, they were officers who would be willing to perjure themselves, plant evidence and fabricate probable cause for searches and put gang members and other presumed criminals in jail.
>
> (2000a:10–11)

Pérez further said that sergeants both condoned and encouraged framing innocent people. He said that, prior to his assignment to CRASH, he had never planted a gun on a person. "When you get to Rampart CRASH, this is something you're taught. This is how it goes" (2000a:11).

CRASH had a reputation for effectiveness. They were expected to bring down the hammer on gang members, and they did. What was astonishing, according to one of Pérez' interviewers, was that officers were able to charge so many people with trumped-up drug crimes. Pérez's response was "All that they cared about was numbers. All they cared about that at the end of the month was . . . how many total narcotics were brought in, how much money, and how many bodies. That's all, really. That was the only concern" (Glover and Lait, 2000a:6).

And their work was liked by many citizens in the Rampart area. A community leader who attended a Rampart Boosters Association luncheon to honor the division said that "Whatever means they used, they justified the ends." And many residents expressed concerns that the corruption probe would allow violent crime to return (Gold and Landsberg, 1999). One of the participants of the luncheon, Margarita Marron, expressed concerns that things would return to the way they were before CRASH started the crackdowns. During the conversation, Marron turned to her 5-year-old son.

> "Leonardo, how do you feel about the police? Are you scared of them?"
>
> "No, *me cuidan* [they care for me]," he said. "They watch out for me."
>
> (Gold and Landsberg, 1999:2)

Though parts of the community were favorable to the hard-edged behavior of CRASH unit members, other parts were not. Their aggressive tactics resulted in much litigation and left hard feelings with many people they came into contact with. In five weeks in 1995, for example, members of the LAPD's CRASH unit were accused of brutalizing two families who were holding gatherings at their homes. Both families complained that they had reported the misconduct to the police. Yet investigations were not conducted into either incident (Connell and Lopez, 1999). Ultimately, the city paid out about one-half million dollars in settlements. In another incident, a mother and daughter with no criminal records were arrested, had drugs planted on them, had their life savings stolen, and were taken to jail on false charges that were later used by their landlord to evict them (Glover and Lait, 2000b).

## *Patterns of Corruption*

Pérez's testimony provided insight into patterns of corruption carried out by the CRASH unit.

*Deportation of gang members.* Pérez said that the unit would work with a unit of the Immigration and Naturalization Service to deport gang members. The LAPD used a variety of questionable tactics, even though the department had a clear policy stating that officers "shall not initiate police action with the objective of discovering the alien status of a person" (O'Conner, 2000:3). And officers were not permitted to turn individuals accused of minor violations to the INS (Immigration and Naturalization Service). CRASH broke these policies regularly.

The relationship between the units had several unsavory aspects. LAPD officers concerned about complaints from citizens would use the INS to have witnesses to the abuse deported. Also, INS agents would accompany the unit on routine street sweeps. They would conduct immigration checks on LAPD detainees even though they had no outstanding warrants. As one INS officer observed, "They were targeting a whole race of people. That's not a gang anymore, that's a culture. They [the LAPD] wanted to do one thing: sweep the street and turn the bodies over to us" (O'Conner, 2000). One agent sent an anonymous letter on INS stationery to the Los Angeles District Attorney's office, in which he accused the LAPD of carrying out "an undeclared war on individuals purported to be associates of the 18th street gang." The agent warned that individuals who were jailed could file lawsuits against both agencies. "The INS," the agent noted, "was just as liable as the LAPD" (O'Conner, 2000).

INS agents said that LAPD officers seemed to have filled out some of the INS's interview forms and, in some cases, inserted incriminating allegations into those files. As one agent noted, there were many denials of citizenship based on LAPD recommendations. As the letter concluded:

> many individuals were catalogued, identified, arrested, placed under deportation proceedings, and sometimes prosecuted and sentenced to federal prison, based on arrests by the LAPD/CRASH. All of the arrests by LAPD were for immigration purposes.
>
> (O'Conner, 2000:5)

*Bogus drug arrests.* CRASH also focused on drug arrests. In cocaine incidents, officers said that drug dealers and users frequently hid rock cocaine in their mouths. When approached by officers, they would spit it out. However, DNA analyses in four drug cases, in which officers testified that they witnessed suspects spit out rock cocaine, indicated that the suspects could not have spit out the cocaine. One of the cases is described by Glover and Lait (2000c):

> the partners (members of the CRASH unit) were watching drug sales from an observation post in the upper floors of an apartment building when they witnessed a drug transaction involving three men. Voeltz wrote in his report that the alleged seller, later identified as Miguel Mongue, was hiding cocaine in his mouth before spitting it into his hand and then passing it to the buyer.
>
> When the alleged buyers were pulled over and arrested by officers on the ground minutes later, the officers recovered two rocks of cocaine from the floorboard of the car—drugs that Mongue had allegedly passed from his mouth to the driver of the car.
>
> A DNA test revealed that the rocks were coated with saliva from two people—neither of whom was Mongue. The case against him was dismissed.
>
> (Glover and Lait, 2000c:4)

*Violence against suspects.* Violence was a part of the unit's armament of corrupt behaviors. Pérez claimed that some officers abused suspects for little more than sport.

> Actually, [Hewitt's] biggest forte was thumping people. He just had this thing about beating up people while they were handcuffed. Between him And Lujan, that was their favorite thing. Just beat people up for no reason.
>
> (Glover and Lait, 2000d:2)

Hewitt was fired from the LAPD for beating up a suspect in 1998. He was accused of grabbing a suspect by the neck, pushing him against a wall, and hitting him in the chest and stomach with his fists repeatedly. The person, Ismael Jiminez, vomited blood and staggered out of the station without being charged. He was later treated at a hospital, but prosecutors declined to file charges against Hewitt. He was beaten, according to the article, because the mother of another gang member filed a complaint against the officers who allegedly beat her son (Glover and Lait, 2000d).

*Bogus testimony—testilying at preliminary hearings*. One of the outcomes of the investigation into Rampart was that several people who pled guilty to charges were later found to be innocent. As Rohrlich (1999) noted, as of 1999, convictions had been turned over for ten individuals who had pled guilty. Because of anti-crime initiatives, preliminary hearings—evidentiary hearings evaluating the quality of evidence for felony cases—have changed. Eyewitnesses no longer have to give testimony. Instead, police officers have been empowered to stand in for them and give secondhand accounts. Moreover, the anti-crime initiatives have provided increasingly harsh punishments for many crimes, especially gang-related crimes. What was discovered in the Rampart cases was that the police regularly lied when giving testimony. Prosecutors would use the police testimony to negotiate plea arrangements with suspects, who were offered either the plea or quite lengthy sentences. Reasonably concluding that they could not get a fair trial, suspects pled guilty and took the shorter sentence. Pérez gave an example of such a case:

> Pérez claimed on the witness stand at Bailey's preliminary hearing that he saw Bailey when he pulled up to the party and recognized him as a gang member on parole. He said that he noticed Bailey had his right hand in his waistband. He said he told Bailey to put his hands up. Bailey, he said, instead pulled a handgun from his waistband and dropped it.
>
> Bailey just listened at the defense table as Pérez perjured himself about the gun. Then the judge asked Pérez how he had known that Bailey was a gang member. "I have interviewed him 15, 20 times," began Pérez. "I have . . ." It was too much for Bailey. He erupted in profanity and called Pérez a liar. "You're a lying ____, you know that? Sorry, your Honor."
>
> The judge quickly reminded him where he stood. "Let me explain something," he said. "You have a right to speak only to your lawyer, and very quietly, and if you do that again, there will be a gag in your mouth." Bailey seemed to get it. He pleaded guilty soon afterward—to possessing the gun that Pérez now says he planted on him—in return for a sentence of two years, eight months in prison.
>
> (Rohrlich, 1999:4)

In another case, Pérez and his partner, Nino Durden, were driving by an alley when they saw Miguel Hernandez. Durden claimed to having locked eyes with Hernandez, at which point Hernandez pulled a gun from his waistband and dropped it. Pérez later said that the gun was a plant. However, Hernandez pled guilty in exchange for a 16-month term. In a third, Joseph Jones was accused by Pérez and Durden of being a middleman in a drug purchase. They purchased $20 worth of rock cocaine. It was the third felony for Jones, who faced life in prison. The prosecutor offered him a deal; plead and it would only count as a second strike. So Jones pled and received an eight-year sentence. Pérez now says that Jones actually refused to sell them the cocaine (Rohrlich, 1999).

During the following nine months, Pérez told his story in more than 50 meetings with investigators, giving more than 4,000 pages in sworn testimony and implicating more than 70 officers. On September 21, 1999, Chief Parks formed a Board of Inquiry to study administration failures and to assess the extent of the corruption associated with the CRASH unit. On March 3, Chief Parks disbanded the CRASH unit.

In April of 2000, the Police Commission formed the Rampart Independent Review Panel. It issued its report in November, concluding that officers needed better supervision and that the department "compromised criminal investigations of officer-involved shootings and major useof-force incidents, and that the LAPD is viewed by the community as excessively hostile and confrontational" (Frontline, 2004:3). Another report, assembled by Erwin Chemerinsky of the University of Southern California, stated that the magnitude of the RAMPART scandal was minimized by the LAPD and that the internal culture of the organization permitted the corruption to develop. On September 9, 2000, the Los Angeles City Council accepted a consent decree permitting the U.S. Department of Justice to oversee reforms in the LAPD, and Los Angeles Mayor Riordan signed the decree in December of that year.

By November, 2000, the city had spent $11 million settling 29 lawsuits. Additionally, it settled a lawsuit with Javier Ovando for $15 million. Ovando, unarmed at the time, had been shot, framed, and then testified against by Pérez and his partner, Nino Durden. He was serving a 23-year sentence at the time that Pérez testified and was subsequently released as the result of the testimony. He was paralyzed from the incident. The city estimated that the total settlement would reach $125 million.

Pérez was released after serving three years of his five-year sentence. He pled to federal charges of civil rights and firearms violations from the shooting of Ovando, and he anticipated a two-year term in a federal prison under the plea agreement (Frontline, 2004).

> MIKE: *You know, I think that most of those cops in Rampart, they were probably fine cops. They started out as good cops. They had the right values. Committed to the good end. You can see this in the patterns of corruption. They did most of what they did in order to be more effective in getting arrests and putting bad guys in jail.*
>
> A captain challenged him on this. "I don't accept that. There were some major problems with those cops. There were hiring problems. There were training problems. They were criminal and they didn't belong in police work. You were right the first time. It was a perfect storm. Everything that could go wrong, did."
>
> Mike looked squarely at him. *You want to believe that you're really different from them. That it couldn't happen here. I bet that some of your*

*line officers talk the same crap that those officers acted out. The difference isn't in kind. It's in degree. Some of those cops had a record of commendation. Noble-cause corruption is rewarded all the time, because it produces what looks like good policing, lots of arrests, good records, promotions—until it gets too visible, too public, and the toilet starts backing up. You lose legitimacy, and you get liability.*

This is the point. We make value-based decisions, and the value we place in the center is the noble cause. Every good cop I know has wanted to push the line to get someone he or she thinks is truly dangerous off the streets. Rampart carried it further than the rest of us are willing to take it. It's like the movie, when the Andrea Gale went to the Flemish Cap, knowing it was the most dangerous area, because they knew it was the most effective place to fish. Rampart shows what can happen when the commitment to the noble cause is transformed into noble-cause corruption in a big way—get the bad guy at all costs. Oh, they were effective. But in the end they were caught. Their boat sank in the frenzy of the media and political storm surrounding them.

One of the officers challenged Mike again. "You know, much of this view of the CRASH unit was based on Pérez' testimony. I'm not convinced that a lot of it wasn't self-serving bullshit to save his own skin. How do we know that the CRASH unit was really as bad as he said it was? I think you just had a few rogue cops who blamed everyone else to save their hides."

Mike looked at him, smiled, and touched his nose, the gesture for "truth." *You might be right. Look at the story of the Andrea Gale. We don't know what really happened to her. The movie,* The Perfect Storm, *was adapted from a book that was historical fiction, with all the unknown details filled in by the imagination of the author. Maybe the media and the prosecutors did the same with Pérez. But it doesn't make any difference. The department still lost legitimacy with the City Council, with its minority communities, and with the U.S. Department of Justice. And they will pay out big, big bucks for liability. Careers will be ruined anyway.*

You've all seen how prosecutors work their magic. You've seen them put people in prison for a long time. Do you think they won't do the same thing to you when the toilet starts backing up? Remember—the system protects itself.

MIKE CONCLUDED THIS SECTION: *Pérez was not stupid. He was smart, and he was doing what he thought the department and the public wanted him to do. I believe that. And it became very easy to go over the line. I want you to listen to his comments when he was sentenced: "Whoever chases monsters should see to it that in the process he does not become a monster himself."*

## Conclusion: I Am the Law

*You've got a nice city here,* Mike observes. *Would you want the federal government to run the police here? That's what a consent decree is.*

*Would that be a good thing for this city? I don't think so. I don't trust the federal government that much. I doubt if you do, either.*

How does the "I am the law" perspective fit the perspectives of corruption discussed in this chapter? In his quote earlier, Pomeroy warned us about police who use force in excess of the law. The examples of lawless behavior described in Box 5.6 suggest that the police acted out of a moral standard aimed at identifying potential offenders, not in order to further some illegal economic benefit. It represented a variety of noble-cause corruption on a department-wide basis, as in Rampart or in Pittsburgh.

Box 5.6

**A Consent Decree in Pittsburgh**

On February 26, the Department of Justice entered into a consent decree with the city of Pittsburgh. A consent decree is an agreement by a defendant (in this case the City of Pittsburgh) to cease activities asserted as illegal by the government. If the court approves the agreement, the government's action against the defendant is dropped.

The decree settled a lawsuit brought against the City of Pittsburgh in 1997 by the U.S. Department of Justice, which charged that Pittsburgh police exhibited a systematic pattern of police brutality. The decree grew out of a lawsuit carried out by the American Civil Liberties Union on behalf of 66 city residents. Incidents included the following: Two women stated that police beat them when they stopped to watch officers beat a man. A disabled woman said that police strip-searched her at a traffic stop while her children watched. And a Baptist minister said he was wrongly beaten and arrested while listening to gospel music at home.

The decree established measures for managing the city's police force. If the police conform to the terms of the agreement for five years, then the decree will be dropped. In accordance with the decree, the City of Pittsburgh agreed to undertake the following reforms:

1. Increase training for officers with multiple complaints against them.
2. Monitor all litigation against police officers.
3. Install and implement an early warning system to identify and track problem officers.
4. Require officers to write a report, to be reviewed by supervisors, for any use of force against an individual or when a search and seizure is conducted.
5. Hire an independent auditor to monitor complaint investigations.

Source: Adapted from "ACLU Opposes City's Move to Modify Consent Decree Governing Police Spying"; Marylynne Pitz, "City to Pay Lawyers in Lawsuit," *Online Post-Gazette*; Claudia Coates, "Police Brutality Forces Pittsburgh to Start Monitoring P.D.," Associated Press.

The takeover of a municipal police organization by the federal courts is controversial under any circumstances. The Pittsburgh Fraternal Order of Police (FOP) has actively resisted the consent decree, stating that the premise of the order, that police violence against citizens was a pervasive problem, was untrue. The FOP has likened the consent decree to a "witch-hunt," has contended that the department should not be punished for the actions of a few officers, and that transfers will undermine the ability of the police to provide adequate public safety. In the active resistance of the FOP, we can see the profoundly divisive effect a consent decree can have on a police organization.

The belief that police are always right, what we call the "I am the law" perspective, can undermine justice in its most elemental sense. In the Rampart case, we saw that, at a certain point, the police simply acted as if they were judge, jury, and perhaps, executioner. Their commitment to the noble cause morphed into noble-cause corruption. Noble-cause corruption morphed into a complete disrespect for the law and opened the door for all kinds of corruption.

In Box 5.6, we again see the pattern of noble-cause corruption at a systemic level, across a department, that is eerily like the events in Rampart. It also progressed to the "I am the law" stage and ultimately resulted in a consent decree against the city.

# 6 Stress, Organizational Accountability, and the Noble Cause

## Key Terms

| | |
|---|---|
| boundary spanner | episodic stress |
| intentional tort | negotiable issues |
| legitimacy | non-negotiable issues |
| logic of good faith | role stress |
| municipal system | Title 42, Section 1983 |
| negligent tort | medical model of stress management |
| *Monell v. Dept. of Social and Health Services of New York* (1978) | de-policing |
| qualified immunity | Stinchcomb's model of organizational stress |
| stress | chronic stress |

## Introduction

This chapter examines the intersection of organizational stress, accountability, and noble-cause corruption in policing, emphasizing the implications for legitimacy and liability. Drawing on Stinchcomb's model of organizational stress, the chapter distinguishes between episodic stress—linked to acute incidents—and chronic stress, which stems from persistent organizational dysfunction. The medical model of stress management is applied to critique the overreliance on secondary and tertiary interventions, while primary sources of stress—such as role stress and value conflicts—remain unaddressed. Officers often experience stress when their commitment to the noble cause is obstructed by courts, the

DOI: 10.4324/9781003626916-9

public, or their own departments, leading to de-policing and cynicism. The chapter explores how boundary spanners, particularly police chiefs, navigate the municipal system to maintain legitimacy among political stakeholders. When legitimacy is compromised, departments may face liability under Title 42, Section 1983, especially following landmark cases like *Monell v. Dept. of Social and Health Services of New York* (1978), which enabled municipalities to be sued for civil rights violations. The chapter differentiates between intentional and negligent torts, emphasizing how qualified immunity and the logic of good faith are often invoked in defense.

In this chapter, we look at some of the implications of value-based decision-making for managers and police organizations. We begin by considering the relationship between stress and value-based decision-making. This is followed by a discussion of the community environment in which police decision-making occurs, how the "system" protects itself, and implications for liability suits against police officers.

## Stress and the Noble Cause

You're in a room full of police commanders. Ask them where their primary sources of stress come from; you might be surprised. Mike did this. Looking across the room after a short break, he asked the commanders.

What is your primary source of stress?

Before we get to what they said, some background is in order. Several years earlier, we collaborated on a paper about police stress. The paper was from research conducted among medium-sized departments in Illinois, but it could have been done anywhere and the findings probably wouldn't have changed much. At the back of the survey, there was what some researchers call a "throw-away" question, added without hope that there would be significant or even interesting findings but inserted to involve the respondent in the survey. In this survey, the question was simply "What is your primary source of stress?"

Findings were surprising—for non-cops. Some reviewers looked at our findings and thought that they represented a bunch of line officers grousing about their work. How would police executives respond?

Back to the room full of police executives. At first, no one answered. But this is itself typical of cops. They don't tend to answer questions quickly. They'll sit back and look the question over, carefully, and warily.

> Mike repeated himself. *What is your primary source of stress? Where does it come from?* One officer finally speaks, shrugging his shoulders at the same time. "Well, the department."
>
> *You're exactly right. That*, Mike observed, *is always the first choice that police make.* Other officers murmured agreement.

> What's another source?
>
> The room was quiet for a minute. Another officer looked at the board, thought for a minute, and said, "The department?"
>
> Mike gave him a long look. *Exactly. The department, the department, the department. It's always the department. Why are you all killing yourselves? It took a moment to digest that and move on. To use an old slang phrase, cops don't like being "put in the trick bag."*
>
> Another officer responded, "rules and regulations," a third, "policy." And so it went. Added to the list were the courts and the media. That was the list. What was missing?
>
> Mike looked over his audience. *Do you realize that not one of you mentioned the dangers of police work?*
>
> An officer in front responded "that's stress reduction." The commanders chuckled at this comment. Danger releases built-up police stress. To get a hot call—a crime in progress—and then show up and discover it's a bogus call, now that's stressful. How do many officers release the pent-up anxiety? They get off work, get a six-pack, and toss it down.

Why isn't danger one of the commanders' sources of stress? It is because danger happens when a police officer is acting on behalf of the noble cause. Burning calories. Pumping adrenaline. Getting bad guys. Complaining about danger is admitting weakness. Danger is not permitted to be a source of stress.

The perspective of these commanders was astonishingly similar to the perspective of the respondents to the survey we conducted in Illinois, although they were separated by a thousand miles from the group Mike is talking to today and although one group was mostly line officers and this is police commanders (Crank and Caldero, 1991).

What source of stress is hard on the commanders in this session? The department. They aren't stressed out about the dangers of police work. One might respond that, because they are managers, they aren't exposed to as much danger as line officers. But their answer was the same as the Illinois line officers. Go into any department and ask the officers there. Are you an officer? What stress is hard on you? When you feel those chest pains in your mid-forties, will it be from the danger of police work, or from putting up with all the organizational hassles?

> Mike continued. *Look at stress. I think it's like this in every department. And what's number two on the stress list? The public. These are supposed to be the good guys, the guys you protect.*
>
> The third source of stress identified by the group was the courts. Mike responded, *Oh, I really love this, especially from cops with bachelor's degrees. "I just busted him and he's already back out on the streets." Mike pretends to be knocking someone in the forehead. Hello in there. These are a series of procedurally regular steps. These steps apply to all citizens. It's the law. You had it in school. Innocent till proven guilty.*

*Released on recognizance. ROR . . . It's how things work. Don't these guys know that? There is a real lack of understanding.*

Let's review this. The organization is the principal source of stress. Second is the public. Third are the courts. Anyone who's read *Alice in Wonderland* can make perfect sense out of this. All the things that are supposed to be the most important, the most valued things in the professional life of a police officer, are the things that they state are the most stressful.

## Research on Police Stress

Stress is broadly defined as any condition that has adverse consequences for an individual's well-being. Adverse consequences include psychological characteristics such as depression, and physical characteristics might be suicide or divorce. An area of stress often studied is **role stress,** which refers to characteristics of a person's organizational role that produces adverse consequences for the individual. Role stress has been of particular concern to police researchers, who have been interested in the unique ways the occupation of policing affects the psychological and physical well-being of police officers.

Stress has been the subject of a great deal of research on the police (Goolkasian et al., 1989; Terry, 1985). Police stress research has historically focused on dangers of police work. This research followed the seemingly common-sense view that police work was dangerous, and danger is, well, danger. Therefore, danger must be a principal source of stress. However, the relationship between danger and stress did not hold up under close scientific scrutiny, though fear of danger did (Cullen et al., 1989).

The authors of this book conducted an investigation into perceptions of stress among eight Illinois Police Departments in the early 1990s. Findings were clear: stress was produced by the organization or factors related closely to the organization. Our findings have been supported by other related research (Launay and Fielding, 1989; Thomas, 1988; Brown and Campbell, 1990; Kop and Euwema, 2001). When stress, police officer burnout, and resignation were studied, the police organization played a prominent causal role.

## Stinchcomb's Model of Organizational Stress

Jeanne Stinchcomb (2004) argued that stress was directly tied to organizational culture. In her research, she said that police culture represented a traditional set of values related to work expectations, officer loyalty, and beat responsibility. Stress emerged because those values were inconsistent with contemporary work expectations. Her special insight emerged from analyzing stress from the point of view of a **medical model of stress management.** She observed that, using a medical model, we can think of primary, secondary, and tertiary interventions. Primary intervention refers to the elimination of the source of the illness itself. Secondary intervention is helping the patient who is exposed to a disease to become less seriously affected by it. Tertiary intervention is the simple recognition that the patient is ill and may include efforts to make the patient comfortable while effort is made to identify the illness or its cure.

When police stress is subjected to this medical model, we see that stress reduction techniques are wholly of the secondary or tertiary kind. Police departments treat the outcome of the disease—the sick individual. Primary interventions—treating the source of the stress—are not carried out. Like a cold in which cough medicine is prescribed to minimize the symptoms, we deal with the coping aspects of stress rather than the curing aspects of stress. Coping is not inappropriate or wrong—programs that aim at counseling may do an officer much good. However, coping is not curing. And police organizations do not cure; they do not do primary intervention.

Stinchcomb also compares episodic to chronic stress. **Episodic stress,** the stuff of old-fashioned notions of stress, refers to violent incidents. However, episodic stress is rare in police work. Far more common is **chronic stress,** or the stress that comes from day-to-day police work. And the bulk of that stress derives from organizational factors.

> Like a continuously nagging cough, chronic organizationally induced stress is an integral presence in the everyday work environment of police officers. In contrast to the immediate pressure of isolated and infrequent events, it is the ultimate product of a slow, gradual process of erosion that, over time, wears away the victim's physical and psychological resistance.
>
> (2004:5)

Why, Stinchcomb asks, has "so little been done to reduce chronic organization stress?" (2004:13). Applying the medical model, she notes that police departments are not engaging in primary techniques, only its symptoms. Many departments provide counseling, thereby demonstrating concern for the well-being of officers. Yet these programs have "managed to quietly and unobtrusively shift attention from the organization to the individual" (2004:14). If agencies were to engage in primary intervention, they would have to admit that it was the organization, not the individuals in the organization, who were responsible for police stress.

Stress, she argued, stemmed from creative and educated individuals trying to adapt to a paramilitary organizational structure. In our work, we tend to look at the moral predispositions of police, particularly as they relate to the noble cause. Yet the message is the same. The organization is the source of stress, but it avoids responsibility by focusing stress reduction techniques on line officers.

The organization is also a source of stress for chief executives. Crank, Regoli, Hewitt, and Culbertson in 1993 found that police chiefs' stress was affected by both organizational and institutional features in their working environment. By institutional stressors, the authors referred to characteristics of their working environment over which they had little control. Together, the body of these findings suggest that, across the ranks in an organization, police are affected by organizational sources of stress, and these sources of stress are endemic to police organizations.

> Mike believes that this stress is closely tied to the noble cause. *Do you see what's going on here? I mean where your stress comes from? Stinchcomb shows how the organization causes, perpetuates, and then ducks responsibility for stress. Holy cow! Then the research Crank and I did showed how hostile many officers were to the courts, the public, and most of all to their own organization. Why?*
>
> Stinchcomb was right—it's about the misfit of both line officers and administrators with the organization. But to understand the officers' stress, you need to see the way they make value-based decisions. These things that cause stress are the things you should care about most. They're stressed about the organization? The public? The courts? What's going on here?
>
> Your officers are committed to the noble cause, and all of these groups they interact with obstruct their ability to seek noble-cause ends. That's stressful. So they blame rules of procedure. They blame their bosses. They blame the courts. This is why you need to understand the values that motivate your officers. And this is why you need to understand yourselves. You're the organization that they blame.

Officers will resolve their role conflicts in a way consistent with their moral predispositions, by seeking noble ends. Hiring procedures and early departmental socialization guarantee this. Mike returns to the whiteboard.

> Do you remember from this morning we talked about value-based decision-making, and about what happened when the line officers thought that the organization resisted good ends? Now, from what we've talked about in the last hour I can add to the list. He puts on the whiteboard:
>
> **VALUE-BASED DECISION-MAKING**
> Police organization ≠ means (tools)
> Media ≠ means (tools)
> Public and politicians ≠ means (tools)
> Courts ≠ means (tools)
>
> If you get this, you see that your officers see the organization, the media, the public, and the courts all as obstacles to their ability to carry out the noble cause. You've hired them with a value perspective, and then placed

them squarely in a situation that interferes with their ability to seek the good end. Now they're secretive. You don't know what they're doing.

So if you could see what is going on in the mind of your street cops, well, they see all these different groups working against their ability to carry out the noble cause. The issue here is moral disagreement, and that is why it's so stressful—so stressful, in fact, that concerns of danger don't even enter the equation as comparable in stress. Sometimes, they see these groups as being on the wrong moral side of things. They're helping the bad guys! The courts let them off! Politicians try to influence how they do their work! The media, oh the media want to stop them from doing any good work at all! They want to expose every little mistake they make.

A commander replied, "I understand that stuff you said about the history of the organization and how it creates problems. And I see how these other organizations are a source of stress. But police departments are all about personal relations between people in the department. You know that. My relationship with someone else is what someone and I make of it. It's not about something that happened 100 years ago. History doesn't have anything to do with it."

Good question. Mike thinks about this. *I'll give you two takes on that. First is that history has everything to do with it. You didn't dream up the command structure of your department. It was there before you arrived. It determines how you interact with other officers. It determines who your friends are likely to be. Do you invite line officers out for beers after work? It determines your responsibilities with other officers. And it goes a long way toward explaining why your officers probably complain about the way commanders use the organization to do this very important thing called police work. History is unimportant? You tell me the American flag first sewn by Betsy Ross has no value, that you have absolutely no feeling toward flag-burners and don't want to throw the book at them if you can, and then I'll agree with you that history is unimportant.*

Second is that all these other groups, the media, the public, and the courts, influence what the way line officers do police work by bringing pressure on the chief. What does the chief do? Chief, what do you do?

"If I have a complaint against an officer, there are formal channels to handle that."

OK, that's good. But line officers don't like internal investigations. Especially when they think they are being punished for doing good for society. You know what they say—no good deed shall go unpunished. What else do you do? For problems that are not really disciplinary but create problems for important constituents, don't you develop policies to say what officers should or shouldn't do? I've heard a book of policies referred to as "100 years of F-ups." So the influence of the public and politicians, the courts, and the media is translated through the chain of command down to the line level. That's the other way the department is seen as acting against the interests of line officers, and why it is lumped in with these other organizations as interfering with line officers' efforts to do good for society.

Another officer asks, "So what if our officers are making value-based decisions? I must admit, I kind of agree with the notion that they should be making such decisions, and believe we should support them. These other groups can really irritate me sometimes. I have seen the press say things that justify what bad people do. That's wrong. Somebody has to take moral responsibility for the well-being of society. Isn't that our job? If it's not I don't want to do it."

Mike responds. *Yes, I completely agree. Line officers do what we want them to do, even if many of us are more uncomfortable than you are in admitting it. The problem is not value-based decision-making. Value-based decision-making is unavoidable. It is one of the universal forces. It's the handgun loaded, ready to fire. People die for their beliefs. And you aim the gun. You have to be very careful how you aim it.* Mike smiles and spreads his arms. *Hey, I'm all for you guys. I'm not going to stand here and say that you shouldn't hire committed cops. But when the noble cause is corrupted, and that's what I am here to talk about, you channel all that force, that very powerful force, to the wrong ends, The problem is noble-cause corruption, when officers break the law or violate policy to carry out their good ends, and that's up to you—your hiring policies, your leadership, your ability to get out in the field and set an example, your memory—you all remember what it means to be a street cop. The value-based decisions made by officers, when they lead to noble-cause corruption, carry two consequences for managers and for the police organization. I call the consequences legitimacy and liability.*

## Organizational Accountability Issues: Legitimacy and Liability

This section looks at police departments' efforts to maintain legitimacy in the municipal arena and what happens when legitimacy is undermined by the improper behavior of street officers. Liability will undercut organizational efforts aimed at legitimacy. This section discusses the overlapping issues of legitimacy and liability and explains how the municipal system will protect itself when the credibility of the organization is undermined.

Mike continues. *Here are two reasons why you might begin to think about the value-based decisions your officers are making. Legitimacy and liability. If your officers are making the wrong decisions, you're going to have legitimacy problems, and you're going to have liability problems.*

### *Legitimacy Defined*

Do your officers understand about legitimacy? Chiefs do. Assistant chiefs do. Sheriffs do. It's when someone tells you that "you no longer represent the public."

This is a statement that riles police officers. Who says that the police don't represent the public? Well, sometimes the press says it. Sometimes a city council member will say it. They will accuse the police of being particularly brutal to some minority group member, or of corruption, or of excessive use of force during a routine encounter. Mothers Against Drunk Driving (MADD) may accuse the department of not stopping and arresting enough drunks on the highway.

**Legitimacy** is whether influential constituents, who can be groups or individuals, agree with the way police do their work. Police organizations are embedded in municipal and county politics, and departments are tied to other community groups who can make police work exceedingly unpleasant at both the executive and line levels. Officers are value-based decision-makers. Their decisions have enormous potential to create problems in the municipal arena of organizational interrelationships. Legitimacy affects police differently, depending on their rank. In the following section, we're going to consider the legitimacy issue at each rank level.

## *Legitimacy and Chiefs*

For a police chief, maintaining legitimacy requires that they balance their expectations with those of municipal and departmental constituencies. Constituencies that they must work with include the mayor, city council, mid-level executives in the department, the public, media, business groups, the courts, the prosecutor's office, school boards and school administrators, police union and non-union labor representation, and sometimes other police organizations and the FBI.

Legitimacy is challenged when one of these constituents questions whether the police are doing their job. A department cannot simply ignore the opinions of people whose views affect the public or important voting constituencies. Chiefs and sheriffs know. They will be fired or voted out of office if they don't address the concerns of powerful constituencies (Crank and Langworthy, 1992).

The chief's role is oriented toward the building of external liaisons with community groups. Chiefs are frequently involved in boundary-spanning activities; a great deal of their activity is in community-relations work with civic and political groups. **Boundary spanners** are individuals who represent the interests of the organization to other organizations and agencies in its environment. As Geller (1985:3–4) observed, chiefs confront the dilemma of balancing their professional autonomy with a need to be responsive to political constituencies, particularly the mayor. This is a large and compelling task.

Chiefs must also have legitimacy within their own departments. The chief may be hired as an outsider but has to demonstrate to the rank and file as well that he or she is a cop's cop (Bordua and Reiss, 1986). Command control is achieved by acquiring personal loyalties as well as demonstrations of leadership skill. The chief, more than any other actor in the organization, must convincingly demonstrate that he or she, too, is committed to the noble cause and to the loyalty that accompanies its moral territory. If the chief cannot gain the loyalty of the troops, even the most reasoned of organizational plans will quickly shatter against the shoals of internal department conflicts and cliques.

## *Legitimacy, Commanders, and Mid-Level Executives*

Legitimacy issues have a direct bearing on the responsibilities of commanders and mid-level executives in police organizations. Police commanders and executives don't work the street unless they are in a small department. They do other kinds of work. Executives have responsibility for planning, management, and budget. Resource allocation is central to their work. The higher the rank of a police officer, the more they are involved in long-range budget forecasting. On a day-to-day basis, they are extensively involved in meetings with other executives in their organizations.

Geller and Swanger (1995:7–10) provide an excellent discussion of the responsibilities of middle managers in police organizations. They observed that, most of the time, middle managers are involved in keeping the promises made by higher-ups. These higher-ups are the chief, a city council member, and the mayor. Police managers consequently become involved in carrying out some of the concerns of people with political clout in the municipal arena. They may act on behalf of the chief to transform those concerns into department policy, strategy, and concrete tactics that can be carried out by lower-ranking officers in large organizations. Box 6.1 is an example described by Geller and Swanger (1995:7).

Box 6.1

**Geller and Swanger: Administrators and Political Needs of Chiefs**

Suppose that the chief or a city council member promises to develop the conflict-management skills of first-line officers and sergeants to help reverse an escalating pattern of violent street conflict between Latinx young men and young Anglo officers during field interrogations. Then the training manager and perhaps a special projects manager from the chief's office will need to explore ways to adjust the in-service and pre-service training curricula to accommodate the new topic without slighting other crucial aspects of education for effective training.

Recall the television series *Star Trek*? Each program began with a vast expanse of space seen through the view-screen of the Starship Enterprise. The view is astonishing. Bells and buzzers suddenly go off, and some sort of problem rapidly unfolds. The second-in-command quickly briefs the Captain about what they have encountered. He suggests a way to identify and correct the problem. The Captain responds, "Make it happen, number 1."

In police work, managers are the chief's "number 1." Managers adapt to a task environment fundamentally different than street officers. Street officers adapt to a task environment made up of unfriendly motorists, troublemakers, misdemeanants, people who can't solve ordinary problems and in need of police assistance, a few serious criminals, and some genuinely dangerous people. Managers adapt to a task environment made up of other managers, politicos, civic leaders, and community organizations. Put differently, the work of line officers is peopled by community non-respectables, and the work of managers is full of community respectables. These respectables want the police to do something about the kinds of problems that are meaningful to them. This means that the nature of the noble-cause shifts. Managers learn about crime from the community itself, or from its elected or chosen leadership. MADD wants to do something about drivers that are drunk. A city councilman wants to make sure some group is treated fairly. Another city councilman wants to find out why police are so rude (his son was just arrested for DUI). The city manager wants police to stop stealth patrolling inside a downtown park because some passed-out drunk was run over by a prowl car with its lights out. The mayor's office wants a written report from the chief, justifying the proposed budget. Or the prosecutor is miffed because a detective blew a crime scene investigation and ruined the evidence.

What do managers do? They are expected to respond to these respectables, to take into consideration their concerns while holding down their own particular responsibilities. So their commitment to the noble cause expands to encompass the views of these audiences. They have to demonstrate their loyalties to police values in the context of community respectables. In essence, they are constantly trying to "make it so," that is, make the organization legitimate in the eyes of powerful people whose opinions count. They are committed to tasks to satisfy political influentials, the mayor or the city council—or to help the chief make good his or her promises to those individuals—even when they think those tasks conflict with their work. They seek to carry out the chief's directives while protecting their small slice of the budget pie.

Although managers often complain about line officers, one can detect the noble-cause theme in their complaints. If one listens to ranking officers talk about line personnel, one might get the impression that they don't think too highly of them—that there's no bond across the ranks or that managers and line personnel are fundamentally different kinds of personalities. Without a doubt, there are rifts and clicks in all police organizations. But managers and line personnel are not different kinds of people, and one needs to read between the lines to understand this.

What are managers' principal grouses? They talk about how line officers are not committed to their work. Line officers won't follow procedures. They're just there for an 8-to-5 job. They can't deal with simple problems. What is the common theme in these complaints? They are saying that line officers today are not committed to the noble cause. Once you understand this, you realize the extent to which managers are themselves still committed to the noble cause. The moral commitment doesn't disappear when an officer moves into the ranks of bureaucracy. For many managers, it's keener than ever.

## *Legitimacy and Patrol Officers*

To understand legitimacy and patrol officers, we need to recognize that they respond to an altogether different constituency than chiefs and managers. Their constituency is primarily the population that inhabits the street or that has been victimized: they deal with victims mostly because they respond to calls about crime that have already taken place. They also deal with disinterested citizens, troublemakers, motorists, small-time criminals, and street people. These groups make up a street officer's social territory, the boundaries of which are determined by their assigned beats. The most important concerns officers have on these beats are maintaining control and preventing problems from getting out of hand. A great deal of their work consists of responding to calls, report taking, and looking for criminal activity. Opportunities for "real police work," which means dealing with dangerous felons, are rare. Legitimacy in this environment is acted out in terms of loyalty to other officers and in commitment to the noble cause.

Line officers also deal with the courts. When they are called to testify, they find that the noble-cause standards of the street conflict with court expectations. As Crank (2004a:70) observed, legitimacy in the courtroom involves "issues of the quality of the evidence and demeanor in front of the judge." The courts are concerned with the technical quality of the evidence and behavior that conforms with the requirements of due process. Police are primarily interested in the factual guilt of suspects—virtually all of whom are presumed guilty (Klockars, 1983)—and consequently view the courts as being soft on crime. Police typically view the courts as untrustworthy; only they (police officers) can make the best determination about factual guilt or innocence. Crank (2004a:308) captures the distinction between police and the court's standard of guilt:

> What is the standard? To get bad guys off the street. To use the law if it will work for them, but to use whatever tools cops have if the law won't. The ideal cop is trickier than the law. Cops know who is bad. When the courts disagree, it is a sorry day for the courts, a sad day for the public. That's the standard.

This quote captures the imagery evoked by the noble cause and the way in which the noble cause has a different standard for justice than the courts. Legitimacy for police thus can put them squarely in conflict with the courts and judges.

Legitimacy has three operative principles. First, the department is part of a system, the municipal system of government. The second is that the system will protect itself. The third is that the toilet backs up.

## *Principle 1: The Department Is Part of a Municipal System*

For line officers, the business of the police is dealing with bad guys. For commanders and executives, the business of the police is not so simple. Chiefs are not politically independent. They are in power at the pleasure of a mayor and city council, and if their organization is involved in scandal, they may be replaced (see Box 6.2).

Box 6.2

**Mayors and Chiefs**

The fate of mayors and chiefs are often closely aligned. Consider the following comments of Donald Frazer, former mayor of Minneapolis:

> In that decade alone (the 1970s) the department changes police chiefs seven times, with an equal number of turnovers at the command level. My own first campaign for mayor in 1979 was dominated by the issue of who should run the police and how best to professionalize the department. The conflict within the department began in 1969, when the head of the police union was elected mayor of Minneapolis on a strong law-and-order platform. He was re-elected two years later, but lost his third election to a democrat. His fourth try found him back in office, but on his fifth attempt, the public returned the democratic mayor, whom he defeated.
>
> This seemingly endless round of musical chairs in the mayor's office kept the department in a high pitch of political ferment. Each new shift in administration brought new shifts in departmental fortunes. Those who had pounded political signs for a losing candidate found themselves pounding remote pavements on graveyard shifts. Choice assignments were regarded strictly as political plums. (Frazer, 1985:42)

And Patrick Murphy (1985:38) notes darkly that "it may be tempting, especially for a new mayor, to place an informer or two inside the department to keep tabs on the chief's loyalty to city hall." These quotes reveal how tightly the fate of police chiefs is tied to municipal leadership in the mayor's office.

**Municipal system** refers to the mutual interdependencies and obligations shared by the various members of the city and county business and public governance. A municipal system is made up of actors and groups who can directly or indirectly influence governance. Consider, for example, chiefs and mayors. What do mayors want from chiefs? Consider the words of William Hudnut III, mayor of Indianapolis, Indiana. He stated simply, "I have replaced two chiefs during my 10 years in office, and I would not hesitate to do so again to insure a responsive police department" (1985:26). But what does "responsiveness" mean? It is a term with an exceedingly vague meaning.

Former chief Patrick Murphy (1985) observed that many issues should be negotiated between a mayor and a chief. **Negotiable issues** include the handling of media relations, issues incidentally related to crime control, such as zoning matters and the management of school integration, and the mayor's role in personnel and organization of the agency. Although, Murphy noted, the chief should draw the line on the negotiability of some issues, he or she should tactfully take the mayor's counsel on those issues. **Non-negotiable issues** include some personnel decisions, such as salaries and promotions. Even with non-negotiable issues, however, Murphy advises that the mayor's counsel should be taken. He observed, for example, that "the mayor should not be making decisions about appointments, promotions, transfers, or assignments; this is not to suggest that he should be deprived of a right to input" (1985:34).

Mayoral input into promotions? Assignments? Undoubtedly, the provision of mayoral input into such areas requires political tact by a chief.

The potential to alienate the troops with ill-advised promotional decisions is substantial. What is clear is the extent to which the police chief is more than a "cop's cop." The police chief is also a citywide policymaker whose decisions are influenced and acted out in the municipal political arena and whose success, and longevity on the job, rises or falls on his or her political acumen. The legitimacy of the police organization is worked out in this arena.

## *Principle 2: The Municipal System Will Protect Itself*

Departments will endeavor to resolve problems before they threaten the working relationships in the municipal system. What kinds of problems can do this? Sometimes only a single incident can create legitimacy problems, for example, a line officer who used too much coercion on a suspect or departmental corruption uncovered by the newspapers. In the case of Rodney King in Los Angeles, a case in which officers were ultimately prosecuted for criminal conduct, the precipitating incident was an instance of brutality captured on camera, released to the Cable News

Network (CNN), and broadcast on national television. The "Rampart Scandal" discussed previously led to a consent decree between the LAPD and the U.S. Department of Justice. The death of George Floyd at the hands of the Minneapolis, MN, police on May 25, 2020, after allegedly using a counterfeit $20 bill to purchase cigarettes, further contributed to the loss of legitimacy. The loss of legitimacy meant that the government no longer accepted the way in which the police organization did its business. Consider Box 6.3.

Box 6.3

**The Ceremony of Legitimacy Lost**

On March 1, 2000, a 362-page report was turned over to Los Angeles Mayor Richard Riordian and members of the police commission. The report documented the Rampart police scandal and accountability failures that permitted the scandal to spread. It stated that central problems that led to the scandal—including poor background checks of recruits, lack of monitoring of officer misconduct and field supervision—continued to be unaddressed. The board of inquiry concluded:

> This scandal has devastated our relationship with the public we serve and threatened the integrity of our entire criminal justice system.

Distrust, cynicism, fear of the police, and erosion of community law and order are the inevitable result of a law enforcement agency whose ethics and integrity become suspect.

The Rampart report was the result of an investigation into the Los Angeles Police Department's Rampart Division anti-gang unit, on which officers were charged with perjuring themselves in court and filing false reports. Up to 3,000 cases would have to be reviewed, according to Gil Garcetti, the Los Angeles County district attorney, who described it as the worst problem he had seen in his 31 years as a prosecutor. Charges included the cover-up killing of gang members by police and the planting of rock cocaine near suspects, then accusing them of spitting it out.

The commission cited the following items in its review:

1. Front-line supervision suffered a breakdown in its ability to control officers.
2. Clear patterns of misconduct were neglected.
3. Complainants were uniformly treated as "recalcitrant," and their complaints were not seriously taken.
5. Personnel and promotional decisions were made with uninformed knowledge about the individuals under consideration.

Box 6.3, *continued*

6. The command team at Rampart Heights lacked cohesive organization.
7. Adequate background checks, a long-term problem, had not been addressed.

The commission stated:

> We have found that the LAPD's pattern or practice of police misconduct includes: the unconstitutional use of force by LAPD officers, including improper officer-involved shootings; improper seizures of persons, including making police stops not based on reasonable suspicion and making arrests without probable cause; seizures of property not based on probable cause; and improper searches of persons and property with insufficient cause. U.S. Department of Justice, Civil Rights Division.

On June 15, 2001, a district judge approved the terms of a consent decree. The city signed the decree in order to avoid a lawsuit with the U.S. Department of Justice (U.S. Department of Justice, Civil Rights Division, 2000) who claimed that there was a pattern of practice of civil rights abuses. According to the decree, the LAPD was required to do the following:

1. Collect data on the race of people in vehicular and pedestrian stops.
2. Install a computerized system to track performance evaluations, complaint, and disciplinary actions.
3. Make the internal disciplinary system more transparent.
4. Provide mechanisms to make the chief more accountable for disciplinary decisions.
5. Increase control over the police units that monitored gangs.

Source: Adapted from Newton et al. (2000), Daunt (2001).

The process of legitimacy lost and regained can be ugly. When legitimacy is lost, a ceremonial process occurs (Crank and Langworthy, 1992). The newspapers and media publicly degrade the police department in front-page exposés. In the earlier example, the loss of legitimacy was so great that the U.S. government no longer accepted the way in which the police department did business. The department was publicly humiliated and required to put into place a wide variety of accountability mechanisms.

Legitimacy lost is also sometimes worked out through the firing of the chief (Crank and Langworthy, 1996). Various groups begin to create pressures for the removal of the chief. Ultimately, the department will be publicly humiliated and the chief likely fired and replaced by a new chief who promises to clean up the department. It is an ugly process carried out in public, providing rich carrion for the newspapers and their readership. Departments will avoid a loss of legitimacy at all cost. This is where the third principle is activated.

## *Principle 3: The Toilet Backs Up*

Meyer and Rowan (1992) observed that public sector organizations operate by a **logic of good faith** (see Box 6.4). They act out powerful values carried by society, and their members believe in what they do. Members have good faith that the organization will do the right thing, and it is difficult for them to understand how their organization can be responsible when problems occur.

Box 6.4

**Good Faith and the Logic of Confidence**

The logic of confidence is what Goffman (1967) calls "face work"—the process of maintaining the other's face or identity and thus of maintaining the plausibility and legitimacy of the organization itself. Face work avoids embarrassing incidents and preserves the organization from the disruption of an implausible performance by any actor (Meyer and Rowan, 1992:90). In a police organization, an "implausible performance by an actor" would be an incident in which a street officer acted in a way inconsistent with the official purposes of the organization, such as using brutality or violating a suspect's due process rights.

It is like this with police organizations as well. It is almost impossible for police officers to think that their department, which in the public mind refers to line officers, is itself morally at fault in some way. The notion rings of disloyalty. So when a legitimacy problem occurs, a police department will not look at what it's doing wrong. It will try to protect itself, believing in the rightness of its purposes. It will blame "rotten apples" rather than look at what the organization might be doing wrong. What line officers don't understand is that the department will sacrifice them in order to maintain legitimacy.

How do police organizations respond to problems that might result in a loss of legitimacy? Principle 3, "the toilet backs up," means that a departmental process occurs in which line officers are initially blamed for problems, with increasingly higher-ranking personnel receiving departmental criticism and punishment until the public spectacle ends.

The Knapp Commission (1972), an investigatory body in New York City in the early 1970s, noted that departments tend to respond with the "individual officer explanation." The Knapp Commission was investigating widespread corruption in the New York Police Department and issued its report in 1972. They noted that, even in the face of pervasive corruption, higher-ranking personnel did not accept the notion that the organization itself was fundamentally at fault. Managers, they observed, were unable to acknowledge the depth of the problem. In Meyer and Rowan's (1992) terms, they were operating with logical good faith. They believed that the problem could be explained by the presence of "bad apples," individual officers who were themselves bad.

So to use the colorful phrase, the toilet begins to back up, as it did during the Knapp Commission investigation. First, individual officers, so-called "rotten apples," were blamed. They were prosecuted. But the toilet was still backing up. The department blamed "rotten pockets": groups of officers working together. If the toilet is still backing up after rotten pockets are corrected, the mayor will fire the chief. If the department cannot maintain its legitimacy, the system will act to protect itself. In the worst-case scenario, such as Rampart, in Box 6.3, the U.S. government will step in and tell the police department how it should do police work. Box 6.5 presents the stages of legitimacy lost.

Box 6.5

**Stages of Lost Legitimacy**

1. Individual officers are blamed: Some officers are fired and/or disciplined. Called the "rotten apple" theory of deviance. Usually ends with individual punished.
2. Toilet backs up. Blame "rotten pockets." Fire or discipline several officers. Call for an external investigation; city calls for audit.
3. Toilet still backing up. Blame chief. Chief is fired; a new chief is hired with "legitimizing mandate."
4. Department loses all legitimacy. Cannot do "police work" right. Consent decree.

## The Liability Issue, or "What Did I Just See on CNN?"

The chief picks up the phone. It's 6 a.m. "Who's this?"

"Chief, I'm sorry to call you at home."

"Yeah, well, what's up?"

"Chief, I think you ought to turn on CNN. The one where they play the same news every half hour. Call me back later on a secured line. We'll talk then."

Outsiders have a mythical idea about the control police chiefs have over police departments. They think that a directive from the police chief can immediately change the behavior of street officers. They think that if a city councilman tells the chief to quit being so tough on Latinos, well, the chief can go down and harangue the troops, and everything will change. Indeed, many chiefs have been fired because city leaders believed that chiefs had more power over the day-to-day operations of their department than they actually did.

Line officers know better. They know that the chief doesn't come down and talk to them and that chiefs have very little effect on what they do. The person that they respond to is the sergeant. And the sergeant is easy to satisfy. Sergeants have their activity that they want line officers to do, they want officers to stay out of trouble, they would like a bit of respect from their officers, and that's about it.

Line officers know what the chief expects of them primarily because they hear new policies being read during roll call. Officers are getting their leads primarily from other officers in the field, and their behavior is motivated by the values of noble cause and loyalty.

> MIKE: *If your officers are taking their leads from other officers in the field, they're making value-based decisions, not law-based ones. How can you know if you have a problem? You'll have a lot of litigation against the department. It's a sure indicator that your officers are using the law to carry out a moral standard.*

Let's review the law regarding litigation against the police. The following discussion on litigation is adapted from Meadows (1996).

Police can be held liable for inappropriate or wrongful behavior, regardless of intent. The most common action that citizens can take against the police is called a Title 42 of the United States Code, Section 1983. It is printed in Box 6.6.

Box 6.6

**Title 42 of U.S. Code, Section 1983**

Every person who, under color of any statute, ordinance, regulation, custom, or usage, of any State or Territory or the District of Columbia, subjects, or causes to be subjected, any citizen of the United States or other person within the jurisdiction thereof to the deprivation of any rights, privileges, or immunities secured by the Constitution and laws, shall be liable to the party injured in an action at law, suit in equity, or other proper proceeding for redress, except that in any action brought against a judicial officer for an act or omission taken in such officer's judicial capacity, injunctive relief shall not be granted unless a declaratory decree was violated or declaratory relief was unavailable. For the purposes of this section, any Act of Congress applicable exclusively to the District of Columbia shall be considered to be a statute of the District of Columbia.

**Title 42, Section 1983** was written originally to protect American citizens against the Ku Klux Klan. ***Monell v. Dept. of Social and Health Services of New York,*** 436 U.S. 658 (1978), also called a 1983 suit, was a watershed moment in litigation against the police. Before *Monell*, only individual police officers could be sued for their actions. These cases infrequently materialized because cops rarely had anything of value to be sued for, and attorneys didn't want to waste their time. Prior to *Monell*, under the Sovereign Immunity Clause, organizations had immunity from civil suits. *Monell* changed all that. *Monell* held that municipalities are "persons" subject to liability damages under the Ku Klux Klan Act of 1871, 42 U.S.C. Section 1983. This allowed for "deep pockets" civil suits against municipalities for violations of civil rights and that municipalities found guilty could pay hefty damages. It is currently the most popular tool to use against the police, for the following reasons:

1. Civil lawsuits are filed in federal court, where discovery is relatively liberal. It is easier to acquire documents and records from the defendant.
2. Cases filed in the federal courts do not have to first exhaust state court remedies.
3. The prevailing plaintiff can recover attorney's fees under the Attorney's Fee Act of 1976. Attorneys consequently may be more inclined to accept these cases.

(Meadows, 1996:105)

Under what circumstances can a "Section 1983," as these cases are commonly called, be filed against a police officer? First, the police officer has to be acting under the "color of law," which means that an individual is acting in an official capacity as a police officer. This includes illegal acts performed while on duty. Second, there has to be a constitutional violation of some federally protected right. Third, the courts will accept both intentional acts by a police officer and acts in which an officer acted negligently. **Intentional torts** refer to a wanton disregard for a person's rights. **Negligent torts** refer to a failure to protect the public from harm. For an incident to be negligent, the following conditions apply:

1. The officer must have a duty.
2. The duty wasn't performed.
3. There must be a relationship between the duty and the failure to perform.
4. There must be damage or injury.

(Meadows, 1996:106)

Use of force is a common type of suit brought against the police. The police are permitted to use nondeadly and deadly force, but the use of force in a given situation must be reasonable and appropriate to that situation. Moreover, an acquittal in a state court does not necessarily mean that a federal case will end the same. As Meadows observed, two Los Angeles police officers acquitted in the Rodney King case, a case involving the use of less than lethal violence, were later convicted in a federal court.

Use of force is not the only kind of incident that can prompt litigation. The other principal causes for litigations are auto pursuits, arrests and searches, employee drug tests, hiring and promotion, discrimination, recordkeeping and privacy, and jail management (McCoy, 1987, in Meadows, 1996:107).

Today, civil liability is a part of a working officer's legal terrain. Kappeler (2001) estimated that the total cost of liability might approach $780 billion annually, with more than 30,000 lawsuits a year.

A 1983 suit is balanced by a series of defenses. **Qualified immunity** applies when an officer is acting in an area in which the law is not clear or in which her conduct was reasonable. Officers may plead that they had probable cause that a crime had been committed or the person was a suspect. Or officers can plead that they acted in good faith; they could not have reasonably known that their actions were in violation of the law (Roberg et al., 2005). Yet these are pleas, and they are invoked in response to a suit, not instead of one. The pressures of a suit, and the way a department can use a lawsuit to investigate an officer, can be immensely unsettling to individual officers.

How widespread are 1983 suits? Hughes (2001) noted that 18.4 percent of all officers have been sued and that 86.4 percent of officers personally knew someone who had been sued. Moreover, officers involved in a citizen complaint are likely to be interrogated, not only about the complaint but about past behavior as well. Their departments may seek to show the public that they are reacting aggressively against complaints, thus alienating involved officers. As Roberg et al. (2005:420) noted:

> officers may interpret these reactions as the organization not "backing" them, citizens being out to "get rich" at the expense of officers, and "no one representing what the police do." Not only does the stress of many officers increase, but these problems may also lead to increased cynicism among officers.

Some officers may engage in **"de-policing"** as well, avoiding the public in order to avoid the likelihood of facing liability issues. Roberg et al. (2005) noted that a police shooting of an unarmed black male resulted in several days of rioting with injuries to both citizens and police officers. A civil lawsuit was filed in federal court alleging the department was engaged in racial profiling. Arrests appeared to drop after the suit, from 5,063 for nonviolent crimes to 2,517 in the month after the indictment. Traffic citations also dropped 35 percent. Yet, overall, crime had increased over this same period.

One of the officers responds to Mike's discussion of liability. "We take liability pretty seriously in this department."

Mike does a double-take. *Oh, you do? I'm glad to hear it. I'm really glad. Because most departments don't. They react two ways. Either they hang some poor officer out to dry, or they cover it all up and promote him.* (audience laughs). *You think I'm kidding? Did you know that officers who are sued are twice as likely to be promoted as to be punished?* (see Box 6.7). *When I say that the department should take these seriously, I mean that they should stop blaming the officer and take a long look at themselves. Don't wait until the Feds do it with a consent decree. You're the department. You're the one pointing the gun. Don't forget that.*

Mike concludes. *If you are being sued and are paying large liability payments, you need to ask yourself why. What kind of case generates liability? Officer incompetence? Sure. Look at the newspapers. Are the big liability settlements from incompetence? Or are they from noble-cause corruption? If you look at them closely, can you see how noble-cause corruption is costing you a bundle? This is why you need to know the value-basis of the decisions your officers are making on behalf of your department.*

Box 6.7

**Police Liability and Lawsuits**

A *Washington Post* investigation (Alexander et al., 2022) into police officers involved in multiple lawsuits and large settlements shed light on the frequency of police officers being named in multiple civil lawsuits, particularly those resulting in substantial payouts. The investigation by the *Post* analyzed data from 25 of the largest police and sheriff's departments in the United States and found that more than 7,600 officers had been involved in more than one settlement related to misconduct claims. Over the course of a decade, these settlements cost over $3.2 billion, with repeat offenders accounting for $1.5 billion of that amount, which means a small number of officers are responsible for a disproportionately high number of settlements. Within the departments surveyed, over 1,200 officers were involved in at least five settlements, and more than 200 were involved in ten or more (Alexander et al., 2022).

According to Chicago PBS station WTTW, between 2019 to 2023, the city paid $384.2 million in settlements, lawyer fees, damages, and other payouts. Repeat offenders (200 of them) resulted in payments that made up $164.3 million dollars. In total, the city paid to resolve 539 total lawsuits during the period (Camp, 2024).

The findings illustrate a systemic issue: repeat offenders within the police departments often face minimal accountability, and cities subsequently absorb the financial burden, usually taken from budgets which had allocated money to citizens needing assistance. This cycle not only erodes public trust but also indicates a need for stronger oversight and disciplinary reform.

## Stress and Ignoble Consequences

*Do you see why these things bother you? The department, the courts? The public?* Mike asks. *You believe in the noble cause. So do I. But you're facing legitimacy problems, and you're being sued. Whose fault is it?*

"The organization again?" offers a captain. The other participants laugh.

*It's always the organization.* Mike responds, smiling. *Always. But you're the organization.*

The room is silent.

The principal sources of stress are not from the organization. Nor are they from the courts, or from the public. These groups are the manifestations of the problem. The problem lies in the commitment to the noble cause, a logic of good faith that all will work out if only officers are committed enough to good ends, and an almost blind failure to recognize how the noble cause is implicated in legitimacy and liability problems. Officers don't recognize that they resent the courts, the organization and the public when these groups interfere with the noble cause, the good end.

Remember that officer I mentioned at the beginning of the chapter? The one who, with his college education, didn't understand how bad guys were back out on the street the day after they were arrested? He was stressed over the courts. And he knew better. That officer's going to get you in trouble. There's your problem. Not the courts.

So my question to you is, what are you doing so that your officers are comfortable with the courts? The administration? The public? The city council? The media? This is where you come into the picture. His stress is your problem, and it can hurt the organization. Legitimacy and liability. You have to take charge here so that he deals with his stress. You're the organization. You take charge. There are a lot of things you can do, and we'll talk about some of them. But the most important will always be simply being a good role model, and being seen. And make sure your other role models, your TOs and POST trainers, are giving the cues you want given.

After lunch, we'll look at the problems of noble-cause corruption. It's not just in any one department. It's across the justice system. Let's break.

7

# Ethics and the Means-Ends Dilemma

## Key Terms

- celebrated cases
- code of silence
- crime control model
- dilemma of ends-oriented-ethics
- due process model
- deontological
- means-ends continuum
- station-house sergeants
- street sergeants
- teleological

## Introduction

This chapter explores the ethical tensions in policing through the lens of the means-ends continuum, contrasting deontological (means-oriented) and teleological (ends-oriented) frameworks. It argues that most police officers operate within a teleological mindset, prioritizing outcomes over procedures, which aligns with the crime control model rather than the due process model. This orientation fosters the dilemma of ends-oriented ethics, where noble-cause motivations can justify unethical or illegal actions. Celebrated cases, often sensationalized by media and misunderstood by legislators, distort public and institutional perceptions of justice, reinforcing a punitive ethos. The chapter highlights how street-level decision-making is shaped by influential figures such as street sergeants and station-house sergeants, who emphasize efficiency and conviction rates over procedural integrity. These pressures, combined with prosecutorial zeal and forensic lab misconduct, contribute to a culture where the code of silence can protect misconduct in the name of effectiveness.

DOI: 10.4324/9781003626916-10

## Ethical Systems

Commanders return from lunch. Mike begins the afternoon's presentation with a discussion of ethical systems. The purpose of this discussion is to distinguish between the types of systems and then to identify the ethical perspective that the police tend to use.

> MIKE: *Ethics is an expression of a person's values. You hire cops that have a common perspective. That's what you hired them for. And that common perspective is underpinned by a common set of values. If we can identify those values, we can predict how they're going to make decisions. If we apply that knowledge, we can lower their stress, save lives, cut down on liability, improve the legitimacy of the organization, and make policy more effective.*
>
> To do ethics, go to the old philosophy books. I did this. You can read in that field for 10 years and not know what you've read. You have to pare it down. I'm going to throw two terms at you. Deontological and teleological.

Deontological and teleological are long-winded terms that describe the way a person thinks through ethical problems. **Deontological,** in its simplest form, means that a person is means-oriented. The Christian maxim "do unto others as you would have them do unto you" is deontological; it provides a basis for behavior regardless of consequences. In a democracy, a belief in due process is a form of deontology. Both Christianity and democracy are grounded in the idea that means—specifically, the way we act—are more important than the ends sought by actors. Deontology is also seen in the behavior of the police commander who "goes by the books," inflexible to changes in situation or unmoved by the morality of the consequences of behavior.

**Teleological** ethics, simply put, means that a person is goal- or ends-oriented. Utilitarianism is teleological. It is grounded in the notion that what is good is determined by what produces the greatest good for the greatest number, regardless of how that end is achieved. Teleology tells us that our behavior has consequences and that we should be concerned not simply about whether or not our behavior is right by some standard but also about what the outcome will be. Less ideally described, a business manager might decide that he or she must focus on profit above all other considerations. If the manager concludes that employee layoffs are necessary in order to maintain a satisfactory profit margin and out-sources American jobs for cheaper jobs in a third-world country, the manager is making a teleological, or ends-oriented, decision. In Box 7.1, Joycelyn Pollock provides the following summary definition of these two ethical principles.

Box 7.1

**Deontological and Teleological Ethical Systems**

A deontological ethical system is one that is concerned solely with the inherent nature of the act being judged. If an act is inherently good, then even if it results in bad consequences, it is still a good act. Teleological systems are interested in the consequences of an act. An act may look "bad," but if it results in good consequences, then it can be defined as good under a teleological system.

The interested reader is referred to Pollock (1998) for an excellent review of these and other ethical concepts and their applications across the criminal justice system.

## *The Dilemma of Ends-Oriented Ethics: You Can Never Know*

MIKE: *The value basis of line officer decision-making is teleological. They are committed to good ends. The problem is that ends-oriented decision-making can be self-defeating. A central problem with ends-oriented thinking is that you may not get the ends you want. Where does that leave you morally? I think it leaves a lot of officers bitter and frustrated about their work. Cynical. Like our officer, the one who didn't understand why someone was back on the street after being arrested, they don't understand, not in their hearts, that means are important, too.*

First, we need to show that ends-orientation is limited as a way to think.

Value-based decision-making means that police officers make judgments about the likely predispositions, behaviors, and social worth of citizens, suspects, citizens, street people, and troublemakers they talk to, and their behavior follows from these judgments. Central to police values are a commitment to the noble cause and the departmental loyalties that reinforce that commitment.

The following imaginary cases are fanciful, but they help to clarify the problems of ends-oriented decision-making. These imaginary cases focus on outcomes that seek the good of the many versus the few, or utilitarian kinds of decisions.

Case #1. You're a switchman. An out-of-control train is barreling down the tracks. If you don't throw the switch, the train is going to run over a drunk collapsed on the tracks. If you do, the train is going to run into a school bus full of children. Are you going to throw the switch?

Case #2. You're a switchman. An out-of-control train is barreling down the tracks and is going to run into a school bus full of children. If you throw the switch, it will change tracks and run over an unconscious drunk instead. Are you going to throw the switch?

These cases are similar in that both involve a decision that seems as if it will end in a loss of life. Case #2 has a more complicated morality for individuals who want to save the bus of children: they must make an active move to save the bus, a move that will kill the drunk. They do not need to do anything in the first case.

A teleological (ends-oriented) ethic will direct most readers to save the school bus full of kids. The good of the many is placed ahead of individual desires. The decision is fortified by a moral sympathy about the kinds of people they are saving and opinions about the social worth of the characters in the example. What could go wrong in a decision to save the busload of kids? In fact, several things could go wrong.

1. The decision-maker misunderstands the design of the switch and throws it the wrong way, sending the train into the busload of kids.
2. The train doesn't change tracks after the decision-maker throws the switch but gets caught on a track spur, derails, and kills everyone.
3. The decision-maker changes the switch away from the bus, but the bus starts up and pulls off the track in time to save the students. The drunk is killed.
4. The drunk is not killed but loses both legs and sues the decision-maker and her department. The decision-maker is also charged with involuntary manslaughter. Convicted, the decision-maker spends a year on probation and the police department settles out of court for $800,000.
5. All of the students in the bus have exited, but they're on the other side of the bus, and the decision-maker can't see them. The "real" choice, though the decision-maker didn't recognize it at the time, was between killing a drunk and killing no one. The decision-maker is subsequently charged with involuntary manslaughter. Though found not guilty, she becomes despondent and commits suicide.

MIKE: *The point here is that, when we are focused on good ends, things don't always work out like we think they will. This does not mean that those good ends are not important. It does mean that, before we decide to throw away the law or go outside department processes in order to achieve those good ends, we should consider our actions very carefully.*

*I'm going to give you four other examples that are still imaginary, but focus on the police.* Mike describes the following four scenarios, and they are discussed by the commanders.

Scenario 1 (see Box 7.2) has a great deal of meaning for police officers. It will boil the blood of many officers, and fear of this kind of event will justify corruption of the noble cause.

Box 7.2

**Scenario 1**

Two officers observe a vehicle containing a suspected drug dealer driving down the street in a high-crime area at 2 A.M. Although the vehicle is exceeding the maximum posted speed limit, the officers only have the legal right to stop the vehicle, issue a traffic citation, and question the driver. Upon stopping the vehicle, the officers' suspicions are confirmed: the driver has been previously arrested several times for drug dealing. However, he has no outstanding warrants, appears to be perfectly sober, and produces a valid driver's license. The officers issue the citation and allow the driver to proceed on his way.

Later that evening, it is learned that the same suspect sold one-quarter ounce of contaminated heroin to two high school students who both suffered fatal overdoses. The suspect was not apprehended.

Scenario 2 (See Box 7.3) is a different outcome for the same event, what we call an "over the rainbow" scenario. The officers acted out of a commitment to the noble cause: the bad guy was put away because they cared enough. The law didn't stop them. It is the way noble-cause corruption is supposed to end: a bad guy is off the street and officers are rewarded. However, it does not always end this way.

Box 7.3

**Scenario 2**

Two officers observe the same vehicle under the exact same circumstances. On this occasion, feeling a strong sense of moral outrage over the death of young victims, they proceed as follows. One officer orders the suspect out of the car and to the rear of the patrol car, where he is patted down for weapons and questioned in detail concerning his activities in the area, a perfectly legal procedure. However, the second officer proceeds to search the interior of the vehicle and locates under the front seat a brown paper sack containing numerous plastic bags each holding approximately one-quarter ounce of a white powdery substance resembling heroin. The officer then removes two of the plastic bags and drops them in plain sight on the passenger-side floorboard. Of course, these actions are entirely illegal.

The second officer then walks back to the rear of the patrol vehicle and begins his own questioning of the driver. The first officer proceeds to the suspect vehicle and looks through the passenger-side window and from the outside observes the suspicious plastic bags. He quite legally retrieves

Box 7.3, *continued*

them and extends the search to the rest of the vehicle, where he discovers the brown paper sack with the remaining plastic bags. The first officer promptly places the suspect under arrest for possession of a controlled substance with intent to deliver. The suspect is convicted. In order to secure a lesser sentence, he reveals information about his drug source. The operators of an illegal lab are quickly arrested and convicted through quite legal procedures. Both officers are officially commended by the mayor.

In Scenario 3 (see Box 7.4), the officers pay a heavy price in terms of their careers. As Mike noted, they had failed to consider the police version of Pascal's wager (see Chapter 1).

Box 7.4

**Scenario 3**

All of the facts of this case are identical to those in Scenario 2, except that during a subsequent trial, a witness surfaces with a videotape of the entire stop and arrest of the suspected drug dealer. Pointing to the illegal search of the vehicle, the suspect's attorney quickly obtains the release of his client. Both officers are severely reprimanded for their conduct and denied the possibility of promotion for several years.

Scenario 4 (see Box 7.5), with unanticipated outcomes like the previous one, also reveals one of the darker aspects of police culture. Officers who will not back up another officer, even when the issue concerns the illegal conduct of a police officer rather than danger on the job, will suffer an unkind fate. Fellow officers are likely to unite against him or her.

Box 7.5

**Scenario 4**

The facts of the case are identical to those in Scenario 2, except that during the trial, the second officer is called to testify concerning the actions of his/her partner. Under unrelenting pressure from the client's lawyer and believing in the oath, the officer gets cold feet and testifies that officer number one illegally searched the suspect's vehicle just prior to the discovery of the illegal drugs. The case is subsequently dropped, and the offending officer is fired.

The second officer is subsequently shunned for failing to back up his/her partner and cannot find a compatible partner for several years. Subsequent difficulties force the officer to seek employment in another profession.

These scenarios describe a central moral **dilemma confronting ends-oriented ethics.** One can never be certain beforehand that the outcome will be what one thinks it will be.

Let's consider a slightly different kind of scenario. This is a "thought experiment." Imagine that you're a patrol officer. Suppose you pull in behind a speeding motorist, and instead of pulling over, he takes off and tries to outrun you. Many departments in the country have an unwritten rule that runners get thumped. It's a question of territorial control. When someone runs, it's considered a form of disrespect, and they get thumped. You are able to force the driver into a stop. You know your partner expects you to thump this guy. What are you going to do? If you don't, your partner might not think that you're trustworthy. If you do, you're acting with brutal force.

Can you say to yourself, "I thought that beating the crap out of this jerk would make the city safer"? Sure, you could, if you were ends-oriented. You made a decision that you thought was good for society. The greatest good for the greatest number. All done by thumping one "jerk." That is an example of a teleological ethical judgment.

Let's imagine that you are videotaped and what you did is broadcast on national news, and the cameras show you beating this troublemaker. Now the world sees you as the bad guy, the problem cop that has to be fixed. The chief may hang you out to twist in the wind. Where can you hide?

This example again reveals the uncertainty in ends-oriented thinking. A police officer can never be certain that the outcome will be what she or he wants it to be. In the "thought experiment" earlier, the outcome could have become a multi-million dollar lawsuit against the city, civil litigation, and possibly, criminal litigation. But it could as easily have been a non-event: the officer might have gone home, feeling good about himself or herself. Box 7.6 describes ends gone wrong.

Box 7.6

**The Death of a Boston Detective**

Consider the efforts of a Boston detective to bring an accused cop killer to justice:

> Recently, charges were dropped against an accused cop killer and three Boston police officers were suspended with pay pending a perjury investigation. The perjury involved a Boston detective who "invented" an informant. The detective maintained that the informant gave critical information which was cited in the affidavit for a search warrant. The "no knock" search warrant's execution led to the death of a Boston detective.
>
> (Barker and Carter, 1999:347–348)

Box 7.6, *continued*

> The officers, subsequently charged with perjury, had "fluffed up the evidence." They illegally invented an informant in order to conduct a search. In this instance, a detective's life was sacrificed in the name of the noble cause.

Mike decides to push the point. He turns to the commanders. *Is there a moral justification for thumping an asshole? It happens all the time. You should look for another explanation. Have you ever done an asshole?*

The commanders don't respond.

Have you seen someone do an asshole? I know I have. Now, if I'm means-oriented, then thumping a jerk is morally wrong. If I'm means-oriented, what am I not doing anymore? No free coffee. No thumping. No free meals. No bending the law to do the right thing.

He looks at his audience. *No one's reacting. Someone react.*

A supervisor responds. "I think that there are a lot of us who believe in doing the right thing. Our cases would be thrown out if we [didn't]. Prosecutors have to review cases. A lot would be thrown out."

I hear both sides. What you said is what supervisors say. They don't see it very often. They've forgotten about the magic pencil. You show me any rules and I can write around them. The report will be fantastic. You won't know. If the decisions are made at the bottom of the organizational pyramid, then how can you check? Have you checked? Do you really understand what's going on? It's nice to think that there isn't much, but do you really know?

You remember this morning we looked at the data, how in that training agency that shall remain unnamed the recruits had become committed to principles of noble-cause corruption by the end of training class? Do you remember that attitudes supporting the noble cause were bound up with organizational secrecy?

I assert that you don't know. You think you know, because you are following department policies that have built in accountability procedures. You are more means-oriented than your officers because you believe in the department and its policies. You have your procedures and policies, you have standard operating procedures, but you don't know how those procedures are being acted out on the street. And I'm here to tell you that they're being used in the service of the good end, and sometimes noble-cause corruption is that good end.

For the first time, the supervisor begins to understand. Mike has brought the point home. They supervise, they help develop strategy, they follow accountability procedures carefully, they periodically review activities with line supervisors, and they review policy to address problems. But they don't know what's going on at the line level, out on the street. Not for sure.

## Due Process and Crime Control Where's Your Department?

In this section, we will develop a **means-ends continuum** and overlay it with Packer's crime control/due process model to describe some of the ethical underpinnings of value-based decision-making.

### *A Continuum of Value-Based Decisions*

> MIKE: *Ethical orientations can be put on a continuum. We're going to do that.*

He sketches a continuum on the blackboard, with means-orientation on one side and ends-orientation on the other. The continuum is reproduced in Figure 7.1.

On this continuum, a score of 1 means that a person is deontological in their decision-making ethic. They are concerned about the way they act, independent of the consequences of their actions. A score of 10 indicates that a person is teleological. The result outweighs the behavior we choose to get there. In Cases 1 and 2 discussed earlier in this chapter, decision-makers tended to be ends-oriented, with scores at the 8 or 9 level. Examples 3 and 4 were more complicated, but they showed that decision-makers still tended to be ends-oriented. An ends-orientation is characteristic of the way police think about their work, as we'll see in the next section.

### *Means-Ends as Crime Control Versus Due Process*

Teleological (ends) and deontological (means) ethics can be observed in Herbert Packer's (1968) models of criminal justice. Herbert Packer

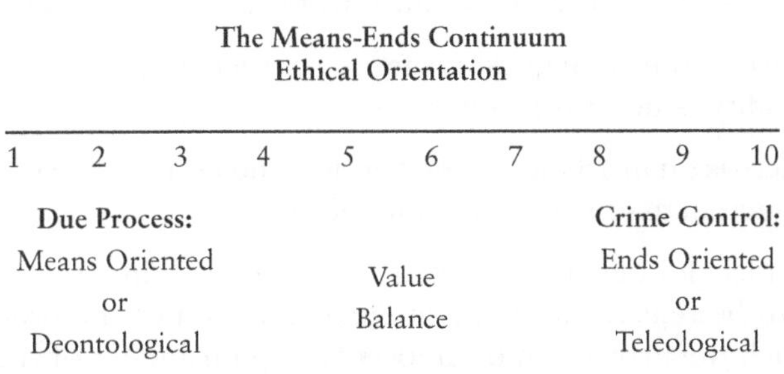


*Figure 7.1* A Continuum of Value-based Decisions

described two models of criminal justice, models that matched widely shared views of how the justice system should operate. The **crime control model** focuses on the ends of justice—obtaining conviction and treating felons harshly. Punishment of the guilty is a primary concern. The **due process model** looks at how the justice system treats suspects and offenders. Protection of the innocent is a primary concern. These assumptions reflect the central values embodying crime control and due process in the United States. They fit a means-ends model as well. Mike uses Packer's models to demonstrate the ends-orientation that characterizes most police officers as well as criminal justice organizations generally. Box 7.7 presents the seven elements of Packer's two models.

Box 7.7

**Herbert Packer's Two Models of the Criminal Justice Process**

*Crime Control Model*

1. Repression of criminal conduct is the most important function performed by the criminal justice process.
2. A failure of law enforcement means a breakdown of order, necessary for freedom.
3. Criminal process is the positive guarantor of social freedom.
4. Efficiency is the top priority of the model. By efficiency is meant the ability to apprehend, try, and convict high numbers of criminals whose offenses become known.
5. There is an emphasis on speed and finality. Facts can be provided more quickly through interrogation than through courtroom examination and cross-examination.
6. The conveyor belt is the model for the system. This is a steady stream of cases from arrest through conviction.
7. A presumption of guilt makes it possible for the system to deal efficiently with large numbers of felons.

*Due Process Model*

1. The reliability of the criminal justice process is closely examined. The model focuses on the possibility of error. It is particularly concerned with the third degree and coercive tactics.
2. The outcome is in question as long as there is a factual challenge. Finality is not a priority.
3. There is an insistence on prevention and elimination of mistakes in factual assessments of culpability.
4. If efficiency demands shortcuts around reliability, then efficiency is to be rejected as a system goal. The aim of the process is as much the protection of innocents as punishment of the guilty.

Box 7.7, *continued*

5. The combination of stigma and deprivation that government inflicts is the end goal.
6. The coercive power of the state is always subject to abuse. Maximum efficiency means maximum tyranny.
7. A person is to be found guilty if and only if a factual finding of guilt is accompanied with procedural rigor in the criminal justice process.

Mike addresses the audience of commanders. *Now we're going to examine the values that characterize your department. We're going to superimpose a model of Herbert Packer's two models of criminal justice over the ends-means continuum.*

What I want you to do is to think a minute, and then tell me where your department falls on this continuum. Consider each of the seven items. Are you on the left? In the middle? On the right? Chances are that, unless you have had a major shake-up in your agency recently, you will have higher scores and be over on the crime-control side. We have seen managers rate their departments up around 9 and 10.

If your department is 8 or above, there is a pretty strong likelihood that you are either having problems you know about or problems you don't yet know about. Let's think about the officers you have in the department. You will have very few if any officers who are means-oriented. If they believe due process is more important than crime control, they have probably self-selected themselves out of the occupation of policing. Or they're in internal affairs.

Recall the nature of the hiring and training process and how the noble cause is at the center of it. The question is not the extent to which your officers are committed to doing something about bad guys. Oh, they're committed, all right. The question is what they're willing to do to get bad guys off the street.

*If your officers are overfocused on the crime control end, you're in an organization that may have some problems. In high-scoring organizations, there is a strong likelihood that there are many complaints against officers. It is also likely that cliques are dominating line-administrative relations. You are getting a lot of litigation. Are you?* Mike scans the room, making brief eye contact with various commanders. Their faces are expressionless, giving nothing away. Mike lets the moment linger, and then continues.

You're probably being trashed by the newspapers.

When problems emerge, police managers are often in denial about what is going on, either from the logic of good faith or because they are out of the information loop. If commanders are intensely focused on crime control, they may not want to admit that too much crime control may have a negative impact on their department. They will not want to think that their golden apples are causing problems, or that the department itself unintentionally encourages noble-cause corruption.

Mike looks over his audience. This group of commanders did not show a strong preference for a crime-control perspective. On the crime-control continuum, they were only slightly on the crime-control side, scoring between a 6 and a 7 on a scale of 1 to 10. *You're only scaling around 6? That's pretty good. That's real good. I've been to other departments that were up to around 9 or 10.*

One of the higher-ranking officers responds. "If you look back 5 years, there are differences. We've had changes in direction, we have a different orientation." Another officer adds, "We've had changes in leadership in our organization."

A third: "The previous chief was pretty tough. He was take charge, no bull. He wanted to change the department. But he didn't know us. The things he wanted to force on people weren't acceptable. The current chief has improved a lot of problems from that administration."

Mike responds. *That's good. It's a tough transition. But I also see commanders scoring further away from the crime-control side than their line officers. If I measure your street officers tomorrow, how will they score? I'll bet that they're more crime-control-oriented, around 7 or 8 on the continuum. Don't be lulled into complacency by the logic of good faith. It's up to you to make sure that your organization isn't surprised.*

## *Where Do Your Officers Get Their Leads?*

One officer, quiet but listening closely, responds. "I don't think we're complacent. We're protective here. You make it sound like we're out of touch. I think we're in better shape than that."

You are? That's good. I think you need to be protective. What I want to emphasize in this section is that there are many sources that push your officers toward noble-cause corruption. This will be uncomfortable, because they involve groups you trust and believe in. They may not realize how they push your officers into corruption. You need to know. Because if you don't protect them no one will.

Mike discusses the development of street officers' crime-control orientations. *Where do your officers get their street ethics? I've made the case that they are hired because they have a particular ethical point of view, and that their ethics are reinforced during training. But why do so few officers ever return to the middle of the continuum? What keeps them over there* (he taps the crime-control side) *so completely? The answer is that their principal referents all push them toward crime control. They don't do it in the same way. But it has the same result. It encourages noble-case corruption. I'm going to tell you about five of them. Some might surprise you. They are their sergeants, prosecutors and the courts, forensic labs, more seasoned officers, and—are you ready for this?—college education.*

Police officers' crime-control values are embedded in a justice environment that reinforces a crime-control perspective and tends to look the other way at the corruption of noble cause. Officers' predispositions toward crime control are constantly reinforced by people whom officers come into contact with in their daily routines and some of whom they admire and respect. Only by understanding how elements in their working environment encourage the corruption of noble cause can we recognize how difficult it is to change police values.

## *Courts and the Prosecutor*

This morning we talked about the way officers are hired with a general value orientation, and it was quickly turned into support for values that justified the corruption of noble cause. It doesn't end there.

Some officers groan good-naturedly. Mike says, *Oh, I know. I groan too. But what you need to realize is that the vulnerability of your street officers to noble-cause corruption is reinforced daily—daily, by groups around them.*

I want to talk about where your officers take their leads from. How about courts? What happens to most of the cases that go before the courts?

One of the commanders responds "Acquitted." Others nod in agreement.

Mike expected this. It is the usual answer. Police everywhere believe that the courts are exceptionally lenient on defendants. They are convinced that bad people are frequently released on legal technicalities. Yet the evidence is compelling: the courts in the United States are harsh by most standards. Less than 1 percent of all individuals charged with violent and property crimes are successfully challenged for due process reasons (Maguire and Pastore, 1995). Moreover, courts are routinely hard on arrestees: If an arrest is made, more than 70 percent of the defendants will ultimately be found guilty (Walker, 1994). This is precisely as it should be, given that the legal standard for conviction of a crime—guilty beyond a reasonable doubt—is more stringent than the probable-cause standard for arrest.

The vast majority of defendants plea to a guilty charge prior to a trial, thereby providing prosecutors with the best of all worlds—a high conviction rate and a small investment of time and precious tax dollars in the prosecution process. When prosecutors don't sustain cases, what reasons do they give? The predictable: lack of evidence, lack of witnesses.

How does our criminal justice system stack up when compared to others around the world? There is compelling if not conclusive evidence that, in terms of the proportion of citizens incarcerated, the United States has the most punitive criminal justice system in the world.

Given the practical, common-sense nature of police, how can they believe something that is so wrong? The answer lies in part in the way the mass media portrays the courts and criminal defendants. The myth of the lenient court system is daily fare on most television news shows. It's great for selling TV and movies, but it's all malarkey.

It is unclear why there is so much misinformation about justice system processes from legislators who should know better and should inform citizens in a responsible manner. In most cases, they may simply not know. Like the rest of us, legislators may form their opinions by the exceptional, **celebrated cases** (Walker, 1994). Walker described celebrated cases as those cases that garner a great deal of publicity yet give a fundamentally wrong impression of courtroom practices.

Legislators see headlines about a Miranda-type case, a person whose conviction is reversed because of illegal police behavior. They have no knowledge of the tens of thousands of cases that typify the criminal justice system nor are they familiar with the circumstances of the approximately 2,247,000 people behind bars (Bureau of Justice Statistics, 2016). They rarely let their views get complicated by messy facts.

The answer also is related to the feelings that police have about due process protections for defendants. It is not important that such protections are rarely used or that they are ineffective. What matters to many police officers is that they exist. There are many officers who feel betrayed by the courts every time they read a suspect their rights. It is a powerful sense of treachery, motivated by their commitment to the noble cause and the corresponding belief that they alone can stem the tide of crime. For some officers, it justifies noble-cause corruption. Consider Barker's conversation with a police officer regarding efforts to gain consent for a search:

> BARKER: That sure sounds like telling a lot of lies.
>
> OFFICER: It is not police lying: It is an art. After all, the criminal has constitutional protection. He can lie through his teeth. Why not us? What is fair is fair (Barker and Carter, 1994:145).
>
> Mike continues. *Acquitted? Really? They're not plea-bargained? They don't plea-bargain cases here? Sure they do. They do everywhere.*
>
> One of the commanders considers this for a moment. "They have to get filed first."
>
> OK, I'll take that. You're not getting them filed, unless they're really, really good. Unless they're solid. What's the prosecutor telling you? That he's worried about someone's constitutional rights? Or that he wants to make damn sure that he gets 'em convicted?

> I'll bet you that the prosecutor in this county tells you that "I have a 95 or a 99 percent conviction rate." Ever hear them say that? Sure you have. They're politicians. It's a political statement. They have to back it up.

With the widespread use of plea bargaining and the scant resources available to indigent defendant offices, there are few checks on the validity and reliability of evidence. It is easy for considerations of prosecutorial efficiency and effectiveness to dominate in such an environment. If due process considerations were taken seriously at all stages, and if full-blown adversarial trials were required for all felony defendants, it would be like adding sand to a Corvette's crankcase. The courtroom workgroup would grind to a halt.

> *You see? Plea bargaining is about efficiency and effectiveness. It guarantees conviction. It guarantees minimal municipal investment. Do you think it's about this? Mike points to the due process side of the means-ends continuum. Or about this?* Mike points to the crime-control side of the continuum. No one answers the question. Mike concludes. *You see. This is the lead your officers are getting from the courts.*

Prosecutors provide one of the primary leads for the police. But prosecutors themselves are often committed to the noble cause and, in their zeal to convict, step across the line in order to prove guilt in courtroom proceedings. Unfortunately, they all too many times strike "foul blows" as well as hard ones. Consider the research conducted by the *Chicago Tribune* on prosecutorial misconduct in murder cases, presented in Box 7.8.

Box 7.8

**Prosecutors—An Example for the Police?**

Do prosecutors engage in misconduct? An investigation carried out by the *Chicago Tribune* found that, since the passage of the 1963 ruling designed to suppress misconduct by prosecutors, at least 381 defendants nationally have had homicide convictions thrown out. These convictions were discarded for the most egregious of prosecutorial misbehaviors: either prosecutors concealed evidence suggesting innocence or because they presented evidence they knew to be false. Of the 381 defendants, 67 had been sentenced to death. And nearly 30 of the 67 death row inmates were subsequently freed.

The *Tribune* articles observed that prosecutors can engage in this sort of conduct with virtual impunity. They cite the convictions of two African Americans in upstate New York. The lead prosecutor withheld information in an eyewitness statement from the victim's brother, who stated that the murderers were white.

Box 7.8, *continued*

Why do prosecutors engage in these unethical behaviors? Part of the answer is because they can. Prosecutors have rarely been punished for their misconduct. In the 381 cases cited in the *Tribune*, not one of the prosecutors was convicted of a crime. The *Tribune* noted many saw their careers advance, becoming judges or district attorneys. There is no reasonable check on prosecutors who misbehave, even in the most serious of cases.

These 381 cases may well be the tip of the iceberg. They represent only those cases where misconduct has come to the court's attention and been reversed. It is likely that many cases of misconduct have gone unnoticed. When cases are reversed for misconduct, the names of prosecutors are rarely noted in the decision.

Most troubling is that these cases represent the worst kinds of prosecutorial conduct for the most serious kinds of cases—cases in which an individual's life hangs in the balance. It appears that the outcomes of capital cases are much more vulnerable to error than is widely thought. Common wisdom is that, because murder cases are so important, these are the kinds of cases where an error is least likely to occur. Yet the opposite may be true. One of the *Tribune's* sources said:

> We generally condone a great deal of misconduct when we think it serves the ultimate ends to justice. There's a feeling that is how it works, that it's legitimate to bend the truth sometimes when you are doing it with—quote the greater good unquote—in mind.
> (Armstrong and Possley, 1999:15)

In other words, prosecutors justify their behavior in terms of the ends produced.

And the ends are the most important in murder cases. The noble cause in this way provides a basis for the corruption of prosecutors as it does for the police and is strongest in the most serious cases. Hence, murder cases, thought commonly of as that area of court activity with the strongest defendant protections, may actually be the source of the most serious mistakes by the system, committed in the name of the noble cause, and doubly egregious because they are intentional.

Source: Adapted from Armstrong and Possley, "Break Rules, Be Promoted," January 14, 1999; Possley and Armstrong, "Prosecutors on Trial in DuPage," January 12, 1999.

## *The Strange Morality of College Education*

Police officers increasingly acquire college education. Their education ranges from a few courses at a junior college to advanced degrees in university programs and departments. These programs influence how recruits think about police work. They have become one of the places where officers get their leads.

A widely shared vision of the universities and colleges in the United States is that they are centers for the transmission of liberal and radical ideology. This idea is exaggerated. Are there liberal instructors? Of course. There are conservative instructors as well. Most college instructors aren't particularly interested in politics. A few politicians, such as the former Speaker of the House of Representatives Newt Gingrich (a conservative), have emerged from the ranks of academia, but this happens infrequently.

Liberal instructors complain about conservative politicians. Conservative instructors complain about liberal politicians. Yet the underlying dynamic in a university environment is intellectual freedom, loosely translated as "Leave me alone!" Teachers zealously guard their right to express their views, whether they are liberal or conservative in their political philosophies. Politics don't mobilize faculty. Issues like tenure denial and merit pay mobilize faculty. Like the rest of the working public, university and college faculty are motivated primarily by bread-and-butter issues—salary, job benefits, and working conditions.

A variety of forces in higher education today emphasize the noble cause and, in some instances, can justify the corruption of the noble cause. Three forces lead academics down the path of noble cause: the moral predispositions of criminal justice students, the use of part-time instructors, and funded research in local agencies.

## *The Use of Local Agency Instructors*

Most criminal justice departments make extensive use of part-time instructors. These instructors are typically drawn from local agencies. Their perspective of criminal justice tends to focus on effectiveness and efficiency in doing something about crime. Most departments cannot survive without the use of local agency instructors. Criminal justice departments are widely viewed as cash cows by administrators who want to fill classes with students the cheapest way they can. And most criminal justice departments are relative newcomers in the halls of hallowed academe and have to compete against established departments for increasingly scarce resources. So part-time faculty, typically drawn from local agencies, provide administrators with the best of all worlds: they are cheap, they are motivated to teach, they often get good evaluations from students committed to careers in criminal justice and admire instructors as future employers or colleagues, and they have no messy job protections that interfere with their firing and replacement.

These instructors have a powerful impact on students for two reasons: (1) they tend to teach large introductory classes, and their views can influence many students; and (2) they represent role models for many students, who themselves are seeking a locally based career in criminal justice. They can consequently have an impact on departments out of proportion with their seemingly low status in academia. They often provide stories and real-world examples that tend to reinforce a crime control view of the world. Indeed, if current trends of low budgets and increasing enrollments continue, criminal justice education at the undergraduate level will be increasingly carried out by part-time faculty.

Some of these faculty may be quite skilled. And their contribution to the classroom is significant. However, unlike academy training or other aspects of justice practice, there is virtually no accountability or oversight of their work in higher education. Hence, there are many opportunities for these faculty to espouse values supportive of noble cause corruption (and perhaps get a rousing cheer from their students). The issues that apply to war stories during training, discussed in Chapter 2, apply with equal vigor and importance to part-time instruction in academe. One can say with reasonable confidence that pre-service training is quite concerned about the content of its instruction, recognizing that what it says carries legal weight. Academics would benefit with similar attention to their instruction, certainly in among part-time faculty, but as well among full-time faculty who often pay little heed to the moral issues facing future criminal justicians.

## *The Moral Predispositions of Police Students*

Criminal justice departments are frequently presented with an anomalous instructional environment. The full-time faculty have often been drawn from educational fields that provided a critical overview of criminal justice institutions and agencies. Yet many of their students are seeking careers in criminal justice, and they are already morally predisposed to the noble cause. Faculty who are openly critical of criminal justice risk alienating their students—and more practically, receiving negative student evaluations. One of the authors recalls a critically oriented instructor whose student evaluation simply stated, “This man is dangerous!”

Faculty critical of criminal justice agencies consequently risk negative student evaluations. And poor student evaluations can have a negative impact on young faculty who are not yet tenured and who need to show that they are competent teachers in order to acquire tenure. Instructors find themselves ceding moral ground, emphasizing areas of the noble cause that they find compatible with their beliefs, or sometimes becoming cheerleaders for local agencies, in order to protect their academic careers.

Criminal justice students are not uniform in their commitments to the noble cause. In a survey of 400 criminal justice students from 12 four-year colleges and universities, Krimmel and Tartaro (1999) found significant differences between students who wanted to be police officers and criminal justice students seeking other careers. Students seeking a police career scored significantly higher in five categories: the relevance of the course content to their desired work, protecting the constitution, arresting bad guys, promotion opportunities, and desires to wear a uniform. The category with the greatest difference between police careerists and others was "arrest bad guys," scoring a value of 3.78 for police careerists and 2.76 for others on a 1 to 5 scale. This suggests that, even within the criminal justice student community, police carry the sense of noble cause to a significantly greater degree than other students.

### *Research and Service in Local Agencies*

Criminal justice faculty are responsible for research and service as well as for teaching. When undergoing review for promotion and tenure, full-time faculty's portfolios will be scrutinized closely for the quantity and quality of their research, and for service, to a lesser but nevertheless important degree. One of the primary paths for the development of research and service goes through local agencies.

Faculty will frequently contact an agency about conducting research. The research will be funded by a major funding source, such as the National Institute of Justice if they are fortunate, though the grant-writing skills for funded research typically come later in one's career.

The opportunity to conduct research in an agency can be a sobering experience for younger faculty. It is a "hands-on" experience with real-world criminal justice, and in order to be effective, they must interact with and understand the justice professionals with whom they work. For seasoned faculty members, it is sometimes an opportunity to renew old acquaintances. For all faculty who must conduct research to gain academic recognition and rank, research conducted in criminal justice agencies will sensitize them to the noble cause and practical agency concerns.

## *Forensic Labs*

Mike continues. *Let's talk about crime labs. What kind of message do officers get from crime labs?*

A commander responds. "Our crime lab has state-of-the-art equipment. I don't see the link to noble-cause corruption. What does the science of the lab have to do with value-based decision-making?"

I've heard other departments say, "we are using DNA, we are double-checking our findings, we've got a well-trained research team." So let's talk about crime labs and DNA. You can trust crime labs and DNA, right? Your forensic labs analyze DNA, which has become the cornerstone of modern police technique. And it produces irrefutable evidence. Right? Let's talk about Fort Worth, Oklahoma City, Charleston, Orlando, and Billings.

DNA (deoxyribonucleic acid), the chemical structure that makes up chromosomes, is one of the cornerstones of modern policing. Crime labs use a technique called DNA fingerprinting, which is done by comparing base pairs. Base pairs are bonded nucleotides on opposite sides of DNA strands. Everyone can be uniquely identified by analyzing the pattern of their base pairs. The entire sequence of base pairs is not studied; identification can be accomplished by studying a relatively small number of pairs. DNA can be used for a variety of purposes: it can establish paternity and maternity, and it is quite useful for establishing criminal identification.

Individuals can be identified with a relatively high degree of certainty with DNA testing. However, the use of population markers to identify members of different ethnic groups is a highly uncertain science. Many of the markers for different ethnicities are distributed in unknown patterns, with a great deal of within-group variation. Hence, DNA is not very useful for identifying race and ethnicity. Also, small samples of DNA material are difficult to work with. Because very small samples are amplified, that is, DNA material is grown from small samples in order to have adequate amounts for identification and testing, the potential for error—a lab technician's cell entering the DNA mix, for example—has been a concern (Brinton and Lieberman, 1994).

In the early 2000s, a new problem emerged with DNA testing and more generally with regard to the work carried out by crime laboratories generally. These problems had to do with the interpretation of DNA findings, particularly in how suspects were linked to crimes. The pattern of these findings was that, in every instance, DNA testing incorrectly identified a suspect who was, in fact, not guilty. We believe these were all instances of noble-cause corruption.

Consider the case of Josiah Sutton. He was tried on rape charges in 1999. The witness was the victim, and her testimony was vague. However, the police had the DNA of the rapist from his semen, and they were told that the DNA from the semen came from Sutton. He was convicted and sentenced to prison for 25 years. In December 2002, an audit of the laboratory concluded that technicians had misinterpreted data and maintained inadequate records. "In most cases, they used up all available evidence, preventing defense experts from refuting or verifying their evidence" (Teeter, 2003). His DNA was retested, and the test demonstrated that the semen could not have been his. In January of 2003, genetic testing was suspended at the laboratory. By March, Houston police had turned over 325 cases involving DNA to the district attorney's office, a number that the district attorney said would likely grow. The district attorney's office said that at least 25, including seven on death row, should be retested.

Montana's state crime lab has experienced similar problems. In 1987, Ray Bromgard was convicted for raping an 8-year-old girl. The victim picked him out of a line-up and identified him at trial. The director of the Montana State lab testified that the hairs recovered from the child's bedroom matched "characteristics" of Bromgard's hair (Bohrer, 2002). He stated that the odds that they belonged to anyone else were less than 1 in 10,000. Bromgard was found guilty and spent the next 15 years in prison. He was released in 2002 after a retesting of his DNA proved he was innocent. The director of the crime lab had subsequently moved to Washington State, where he was employed since 1989. In Spokane, an audit was being conducted of about 100 cases on which he had worked.

Next, consider Oklahoma. An Oklahoma City police laboratory scientist was involved in about 3,000 cases from 1980 to 1993. She was hired in 1980 after training at the FBI academy in Quantico and the Serological Research Institute in Emeryville, California. Both Oklahoma State and the FBI were conducting separate investigations after an FBI report contradicted her findings on a 16-year-old case in which a man had been convicted of rape based on her testimony of the similarity of his hair to hair found at the crime scene. The man was exonerated and was due to be released.

Of particular concern were 23 capital trials in which the testimony of the Oklahoma City lab scientist helped gain convictions. Eleven of the inmates had been executed. The other 12 were on death row. All cases were being reassessed, and the governor stated that no inmates would be executed until the scientist's role was reviewed (Yardley, 2001).

The scientist's work had even been criticized by other forensic scientists. The chief forensic scientist at the regional crime laboratory in Kansas City, Missouri, had lodged a complaint about her to the Southwest Association of Forensic Scientists and had offered conflicting testimony to Ms. Gilchrist's in one case. She was warned by the association to distinguish personal opinion from fact. And the Association of Crime Scene Reconstruction had expelled her for unethical behavior. As Barry Scheck, of the Innocence Project, noted, she had long been recognized as a problem. He attributed some of the blame to a "failure of oversight by the district attorney's office" (Yardley, 2001).

In Charleston, West Virginia, Fred Zain, a crime lab chemist, was being investigated, and seven of his convictions were overturned, with several lawsuits pending. The state had paid "at least 6.5 million to settle lawsuits" (Associated Press, 2001). Troubles regarding the chemist first appeared in 1992, when DNA testing showed that a man convicted of two life terms plus 335 years could not have committed the crimes. The chemist had claimed to use a test that, according to a report, the State Police did not have the ability to perform. The man was exonerated and received a settlement of $1 million. In another case, two men were accused of killing three people and were convicted in part because the chemist testified about blood found on an axe. In a 1997 hearing on whether one of the men should receive a new trial, the chemist refused to discuss his tests. Another scientist hired by the defense found that the blood was not human and the axe had not been tested. Fred Zain died of cancer in December 2002. His trial was postponed indefinitely.

In Orlando, Florida, a state crime-lab analyst falsified DNA data involving an unknown number of criminal cases in Florida. The analyst, John Fitzpatrick, worked as a blood and DNA specialist at the Orlando crime laboratory of the Florida Department of Law Enforcement. He has admitted to "switching DNA samples and changing data in a test designed to check the quality of work at the lab, according to an internal investigative report. He was either fired or dismissed shortly after that—the agency would not say which" (Stutzman, 2002).

One of the cases in Orlando involved a triple homicide. The Circuit Judge temporarily delayed for two weeks a DNA hearing in the case of suspect Michael Reynolds because of concerns that the analyst handled the evidence. Prosecutors did not have eyewitnesses or a murder weapon, and there was scant evidence to link the suspect to the crime. Their case was largely based on the testimony of the lab in Orlando, who said that blood spots found near two of the victims contained Reynolds' DNA. As Stutzman (2002:1) noted:

> the reason the judge halted Thursday's hearing was because David Baer, the FDLE senior analyst who pegged Reynolds as the likely source of DNA at the crime scene, could not say whether Fitzpatrick had been involved in any of the lab work. During the test that Fitzpatrick admitted rigging, he changed data in a computer unbeknownst to Baer, who also was involved in the test. "The bottom line is he flat-out cheated," said Steve Laurence, Reynolds' lawyer. "There should be a major investigation going on down there."

These cases bear certain features in common. They tended to involve individuals with known problems among their own staff but who had risen quickly in their organizations because of their work supporting the prosecutors and police. At least two were trained at the FBI academy in Quantico. Problems with their work had earned reputations among judges and professional associations. However, oversight by local prosecutors was inadequate; they continued their work until problems became so egregious that they could no longer be overlooked.

MIKE ASKS: *What do these cases have in common?*

A Captain responded. "These labs were doing sloppy work. They were unprofessional and undertrained." Mike thought about this for a moment. *No, the problem was not that they were undertrained. Look at the outcome of all these cases. In every instance, there was a finding in favor of the guilt of the suspect without evidence or with inconclusive evidence. It wasn't like we have an unprofessional group who are contaminating evidence, the result of which would be that too many people are having their DNA ruined and bad people are being released. The opposite is happening. No one's getting off. No, the issue is not that lab scientists were untrained. The issue is that they were caught.*

Another officer says, "These are just a few big-city cases. We have well-trained forensic chemists in our state lab. We use them all the time and we can count on their work."

Oh, I agree. There are many talented forensic scientists out there. I've seen them do magic with evidence. But what you need to ask yourself is, what are they using their talent for? Are they producing findings that match the science or are they producing findings to get bad people off the streets? You have to be very careful here. Maybe you have no problem with the crime lab you use, but how would you know if you did? Can anyone here tell me how much your crime lab paid out in settlements last year? How many cases did they testify for that have been overturned in the past five years?

What you should be beginning to realize is that you are embedded in an environment dense with noble-cause temptations. Everyone wants to get the bad guy off the street. Here, we see that your crime labs are helping you. They're doing a good job. Sometimes they come up with results that they think the police and the prosecutor want. They are rewarded for good work that leads to convictions. Careers are made. And sometimes innocent people are going to prison for very long times. Are you uncomfortable yet? You should be.

## *Sergeants*

What kind of lead do officers get from their supervisors? Not from brass, but from their sergeants? Don't they get efficiency and effectiveness? What do sergeants want from officers? Good reports, right? Good, legal, case-solid reports. Reports that aren't screwed up but get convictions.

You have to make sure that you write up the report just right, to get the conviction. None of this "But Sarge, that's not exactly what happened." Sarge'll look at that. "I don't give a shit," he'll say. "You've got to do this, and this, and this."

You're putting pressure on your people to be efficient and effective. No messy complicating factors. Suppose an officer writes it up like it really happened. You pat 'im on the back when he goes out and tries real hard, and the case gets dropped. And the sergeant says to him "Dumbshit. If you'd done what I'd told you to do, you'd have a conviction." So the case is dropped, the sergeant's pissed, the prosecutor's pissed. What's this good officer going to do the next time?

Sergeants are line supervisors. They straddle two worlds, the world of administration and the world of the street. Their loyalties may reflect one or the other of these domains but typically not both. **Station-house sergeants** tend to see their work in terms of controlling the conduct of their officers on the beat. They are interested in the production of reports, quotas, rules, and regulations (Van Maanen, 1997). **Street sergeants,** on the other hand, take a more active role in their officers' assignments. Station-house sergeants are also more likely to be promoted. Once promoted, they focus on the production of statistics rather than craft excellence.

> Selection procedures favor administratively inclined candidates, and those candidates, when bestowed with the sergeant rank, tend to take a relatively remote supervisory stance toward the supervised. Matters of subordinate craft and competence in the field are not of great interest to station house sergeants. More often than not, these sergeants direct and evaluate the performance of their men on the basis of official, albeit indirect, productivity measures (e.g., calls answered, tardiness, tickets amassed, arrests logged, citizen complaints filed, street stops, miles logged, sick or vacation days taken, etc.).
>
> (Van Maanen, 1997:180–181)

Station-house sergeants are not responsible for quality in the production of police work. This is not because sergeants don't like good work; like other officers, they appreciate a good bust and a difficult case solved. But sergeants need to accumulate the kinds of numbers and the reputation for toughness that will get them promoted. Officers everywhere know that they have to produce activity for their sergeants. It is a characteristic of the authority and promotional structure of American police organizations. In Box 7.9, Skolnick and Fyfe (1993) capture the implications of the way authority is number-driven.

Box 7.9

**The Numerology of Authority**

[The] objectification and quantification of police work—How many arrests? How many field citations? How many tickets? How many minutes and seconds responding to calls? How many pounds and ounces of drugs seized? How many dollars was it worth? How many outstanding robbery cases did the shooting solve?—trickles down to the department's lowest level, its patrol cars and hoof beats. When that occurs, everybody up and down the line becomes driven by what the New York cops used to call "big numbers," without regard to whether they accomplish any desirable end. When that happens, street cops, who know from every source that they have been assigned to their department's dirtiest job, also learn that their supervisors are interested only in the figures on their activity reports, not in what the police may have done to put them there.

Those are bad messages to give repeatedly to people who are expected to serve professionally as first responders to some of society's most pressing and sensitive crises. It tells them that the cardinal sin is not to break the rules but to be caught breaking the rules.

Source: Jerome Skolnick and James Fyfe, *Above the Law*, 1993:189–190.

## *Other Officers: Ends Control and the Code of Silence*

MIKE: *We saw this morning* (see Chapter 4) *that officers quickly become committed to good ends and rapidly learn to disrespect due process. They get this from other officers. They get it during and after pre-service training.*

New officers go through a socialization process. It's like family. When we look at who is most responsible for the behavior of a young person, we look at the family. The police are the same way. Look at the family. Officers are socialized by other officers, and these other officers have been embedded in this crime control environment for a very long time. So officers look to family, and they learn values that support the corruption of noble cause. And they learn to be secret.

"That sounds like my teenagers," says one commander. Officers laugh.

I'm not saying your officers are like children. I'm saying that they're new to the actual practice of police work. A lot of bad things can happen to them. And their family takes care of them.

Many observers of the police have described what they call a code of silence. By **code of silence,** we mean the inability of outsiders, including police managers, to find out information about incidents involving line officers. The code of silence is marked by officers who refuse to talk about what other officers do, even when it involves illegal behavior. It is viewed by managers as a principal source of resistance to police reform.

The code of silence, we think, is closely linked to efforts to control "ends." It represents an effort on the part of officers to control the outcomes of events. By erecting a "code of silence" around street happenings involving officers, a principal threat to ends-oriented behavior is removed; managers and the public will not know about questionable police behavior that might result in review or negative publicity.

The code of silence, in other words, is a mechanism to control information. Yet even the code of silence may sometimes fail. Box 7.10, an example of a crack in the code of silence, shows how ends cannot be controlled.

Box 7.10

**The Wall of Silence and Perjury**

Sometimes the wall of silence cracks. Under enough pressure, it can crumble. In the following incident, officers tried to cover up the beating of a suspect who was actually an undercover officer.

The incident began when a large number of officers rushed to the scene of a shooting, having mistakenly heard that a police officer had

Box 7.10, *continued*

been injured. The suspects led the police officers on a ten mile chase and eventually were cornered in a cul-de-sac. In the ensuing mêlée, some of the officers confused an undercover officer for one of the suspects and attacked him. He was treated for a concussion, kidney damage, and multiple cuts to his face.

The official report did not report the attack by police. Instead, the official report stated that the undercover officer had lost his footing and cracked his head. None of the officers on the scene came forward to tell the truth at a subsequent hearing, in spite of the fact that several of them were in the vicinity and were involved in the pursuit. Two dozen officers reported that they saw no beating. One of the officers on the scene, however, testified that he had not seen the undercover officer pursue the suspects. He was subsequently convicted of perjury and obstruction of justice in a federal court.

The event has all the indications of noble-cause revenge—emotionally charged officers, acting on erroneous information that another officer was injured, attack a suspect. Two mistakes were made, however. No officer was injured, and the suspect was another officer. The wall of silence descended to protect the officers in the case. Yet it was not enough to protect all the officers; one was convicted of serious federal charges. This example shows that, even when the wall of silence is invoked to control outcomes, outcome control is not always possible.

Source: Adapted from the *New York Times* Online, "Officer Convicted of Perjury."

Mike continues. *If you are having trouble with an officer you are probably not going to hear about it until all hell is about to break loose. Here's what you will hear. One of your sergeants comes up to you and says "Officer Hardy asked for a transfer." That may be the only thing you hear.*

Mike concludes this section of ethics training. *You have academia leading people to believe that all they have to do is unfurl their moral flag and everything will be fine. You have the courts and prosecutors telling them that all they have to do is be efficient and effective. Then everything will be fine. Their Sergeant is telling them to do the paperwork right, make the arrests, be efficient, and everything will be alright. Sometimes their own crime labs are willing to bend the rules to make their evidence work. Educators aren't watching what officers are taught . . . who knows what is learned there? And their family is taking care of them, and the family has been in the crime control environment for a very long time. They're getting their leads from these groups. How can they NOT*—Mike taps the crime-control side of the curve all the way over on the crime-control side—*be way over here? How can they be any other way?*

When officers are hired, they are already on the crime-control side. Important references in their environment encourage behavior that is focused on the ends of crime control. Prosecutors, sergeants, crime labs, college educators, and other officers—all people that in different ways represent authority and command respect from line officers—emphasize work that is passionate and effective. It all reinforces the temptations for noble cause corruption. Consequently, from an organizational point of view, something has to go wrong for line officers to move back to the middle of the crime-control/due process continuum, toward a balanced perspective. There's not a way for them to get there in their natural working environment.

# 8

# Police Culture, Ends Orientation, and Noble-Cause Corruption

## Key Terms

| | |
|---|---|
| avenging angel syndrome | police culture |
| boomerang effect | George Floyd |
| the code | rotten apple theory |
| crevasse | scientific management |
| deceptive practices | street cop culture |
| excessive force | street environment |
| management cop culture | Type 2 drug corruption |
| operative assumption of guilt | victimless crime |
| police brutality | warping effect |
| | solidarity |

## Introduction

This chapter explores the complex interplay between police culture, noble-cause corruption, and the ethical dilemmas that arise in the pursuit of justice. Central to the discussion is the crevasse—a deep divide between street cop culture and management cop culture—where solidarity among line officers fosters a code of silence that shields misconduct from oversight. Within this environment, officers often adopt an operative assumption of guilt, justifying deceptive practices and excessive force as necessary tools in the war on crime.

DOI: 10.4324/9781003626916-11

## Part I: The Crevasse and Police Culture

### *The Crevasse*

> Mike thinks for a minute. This is always a difficult topic. *Do your officers understand the crevasse in your department?*

Note that Mike does not ask commanders if a crevasse exists in their department. It exists in all departments, yet every department thinks that it is uniquely their problem. He has noted that outsiders like himself are often brought in to talk about ethics when managers are having problems with line officers and they don't know how to deal with them. Nor, when he gives the same talk to line officers that he does to commanders, does Mike ask if they know about the crevasse. They live it. Do they understand it? Usually they do not; they think of the crevasse in terms of promotional unfairness and special favors from the command staff.

Every department that we know about has some sort of a crevasse in it. Call it a chasm, a barrier, a conflict, management versus street culture, it describes the same thing. Line officers are on one side of the crevasse. Managers and commanders are on the other side. New sergeants fall into it, and they often don't understand what happened. They don't yet comprehend the distrust their lower-ranking officers feel in their presence, the silence with which sometimes they are now greeted, or how their former friends are off talking to each other when he walks down the hall. They can't believe that they are no longer one of the guys. They will learn in time.

Managers don't know about their agency problems because these problems are on the other side of the crevasse. What's the **crevasse?** By crevasse, we mean two things: the "official" rank-determined boundary between line officers and everyone with a rank of lieutenant and above, and the antagonisms and conflicts that occur across that boundary. We use the word "crevasse" instead of a more neutral term like "space" or "distance" because a crevasse is a wide, treacherous rift whose dimensions can't be seen by outsiders and because its glacial connotations are an apt description of management-line relations in many police departments.

The crevasse can be almost undetectable. Managers often do not hear about problems at the line level. But it can be present nevertheless. However, it is not always a silent barrier. In its strongest manifestations, line personnel will openly challenge commanders in the organization.

Unfortunately, crevasses are present in varying degrees in most municipal police agencies in the United States. A recruit's first exposure to the crevasse is when he or she is told by a TO to "forget everything you learned in Peace Officer Standards and Training (POST): I'm gonna show you how we really do it on the street." What this means is that the TO is going to show them how to act outside department policy and get away with it. It is also, as we have described in this book, the first loyalty test that really counts.

Elizabeth Reuss-Ianni (1983) captured the idea of the crevasse in her book the *Two Cultures of Policing*. Her core notion of the conflict across the crevasse—across the two cultures—is presented in Box 8.1.

Box 8.1

**The Two Cultures of Policing**

The organization of policing is "best described and understood in terms of the interactions of two distinct cultures: a street cop culture and a management cop culture. These two cultures are increasingly characterized by competing and often conflicting perspectives on procedure and practice in policing."

Source: Reuss-Ianni, E. (1983). *Two Cultures of Policing: Street Cops and Management Cops.* New York, NY: Routledge, p. 1.

These two cultures, she argued, are marked by conflicting value systems. The **management cop culture** is characterized by a belief in principles of scientific management. **Scientific management** means that the department should be organized hierarchically and that employment and advancement should be based on merit. An individual's formal role on the organizational chart is written and documented. Managers are concerned with crime but have a different perspective on it than do line officers, who have to deal with its immediate impact. Managers have a citywide focus. They have to allocate resources throughout the system based upon a system of priority. They must "weigh and establish those priorities within political, social, and economic constraints and justify them within each of these contexts as well as within the police context" (Reuss-Ianni, 1983:7). Law enforcement is a carefully planned, well-designed, and efficiently implemented program in which individual officers' patrol units are impersonal resources to be used for the advancement of interrelated organizational goals.

**Street cop culture,** on the other hand, finds its meanings in the traditions of the department. The organizing ethos of street police is the idea of the "good old days" of policing when police were respected by the public, officers could count on each other, and managers were part of the police family. Relationships are familial rather than bureaucratic, and officers count on informal friendships and alliances to do their work. Officers believe that they must protect each other from administrative oversight. A central organizing principle of line officer behavior is called CYA (cover your ass).

Mike discusses Reuss-Ianni's concept of culture. *Your officers have rules. You used to play by these rules. A lot of times commanders forget these rules. An observer of the police once wrote them down. Let's go over them.*

Reuss-Ianni identified 21 precepts of police work. The first 12 define relationships with other cops. The second nine describe relations to superior officers. Her precepts are presented in Box 8.2.

Box 8.2

**The Cops Code: Reuss-Ianni**

*Rules Defining Relationships with Other Cops*

1. Watch out for your partner first and then the rest of the guys working that tour.
2. Don't give up another cop.
3. Show balls.
4. Be aggressive when you have to but don't be too eager.
5. Don't get involved in anything in another guy's sector.
6. Hold up your end of the work.
7. If you get caught off base, don't implicate anybody else.
8. Make sure the other guys know if another cop is dangerous or "crazy."
9. Don't trust a new guy until you have checked him out.
10. Don't tell anybody else more than they have to know; it could be bad for you, and it could be bad for them.
11. Don't talk too much or too little. Both are suspicious.
12. Don't leave work for the next tour.

*Rules Relating Street Cops to Bosses*

1. Protect your ass. (If the system wants to get you, it will.)
2. Don't make waves. Supervisors pay attention to troublemakers.
3. Don't give them too much activity. Don't be too eager.
4. Keep out of the way of any boss from outside your precinct.
5. Don't look for favors just for yourself.
6. Don't take on the patrol sergeant by yourself.
7. Know your bosses. Who's working and who has the desk?
8. Don't do the bosses' work for them.
9. Don't trust bosses to look out for your interest.

Source: Reuss-Ianni, E. (1983). Two Cultures of Policing: Street Cops and Management Cops. New York, NY: Routledge.

Mike continues. *Do you remember these? You may no longer be line officers, but your line officers still think this way. And they're applying these rules to you. Just like you did 10 years ago to your supervisors.*

The crevasse is a barrier created and sustained by line officers to protect themselves from managers. It is maintained by their practical code of departmental conduct, a code that provides rules of thumb regarding who to talk to, who to avoid, how much work to do, and how to treat other officers. It limits the ability to influence them.

*I'm making the case that your officers make value-based decisions. You don't hear about it because the code keeps you from hearing about it. So if you aren't hearing about problems, don't think that everything is OK.* When Mike says **the code,** he's referring to the code of secrecy stated by Reuss-Ianni above. The code, in its most general sense, means that the activities of line officers (and their closest friends) on a particular shift are not to be discussed with others.

The crevasse is in place, in large part, so that line officers can protect themselves from managers. What are they protecting themselves from? To answer this question, we will spend some time discussing police culture.

## *The Crevasse and Police Culture*

In Chapter 1, we discussed police culture, focusing on how imported values are framed and intensified in the conduct of daily police work. Manning (1989:360) has described **police culture** as the "accepted practices, rules, and principles of conduct that are situationally applied, and generalized rationales and beliefs." Culture emphasizes particular "contours" of its environment, that is, particular aspects of daily work activities that are important for defining police culture. These contours include uncertainty, personal autonomy, and authority.

Culture, in the form described in Chapter 1, is a particularly street-level phenomenon. It is not uniform across an agency. Indeed, some authors argue that there are different cultures in a police department, and these cultures are determined by rank. As we noted earlier, Reuss-Ianni distinguished between street cop and management cop culture. These cultures were antagonistic to each other, and elements of street culture focused on beat responsibility and protecting officers from command oversight. Manning (1989) suggested that police organizations contain three distinct but overlapping cultures, a command or executive level culture, a middle-management culture, and a line-level culture. Police culture, as Manning (1989) observed, tends to isolate its members and emphasize their shared identity. Officers are isolated from the friends they grew up with, mostly because rotating and late shifts segregate the police from the 8-to-5 work-a-day world that most of the working world inhabits. In the conduct of their daily routines, however, they are separated from the public they serve in a moral way: they believe that it is their responsibility to control their assigned territories, including all the people and places in it. In that world, citizens are to be protected, the public served, and evil overcome. It is about placing one's life on the line for strangers and running toward the tower. Police do these things for citizens, not with them. Cops consequently inhabit a world of their own, separated morally from the citizens they serve, from the day that they enter the police academy until the day they retire. Their primary identity is a shared sense of copness (Ahern, 1972). They look in a mirror, adjust their belt and their hat, and they see a cop looking back. They are the police, and they protect and serve.

## *Layers of Street Culture*

Think of police culture as an onion. It has a heart that animates every police officer and gives meaning to police work. The heart is how police officers feel and think about their work, how they celebrate their victories and mourn their losses. It is how they do their work and how it is meaningful to them. Mostly, it is about their commitment to the noble cause and how that commitment is animated in training, in daily police work and in conversations with other police officers.

The "heart" of officers' values, particularly their commitment to the noble cause and the belief that they can make a contribution to society, are imported from broader society. The layers over the heart of the onion, however, are cultural creations, which means that they come about from the daily experiences of police work and how the experiences are shared by officers.

The first layer, the layer that encloses the heart and animates its pulse, is their assigned beat, romantically called the **street environment.** This is where patrol officers and detectives carry out their daily work, and the term refers to the various kinds of people line officers come into contact with. Meaningful street work is about suspects and troublemakers. It is doing something about bad guys—responding to calls, being involved in the chase, making an arrest, the "huff and puff of the chase" as some have called it. Police territories—their assigned spaces—are accepted in a profoundly moral sense. They are responsible for their assigned geography. All of its problems are their problems. Their reputations and self-esteem rise and fall on how well they control their territories. "Many officers want to be considered part of the police family and, in some instances, will go to great lengths to obtain such an honor—a distinction that often requires unconditional loyalty, occasionally demonstrated by an officer's willingness to violate the law or department policy, including the application of coercive force" (Elliott and Pollack, 2014:243, in Fitch, 2014).

Suspects are bad guys, and troublemakers are frequently called "assholes" (Van Maanen, 1978a). Cops don't see a lot of differences between criminal suspects and troublemakers, who are often believed to be criminal wannabes or whose crimes aren't yet known to police. "Assholes" are troublemakers who openly criticize the police, who are deliberately rude, or who do not show adequate respect. Sometimes, in racially divided communities, police use ethnicity or skin color to identify who they think is an asshole.

For a few officers, all citizens are assholes and potential criminals. These officers have what is called a "siege mentality." For them, there are no friends other than brother and sister officers. The world contains no joy, only dark threats everywhere. For "siege mentality" officers, police culture has ceased to be a source of celebration and growth and has become a psychological prison.

The second layer around the heart of the onion is uncertainty. Manning (1989) recognized the central role uncertainty played in police culture. A psychological sense of uncertainty was intimately tied to the external world of disorder and risk. An officer's external focus on order protected him or her from the unpredictable. Crank (2004a) identified five different aspects of uncertainty that he called "themes of the unknown." They are presented in Box 8.3.

Box 8.3

### Themes of the Unknown

**Suspicion**. Police work carries two different, opposing kinds of suspicion. Legal suspicion is based on a legal standard of reasonableness and is determined by an officer's ability to articulate reasons why he or she thinks that a suspect might be a danger to a police officer or might have committed or is about to be involved in a crime. On the other hand, sixth-sense suspicion is the ability to identify wrongdoing from the most trivial of clues. It is based on intuition, not fact, though when it is highly honed, it will produce solid evidence. This latter type is the special craft of police work, and officers who construct cases from the most seemingly innocent of clues gain a great deal of status in their organization.

**Danger and Its Anticipation**. Thinking about and preparing for danger are central features of police work. Police officers confront not only real dangers but also operate in a working environment where danger can occur unpredictably. The threat of danger, Crank noted, mobilizes much of what the police are about, and danger realized unifies the police.

**Unpredictability and Situational Uncertainty**. Situational uncertainty refers to the ambiguity police face both with regard to their daily work routines and with regard to the organization itself. The unpredictability inherent in all police work underscores the need for apprenticeship-type

Box 8.3, *continued*

training. Common sense among the police lies in their abilities to negotiate their way through uncertain settings to a successful, injury-free conclusion.

**Turbulence and Edge Control.** Turbulence means two things. First, in a police-citizen interaction, a great deal of activity can happen in a short period of time—in bursts of energy. Second, activity unfolds unpredictably. Turbulence can be fun, up to a point, and make police work exciting. However, activities can become so turbulent that they are physically dangerous. By the "edge" is meant the point at which turbulence turns into physical danger. Police do not like to go beyond the edge because events can escalate up to the point where someone is killed. Edge control refers to the skills police officers have to contain turbulence below the edge of significant danger. It is a central skill to police work and important to understanding the way police officers view danger. A great deal of police work is about edge control.

**Seduction.** The theme seduction conveys the idea that police work, especially danger and the thrill of the chase, is attractive to police officers. It's more than excitement. Crank (187) describes a retiring officer looking back over his career: "It is a view that still triggers in him a brief surge of adrenaline, a sense of being in special places, dark corners, dealing with wild things, and riding the wind."

Source: Adapted from John P. Crank (2004). *Understanding Police Culture*. New York, NY: Routledge.

The third layer around the onion's heart is the strong sense of solidarity that police officers feel. Their sense of **solidarity,** what we call the "mask of a thousand faces," is often attributed to camaraderie, the sense of coming together in the face of danger. Certainly, individuals who share dangerous work have high levels of camaraderie (Lyng, 1990). The perceptions of real and potential danger are a shared bond among police officers. Solidarity is also reinforced by the perceptions of many officers that they are isolated from and in conflict with many elements of the public. Both the isolation felt by officers and the conflict and resentment they feel toward many outside groups is a powerful stimulus to a shared sense of identity (Coser, 1956). Constant daily contact with such groups as the courts, criminals, media, and unfriendly motorists contribute to police solidarity.

The fourth layer is described by themes (strategies and tactics) used by line officers to protect themselves from external oversight. These themes represent ways, widely observed in many police organizations, that line officers avoid observation and control. These themes emerge when line personnel think that particular groups interfere with their ability to do their day-to-day work. One such group is the court system. Police everywhere tend to believe that the legal system is soft on crime, and some of them develop a repertoire of "street justice" skills and techniques so that they can both punish offenders and avoid the courts. Police officers also develop strategies to get around due process constraints on their behavior.

The most important group that line officers protect themselves from are their own administrators and commanders, sometimes simply called brass. Officers tend to have a powerful distrust of their departmental managers (Crank and Caldero, 1991). The influence of influential outside groups, the mayor for example, or the press, is translated into policy through the department's chain of command. Consequently, many of the frustrations line officers have toward outside groups are also focused on the department itself.

By recognizing layers of culture, an observer can understand how the working world of the street officer is insulated from and resistant to control by police supervisors. The values most central to line officers, the "noble cause" heart of the onion, are encased by the first layer, which is their daily work, dealing with bad guys, and the moral sense of responsibility they feel over their territories. The middle layers create a special identity, a sense of solidarity in the "outsider" status felt by many officers and from the unpredictable danger that characterizes their work. The outermost layers of the onion enable police to protect themselves from external influences, particularly the upper management levels of the organization itself, so that they can maintain their moral control over their territories.

## *Culture and Secrecy*

When we look at street officers as inheritors of a cultural setting distinct from managers, the difficulties that reformers have encountered in their efforts to change the police become apparent. The outermost layers of police culture protect line officers from oversight so that they can continue to focus their day-to-day energies on that which is closest to their heart—the noble cause. Efforts to change the police, vis-à-vis the courts, departmental policy, chain-of-command, or due process procedures, will tend to have either a boomerang or warping effect. The **boomerang effect** occurs when efforts to change the police increase the resistance of line officers, who develop strategies that makes change more difficult in the long term. Many observers, for example, have noted that the effect of the "due process" revolution of the Warren Court in the 1960s, aimed at controlling police misbehavior, was an increase in police strategies designed to circumvent the Court's decisions.

The **warping effect** is created when police culture adapts to and assimilates proposed and intended changes into its own values, thus shifting the effects of changes in unplanned ways. For example, states increasingly require due process to be taught as a component of POST training. Due process instruction is typically taught in two-hour or four-hour blocks of classes. Sometimes an instructor will make a derogatory comment about rights for criminals, or tell a story about how Joe Bum was released on a technicality, only to commit a more serious crime. These stories subvert the purpose of training by emphasizing that, while it is important to follow the letter of the law, at least on paper, it is more important to believe in the noble cause. POST training thus can become a tool for the subversion of the law through the telling of stories hostile to due process. It's not an optimistic vision for people who want to reform the police by changing the training they receive.

Let's put this discussion in perspective. The hiring process results in police recruits with a general worldview and a POST and TO training process which selectively highlights elements of that worldview. The result is an officer committed to an end, not a means. Police culture nurtures noble cause and protects officers from efforts to control it. When the "means" of policing—due process, civil rights, and department policy—interfere with the noble cause, then the culture shrouds police behavior in protective secrecy. Reform efforts, whether through POST or through department policy, tend to boomerang or warp.

We can see from this discussion that the crevasse between police managers and line personnel is an important aspect of police culture. If managers want to change policing, if they want to do something about the crevasse, they must work with, not against, police culture.

> Mike describes police culture, its relationship to hiring, and the role of commanders in the hiring process. *If you understand police culture, if you really, really understand it, you see how it is constructed around the noble cause. Police officers are hired so that they can protect the weak and hurt the mean and the bad.*

For a police officer, local police culture can be a wonderful thing. It is how police celebrate their work. It carries all the stories, the successes, the tricks and gambits, the history and habits of a department. But it also can be a dark master. When culture is in the service of noble-cause corruption, police departments have a problem with line behavior that they can't control.

For commanders in departments where police culture hides corruption, it's almost impossible to find out. Commanders find themselves operating on the logic of good faith, hope against hope that they aren't hearing about problems at the street level because there aren't any.

> Mike provides the following warning for commanders. *You may hear a request for assignment change and ignore it. Yet this may well be the only sign of internal problems. Here's a sign that problems are emerging: a few officers begin quietly requesting changes of assignments. Has this ever happened to you?*

The corrupted noble cause is the source of a great deal of secrecy that is associated with the "dark" side of police culture (Kappeler et al., 1994), which is why commanders don't hear about problems.

*Let me ask you a question*, Mike says to the commanders. *Do you have patrol officers wolf-packing routine stops?*

One of the commanders responds. "We have some dangerous stops sometimes. We went off two-person vehicles a few years ago."

Mike pauses for a moment. A thin, dark smile creases his lips. *I get that a lot. If your officers are wolf-packing, you've got a problem. And none of them are going to tell you.*

## Part II: What Happens on the Other Side of the Crevasse: Kinds of Noble-Cause Corruption

Managers, though having worked their way up through the rank and file, adapt to the needs and philosophies appropriate to their current rank. They adapt to management culture, as Reuss-Ianni noted, and use the organization to carry out the values that make good policing. They sometimes forget what happens on the other side of the crevasse. They know that line culture can be a powerfully insulating force, shielding line officers from the scrutiny of commanders, but they tend to forget why. This section examines what it is that is being shielded.

In this section, we discuss various types of noble-cause situations. All of these situations represent efforts to achieve good ends. But they also create many opportunities for noble-cause corruption. Some are clearly illegal; others are in grey areas, in a netherworld somewhere between legality and illegality. But they create temptations to go after good ends that can involve illegal behavior.

### *Racial Profiling*

Mike broaches a topic that is always controversial. He takes a minute to begin. *Do you ever read in the local paper that cops are making racially motivated stops? That they're racist? Do your papers ever say that?* He knows this topic angers officers and commanders. Their patrol officers may be using race to make stops, but they don't recognize it.

One commander responds. "I read that. Our officers are making good stops. They're finding drugs and getting drugs off the streets."

Another: "I really get irritated when I hear that we are racist. I think it shows a real lack of understanding. We are making good stops and good arrests."

Mike recognized the implication: Be careful here.

Mike is not careful. *It is time to get it all out on the table. You are facing editorials that accuse you of racism. The city is paying money to litigants because of the stops you make. The press and lawyers, maybe the State Police, and maybe the Feds, are combing through your records to see if they can find a pattern of stops that suggests racial motivation. If it's not happening to you, well, it could. It could happen to any department.*

"Are you saying that we are making stops based on race?"

You're not making stops based on race? Race is not involved when an officer decides to make a stop? Let's see. You have a patrol officer flashing vehicles. A vehicle drives by with a driver with dark skin, and it's an expensive vehicle. The vehicle is on a highway known to be a drug courier route. It catches his interest. He follows it, and he notices that the license is partially covered with mud, even though the rest of the vehicle is clean. Should that officer make a stop?

"The license is inconsistent with the vehicle. That's a good stop. We train for that. I would want a look at the interior."

Mike looks at him. *It was a good stop?*

"You bet. Maybe courier activity on the highway. Expensive vehicle. Dirty license."

Let's take a step back. *Why did the officer make the stop?*

"The officer was trained to look for drugs. He acted out of his training."

*What was that thing* (Mike opens his hands widely) *that motivated the stop? Why was the officer interested in that car? If Lieutenant Johnson over there was driving the car, would you make the stop?*

The officer looks over at the Commander. "I'd cavity search him too." Everyone laughs.

Mike continues. *The car was stopped because the driver was black. Isn't that the case? You have all your ducks lined up. Professional training, drug courier indications. But the stop was because he was black.*

"We can use race if it is a part of a broader drug courier profile. We can look for gang members carrying drugs."

Sure, sure. But that's not what happened. He was selected for the stop because he was black. That was the reason. If he had been white, the officer would not have given him a second look. What you need to understand is that your officers are racial profiling, and they're doing it all the time. Are they racist? No. They're doing what they were trained to do.

"Wait. We don't train to racial profile."

Didn't you just say that race is OK if it is part of a drug courier profile in which a number of indicators are used? Whether you realize it or not, you're training your young recruits to use race to initiate a stop. Race is the first thing they notice, and once they see that, they take a closer look. It's not racism, but race is what it's all about. Your officers are doing drug courier profiling by profiling for race. And that's why, when the press and the attorney general's office looks for a racial pattern of stops, they will find that pattern.

Profiling is traced to the 1970s, when it was originally developed to identify potential airline drug couriers. A DEA agent, Paul Markonni, developed a profile to facilitate surveillance use at Detroit Metropolitan Airport (Lersch, 2002). Markonni did not use race as a component of the profile but used a mixture of other attributes, such as nervousness, paying for tickets in cash, traveling to or arriving from a destination considered a "place of origin for cocaine, heroin, or marijuana" (Lersch, 2002:68).

Drug profiling on the highways can be traced to the early 1980s (Crank and Rehm, 1994). The New Mexico State Police, in 1983, was the first department to formally use courier profiles as a component of its highway interdiction policy. New Jersey and New York followed in 1985. Highway profiling, it should be noted, is fundamentally different from airport profiling. Unlike airports, stopping a vehicle on a highway is a seizure and consequently protected by the Fourth Amendment of the Constitution. Officers have to establish suspicion both for the stop and for a subsequent search. Generally, a stop itself does not constitute reasonable suspicion for a subsequent search. However, after a stop, officers are frequently trained to look for particular items. The Illinois State Police (ISP), for example, received drug intervention training that included the following:

> (1) observation and stopping techniques, (2) conversational approaches to suspected violators, (3) discussion of legal issues related to search and seizure, (4) common concealment locations, (5) use of drugscreening canines, (6) methodology used by drug traffickers, (7) discussion of seizure and forfeiture alternatives, and (8) discussion and utilization of information provided by El Paso Intelligence Center (including EPIC checks during routine stops).
>
> (Crank and Rehm, 1994)

The ISP claimed a high rate of success for their hits. However, one should ask what constitutes a successful "hit." Crank and Rehm (1994) noted that the Illinois State Police, under "Operation Valkyrie," were able to show statistics suggesting overall success in drug interdiction stops. Their reanalysis of data suggested several qualifications to this success. They noted that, in 65.4 percent of the stops, the estimated street value of the drug found was $50 or less. At the other end of the spectrum, 18 percent recorded hits in excess of $500 street value. They also noted that the program expanded 553 percent between 1985 and 1989, the years for which they had data. However, the value of the average hit dropped slightly but significantly over this period. Moreover, the ISP identified several successful stops even when drugs were not found; in 27.8 percent of the cases, the estimated street value of the confiscated drug was 0, suggesting no drugs were found. Under the category "Confiscated drug type,

"None reported" was noted in 35.1 percent of the cases. Crank and Rehm concluded that Operation Valkyrie, as practiced in Illinois, fell disproportionately on small-time users, and though some large confiscations were noted, these were exceptional.

**War against drugs or war against minorities?** To what extent does race play a part in these stops? Certainly, race was a part even from the beginning. As Crank and Rehm noted, the New Mexico Highway 40 Cocaine Courier Profile used ten indicators. The first was "The vehicle occupants are usually resident aliens from Colombia." Similarly, the Florida Department of Highway Safety and Motor Vehicles developed a set of guidelines for identifying motorists carrying drugs. These guidelines included motorists who were members of ethnic groups tied to drug trafficking (Lersch, 2002; see Harris, 1999). Since then, many departments have been accused of using race as a basis for a stop and for subsequent searches. Some examples are presented in Box 8.4.

Box 8.4

**Racial Profiling?**

Many instances of police behavior have been documented in which a disproportionate number of minorities are stopped and/or searched subsequent to a stop. Are they racial profiling? Or are there other dynamics at work?

In East St. Louis, Latino motorists were disproportionately stopped. Latinos, though accounting for only 1 percent of the population, made up 41 percent of the vehicles searched.

In North Carolina in 1995, the Special Emphasis Team (SET) assigned to drug interdictions comprised of 12 state troopers pulled over African American drivers at twice the rate—45 percent—as did regular state patrol officers.

In New Jersey, a state court found that 73 percent of the motorists pulled over and searched along I-95 were African American, even though they made up only 14 percent of motorists. Moreover, 4.7 percent of out-of-state drivers were African American, 80 percent of the stops were of such persons. African Americans in Mercer Island, Washington, complained that they are routinely stopped by the police. The chief said that officers are trained to look for anything unusual. However, as the authors noted, being black in Mercer Island is unusual; they make up only 300 of the 21,000 residents.

In New York, the attorney general initiated an investigation into stop-and-frisk practices in New York City. The study showed that blacks and Latinos were much more likely to be stopped and frisked even accounting for differential criminal participation rates in neighborhoods. He found that blacks were stopped six times more often than whites, and Latinos were stopped four times more often. "Blacks made up 25 percent of the city population but 50 percent of the people stopped and 67

Box 8.4, *continued*

percent of the people stopped by the New York City Street Crimes Unit" (Ramirez et al., 2000).

In Maryland, a suit by the Americans for Civil Liberties Union uncovered a confidential police memorandum that stated that dealers and couriers were predominantly black men and women. For this, the Maryland State Police were required to maintain records of stops and searches.

Do these events occur because of a racial profile? Lersch noted that departments receive substantial rewards for stops that net drugs. An individual officer may receive a commendation, and the department may be permitted to retain up to 50 percent of the value of goods received, to be used for training and related expenses. And there are few costs associated with stops that yield no drugs. Crank and Rehm (1994) observe that race is associated with courier behavior in the training officers receive and can be used to justify a stop. Moreover, officers may be trained that a particular ethnic gang always couriers drugs using two vehicles; hence, based on officer safety, the subsequent search as well as the originating stop can be justified on the basis of race.

Source: Adapted from Lersch, 2002; Roberg et al., 2000; Russell, 1998; Crank and Rehm, 1994; Ramirez et al., 2000.

One might be tempted to respond that a higher focus on minorities is justified because of the simple fact that minorities are more likely to carry drugs. Using this logic, police would be neglectful if they failed to recognize the racial dimensions of drug courier activity. However, this logic collapses in the face of empirical research. Ramirez et al. (2000) note:

> In [John] Lamberth's study on I-95 in Maryland, he found that 28.4 percent of Black drivers and passengers who were searched were found with contraband [compared to] 28.8 percent of White drivers and passengers. . . . According to the New Jersey Attorney General's Interim report (April 1999) the "hit rates" at which contraband was found among those searched did not differ significantly by race. Similarly, in the New York study of "stop and frisk" practices, between 1998 and 1999, the attorney general found that 12.6 percent of Whites stopped were arrested, compared to only 10.5 percent of Blacks and 11.3 percent of Latinos. [In a U.S. customs survey of stops and searches in airports], nationwide data revealed that, while 43 percent of those searched were either Black or Latino, the hit rates for Latinos were actually lower than the hit rates for Whites. The study found that 6.7 percent for Whites, 6.3 percent of Blacks, and 2.8 percent of Latinos had contraband.

Similarly, Meehan and Ponder (2002) found that African American stops were highest in predominantly white areas, especially in white nonborder areas. Yet it was in these areas that the hit rates for stops were the lowest. They looked at "first query" only, testing the extent to which police discretion was used to make an initial stop. In other words, they concluded, "considerations of place, not the productivity from hits, drives the African-American query rate" (2002:420). Further, they noted a strong relationship between the proactive race-based stops and the use of Mobile Data Terminals (MDT) technology. Officers who used the technology more also made more stops inside predominantly white areas. In this way, surveillance vis-à-vis background checks, which provided officers the ability to surveil apart from using dispatch, also accompanied the likelihood of stops. High MDT users were high stoppers. Modern technology facilitating officer autonomy also contributed to higher rates of racial stereotyping.

In their overview of racial profiling, Engel et al. (2002) identified 13 sites with published racial profiling data. A racial disparity was noted in all sites, though the degree and type of disparity differed in each site. Only the data collected by Texas led to a conclusion by the site collectors that no discrimination existed, though some disparity was noted for drug interdictions and searches.

The selective use of discretion to stop and search minority group members should be considered against the backdrop of a broader shift in the practice of selective enforcement of the drug laws in the U.S. in the past several decades. Blumstein (1992) observed that arrest rates per hundred thousand for drug offenses among whites exceeded nonwhites from 1965 to 1982 and that arrest rates for both declined from a peak in 1974. He attributed the decline to the tendency toward decriminalization from the early 1970s to the early 1980s. The modern drug wars began in earnest in 1982, with a sharp rate of increase in arrests. This increase occurred wholly in the nonwhite community, increasing from less than 200 to more than 400 per 100,000 between 1974 and 1989. Among whites, the arrest rate continued to decline, following the trend begun in 1974. In other words, by the early 1990s, the drug war had shifted its focus and was being waged wholly against nonwhites, while whites continued to experience a de facto practice of permissive decriminalization. And this has occurred in an absence of evidence of any change in broad racial differences in the use of drugs.

The war against drugs, seen in the larger context provided by Blumstein and in the Federal context of the history of the DEA training for Operation Valkyrie in the early 1980s, thus turned into a war on minorities. The practice of racial profiling should be understood in those contexts. Yet one cannot make sense of racial profiling as a product of racial intent on the part of individual officers or departments. It is the product of a way of thinking about doing good police anti-drug interdiction that involves value-based decisions about where officers have the greatest impact. But it does carry with it a presumption that minorities are more likely to be in gangs that are drug oriented, a presumption that was constructed into the early training for interdiction and continues to this day. It translates into a predisposition for suspicion about minority group members whenever encountered during routine police work.

> Mike concludes this section. *What you've got is a policy at the department level that permits race to be included in a broader profile if it is a characteristic of a dangerous group. That's legal, sort of, but it sets you up for major problems. This policy is translated at the street level into a reason to pull over black people because they're black and then see if you can find anything on them. That's illegal. That's noble-cause corruption.*
>
> Using race to pull people over—and that's what your patrol officers are doing—leads to a way of thinking that is going to cause you real problems up the road. Pretty soon, your good officers are thinking that if a black person is in an expensive car, he may be a member of a drug gang, pull him over. If a black person is in a cheap car, he probably doesn't have current insurance, pull him over. If they're in a white neighborhood, they probably are looking for a house to burglarize, pull him over. If they're in a black neighborhood, they're probably recently released or out on parole and up to no good, pull him over. Better see what's going on.
>
> Is there a slippery slope to racial profiling? Batton and Kadleck (2004) suggest that there might be. They describe the process in Box 8.5.

Box 8.5

**The Slippery Slope of Racial Profiling**

The use of racial profiling as an indicator of criminal propensity may function as a "slippery slope" that facilitates more aggressive policing, especially in interactions with minorities (Kennedy, 1997). It also contributes to the development of a self-fulfilling prophecy for police about "who" criminals are and "where" crime is likely to occur. To the extent that minority communities are targeted with increased surveillance and patrols, the likelihood of actually finding crime in these areas is increased (Donziger, 1996). At the same time, the ability of the police to effectively combat crime is reduced by racial profiling because it results in a loss of trust and respect for police by minorities (Decker, 1981).

Source: Candice Batton and Colleen Kadleck (2004). "Theoretical and Methodological Issues in Racial Profiling Research." *Police Quarterly*, 7(1):34.

> I absolutely believe you when you tell me that you and your officers are not racist. But this isn't about race. It's about the noble cause. Your officers are trained to make these stops, and they are rewarded when they do. But in the name of the noble cause, getting bad people off the streets, you are letting race in through the back door.
>
> Your officers are making a value-based decision when they make a stop, and being black carries a penalty. It means that someone will be pulled

> over. To you this isn't about race, but you'll never convince the courts that. They'll subpoena all your records. The attorney will say, "Yeah, but look at this pattern, and look at this one, and why was this guy pulled over 50 times?" By the time the courts are done with you, they'll be telling you what to think and what to do. They'll track everything you do. You will have lost legitimacy, and it will take a very long time to get it back. This is a nice department. Don't do that to yourselves.

At this point, more than quarter century since the term "racial profiling" was first used, we now have a body of rigorous research and a history of litigation. What we've learned, at least from an ethical perspective, is that one's perception of racial profiling lies largely within one's perspective. In the absence of evidence that an officer actually knew the race of the driver prior to initiating the stop and corroborating evidence of *racial animus*, it is exceedingly difficult (maybe impossible) to objectively prove that a traffic stop was based on the race of the driver. Even so, some drivers strongly believe that they were stopped merely because of their race, and no amount of empirical evidence is likely to convince them otherwise.

In 2014, Michele Quinones published the results of a research project (her dissertation) that was designed to identify the officer behaviors occurring during a routine traffic stop that increased the potential for the perception of a racial motivation. In this research, she showed young, mostly minority, students several highly scripted videos of routine traffic stops. The officers in these videos adhered very closely to the traditional seven-step violator contact. She found that many of the routine behaviors exhibited by the officer, and even encouraged by his training, were perceived to be racist. For example, if an officer asked the driver, "Where are you headed to today?" the observers considered this none of his business and likely racist. More ominously, when the officer glanced into the back seat while approaching the driver's door, the students perceived this as an illegal search and likely racist. Her research suggests an opportunity for addressing the racial profiling controversy through an open dialogue with the affected communities. It is likely that when minority drivers are presented with the justification for routine behaviors during traffic stops, many of which are predicated on the need for officer safety, that they will be less likely to perceive these behaviors as racially motivated.

## *Police Violence*

The topic of police use of force is large and its use by the police is commonplace. Many have argued that it is the defining element of police work (see Bittner, 1970; Westley, 1970; Klockars, 1991). Police use of force varies widely in intensity, from the relatively mild use of "command voice," where officers speak directly to citizens as "adults to adults" in order to steer their behavior, to deadly force, where suspects may be seriously injured or killed.

Officers sometimes use too much force. **Excessive force** occurs when officers use a greater degree of force than is necessary to counter a suspect's resistance. If an officer were to use forceful grips, for example, to restrain a suspect when the officer could have accomplished the task with command voice, the officer is using excessive force. **Police brutality** is more severe and represents a gross imbalance between citizen noncompliance and level of police force. The use of a baton to strike a compliant handcuffed suspect, for example, is an example of police brutality. The choke hold used by the Minneapolis police in the killing of George Floyd in May 2020 is another example of what is considered now to be police brutality. The police officer knelt on Floyd's neck for almost nine minutes, despite him pleading with the officer that he could not breathe. A bystander's video captured the incident, which went viral and sparked widespread outrage. The Black Lives Matter (BLM) movement, which had been advocating for police reform and racial justice for several years, gained significant momentum after Floyd's death.

Police executives tend to use the **"rotten apple" theory** to explain excessive force and police brutality. If circumstances are compelling, the department will blame the misuse of force on some sort of psychological or moral weakness of the offending officer. Recall the principles of legitimacy stated in Chapter 6: the system will survive, and the toilet backs up. Newspapers always want to dig deeper, find the dirt, embarrass the department, and sell copy. Reporters and the media whom they represent also tend to think simply about problems and succumb to the rotten apple theory. They know that the best way to sell a story is to emphasize the "personal element." So they will try to find out about the personal background, family life, and the psychology of the offending officer. Reporters will publicly wonder what there was about the officer that led to such an explosion of violence. They will question the officer's motives.

Noble-cause violence, however, is not so easily explained. John Van Maanen (1978b) described what we consider to be noble-cause violence in his article "The Asshole." Police violence, he observed, emerged in concrete street encounters and was about asserting moral authority over individuals that, simply put, gave the police a difficult time. Van Maanen noted that police officers identified some individuals as "assholes." Those so labeled were vulnerable to rough street justice. When police roughed up assholes, they were acting out a moral judgment. Moral?

The asshole, according to Van Maanen, represented an individual whose behavior was viewed as a challenge to the authority of the police. It might have been a motorist that rudely questioned why a police officer is not out chasing dangerous criminals. Assholes, Van Maanen concluded, to a great extent represented what the police were about. The physical violence carried out against an asshole re-affirmed on the body of the victim the rightness of the police to control their territories.

Barker (1996:19) characterized moral violence acted out against certain individuals or groups as the **avenging angel syndrome.** The avenging angel syndrome is the idea that officers exact their sense of street justice on individuals or groups they personally dislike. When citizens acted rudely or disrespectfully, they sharply increased the likelihood that they would go to jail or get citations for "contempt of cop—COC" (Barker, 1996:19). Street justice communicated the message that an officer was above the law.

Noble-cause violence, however, occurs in situations that do not always fit well into Van Maanen's model. Some police officers initiate police-citizen interactions with the assumption that a citizen is an asshole and under some circumstances will allow a citizen to prove that he or she is not (Crank, 2004a). Sometimes racial stereotypes are enough for police to label someone as an asshole and to act violently against them.

Secondly, the argument put forth by Van Maanen underestimated the extent to which police violence can be explosive, sometimes well beyond any possible need to rectify some "out-of-kilter" situation. Consider Box 8.6, a description of the case involving Manuel Villa.

Box 8.6

**Noble-Cause Violence: A Case Example**

When police officers took Manuel Villa to St. John's hospital in Queens on November 10, 1994, his face was so bruised that doctors thought he had been in a car wreck. Villa, a mechanic with no criminal record, said he had been pummeled by dozens of blows from two detectives questioning him about his brother's role in a shooting. The police officers who brought Villa to the hospital after he was beaten told doctors that he had slipped and hit his head on a desk. But once the officers had left the room, Villa told a nurse that he had been pummeled by two officers and two detectives, who handcuffed him, pinned him to the floor of the 106th Precinct detective squad room, and took turns punching him in the face, hitting him with more than 50 blows.

Source: David Kocieniewski, the *New York Times*, April 23, 1988.

Was Villa an "asshole," as described by Van Maanen? He was certainly treated violently. However, as the author of the article cited earlier notes, Villa was a volunteer auxiliary police officer, had passed the Transit Police Department's examination, and was scheduled to take the city exam. Villa was hardly a likely candidate for an "asshole" list.

Perhaps the most disturbing part of the incident involved the circumstances that sparked the beating. Villa had been asked to come to the 106th Precinct station house to pick up his brother's belongings. An angry interrogation began when he arrived. He was hit in the face with a ruler.

After several blows, Villa threatened to file a brutality complaint. It was at that point that he was cuffed and beaten.

In what way did Villa bring into question the police detective's notion of moral order? The answer is clear. He suggested that they were responsible to the law. By threatening to file a brutality complaint, Villa was suggesting that they weren't above the law but indeed had a responsibility to it. The beating quickly followed, a demonstration acted out on Villa's body that he was factually wrong.

## *Testimonial Deception or Perjury*

Rarely will police administrators admit, and indeed few believe, that officers perjure themselves giving sworn testimony in the courts. However, it may be that perjury is commonplace, a widely shared characteristic of many local police cultures. In a survey of drug cases in the late 1960s, Skolnick (1988) was able to provide a glimpse into the pervasiveness of police perjury. He noted a dramatic increase in "dropsy" testimony, where individuals apprehended for drug possession after the *Mapp* decision were dropping drugs on the ground rather than being caught holding them. Findings were striking; looking at the Narcotics Bureau in New York, Skolnick observed that prior to the *Mapp* decision (concerning the exclusionary rule), the narcotics bureau claimed that 92 percent of the narcotics found were hidden on the person, 8 percent on the ground. After the *Mapp* decision, only 28 percent were found on the suspect's body, with 72 percent found on the ground. As one of the authors of this book observed elsewhere:

> If, as some argue, criminals rationally adapt their behavior in order to take advantage of the criminal law, why then would criminals, as suggested by these numbers, modify their behavior in such a way to dramatically increase their likelihood of arrest?
>
> (Crank, 2004a:296)

Some readers might consider Skolnick's data to be outdated. Not by a stretch! Our concern is that testimonial deception is a widespread contemporary problem. Thomas Barker conducted a questionnaire survey of police behavior in a city he called South City, his findings published in 1994. The survey was conducted in a small city with a population of about 25,000. The questionnaire he used was designed to measure the pervasiveness and support for various aspects of police deviance.

One of the topics presented on the questionnaire was testimonial deception. Police officers reported that they thought that about 23 percent of their fellow officers had lied in court. When asked about how often an officer would report another officer for perjury, 28 percent, slightly more than one in four, stated "always." Sixty-four percent of the officers stated that they would report another officer for perjury either rarely or never.

Keep in mind that the findings on this survey were reported by the police themselves, not an outside group who might have motives different from the interests of the police. Perjury was defined as those who have "lied in court." The clear conclusion, at least in this small city, was widespread tolerance—nearly three-fourths of the officers in the survey—for police perjury.

> Mike discussed this research with the commanders. It is always uncomfortable. Mike lightly laughed. *You may think that you know your officers. But do you? You know the song and dance that you put on for reporters? Where did you learn it?*

Barker's research, some observers might contend, represents an isolated and atypical example. Consider another assessment of police lying by Barker et al. (1994). The findings of this research reveal how central the noble cause is for young recruits and how willing they are to set legal means aside in order to achieve noble causes.

Barker, Friery, and Carter conducted their research among rookie officers in five academy training sessions. The majority of these officers had field experience, with a few having up to five years. The authors found that "58 percent of the respondents gave moderate acceptance to deviant lies that were told for legitimate purposes" (1994:161). What were legitimate purposes? Barker and his colleagues (1994:161) cited "frustration with the criminal justice process" and "get the bad guys off the street." In other words, lying was an acceptable strategy if it contributed to the noble cause.

The Officers in Barker and his colleagues' study were in training. The majority had limited exposure to their organization's local cultures, though most had been in their departments for a year or more. Yet they were prepared to lie if it would put bad guys behind bars; the noble cause was firmly instilled in them. These officers were in POST academy. What were they learning?

## *Drugs*

The use and sale of illicit drugs is one of the most grave violations of ethical conduct that a police officer can commit. As we noted in Chapter 4, Sherman (1985:259) presented drug corruption as the final stage in an officer's moral decline. An officer that used drugs had slid all the way down the slippery slope, had effectively lost all personal dignity.

Some officers may be morally vulnerable to illicit influences in their agency or on the "street," as Sherman's model suggested. However, we believe that drug corruption is more ethically complex than suggested by his model. Some officers find that narcotics use and sales are part and parcel of police work. Indeed, their effectiveness as police officers requires that they be intimately involved with illicit narcotics.

In other words, in order to understand the way in which officers can become "bent" in the use and sale of narcotics, we recommend that the reader not start by trying to figure out what's wrong with individual officers corrupted by greed. One should begin by taking a look at the organizational and personal pressures on narcotics agents.

Consider the investigations of Manning and Redlinger (1977). These authors found that there were departmental pressures on agents that compelled them to commit noble-cause corruption associated with drug use and sales. Pressures to corrupt officers, they observed, were of two types: pressures to violate laws to enforce narcotics laws, and pressures to obstruct justice. These pressures are listed in Box 8.7.

Box 8.7

**Pressures to Enforce Narcotics Laws and Obstruct Justice**

***Departmental Pressures to Violate Laws to Enforce Narcotics Laws***

1. Aspirations for promotion and salary. Officers need a good track record of busts.
2. Implicit quotas for arrests.
3. Directives from administrators.
4. Self-esteem maintenance. It feels good to be good at your work.
5. Moral-ideological commitments. You're "protecting the kids" in winning "the war against drugs."

***Pressures to Obstruct Justice***

1. Protect informants.
2. Create informants through threats of prosecution and its abeyance if they cooperate.
3. Suppress information on cases pursued by other officers.

Source: P.K. Manning and L. Redlinger (1977). "Invitational Edges of Corruption: Some Consequences of Narcotic Law Enforcement." Pages 288–289 in P. Rock (ed.) *Drugs and Politics*, pp. 279–310. New York: Routledge.

A casual inspection of this list might lead one to conclude that there's nothing particularly wrong with organizational pressures that encourage the suppression of illicit drug activity; after all, don't these pressures simply reflect how the organization encourages good police work? However, let's think about these pressures in the context of narcotic suppression. See Box 8.8 on simulation.

Box 8.8

**Simulation**

Trainers will emphasize to their officers that it is never appropriate for them to taste drugs. They will insist that good undercover work can be done without using drugs. That you can simulate drug use, you don't actually have to do it. Poppycock! Consider the words of one of Carter's (1999) confidants:

> Simulation is crap—any user knows if you're smoking or faking, and you can bet they're watching the new guys to see if you're taking a real hit. If I'm at a [drug] deal and I try to simulate, I might as well be wearing a sign that says COP . . . so you've got to take a real hit of marijuana—it's got less bite than tequila.
>
> (Carter, 1999:320)

Source: Carter, D.L. (1999). "Drug Use and Drug-Related Corruption of Police Officers." Page 320 in L.K. Gaines and G.W. Cordner (eds.) *Policing Perspectives: An Anthology*, pp. 311–323. Los Angeles, CA: Roxbury Publishing.

Pressures to carry out narcotics enforcement occur in a crime control environment in which agents have to find ways of obtaining information that aren't victim-centered. Drug crimes are often **victimless crimes.** This means that information about drug-related crime is not obtained from "victims" who report crimes to the police. Police consequently have to resort to other techniques—usually informants or undercover activity—in order to unmask illegal activity. They have to have informants that are willing—or can be coerced—into giving information. To make cases, they have to be able to buy or sell. They have to know what marijuana smells like. They have to be willing to taste it and know what it should taste like. If they want to be effective, they have to move up in the criminal organization. They have to be prepared to "turn on" individuals, introducing outsiders or non-users to techniques of narcotics use. In short, they have to be better at being bad than the bad guys. And they will be. They believe in their work. They are "morally and ideologically" committed, to use Manning and Redlinger's (1977) phrase. The noble cause is in their hearts. An inspection of departmental and obstruction of justice pressures listed earlier shows that they focus on the "good end." In a word, the police organization itself encourages noble-cause corruption. How can officers, already committed to the noble cause, resist these pressures?

Agents corrupt themselves in order to be good agents. They desire to be golden apples. What are the patterns of agent corruption that Manning and Redlinger identify? They are listed in Box 8.9. The reader will not find them comforting.

Box 8.9

**Patterns of Corruption**

1. ***Taking Bribes***. This can be in the form of payoffs from dealers to officers. If an arrest is already made, an officer can "make the case badly." This kind of corruption was reported to be widespread by the Knapp Commission (1972) in New York.
2. ***Using Drugs***. Undercover agents, to show their loyalties to those on whom they are doing surveillance, have to "turn on" with them.
3. ***Buying/Selling Narcotics***. Narcotics can be used to pay off informants. Potential customers can be introduced to dealers.
4. ***Arrogation of Seized Property***. This is a complicated way of describing the disappearance of narcotics, and sometimes cash, in police lockers.
5. ***Illegal Searches and Seizures***. Smoke can be smelled. Drugs can be seen in "plain sight," later planted in plain sight to prove the point. Drugs can be flaked, that is, planting illicit drugs on someone. Padding is where drugs are added to an already confiscated seizure.
6. ***The Protection of Informants***. All major agencies provide money for informants. This has a number of negative consequences. Informants can be protected from other charges while they are working. Manning and Redlinger cited one case in which:

> the confidential informant was caught breaking and entering a home, but the agents "fixed" the charge with the Prosecuting Attorney's office on the basis that the informant was "one of the best." The prosecutor then added five cases to the informant's caseload.
>
> (Manning and Redlinger, 1977:162)

Source P.K. Manning and L. Redlinger (1977). "Invitational Edges of Corruption: Some Consequences of Narcotic Law Enforcement." Pages 290–298 in P. Rock (ed.) Drugs and Politics, pp. 279–310. New York: Routledge.

The message in Manning and Redlinger's research is clear. To understand how officers become corrupted by narcotics, we should not look for flaws in their character. To understand narcotics corruption, one should consider their commitment to the noble cause and how the organization reinforces that commitment with pressures to put bad guys away through the circumvention of legal due process. Some officers become corrupt, not because they have character flaws but because they are carrying out organizational purposes efficiently and effectively.

Carter (1999) described noble-cause drug corruption as **Type 2 drug corruption,** or corruption in the pursuit of legitimate goals. It is consistent with our definition of noble-cause corruption. Box 8.10 presents Carter's definition of Type 2 drug corruption.

Box 8.10

**Type 2 Drug Corruption**

There are persons whom officers "know" are involved in drug trafficking; however, the police are consistently unable to obtain sufficient evidence for arrest. Similarly, there are "known" criminals who have been found not guilty in court because the government has not been able to prove its case—frequently because evidence has been excluded on "technicalities." The officers see these recurring circumstances and become frustrated because the trafficker is "beating the system."

It is argued that in the case of Type 2 corruption, the acts are committed not only for the personal psychological gain of the officer but also in support of organizational goals through which the officer may be rewarded by commendations, promotions, and/or recognition.

Type 2 corruption is further compounded because this behavior is not traditionally perceived as being corrupt. There is a degree of informal organizational tolerance for behavior which gets "known" traffickers off the streets or seizes the trafficker's cache of drugs.

Source: David Carter, "Drug Use and Drug-Related Corruption of Police Officers," 1999. In Quint C. Thurman and Jihong Zhao (eds.), *Contemporary Policing*. Los Angeles: Roxbury Publishing.

It is difficult for commanders to believe that their officers will be involved in drug-related corruption and will resent the suggestion that they might be. For many commanders, it is unthinkable. You may think that this research discussed earlier is outdated, that this kind of thing doesn't happen today. Consider a case in Chicago described in Box 8.11, the case of the Austin 7.

Box 8.11

**The Austin 7**

Seven officers were arrested in December 1996, on federal charges of conspiracy to commit robbery and extortion for shaking down undercover agents they thought were drug dealers. In their lockers were found crack cocaine, powder cocaine, marijuana, and possibly heroin. The indictment included the following charges:

1. Robbing an apartment used as a safe house by drug dealers.

Box 8.11, *continued*

2. Revealing the identity of an informant to an undercover agent thought to be a drug dealer.
3. Payments for escorting a cocaine shipment.

This case also produced some new language into the argot of drug interdiction. Planting drugs on defendants, stated by one of the officers to be common, was called a "blind date." Another practice was called "reintroduction." If someone dropped drugs during an encounter with a police officer, the officer would put it in his pocket until the next time they met. Then the officer would make an arrest and "reintroduce" the drugs.

Source: Adapted from the *Chicago Tribune*, December 21, 1996, "7 Chicago Cops Indicted in Shakedowns." the *Chicago Tribune*, January 29, 1997, "1st Break in Austin Code of Silence."

Former Houston Police officer Gerald Goines was convicted in November 2019 of felony murder for his role in a January 2019 drug raid that killed two civilians. The raid was based on falsified information, and Goines was later indicted on multiple federal charges, including civil rights violations and obstruction of justice. The indictment detailed how Goines fabricated evidence and made false statements in official reports to justify the raid (USDOJ, 2019). In Antioch and Pittsburg, California, in 2023, ten current and former officers were charged in a federal corruption case involving drug distribution, fraud, and civil rights violations. Among them, former Antioch officer Devon Wenger was convicted of conspiring to distribute anabolic steroids and obstructing justice by deleting evidence (USDOJ, 2023a). And in Phoenix, Illinois, in 2023, police officers Antoine Larry and Jarrett Snowden were indicted for conspiring to steal drugs and cash during traffic stops. They allegedly sold stolen drugs and falsified police reports to conceal their actions (USDOJ, 2023b). These cases reflect a pattern of drug-related corruption within law enforcement, often involving falsification of evidence, abuse of power, and systemic failures in oversight.

These are big cities. You might feel relieved that you are from a smaller place. You shouldn't. Consider Cicero, Illinois, population 67,000. Nearly one-third of the officers have been suspended or forced to resign. The acting police chief was suspended because he had ties to a former Stone Park, Illinois, officer (Stone Park—population 4,383) convicted to helping run a large, mob-linked, marijuana-growing operation. Where was internal affairs? The captain of internal affairs was removed after he blocked the investigation of two officers who were involved in an attempted theft at an electronics store.

We are concerned that drug-related noble-cause corruption is becoming more frequent in the United States. Chuck Wexler, the former executive director for the Police Executive Research Forum, stated that the drug trade was behind a "sea change" in the growth of corruption among the police (Johnson, 1998). He attributed the problem to the tremendous amounts of money available to tempt officers into corruption. We think that some of the growth in the corruption is associated with the noble cause. A commander should ask him or herself: What motivated officers who later faced corruption charges to become involved in anti-narcotics activity in the first place?

If the reader is a commander, he or she knows that narcotics vice is among the most popular assignments for detectives. It is an elite unit. Why is that? The answer, we believe, is that an assignment in narcotics vice enables police officers to act out the noble cause against a clear moral wrong—drug use and sales. It also allows them to act without a great deal of messy bureaucratic oversight and with easy opportunities for arrests. As Manning and Redlinger (1977) noted, the sense of moral fulfilment for successful undercover drug work is great.

> Mike expands on this theme. *Commanders, do you understand how your officers think about undercover work? I know. I've done it. It's exciting. I'm out there doing something about bad guys and no one's watching me. Do I believe in getting the scum off the streets? Oh yeah. I believe.*

To understand the extent to which drug enforcement officers are committing this kind of noble-cause crime, one needs to recognize the compelling nature of the noble cause and how organizational pressures reinforce it in narcotics cases. One has to recognize how the organization's values can be used to compel officers to become involved in a wide variety of illegal drug activities.

Finally, if the reader is a commander and is absolutely convinced that this couldn't happen in their agency, consider the following words of another commander, from Carter (1999:319):

> The last problem I ever thought I'd face is my officers robbing drug dealers for drugs. I mean, the reports are here—but my mind just can't accept it. I don't know if I let [the officers] down or they let me down. Something definitely went wrong in the system.

Consider yourself warned.

## Confessions and the Operative Assumption of Guilt

> MIKE CONTINUES: *I bet most of you were detectives at some point. Didn't you interrogate suspects? I bet you all knew someone in your*

*department who had a reputation for interrogation. Someone who could really peel back a suspect's story and get at what really went on. Tell me: do you think they were trying to find the truth, or were they trying to get a confession?*

Klockars has noted that police operate under an **operative assumption of guilt** (see Chapter 1). What he means by this is that police, having arrested someone, believe that the person is guilty. This belief will be steadfastly maintained even in the absence of evidence of guilt. What, then, can a detective or interviewing officer do, when dealing with someone he or she strongly believes is guilty, but lacking evidence? The answer is straightforward—obtain a confession. Confessions make good evidence. "Confession," Brooks (2000:9) noted, "has for centuries been regarded as the 'queen of proofs' in the law; it is a statement from the lips of a person who should know best."

The operative assumption of guilt affects the interrogation process. If the belief is already in place that the suspect is guilty, interrogation subtly shifts from a fact-finding process to a guilt-finding process. To rephrase Brooks' observation about judging individuals (2000:164), once one has eliminated the very possibility of innocence, one can go about the process of interrogation with a certain relish.

The guilt-finding process can be seen in the case of the rape of a jogger in New York's Central Park. One of the big stories of 1989 was the rape of a jogger in Central Park by five African American youths. The case was racially incendiary; five youths were "wilding," a term that entered American crime discourse from the incident. Wilding referred to a frenzied crime spree carried out by juveniles roaming in packs (Getlin, 2002). It also carried a racially charged connotation: African American youths in groups are hunting pack animals preying on innocent white women.

The case was always controversial because of the lack of evidence. The victim, a white, 28-year-old jogger on a well-known path, was dragged to the side of a ravine and raped. Her skull was crushed, and she was expected to die. She recovered only after months of intensive care and therapy. She had no memory of the incident.

Police officers, responding to the incident, came up with the names of five young men who lived in nearby Harlem. All made videotaped confessions. No forensic or DNA evidence linked the youths to the crime, though the victim bled profusely. None directly admitted guilt, but all implicated each other in the confessions. For example, one youth noted, "We all took turns getting on top of her." Another said, "This is my first rape" and also said he "witnessed, but did not participate" (Getlin, 2002). Another said, "We cut her clothes off with a knife" and another claimed that a knife was plunged into the victim repeatedly (no sharp object wounds were found on the victim) (Dwyer and Flynn, 2002). In three of the confessions, parents were present when the confession was videotaped. All five were found guilty and served prison terms.

Thirteen years later, another man, Matias Reyes, admitted guilt to the rape and beating. DNA testing identified him, then serving 33 years to life in prison, as the rapist. The tests showed that he carried out the act alone. He cannot be charged for the crime because the statute of limitations has expired for the crime. A review of records showed that he had been identified as a suspect in a rape case in Central Park two days before the jogger was raped. However, he had not been interviewed about the jogger.

On December 19, 2002, a judge vacated the convictions of all five men. The convictions were set aside at the request of the Manhattan District Attorney's Office. The District Attorney agreed with a defense motion that the guilty verdicts should be overturned, as the confessions had significant weaknesses that came to light when Reyes confessed to the crime (Dwyer and Saulny, 2002).

Several troubling elements were noted about the confessions. Though they were videotaped, the youths had been in custody and interrogated before the videotaping for up to 28 hours. And much of what the youths said about the incident was factually wrong: the description of the location, the clothing worn by the victim, and other elements that made it seem as if they were talking about a different crime (Dwyer and Flynn, 2002).

The operative assumption of guilt continues to be maintained by many involved in the case. In spite of the new evidence and the decision of the prosecutor and the judge that the sentences should be vacated, many individuals continue to insist on the guilt of the five African American men. The New York Police Department said that it had acted properly and that the five defendants were "most likely" guilty (Associated Press, 2003). One former New York investigator said that it was possible that both Reyes and the youths were guilty, that they were raping her until Reyes came along. Another detective, who handled the case, "angrily disputed the notion that savvy cops had tricked or scared, impressionable youth[s] into a confession." "Where's the coercion?" he asked.

The young men charged with the crime were not "innocent" in a worldly sense. One of them was, by all accounts, involved in a mugging in another part of the park when the jogger was raped. Witnesses also had said that the youths had attacked several bicyclists around the time of the crime. Another person said that the youth had tried to block them when they were running and had grabbed at her when she ran by (Dwyer and Flynn, 2002).

However, in spite of the protestations of those who obtained the confessions, the youths were innocent of the crime for which they were charged. The prosecuting attorney concluded this, and prosecutors rarely side with defendants in such circumstances. The judge threw out the convictions. The guilt of Reyes is clear and indisputable. The police department is trying to save face and correctly observed that its officers acted legally. Yet the issues here are about the noble cause and cannot be understood only in terms of the legality of the behavior of the interrogators.

The noble-cause question is this: Were the youth interrogated in order to find out the facts of the case, or were they interrogated in order to acquire confessions? If they were interrogated in order to acquire confessions, then the interrogators are carrying out an interrogation whose purpose is the "good end," the finding of guilt when no other means provided a way to find guilt. In the example earlier, the interrogators extracted confessions, the guilt finding, in spite of the innocence of the accused of the crime for which they were charged.

The New York jogger case is perhaps the most prominent case of noble-cause interrogations. It is certainly not the only one. In another example, the *Miami Herald* described 38 questionable murder confessions thrown out by Broward County courts. These are discussed in Box 8.12.

Box 8.12

**Murder Cases Tainted by False Confessions**

Since 1990, according to the *Miami Herald*, 38 murder cases have been rejected by the courts in Broward County, in South Florida. According to the *Herald*, detectives:

1. Put people in jail for confessions incorrect on basic facts of the crime, such as the year in which it occurred, who the victim was, or what kind of weapon was used.
2. Obtained illegal confessions from individuals who had asked for their attorneys or had insisted on their right to remain silent.
3. Obtained confessions from people who were incoherent. One such individual was high on morphine when his confession was obtained, and it was later thrown out.
4. Acquired confessions from very young individuals and the mentally retarded. One individual, with an IQ of 58, "falsely confessed to murders in Broward, Miami-Dade, Tampa, and San Francisco."

(Herald.com, 2002:1)

One such confession was described by the *Herald* as follows:

One "confession" . . . that of Frank Lee Smith, turned out to be no more than an oblique admission of guilt—at best. Detectives claimed that Smith blurted out that a witness couldn't have seen him at the crime scene because it was dark. He never told the police he was the killer. But court papers characterized the outburst as a confession, and the statement helped put an innocent man on Death Row for 14 years. Smith died of cancer months before his exoneration.

(2002:3)

Box 8.12, *continued*

Not all instances of false confession are examples of noble-cause corruption.

In some of these instances, the department identified the falseness of the confession; in these instances, we can conclude that possible overzealousness to gain a confession was offset by other factors that operated in the interests of justice. And in some of them, judges did not accept the confessions as credible. Moreover, the Broward County department faced legitimacy problems: in nine instances, Broward County juries acquitted murder defendants who confessed, including one in which detectives took the stand and said that a defendant had confessed to the murder.

Contradictory or inconsistent details are not unusual in confessions. Some detectives argue that the presence of such details is proof that they do not coach suspects to provide consistent testimony to make confessions letter perfect. Moreover, many individuals commit their crimes in the heat of passion and do not clearly remember what happened. And in two cases where the police had obtained false confessions, detectives point out that their work was responsible for freeing the suspects.

In some of them, however, one is led to conclude that some of them are instances where the interrogator was motivated to gain the confession, that critical element of testimony that would ensure a court finding of guilty if held up. These are instances of noble-cause corruption, the commitment to the good end—getting the bad guy off the street by focusing one's efforts on acquiring the confession, not finding truth.

Source: Adapted from the *Miami Herald,* 2002, December 22: www.miami.com/mld/hiamiherald/4791670.htm.

An outcome of a false confession is not only the collection of evidence to prove guilt. Out there somewhere, a guilty offender goes free to commit more crime. Witt (2001[1]) described the case of Keith Longin, who was arrested for murder and falsely confessed, according to the Prince George homicide detective unit. As Mr. Longin observed:

> The detective said "well, thanks for making the confession." Longin recalled. I'm like . . . "What? I didn't admit to anything." . . . He said "Yes, you did."

He spent the next eight months in jail. Other investigators identified the true killer with DNA. During that eight months, the man allegedly sexually assaulted seven more women.

> An officer responds to Mike's discussion of confessions. "You know that I might interrogate someone, and I know he is guilty because this was

his MO and he was in the area of the scene of the crime. He's got a prior conviction record a mile long. There's this woman who was beaten in her apartment and she's a bloody mess, can't remember anything, can't see well enough to identify anyone. The apartment is ruined. She can't afford hospital bills. It could be my mother. There was a picture of her kids in a busted glass frame on the floor. Are you saying I should be nice to this guy?"

Mike hesitates, then smiles broadly. *Exactly. Cops smell the blood of victims. It's a central part of value-based decision-making. What you are saying is exactly what I have been saying all along. You are committed to getting this guy of the streets. How could you use the law to get this bum off the streets?*

The officer starts to respond, then stops, catching himself. Mike looks at him. *You see? See how easy it is? You remember how to do it. That's what your officers are doing.*

Many of you are remembering cases like this, where you were dealing with someone who you know was guilty. Some of you are thinking that they weren't innocent in any sense of the term. They had a long list of priors and there was no question they were implicated in the crime in some way. You don't want to talk about it, but you're thinking it. But if you carried out the interrogation in order to prove guilt, that's noble-cause corruption.

ANOTHER OFFICER CHALLENGES MIKE: "A lot of what you say is right, but I take offense at your suggestion that we are morally corrupt because we think this way. The reality of police work is that we are dealing with people who are secretive, do hurt people, and who want to get away with it. You know that. Do you think they want to tell us the truth?"

MIKE: *OK. Let's take a step back. You've got cases where a detective has interviewed someone and by golly, they've managed to get a confession on tape. High-fives all around. The detective has spent a lot of time on the case, and the department has invested a lot of resources. The confession holds up, and the suspect goes to prison. Five years later, DNA shows he couldn't have done it. Someone else out there has been free to commit more crimes, and you've closed the case. Are you going to reopen it? No. You're facing legitimacy problems and now the public thinks you're the bad guy. Your PR man has to spend a lot of time defending the department. Judges and juries are taking a second look at your work. You're being sued by the family of the released suspect—who your detective probably still believes is guilty. Here we go again, legitimacy and liability, and you're dragged through the gutter of media attention. You may not like it, but it happens.*

I'm not here to throw stones at you. You're the good guys, number one in my book. I'm working through a very complicated moral problem that you face on a day-to-day basis. It has a lot of different aspects, and any one of them can backfire and cause you a lot of grief. It's all about a way of thinking and its consequences. We're going to do an experiment that is about that way of thinking. This experiment is about the way we do deceptive legal practices—all totally legal—but about how such practices can confuse us about how we should live our life.

## The Treacherous Psychology of Deceptive Legal Practices

For those of you who are police officers, recruits, or students who want to become police officers, it is unreasonable to think that there could be problems with anything you do that is legal. After all, the law is what the legislature says it is, and the police carry society's responsibility to enforce it. We believe, however, that there are deceptive practices that the police use, that are themselves legal, but that create a working environment that both justifies noble-cause corruption and alienates the public.

**Deceptive practices** justify morally questionable behavior in terms of the ends that are gained. These practices contribute to an ethical environment that encourages a focus on policing's "good ends." If a police department uses deceptive practices without thinking about their ethical implications, its officers are working in an organizational climate fertile for the growth of noble-cause corruption. Deceptive practices are an invitation to ethical chaos.

Deceptive practices can take a variety of forms. Skolnick and Fyfe (1993:61) describe several types of deceptive legal practices commonplace in police organizations. Consider the following examples having to do with the fabrication of evidence:

1. Tell a suspect falsely that he has been identified by an accomplice.
2. Present a suspect with faked physical evidence, such as fingerprints, bloodstains, or hair samples, to confirm the suspect's guilt.
3. Tell the suspect that he or she has been identified by an eyewitness.
4. Stage a line-up where a pretend eyewitness identifies the suspect.
5. Have the suspect take a lie-detector test and then tell the suspect that the test proved that he or she was guilty.

How would the practices listed earlier be analyzed from an ethical perspective? They are clearly ends-oriented. They seem to offer the best of all ethical worlds; they are legal and they are ends-oriented. They are faithful to the noble cause but are acted out in accordance with the legal requirements of police work.

So what's wrong with them? Let's conduct another thought experiment about suspected spousal infidelity. The thought experiment is presented in Box 8.13.

Box 8.13

**A Thought Experiment: Jealousy and Uncertainty**

Imagine that you are a married woman, a street cop, and you come home late, and your husband wants to know what you've been doing. He doesn't trust you, and he is certain that you're cheating on him. He absolutely believes it. So he tells you that a friend called and said that he had seen you with another man. You deny it. He pulls out a pair of your panties that were supposed to be in the wash and tells you that they've got semen on them. WHO IS IT? You deny the accusation a second time. He says that a friend of his has seen you having lunch with this man. You deflect the comment, responding, "So what? What's wrong with having lunch with someone?" This third response to his accusations only makes him angrier, convincing him he's right. By now, you are in the midst of a raging fight. He continues, "I followed you yesterday. I saw you and him together. I know his name. I want to see if you'll admit it." He's bluffing to see if you'll admit being with a man that a friend says you had lunch with. You deny it for the fourth time. He says, "Look me squarely in the eyes and tell me that you aren't having an affair." In response to this fifth accusation, you blow up and storm out of the house, your relationship severely damaged by his crude harassment.

What can we learn from this thought experiment? We have a jealous husband, consumed by his passion but with no real evidence of his wife's betrayal. He knows it, is certain of it. How can he uncover the truth? His options are limited. So he becomes deceptive in order to try to uncover the guilt of his wife.

How would you react if your spouse treated you this way every time you worked late—when, ultimately, the act of working late itself became the proof your spouse needed to prove that you were guilty? We don't think you'd like it very much. But what is it about the husband's behavior that's troubling? We suggest that it begins with the certainty of guilt in the accuser's eye and proceeds to use deception to verify the guilt. Indeed, if each of the husband's accusations are reviewed, the reader will note that they are examples of #1 through #5 of Skolnick and Fyfe's (1993) deceptive practices described previously in this chapter. Not much of a way to value a relationship, is it? Yet it's how we conduct this business we call policing; we, too, often start with an operative assumption of guilt and proceed to "trick" or badger a suspect into confessing. It's no wonder that some officers get confused and act out the noble cause at home, destroying their relationships. They carry principles of distrust into their family life, acting them out on their wives or on their children. And it's no wonder that citizens subjected to these techniques, guilty and innocent alike, end up disliking the police.

In the thought experiment in Box 8.13, what has the husband accomplished? He has created an environment where the most important consideration is the noble cause—in this instance finding guilt of which he is certain—but in his spouse, not a criminal suspect. Does the husband ever wonder that sometimes accused individuals are so overwhelmed with the deceptive accusational practices that they finally admit guilt just to get on with their lives? And, reader, have you ever done this to anyone?

There are two ethical questions evoked by deceptive practices, and we will end this section with the recommendation that the reader consider them carefully.

1. When deceptive practices are used, do they uncover truth or create it?
2. Does the reader understand how deceptive practices, legal though they be, encourage street officers to cross the line to noble-cause corruption?

# Ethics and Police in a Time of Change

# Part 3

Rarely in our history have Americans invested their internal security so completely to the trust of the police and never before has so much been at stake. The legal authority of the police to intervene in citizens' affairs is increasingly relaxed by a congress and court system panic-stricken over media-amplified images of terrorism, crime, and social decay. Police expansion of legal and extralegal authority is supported by a crime-fearing public and academics who champion innovative police strategies.

The early twenty-first century is a time in which the social fabric of the country is dramatically changing. The age of Anglo-Saxon demographic dominance is giving way to a polyglot society, for better or for worse. Urban and rural spaces are increasingly characterized by different kinds of groups sharing the same local geography. Ethnic, religious, cultural, and age-based conflicts are possible. These conflicts and their resolutions will define the "order" that the police must deal with in our emerging future. On the one hand, public order problems are increasingly defined in terms of relations among diverse groups. On the other, large numbers of immigrants live in the United States, and approximately 30 million alien visitors travel to the United States on visas yearly. The notion of a core ethnicity, characterized as Anglo-Saxon or put simply, white, is dissipating into a polyglot of ethnic variety. We are, like it or not, a true world civilization. What kind of police organization does this civilization need?

The police, Mike has argued, are authorized representatives of a moral standard and use the law to advance that standard. The standard is the noble cause. How will this moral authority mix with the needs of policing in a polyglot society? Asserting their own brand of noble-cause morality, they may lose legitimacy in those same communities they try to protect.

We will describe a different way of thinking about public order. In a society marked by diversity and conflict, successful maintenance of public

DOI: 10.4324/9781003626916-12

order will require powerful skills in negotiating order among contending groups. Police will be prepared for the future if they possess the skills, and morality, and the patience to weave threads of order together from differing racial, ethnic, and religious accounts. In other words, they must negotiate order rather than assert it.

We believe that policing in the U.S. is at a crossroads. The second half of the twentieth century was what we call the era of citizen-based policing. By citizen-based policing, we mean that police officers saw their primary role in citizen protection terms, and their work was organized around responding to citizen calls for assistance, rapid response, random preventive patrol, and protecting the public generally. The height of the citizen-based policing era is the first half or "velvet glove" period of the community policing movement, from its incipient form as team-based policing in the early 1970s to the early 1980s. It was characterized by colorful strategies, such as "police community reciprocity," which promoted a notion of the police and public working as equal partners for community self-protection.

The second half of the community-based policing movement, from Wilson and Kelling's "broken windows" article in 1983 until 2000, is probably better characterized as a victim-based policing movement. It was characterized by hardening responses to criminals, dramatic expansion of penal sanctions for drug and alcohol offenses, lowered concerns about the impact of aggressive practices on minority groups, and sharp expansion of prison populations. The victim-based movement had consequences—large numbers of offenders returned to the streets with no employable skills, overburdened parole and probation, and increasingly economically burdened minority communities. In this era, police justified their work in terms of victims' concerns and tended to take a very hard or "iron fist" attitude toward criminals. This response has continued into the early twenty-first century, amplified by technological developments of real-time intelligence through COMPSTAT and crime mapping technologies.

The community policing movement, never particularly popular among the police, collapsed with the presidency of Bush in 2000 and the consequent sharp disinvestment in federal community policing grants. Today, we are increasingly moving into what we call "neo-professionalism." The tactical and strategic purposes of the police are increasingly focused on aggressive law enforcement. The purposes of policing are couched in and justified in terms of a "security" rhetoric, and police work is about protecting government at all levels from disruption, be it in the form of crime, disorder, external threat, or fiscal emergency brought about by natural causes. A "broken windows" philosophy permeates this approach because it resonates with ideas of police response to external threats. Practices such as intelligence-led policing, COMPSTAT (with its focus on real-time crime intelligence), and a blended intelligence-investigation function justified in terms of "connecting the dots" are important elements of this policing.

Chapter 9 looks at the notion that police work is citizen-based. It claims the citizen-based approach to policing is important but has become less viable in the early twenty-second century. Chapter 10 looks at where police work is going. A section called the "Noble Cause Ascendant" is a cautionary tale to managers about what can happen when the law can be justified in terms of the noble cause. This is followed by a review of the most popular police operational tactics in the current era, which focus heavily on aggressive enforcement practices.

# 9

# Policing Citizens, Policing Communities: Toward an Ethic of Negotiated Order

## Key Terms

| | |
|---|---|
| cognitive dissonance | police-community reciprocity |
| informal norms | quality of life |
| iron fist | melting pot |
| middle-ground institutions | social distance |
| order maintenance policing | velvet glove |
| "Broken Windows" | incivility |
| globalization theory | distinctiveness theory |
| disorder | order negotiation |

## Introduction

This chapter explores the evolving role of policing in diverse democratic societies, emphasizing the ethical and practical challenges of community-based policing. Drawing from the "Broken Windows" theory, it examines how incivility and disorder signal declining quality of life and erode informal norms that sustain neighborhood cohesion. The chapter contrasts the velvet glove of community engagement with the iron fist of aggressive enforcement, highlighting the tension between order maintenance policing and democratic values. As globalization theory and distinctiveness theory suggest, increasing diversity intensifies group identity, challenging the melting pot ideal and complicating shared notions of public order. In such contexts, police must navigate cognitive dissonance between their moral predispositions and the heterogeneous values of the communities they serve.

DOI: 10.4324/9781003626916-13

The commanders return from the 2:30 P.M. break and prepare for the final discussion. Participants had taken a long break, and only two hours of presentation remain. This is where Mike presents his pitch for a citizen-based ethic of police work.

*Mike: I remember when someone said to me once "You don't represent citizens." I was stunned. It made me really mad. What did they think I was doing out there on the streets? I really had to think hard on that one.*

You know something? They were right.

## Part 1: Citizen-Centered Policing: Moral Issues

The United States is in the midst of a sea change in policing. Federal funding for community policing through the National Institute of Justice dropped off dramatically after the terrorist attacks of September 11, 2001. And federal requirements to develop local counter-terrorism practices were inadequately funded, requiring a re-channeling of funds away from other programs into counter-terrorism. Many U.S. agencies, particularly at the federal level, began the process of re-framing the police mission toward state-protective policing organized around a security mandate, and in which all citizens were deemed potential security hazards, something which was not even a consideration prior to the 9/11 attacks. Yet the notion of policing for citizens, and acting on their behalf in the maintenance of community order, is strong. Police officer moral commitments to the noble cause—to doing something for citizens and victims—help tie police to local communities. This chapter is about policing for citizens and communities, which was the principal form of policing in the twentieth century. This chapter looks at the way the noble cause facilitates but also sometimes disrupts police abilities to "represent citizens."

## Citizen-Based Police Work in the Twentieth Century

Policing for citizens, with its tripartite functional structure of service, order maintenance, and crime prevention, was central to policing through the twentieth century. It particularly emphasized the way police can maintain public order, either through direct action on their own or with the assistance of citizens. The most important of these three functions was order maintenance (Wilson, 1968). Regoli and Hewitt (1996) defined **order maintenance** as follows:

> When order has been disrupted, it is the police officer's job to restore it. Police intervention is intended to stop whatever has disturbed the peace whether it is the peace between a citizen and a neighborhood or the peace between two people.
>
> (Regoli and Hewitt, 1996:265)

Wilson's (1968) notion of order-maintenance, it should be emphasized, located most police work at the discretion of citizens, who regularly invoked police to address local disorder problems, through calls for service. In Wilson's model, police calls for service were dominated by those related to misdemeanor offenses, and they relied on the willingness and energetic actions of citizens to ensure the law was enforced. Black (1973, 1980) extended this notion to felony calls as well, which he noted often were only enforced when citizens wanted them to be. Citizens consequently could be thought of as a moral filter through which police acted to maintain community order, as a direct response to a citizen request.

In May 2020, George Floyd, a 46-year-old Black man, was killed when a Minneapolis police officer knelt on his neck for nine minutes. The type of choke hold used on Floyd was approved and taught at the time in police officer training. However, the killing of Floyd in addition to the prior deaths of Breonna Taylor in Louisville, KY, Freddie Gray in Baltimore, MD, Tamir Rice in Cleveland, OH, Michael Brown in Ferguson, MO, and Eric Garner in New York, NY, triggered a broad social response: a noticeable shift in public opinion of policing. Polls taken at the time, including a Fox/Data for Progress poll, indicated that a majority of likely voters supported some reform ideas such as collecting better data on police use of force, mandatory use of body cameras for police officers, and banning choke holds, such as the one used on Floyd. Since policing in a general sense is dependent upon cooperation from the public, a logical question at the time was whether the shift in opinion resulted in an effect on police calls for service. According to a study by the National Academy of Sciences (2022), data from New York City and Los Angeles related to calls on violent crime, property crime, and quality of life disorder were compared to address any differences prior to and after Floyd's death. In New York City, after his death, property crime, violent crime, and quality of life calls all increased significantly. The statistically significant number of calls related to violent crime in New York was greatest in areas of the city where the majority of residents were black, but the increase in property crime calls was greatest in areas where most of the of the residents were white. In Los Angeles, the calls related to quality of life decreased significantly but only in areas with a white majority of residents. In both cities, however, the effect was relatively short-lived (Brantingham et al., 2022). One reasonable conclusion from the study was that there was a temporary emotional public reaction to Floyd's death, but civilians in an emergency need to call someone for assistance, and people call the police because they have no credible alternative.

Black Lives Matter (BLM) is a social movement that advocates for racial justice and equality, particularly focusing on issues of police brutality and systemic racism. It began in 2013 after the acquittal of George Zimmerman in the killing of Trayvon Martin and gained recognition following the murder of George Floyd in 2020. The movement seeks to address disparities in law enforcement, criminal justice, and economic opportunities for black communities. BLM has been instrumental in raising awareness about racial injustices, inspiring protests, and influencing policy discussions on policing and civil rights. It promotes initiatives such as criminal justice reform, educational equity, and voting rights.

Despite its impact, BLM has faced criticism regarding its leadership structure, lack of financial transparency, and the role of certain protests that have led to unrest. Some opponents argue that its call to defund the police is too extreme, while supporters believe it is necessary for reallocating resources to social services. Regardless of differing opinions, BLM has sparked meaningful conversations about race and justice worldwide. It continues to shape discussions on equality, pushing governments, institutions, and individuals to confront longstanding racial disparities and seek solutions for a more just society.

Order-maintenance activity is closely associated with neighborhood quality of life. By **quality of life** is meant two things: citizen attitudes, such as fear of crime and the related fear of participating in outdoor activities, and declines in the physical quality of neighborhoods, indicated to a certain extent by the accumulation of trash and graffiti. Some departments act on the belief that aggressive enforcement of public-order laws can protect communities from future "quality of life" decline and the onset of more serious crime problems. Consequently, under a community policing mandate, police departments and officers may aggressively suppress public-order problems in order to improve what is perceived as community quality of life.

## Communities, the Velvet Glove, and the Iron Fist

The last third of the twentieth century was widely described as the era of community policing, which can be characterized as the highest expression of citizen-based policing. However, one can identify two separate and conflicting themes in that era: the velvet glove and the iron fist (Kraska and Paulsen, 1996). The **velvet glove** refers to "soft" police strategies and tactics, such as door-to-door crime prevention initiatives, community watch groups, and block meetings. Velvet glove initiatives encourage public participation. These and related practices were at the core of the community policing movement from the early 1970s until the mid-1980s. Community policing practices in this era, spurred by the Crime and Kerner Commission reports in 1967 and 1968, represented an effort by local political groups, often with the support of federal grant monies and with a nascent but highly interested academic research support, to build positive and sustainable relations between the police and minority communities (see Crank, 2003).

The **iron fist,** on the other hand, represents the hard edge of law enforcement. Iron fist tactics, such as street sweeps and aggressive enforcement of public-order statutes, are designed to assert police control over crime-ridden areas. In one of its most aggressive forms, the iron fist refers to the militarization of police units and their use in routine police activities. This retooling of the community policing movement was initiated with the widely cited "broken windows" paper in *Atlantic Monthly* (Wilson and Kelling, 1982) and was in force through 2000. During this period, community policing shifted from a notion of policing organized around citizen empowerment to policing organized around the control and surveillance of risk populations.

Crank and Langworthy (1992) argued that one could see within the community policing movement the competing influences of conservative and liberal crime control agendas. Conservative themes aimed, according to the authors, at expanding police authority to intervene in crime and public-order problems that appeared to be endemic in many cities. Liberal themes were concerned with providing broad police services for residents of poverty-stricken minority neighborhoods and ensuring that the police treated minority citizens fairly. In the aftermath of George Floyd's death in 2020, progressive liberals lobbied to "defund the police" among many demonstrations after his death. However, to date, no city has done this, although many departments have outlawed the type of choke hold used against Floyd.

Many observers of the police are fearful that if the police are granted increased authority to intervene in the affairs of the citizenry on behalf of public order and the quality of life, United States democratic traditions will be seriously compromised (see Box 9.1). They may be right; we don't know. The United States is, in many ways, an innocent among world powers; unlike most countries in the world, we have never experienced a history of autocratic rule or military dictatorship. We might not know how to recognize either encroaching totalitarianism or advancing socialism.

Box 9.1

**Community Policing and the Expansion of State Power**

Because government is deeply distrusted in Anglo-American tradition, the powers of the police are circumscribed; their activities closely monitored. . . . Seen in these terms, community policing, which is community-based crime prevention under governmental auspices, is a contradiction in terms. It requires the police, who are bound by law, to lead communities in informal surveillance, analysis, and treatment. Community policing is a license for police to intervene in the private lives of individuals. It harnesses the coercive power of the state to social amelioration. This represents an expansion of state power and is much more in keeping with the continental European than with the Anglo-American traditions of policing.

Source: D.H. Bayley and C.D. Shearing (1998). "The Future of Policing." Pages 158–159 in G. Cole and M. Gertz (eds.) The Criminal Justice System: Politics and Policies, Seventh Edition, pp. 150–168. Belmont, CA: West/Wadsworth Publishing Company.

Mike describes his thoughts on community policing to the commanders. They've heard most of it before—many of the ideas aren't new. He then discusses how a value-based decision-maker might look at citizen-based policing.

Think of a value-based decision-maker—which, you'll recall, is who you hire when you recruit a police officer. She or he is a hero type, a tower runner. He's got all the symbols of authority—the badge, helmet, the insulating sunglasses, Sam Brown, pepper spray, 9mm, PR24, shotgun in the trunk, Taser, running for cover, ready for war. Whose values do they represent? The public? Not exactly. They are value-based decision-makers, committed to the noble cause, and they use the law to advance that cause.

Mike waits for an answer. No one answers. *Where do his values come from?*

"Their upbringing," one of the commanders responds.

*Right.* Mike smiles. *Their values. It always comes back to that.*

If we are policing for communities, we then ask this officer to enforce neighborhood order. Whatever that is. We recommend to them not to take a "what the hell" attitude just because the law hasn't been technically broken. We want them to get involved in the community. What're we really asking them? We're asking them to apply their moral standard to this whole new area. We have to be very, very careful about this. How are you going to react when a citizen tells you "you don't represent citizens"? Well, do you? Maybe you don't.

## *Informal Community Norms and Police Values*

A central tenet of community-based policing, as Wilson (1968) (see also Wilson and Kelling, 1982) noted, is that in maintaining public order the police enforce the informal norms of their local communities. By **informal norms** is meant that a community has its particular ideas of acceptable behavior, ideas that are not written down but taken for granted by community members. Informal norms are different from laws, which are written down and provide the basis for law enforcement. For example, a community may think that it is unacceptable for homeless individuals to sleep in a particular park, even though there is no law that technically forbids it. Police officers might consequently roust out the homeless, arguing that by doing so, they diminish the sales of drugs in the park. Reformers worry that informal community norms might include racial norms as well. What if, for example, an African American community wants police to stop and question all young Asian males in their neighborhood? What, then, would be the police role? Finally, does the policing of informal norms "condition" the police to extra-legal actions against citizens on behalf of state security?

By enforcing the "informal norms of the community" the police will, in the day-to-day practice of their work, theoretically enforce the same values as the communities they police. Whatever predisposing values or ethics an officer has, he or she may set these aside and adopt the standards of the communities for which they are responsible. Yet, as we have argued, this is precisely what many police officers don't do. The values that motivate police officers tend to stem from moral predispositions and sometimes override the standards of the community. Many cops, the value-based decision-makers, are committed to the noble cause, and they use the law to advance that cause. And where do their values come from? Their upbringing. Something which is difficult, if not impossible, to override.

Under a community policing philosophy, are we simply providing them with an expanded authority to exercise their moral predispositions over citizens? The danger is that community policing carries in it the seeds for noble-cause corruption justified in terms of community protection. The noble-cause corruption problem for community policing, simply put, is this: "If community protection is a higher moral principle than the lawful constitutional protections given to individual citizens, why should we pay attention to the law if we can do something to protect communities?"

> Mike taps the continuum with his knuckles. *Remember the continuum? With police values way on the right and community values on the left? If we just power up line officers with more authority, what do you think is going to happen? Do you think that they'll get along better with citizens? Giving them more power is not enough. You've got to get the police and the public on the same side of the continuum.*

Let's replay this dilemma as an ethical question. How can we provide police with a wider mandate to intercede in the affairs of citizens and at the same time instill ethical protections against noble-cause corruption? This is a difficult question, yet one that must be answered if we want to both preserve our democratic heritage and expand the police role.

> Mike presents his vision of community policing. *When we police for communities, and when we go out and try to maintain public order in these same communities, it has got to be done right. Let's think about it for a minute. When we do community policing, we have to make sure that all officers are doing it. Not a special squad within the department, there's no commitment there. And they all have to get out in the public and mix with citizens. That's got to be part of the package.*
>
> The other part of the package is command. Commanders have to be on board. They have to be supportive, and they have to know what they are doing in relation to the communities their officers are policing. If you do this you've done two things important to citizens. First, you reduce the social distance between the police and the policed. Second, you empower the police and the policed alike, together.

## *Proposition 1: Policing on Behalf of Citizens Can Reduce Social Distance*

The first proposition is that community-based policing can reduce the social distance between the police and the policed. **Social distance** refers to the degree of friendliness and sense of comfort between two people or two groups. Social distance is small between two families, for example, if they would permit their children to intermarry. Social distance is large when a family would not permit one of their members to talk to someone or would not be willing to live in the same neighborhood with that person.

Consider the crime control/due process continuum again. The police, as we noted earlier, tend to be on the right side of it, on the crime control side. The policed tend to be more toward the middle or on the left side, the due process side. This is what the Rokeach et al. (1971) data show us in Chapter 4. Members of ethnic and racial minority communities tend to be on the due process side, not because they are sympathetic to criminals; they tend, in fact, to be victimized more frequently than middle-class Anglo citizens. It's because that abuse by the police is historically greater among minority group members than among white middle-class citizens, and minority group members are consequently more afraid of them (see Cao et al., 1996; Williams and Murphy, 1995; Powers, 1995; Kappeler et al., 1994; Kerner and the National Advisory Commission on Civil Disorders, 1968).

What is the social distance between the police and the population policed? It tends to be large, particularly in minority neighborhoods, for two reasons. First, the police and the policed don't share the same values. This is particularly the case when the policed are also minorities. Our data often show that the areas most heavily policed are minority communities, particularly African American communities. In such communities, the police sometimes develop their images of crime, criminals, and appropriate police response, according to prevailing racial stereotypes. Consider Bouza's observation in Box 9.2.

Box 9.2

**Racial Stereotyping and Police Practices**

In Los Angeles, the police were forced to abandon choke holds, not because they were ineffective but largely because of a stupid comment made by the chief following the death of a black man who'd been subdued by the grip, which temporarily cuts off the flow of the blood to the brain, causing the suspect to pass out. The chief created an uproar when he blurted out that blacks were somehow physiologically different from

Box 9.2, *continued*

> "normal people" in the flow of blood to the brain. The resulting clamor was so intense that an aggressive agency, and an aggressive chief, had to abandon the practice.

Source: Anthony Bouza (1990). *The Police Mystique*, p. 94.

Second, police of necessity act out their role in an authoritarian manner; they don't take a vote of citizens when deciding to make an arrest. Indeed, the authority of the state is specifically granted to permit total control of citizens under specific circumstances. Many police officers make peremptory decisions about the likely guilt or innocence of a suspect, and their subsequent actions stem from that decision. They may decide, for example, that the person they are dealing with is an "asshole" and needs special, physical "treatment"—a beating or rough search. Such decisions, when linked to racial stereotyping, will sharply increase the social distance between the police and the policed.

Policing as though people matter, to borrow Guyot's (1991) wonderful phrase, has the potential to lower the social distance between the police and the policed. It can do this by building relationships between the police and the policed in ways that do not depend on police authority but instead are constructed around a shared capacity to solve community problems. One of the best discussions of the idea of a shared problem-solving is presented by Skolnick and Bayley (1986). They used a phrase, police-community reciprocity, to describe this idea. By **police-community reciprocity,** they meant that the police and community members work together to solve crime problems and to develop crime prevention tactics. What does reciprocity contribute to the police mission? Skolnick and Bayley (1991) suggested that "police who are substantially involved in reciprocal community crime prevention programs will experience significantly less fear of those communities." With regard to community members, they observed: "The general reaction to community contact seems to have been 'Where have you been all along?' or 'It's about time.'" This also makes for good policing:

> Like policemen themselves, the public is tired of police arriving after harm has been done, understanding all too well that little can be done then, particularly with respect to catching the criminal.
>
> (Skolnick and Bayley, 1991:501)

Community-based policing increases the number of non-enforcement contacts between police and the policed. Police, we believe, will cease being faceless uniforms to citizens, and the public will cease being treated as potentially dangerous strangers by the police. In short, the police and the policed become humanized; they are received as individual citizens to each other, seeking acceptable solutions to common problems. Guyot (1991) captured the way in which nontraditional policing humanizes the police by changing the social distance between the police and the policed in Box 9.3.

Box 9.3

**Toward an Understanding of Common Humanity**

When officers repeatedly assist diverse individuals and receive heartfelt thanks, they come to see beyond the jumbled fragments of others' lives to recognize the common humanity they share with people who ask for their help and even with many of the people they arrest. In learning to care for the people they serve, officers develop a tragic perspective on life that makes them less susceptible to cynical views. They become strengthened by their personal commitment to helping people. By contrast, if officers narrow their responsibility to dealing with crime—to attacks that people make on each other and their property—and focus on lawbreakers, then they have fewer opportunities to feel kinship with their clients.

Source: Dorothy Guyot (1991). *Policing as Though People Matter*, Philadelphia, PA: Temple University Press. p. 271.

Guyot also noted that early contacts with citizens can have an amplifying effect on officers' attitudes. Officers who initially felt sympathy for their clients tended to find satisfaction in their work and develop a wide repertoire of social skills. On the other hand, those who started with distrust tended to cause distrust in the public as well and become vindictive in their police work. The responsibility for a TO was clear: to ensure that officers start in the right direction.

## *Cognitive Dissonance and Community Policing*

At this point, Mike decides to develop one of his favorite themes. He pauses for a minute, rubbing his hands together, composing his thoughts. It's important, he believes, that the audience understand this aspect of the training seminar.

If I bring different groups together in a non-arrest circumstance, what do you think is going to happen? It's going to lower the social distance between them. There is a psychological term for the way social distance is affected when people interact. It is called cognitive dissonance.

Cognitive dissonance is a concept that has been around for more than 65 years. First published by Leon Festinger in 1957, and reaching its height of popularity in the late 1970s, the theory of cognitive dissonance has generated a great deal of discussion. Let's review the central ideas of cognitive dissonance (see Box 9.4).

Box 9.4

### Elements of Cognitive Dissonance

Cognition refers to knowledge that we have. They can be specific bits of information or general concepts. Sometimes we have cognitions—pieces of knowledge—that seem to be inconsistent or "dissonant" with each other. When this happens, the person is in a state of **cognitive dissonance** (Wicklund and Brehm, 1976). They have two (or more) cognitions that conflict with each other.

Let's say that someone is eating a strange food. The food is a mash that tastes like potatoes but more meaty. The eater thinks that it tastes good. Then the eater is told that she is eating mashed insect grubs. The eater might have a cognition of what bugs look like, and what they don't look like is good food. Consequently, at that moment, there are two cognitions—(1) one is eating bugs, and (2) bugs aren't food—that are dissonant to each other.

The more important the cognitions that are in disagreement, the greater the cognitive dissonance. Hence, the greater the motivational pressure to resolve the dissonance. Most people are extremely uncomfortable with high levels of cognitive dissonance. Eating bugs is highly dissonant for many people. How can the dissonance be resolved?

There are three general principles that describe the resolution of dissonance. First, when dissonance is too great, the reduction in dissonance will occur toward the cognition least resistant to change and away from the one most important to the individual. For example, in the previous "eating bugs" example, it may be far easier to simply stop eating bugs than to convince yourself that bugs are good food. If, on the other hand, the only food available was bug mash, one might reconcile oneself to the notion that bugs are, after all, good food and resolve the dissonance by munching away.

Second, all things being equal, when a recent behavior and a more distant behavior are dissonant, the dissonance is more likely to be resolved in terms favorable to the more recent behavior.

Third, personal responsibility is central to the resolution of cognitive dissonance. If a person acts freely, without sense of external constraint, s/he has a sense of personal responsibility for the relationship between the dissonant elements. Without the element of personal responsibility, the dissonant elements are psychologically irrelevant to the individual (Wicklund and Brehm, 1976). In other words, if someone is forced into a situation where they have to endure dissonant cognitions, the sense of disagreement between them will not go away. For example, if I am forced to eat mashed bugs, and I already know I do not want to, I am likely to continue to dislike it. But if I eat them voluntarily, I am more likely to decide that I like eating them.

> Mike taps the board on the right side of the continuum with his knuckles. *If your street officers believe that they are morally different from the public, and I'm making that argument that police are value-based decision-makers, why should they want to pay attention to what citizens think? If there's a lot of cognitive dissonance, if your officers are over here*—he taps the right side of the continuum on the blackboard—*and the policed are over here*—he taps the left side of the continuum—*they aren't going to like each other. That's the point. It's up to you to see that they not only work together, but that they want to work together. Otherwise your efforts to reach out to citizens are probably going to fail.*

Cognitions include beliefs about people. For the police, cognitions can include stereotypes about those policed. We have argued that many police officers believe themselves to be morally different, on "the side of angels," as Bouza (1990:17) put it. Moral difference transforms easily into racist stereotyping when the population policed is different in some ethnic, religious, or racial way (Crank, 2004a). Moreover, cognitions are emotionally charged by a person's somatic markers, infusing their behavior with predispositive emotional content. When a police officer views his or her responsibility through the lens of moral righteousness and believes that they have the authority of the state on their side, will they feel cognitive dissonance in arresting or mistreating someone whom they have negatively stereotyped? No. They'll enjoy it.

Programs that are designed to bring the police and the community together in non-traditional ways have the potential to lower the impact of moral differences between the police and the policed. Skolnick and Bayley (1986) maintain that the police must convey to the public that they have something to contribute to the community and that the police must recognize that the public is an equal partner. But what kind of behaviors can change the traditional authority imbalance between citizens and police?

Bringing the two groups together will cause a state of cognitive dissonance for the police and the policed alike. The police must treat as problem-solving partners a group previously thought of as morally inferior. The police, as Skolnick and Bayley (1986) noted, must be prepared for constructive criticism from the public. How will the dissonance be resolved? Let us return to the three principles for the resolution of dissonance in Box 9.4.

The first principle was that dissonance would be reduced in the least resistant direction. For a line officer, which of the following is least resistant: to work in a crime preventive capacity as equals with a formerly distrusted group or to refuse to work, request a shift, and ignore the expectations of superior officers? The tendency, we argue, will be to conform to managerial expectations. Forcing people to work together does not, in itself, reduce dissonance, however. Experiences with minority hiring programs in some police departments have taught us that laws requiring occupational integration can backfire, intensifying hostilities between

Anglo- and African Americans. Recall the third principle of dissonance in Box 9.4: Forced relations do not reduce dissonance.

Commanders, in order to resolve dissonance in a non-forced way, must be practically involved in the day-to-day implementation and activity of community policing. Line officers have to understand that the community policing program carries the moral weight and real commitment of its leaders. Active command level support is important for successful implementation of the kind of value changes that will enable community policing to prosper. Commanders must take the lead through the art of example and persuasion, not punitive policy.

Commanders have to take the lead in bridging the gap between the policed and the police. If they abandon this work to their sergeants, the program will collapse under the weight of line resistance. Commanders have to get out into the field, work with the troops, be highly visible, and sell the program with their own commitment. Commanders may be the single most important and undervalued link in the implementation of community policing programs (Geller and Swanger, 1995). Through the aggressive and supportive activity of executives, including the chief or sheriff, commanders can begin to change the leads followed by line officers.

The second principle is that dissonance tends to be resolved in terms of more recent behaviors. This principle suggests that, even for officers with a tradition of negative feelings for particular groups, more recent positive behaviors or "good works" can result in a change in sentiments toward the groups policed. Here, we again consider the question "Where do your officers take their leads from?" If they're being shoveled from assignment to makeshift assignment, or aren't being provided clear responsibilities and receive no command support, they're likely to end up despising community policing and the populations being policed. If, on the other hand, commanders are out in the field with them, their TO is preparing them to work with other groups, their performance evaluations are linked to their relations and activities with the policed, they have a clear set of job expectations and they are learning specialized skills for their craft, then they are gaining a set of behaviors that will encourage positive relations with community groups.

The third principle is self-responsibility. If a person is arbitrarily assigned to work with others they don't like, their sense of personal responsibility for the policed is absent, and there will be no reason to resolve the dissonance. Arbitrary assignments can have backfiring consequences, with officers increasing their disdain and moral distance for the policed. Police officers doing community policing must be involved in the decisions about the kinds of assignments that they have or the way the assignments are organized. Again, to use the words of Skolnick and Bayley (1986), officers need the opportunity to do "creative, customized police work."

## *Proposition 2: Policing on Behalf of Citizens Empowers the Police and the Policed Alike*

Empowerment means that the police work with citizens at the neighborhood level to cooperatively alleviate the root causes of criminal behavior (Frank et al., 1996). Community policing focuses on what are sometimes called the **middle-ground institutions** of American life: local neighborhoods and neighborhood organizations that are midway between individuals and large-scale governmental enterprises. Citizen empowerment at the neighborhood level is different from both conservative and liberal solutions to crime and public-order problems, though it contains features of both. Traditional strategies have sometimes used large-scale governmental intervention to change the social structure of equality or opportunity. The unanticipated consequences of these policies as a spur for central state growth have rarely been examined by their proponents. On the other hand, policies aimed at individuals have typically taken the form of crime suppression efforts. These efforts have been designed around deterrence and arrest production, without thought given to the long-term consequences of mass incarceration practices on individuals, their families, their communities, and ultimately, on re-entry post-incarceration.

It is in the arena of **middle-ground institutions** that we envision a continuing role for community policing. The middle-ground institutions—the social, geographical, and economic arenas where we act out our daily lives at home and at work—are the proper focus of community policing. Community policing empowers line officers to make decisions about how normal affairs in their assigned area are carried out, with an eye toward the contribution of their efforts to the well-being of those communities. A guiding premise of community policing is that, by granting line officers wider authority in the way in which they carry out their daily routines, they will develop imaginative solutions to the problems of crime and its prevention (Trojanowicz et al., 1990; Greene and Mastrofski, 1991). Crime and public order are intricately tied to the social and economic well-being of local communities, particularly in quality-of-life issues. For this reason, community policing, by empowering officers to assist communities in quality-of-life issues, helps protect and preserve the middle ground.

Some observers of the police have been concerned that the language of community policing is little more than a veil for the expansion of the criminal justice system into areas of activity traditionally private (Kappeler and Kraska, 1998). This literature asks a question important to the perspective we develop here: Is empowerment any more than the expansion of police authority in the lives of citizens? We believe that the answer to this question depends on how community policing is practically implemented. Empowerment is a community property shared by police and policed alike.

For police officers, empowerment is the ability to act in concert with the community and with other officers in order to achieve what cannot be done alone. It is the cooperative dimension of human interaction that seeks to engage our imaginations, to enable us as collective actors to participate in the shaping and enrichment of our lives (Ferguson, 1987). Citizens can also be empowered through an effective community policing program. Through the organization of community groups—the lifeblood of community policing, as Skolnick and Bayley (1986) described them—citizens can reassert their control over the spaces in which they live. For the police and citizens alike, empowerment is the enabling process that reaches beyond traditional reactive policing in order to address larger social and environmental problems that create the conditions for disorder and crime. Empowerment affirms the middle ground institutions that, as de Tocqueville (2009) noted 200 years ago, are the foundations of democratic participation in American social and political life.

## *Common Good and Individual Rights*

Some scholars perceive the array of constitutional "due process" protections to be a threat to community order. By focusing too much on individual rights, it is argued that we overlook the common good and inadvertently allow public-order conditions to emerge that damage community life and viability. Public-order problems that endanger communities may not technically be against the law or, if they are, may seem not to warrant a large investment in police services. Yet, it is suggested, a failure to deal with these problems will lead to more profound crime problems in the future. The police should be encouraged to become involved even in seemingly unimportant public-order problems, for these problems can lead to community deterioration and serious crime. This often leads to "zero-tolerance" crackdowns on minor disorders or other misdemeanor crimes.

We have a different view of the relationship between the common good and individual rights. We take a historically Republican view that due process protections provide the primary bulwark against the growth of central state power in the United States (see Klockars, 1995). By focusing on the responsibilities of individuals to participate in the civic life of their communities, and by empowering local and community institutions to deal with their problems, we can deal meaningfully with the crime and public-order problems that tear at the fabric of community life. The basic question is this: What police tactics and strategies contribute to the common good of communities, and what tactics detract from it?

Some aggressive policing tactics, particularly those associated with drug suppression—intensive use of arrest to deal with public-order problems, sweeps, zero-tolerance, or the use of battering rams to break into suspected drug houses, for example—may carry in them the seeds of long-term neighborhood destruction rather than revitalization. Other tactics that fall into this category include sting operations and stakeouts (Bouza, 1990). It is not that these police tactics are ineffective or illegal; they frequently are seen by the police as the only reasonable way to deal with entrenched drug and/or crime problems. But they can alienate many citizens in precisely those neighborhoods that police are trying to "save." As Bouza observed, stakeouts sometimes end in a deadly force incident, which may be viewed by the surrounding community as an "execution." Street sweeps are seen as blatant harassment. Community members often view stings as unfair entrapment, even when conducted legally. These kinds of tactics empower police while weakening the policed. If the reader doesn't believe that, watch one sometime. Tactics such as these isolate the police from the communities they are intended to protect. They delegitimize the police to citizens.

It is difficult to see the long-term good in police tactics that, in some of our cities, have resulted in as much as 50 percent of the African American youths under correctional control or sought by the police on warrants. The focus on individual-level crime has led us away from an understanding of crime's environmental and community roots (Felson, 1994). Without understanding how crime is rooted in everyday life, the police are and will continue to be ill-equipped to adapt to the profound changes that are occurring in the economic and social lives of citizens today, including the growth of groups such as Black Lives Matter.

Citizen-based policing, by focusing on the empowerment of neighborhood institutions rather than a strategy of individualized suppressive crime control, provides the conditions for organized neighborhood involvement in the political life of cities, a condition essential for the long-term well-being of democratic society. When we organize citizens into community groups, we are harkening to the traditions of grass roots democracy in the United States. Citizen-based policing, using community-based policing and other dissonance-reducing practices, adapts that tradition to the emergent needs of the twenty-first century.

## Part II: Policing in Transition: Who We Are and Who We're Becoming

The United States is in the midst of dramatic population transformation, both in terms of the kinds of people emigrating to the United States and in the way various groups are distributing themselves across the American landscape.

Consider the extent to which the U.S. receives foreigners on a yearly basis. In 2000, immigrants numbered about 850,000, a number that is anticipated to increase. Most come to be with family members, with the second largest numbers coming for work. Further, 33 million nonimmigrants arrived in 2000. Thirty million of them came for business or pleasure. At that point, about 8 million illegal immigrants were in the U.S. These included illegal entrants, legal entrants who overstayed their visas, and those who committed crimes. With President Biden's open border policies, in effect since his election in 2020, the United States has allowed more than 11 million illegal immigrants into this country (USAFacts, 2024). This has crippled many cities in America, in terms of attempting to provide social services, including education and health care, for both citizens and immigrants. The absence of federal funds to help with state and local costs, large numbers of migrants arriving without any connections to this country, and long waits for migrants to work legally have combined to create a major burden for several "sanctuary" cities, which have spent millions or billions to try and meet immediate needs of immigrants. New York City spent an estimated $1.7 billion on illegal migrants through July 2023, Chicago expects a bill for $256 million between August 2022 and December 2023, and Denver has spent $24 million as of September 2023 (Chishti et al., 2023).

We're also witnessing a broad change in general migration patterns. In the 1980s, one-half as many people emigrated from Europe to the United States as in the 1960s. More than five times as many came from Asia, twice as many from Mexico, the Caribbean, and Central America, and nearly four times as many from Africa (Roberts, 1994:73). These general geographic identities themselves mask astonishing ethnic diversity. The current census counts 179 ancestry groupings for the "Hispanic" category alone (Roberts, 1994:73). And the most recent wave of immigration has seen the numbers of Asians more than double. For example, according to Suburbanstats.org (2020), in Minnesota, Asians total 214,234, with slightly more than half of them female (110,295). Diversity in some places is remarkable. In Los Angeles, more than 80 languages are spoken (Kaplan, 1998). The long-term implications are clear. By 2050, no racial or ethnic group will constitute a majority (Roberts, 1994:246).

The United States is in the midst of a dramatic internationalization of its population. Kaplan (1998) argued that the United States is in the process of becoming the first true international civilization. The century of European political domination is fading. The United States is "shedding its skin," becoming truly multi-civilizational. According to the U.S. census:

> the projections show that the U.S. population is expected to rise from 305 million people to 439 million by 2050, but it will be a population that looks quite different both in age, race and ethnicity. According to the census bureau's statistics, people who regard themselves as Hispanic, African-American, Asian, American Indian, Native Hawaiian and Pacific Islander will become the majority by 2042.
>
> (*LA Times*, 2008)

Kaplan's (1998) description of Los Angeles in Box 9.5 recalls the complex diversity that characterizes urban America.

Box 9.5

**Kaplan and the Internationalization of the American Population**

Immigrant dynamism coupled with Asian as well as Latino mestizoization are the central facts of late twentieth-century Los Angeles. And the reality is richer still, as Indian Immigrants buy up Artesia, next to Cerritos, and Iranian immigrants, after buying many properties in Beverly Hills, buy now in nearby Westwood (Kaplan, 1998:42).

Walking down streets in Vancouver, Kaplan observed:

> I saw many signs in Punjabi, Hindi, Farsi, Arabic, and Khmer—but almost none in French, an official Canadian language.
> (1998:52)

And in Portland, Kaplan cites another informant:

> "The early settlers here recreated the New England village," Seltzer explained. "Since then we've been good at space arrangement and streetscapes. Our next challenge will be to get along with each other." The white population is aging, and twenty years hence Portland will be like greater L.A. in terms of ethnicity.
> (1998:61)

Source: R. Kaplan (1998). "Travels Into America's Future." *Atlantic Monthly*, August 1998.

One of the driving factors behind these changes is the dramatic internationalization of the economy that occurred between 1980 and 2010. It is cheaper, Kaplan observed, for companies to hire educated immigrants than to educate them in the United States. Weak national standards in the United States and low taxes have intellectually and financially impoverished many local school systems, making it far easier to import intellectual capital needed to compete internationally and lessening the Anglo-European influence over the economy. The United States is consequently internationalizing, united not by a common morality but by its commitment to its economic system.

## *Change and Conflict*

Foreign in-migration, substantial though it is, is only a small part of overall migration in the US. Internal migration is high, fluid, and dynamic. Blue-collar workers tend to migrate at a much higher rate than white-collar workers. City dwellers relocate to the suburbs or rural hinterland, the rural area within automotive access to city services and employment, seeking a more comfortable lifestyle. Religious groups seek divine meaning through rural settlement. All of these are groups on the move in the

United States today. We not only have broad shifts in ethnicity and race but in income, education, and age as well. And not only Anglo citizens migrate internally but so do African Americans, Latinos, and other indigenous citizens. Will all these different groups "melt" together, as suggested by the storied melting pot idea? Or will they conflict?

Our history books have described the pattern of ethnic assimilation in the United States groups in terms of a **melting pot** metaphor. This means that groups are assimilated after immigrating to the United States, their distinctiveness and cultural uniqueness gradually disappearing. Over time, immigrants share common values and beliefs. Yet the opposite may, in fact, occur. Huntington (1996) observed that cultural identities become more important with increased interactions between groups. He described this as **distinctiveness theory** (McGuire and McGuire, 1988), which means that people define themselves by what makes them different from others. Ethnic self-consciousness is intensified as diverse ethnic and cultural groups become more interdependent, a phenomenon Huntington called **globalization theory** (Robertson, 1987).

Both globalization and distinctiveness theory describe a very unmelting-pot notion—that groups become more different as they interact with each other. Core cultural identities are based in religious beliefs, and increased contact has resulted, Huntington argued, in the rise of fundamentalism in and conflict between many of the world's major religions. A global religious revival marks the onset of a "return to the sacred," in response to peoples' perception of the world as a single place (Huntington, 1996:68). If this is the case, there is a possibility that ethnic, religious, and cultural diversification will similarly result in internal conflicts in the United States. Certainly, we have witnessed a great deal of violence against Muslims in the United States since 9/11, though the specific numbers of hate crimes are unclear. Should the police try to reinforce or to enact that traditional community's local standards of order?

Let's present this question in a different way. What if the police were to adopt the position that they were responsible for reinforcing the will of the "traditional" community? Would they then encourage further acts of violence against newly arrived minority group members? The notion is, of course, offensive and reveals a fundamental flaw in contemporary ideas of public-order policing. The very presence of public-order problems stands as stark proof that the idea of public order is itself an open question. When we ask the police to carry out some idea of "underlying order," we may be unintentionally asking them to take sides in conflicts. This is an inappropriate role for the police, especially in a democracy increasingly polyglot in every religious and ethnic sense of the term.

The police will be best served by a citizen-based ethic that will promote community security during the current age of demographic transition and social change. As the American people become more diverse, the police may be the critical mechanism that enables us to get along. It will fall to them to decide how and whether we get along. If they seek balance through negotiation in our complex cultural relationships, we just might succeed. If they view their task as the imposition of morality, we will not.

## Policing Communities in Conflict

One of the problems police must negotiate has to do with the way in which a highly segmented and diverse society lives, works, and recreates. How will groups coexist, where will the fault lines of conflict and dissent be, and in what constructive way can the police contribute?

### *Mastrofski and the Problem of Shared Order*

Mastrofski has studied the problems of shared order in communities and in neighborhoods. The following discussion is adapted from his analysis of these problems. His findings are insightful (1991:517):

> A basis for police action requires a demonstration that a group of people—say a neighborhood—shares a definition of what constitutes right order, threats to it, and appropriate methods for maintaining it. . . . There are undoubtedly neighborhoods that possess a high degree of homogeneity and group attachment. But it is in precisely the most afflicted areas that community is problematic in the sense required by the reform.

In other words, in those areas where we want the police to enforce some standard of existing public order, we are least likely to find it. Isn't it inevitable that the police, if they have the responsibility for carrying out some community standard of order in these communities where no standards exist, will retreat to their own moral standards? Problems of noble-cause corruption can only intensify in such circumstances.

Even the presence of a common ethnicity and shared customs does not guarantee common interest. Reviewing Horowitz (1984), Mastrofski described an old Chicago neighborhood that, by all appearances, looked like it would share a common heritage of values. It, in fact, did not. Neighborhood residents held widely differing views on two concerns important to public-order policing: what constituted public disorder and gang membership.

Rieder's (1985) study of Canarsie similarly revealed stark disagreement in residents' assessments of public order. This case was marked by overt racial conflict. Jewish and Italian residents mobilized in order to resist African American in-migration. They used confrontational strategies such as arson and vigilantism to keep African Americans out of their community. Block associations and crime patrols were employed to resist African American in-migration—a lesson in human relations for community policing advocates. In this case, any effort by the police to support traditional community norms would have resulted in openly discriminatory practices.

Block organizations, like other organizations that community police are supposed to work with, may not represent broad-based community interests. As Bohm (1984) observed, block organizations are heavily influenced by the distribution of power and influence in their community, particularly married homeowners with children. Nor do the views of block organization participants necessarily correspond to the interests of a representative population of residents. Research has shown that the attitudes of people active in neighborhood associations are not closely associated with the views of the larger neighborhood. They are, however, significantly correlated with those who have wealth and status (Rich, 1986).

What should be the police responsibility in places where the idea of order is itself problematic? We believe that the police role is to negotiate public order on behalf of citizens, not superimpose it based on some ill-defined notion of informal community norms. The distinctive mark of neighborhoods where public-order problems are the worst is that they are often places of high population mobility and where residents carry diverse notions of acceptable order. Common ground for order will itself change as migration patterns change. There is not a common level of public order that an officer can use as a standard for behavior. Contending and competing notions of order, changing over time, may be the standard with which the police must deal. The best contribution that an officer can make is to act as an arbiter among contending groups and work to negotiate an acceptable resolution to problems. That contribution, however, is truly democratic. It is order derived from within, not imposed from outside.

## *Skogan and the Limits of Police Authority*

In compelling research, Wesley Skogan (1990) examined the causes and consequences of disorder. His work is valuable for anyone trying to understand the many facets of disorder, and we will review it at length here.

Skogan assessed residents' perceptions of public-order problems in 40 neighborhoods in six major American cities. His team interviewed 13,000 residents on topics of disorder, crime, satisfaction, victimization, and neighborhood stability between the years of 1977 and 1983. He defined **disorder** as both individual behaviors that threatened the public order, and signs of physical decay to neighborhoods. To assess disorder, he examined individual behaviors, such as public drinking, corner gangs, street harassment, drugs, and noisy neighbors, and signs of physical decay, such as vandalism, dilapidation and abandonment, and rubbish.

Skogan found that neighborhood residents tended to agree on what constituted disorderly conditions. Renters as well as homeowners were likely to see the same sorts of things as disorderly. Interracial agreement was also observed: "Blacks and Whites agreed in their views of their communities to a surprising extent" (Skogan, 1990:57).

In what sort of communities was disorder a problem? Skogan conducted several analyses to determine where disorder was most likely to occur. His findings indicated that the best predictors of disorder were poverty and instability, that is, the extent to which the neighborhoods had more long-term residents, more owner-occupied residents, and higher levels of employment. What was the best predictor of poverty and instability? As Skogan notes, "The 'bottom line' is that racial and linguistic minorities in these 40 areas report the most significant disorder problems" (Skogan, 1990:61).

Skogan reviewed several evaluations of efforts to deal with disorder. His assessment of the capacity of community policing to do something about disorder was pessimistic. In Houston, the police had started programs aimed at citizen contacts, storefronts, and community organization. Disorder of all kinds went down after the programs were put into place. However, program successes were reported only for whites and homeowners. Blacks, Hispanics, and renters were unaffected by the program. In other words, "the better off got better off, and the disparity between area residents got deeper" (Skogan, 1990:107). The implications of the findings are bleak:

> The police are likely to get along best with the factions that share their outlook (Morris and Heal, 1981). The "local values" they represent are those of some of the community, but not all. In heterogenous neighborhoods, some residents can easily become the targets of the programs, and are not likely to be happy about that. . . . Equitable community policing may depend on a degree of homogeneity and consensus that does not exist in many troubled neighborhoods.
>
> (Skogan, 1990:109)

In our words, police officers who were carrying out community-based ideas of policing tended to find justifications for viewing public-order problems through the lens of their own morality.

Could communities confront disorder on their own, without police assistance? Consider Skogan's review of community efforts to control disorder in Chicago. The Ford Foundation paid ten community organizations $550,000 to organize block watches and other crime prevention measures. These were dubbed by Skogan as disorder reduction projects. Like the community policing experiment in Houston, evaluators found that those who were already better off were most likely to take advantage of the programs. More disturbingly, evaluators identified very few positive and many negative outcomes. Interaction and solidarity among community members either remained the same or declined. More troubling, residents' perceptions of social disorder, physical disorder, and fear of crime either remained the same or went up. In short, efforts aimed at reducing disorder seemed to be equally unsuccessful whether it was accomplished by the police or by the community itself.

If the community cannot deal with disorder by itself, what could the police have contributed? Very little, suggested Skogan. He concluded that the most the police can hope for is to make their best case to community groups. The police can appeal to the wisdom of community members, but their ability to assert their views on neighborhoods is severely constrained. In the United States where diversity and freedom are highly regarded values, the voice of the police is unlikely to be "automatically accepted as authoritative" (1990:160).

When it comes to a great deal of disorder, police and community organizations are just additional interest groups jockeying for attention. Order is more likely to be negotiated than imposed (Skogan, 1990:160).

Skogan identified three limits on the policing of disorder.

1. Can legislators write constitutional statutes concerning disorderly behavior? Our traditions of rights and limited governments suggest fundamental limits on the ability to legislate away disorderly behavior.
2. The use of discretion in controlling disorder is a problem. Officers are free to act upon their prejudices or stereotypes in virtually unchecked fashion when they are the upholders of order who must be satisfied.

(Skogan, 1990:164)

The use of discretion to control disorder in a community-policing context can inadvertently justify the kinds of violence that are consistent with our ideas of noble-cause corruption:

3. Limits on policing disorder are imposed by other elements of the criminal justice system. It is, Skogan observes, difficult to sustain the interests of judges and prosecutors in disorder cases. If arrest does not lead to prosecution, then disorder arrests are simply an extralegal form of harassment. And if they are not prosecuted, then they provide the basis for legal actions against the police.

In short, there may be limits on what the police can hope to accomplish by taking an active role in disorder reduction, even if and when a local community agrees on disorder's root causes. Police efforts to reduce or contain disorder are particularly likely to be ineffective when they try to assert their standard of morality to determine what acceptable order is. It puts them out of touch with other elements of the criminal justice system, it threatens to undermine their legitimacy in the community, and it does not reduce disorder. Are we entering a new era of policing? See Box 9.6.

Box 9.6

**Are We Entering a New Era of Policing?**

Most observers label the early years of American policing, mid-1800s to early 1930s, the Political Era. During this time, most police agencies were closely connected, and heavily influenced, by local politicians. Police officers were often hired on the sole basis of their individual political affiliations or connections with powerful political figures. The mission of most police departments reflected the goals and aspirations of local political leaders. Sometimes an entire police force was replaced when a new political party assumed control of city hall. Police officers routinely made enforcement decisions on the basis of what pleased their political bosses. As one might imagine, corruption was common.

The Reform Era (1930s–1980s) was largely a response to this political corruption. This era of American policing focused on professionalism and crime fighting. Political influence of any form was considered contrary to the effective management of police organizations. Technological advances, like the two-way radio and motorized patrol, substantially affected the policing function. Civil service testing, designed to identify the best qualified candidates (regardless of political affiliation), became commonplace. Often, measures of police effectiveness were based on objective criteria, like response times to calls for service and crime clearance rates. This era, despite all of its advances, began to end when influential policing leaders observed that police forces had all but separated themselves from the communities they served.

The Community Era (1980s to 2001) emerged when policing leaders observed that most crimes were solved by input from the community. Out of a desire to improve crime clearance rates, the police engaged in programs that encouraged community members to take a more active role in routine decision-making relating to the management of the police organization. It was during this era that the problem-oriented policing strategy came to fruition. This strategy encouraged police agencies, with the input from the community, to address the underlying conditions that caused criminal behavior.

In 2001, the Community Era abruptly ended when Islamic terrorists destroyed the World Trade Center in New York City, damaged the Pentagon in Washington, DC, and crashed an airliner near Shanksville, Pennsylvania (that likely was intended to be used to destroy the White House in Washington, DC). This new era focused on national security and counter-terrorism. Local police agencies, anxious to avoid another terroristic attack, actively focused resources on intelligence gathering and target hardening. Law enforcement agencies at the federal, state, and local level organized themselves into multi-agency task forces that were intended to share information and support a comprehensive approach to the threat of terrorism.

There is some suggestion that on May 25, 2020, American policing may have entered yet another era. On that day, George Floyd, a 46-year-old

Box 9.6, *continued*

black American man, was murdered in Minneapolis, Minnesota, by Derek Chauvin, a 44-year-old white police officer. This murder occurred while Chauvin attempted to arrest Floyd for allegedly using a counterfeit bill to make a purchase. Chauvin knelt on Floyd's neck for nearly ten minutes in an attempt to subdue him. As a result, Floyd died and Chauvin was later convicted of murder and sentenced to prison. The three officers with Chauvin at the time were also convicted of civil rights violations.

Indeed, the murder of George Floyd is a tragedy of epic proportions. But the incident might become a watershed moment in American policing. The public response to this incident throughout the nation was intense. The Black Lives Matter organization rose to prominence and led much of the controversy. Elected officials, particularly those serving on city councils, seriously questioned the value of policing services. Some advocated for the total defunding of entire police agencies and replacing them with unarmed social workers. To be fair, no police department in America was totally defunded, at least not directly. Demoralized by a perceived lack of support from elected officers, many police officers retired or resigned. Police chiefs reported that it became difficult to hire new police officers to take their place.

It is too early to know whether this incident, by itself, is the beginning of a new era in American policing. Likely not. Throughout the history of American policing, there were numerous other incidents, just as controversial, that in the long run did not appreciably affect how police agencies are managed or fundamentally erode public confidence in police officers. Citizens still call the police when they need help. Most public opinion polls report support for police officers. What is unclear at this point is whether or not this and other related incidents will fundamentally change the relationship between police departments and all of the diverse communities they serve. At issue is whether the polarized political discourse that arose after this incident will diminish the relationships between police departments and the diverse communities they serve. At risk is a police strategy that is overly responsive to a dominant political ideology within a community at the expense of other perspectives. And that is dangerously close to a return to the Political Era.

## Learning the Right Lessons of the Past

What image of policing is appropriate to the future of the United States? Some advocates of citizen-based policing would have us look to America's past to find a model for the police. Wilson and Kelling's widely cited paper "Broken Windows" (1982) recognized that fear of disorder and crime ran high in neighborhoods confronting incivility and provided an important contribution to our understanding about how migration can undermine social institutions (see Box 9.7).

Box 9.7

**The "Broken Windows" Perspective**

Wilson and Kelling present an important argument about the relationship between disorderly behavior and serious crime. In simplified form, the **"Broken Windows"** perspective is as follows. When neighborhoods experience increasing levels of disorder, residents become increasingly fearful. Disorder is characterized by incivility and physical decay. Once disorder reaches a certain intensity, residents change their behavior, avoid strangers, and stay off the streets. This change in residents' activities marks a loss of traditional control over public places—the parks, the streets, shopping, and parking areas in their neighborhood. Residents' loss of social control results in further declines in the quality of life and the onset of serious criminal activity. The way to stop this is to have the police aggressively intercede in public-order problems before citizens become fearful and avoid public areas. Interceding at an early point is the best means to preserve natural, informal social controls.

"Broken Windows" focused attention on the concept of "fear of disorder." Disorder has subsequently emerged as a popular area of study in contemporary research (see Lewis and Salem, 1986). The literature on disorder and crime is wide, and the government regularly contributes to research through federal granting programs. We believe, however, that there are three issues important to "Broken Windows" that complicate the issue of shared order: the causes of incivility, the capacity of the police to do something about disorder, and the changing and unstable demography of local communities where order problems are the most significant.

In the following discussion we will consider (1) what incivility means, (2) the implications of demographic changes for "Broken Windows" notions of policing, (3) the role of the police in the maintenance of public order, and (4) the police as peacekeepers. This discussion will provide the basis for our vision of the future of public-order policing.

## *(1) Incivility and Commonly Shared Order*

First, let us consider the notion of incivility. What does incivility tap? What is uncivil to people? Certainly rudeness, though rude behavior in and of itself is not against the law. Incivility can cover a wide variety of things. Lewis and Salem (1986) suggest that **incivility** is an indication of the following:

> a variety of circumstances which suggest to neighborhood residents that all is not well in their neighborhood. . . . They may include unacceptable behavior by teenagers; physical deterioration in homes, commercial areas or public spaces, the intrusion of "different" population groups into the area, or an increase in marginally criminal behaviors such as

> drug use and vandalism. Although the events or conditions captured in the incivility term may vary in each neighborhood, they elicit the same concern among area residents that the mechanisms for exercising social control are no longer effective, and the values and standards that in the past characterized the behavior of local residents are no longer in force.
>
> (Lewis and Salem, 1986:10)

This long quote can be simplified to some basic ideas. People tend to fear change. When they are in changing environments, they react by withdrawing or by becoming hostile toward outsiders, recognizing that the ways of the past are not going to guide the future. In-migration is a symbol of that change. Yet American history tells us that migration is inevitable. Indeed, American history is in large part written by patterns of migration.

It is precisely a common notion of order, what people might regard of as uncivil, that will become increasingly problematic in the coming years. If the police assert their idea of order or align themselves with like-minded community "respectables," they will contribute to social friction and disorder over the long term.

## *(2) Demography and the Preservation of Order*

Can the police control public order? In our review of pertinent literature presented in the previous section, it appeared that they could do very little. They lack the resources to prevent neighborhood deterioration. Broad economic factors determine the fate of neighborhoods, and if the economics are not there, the physical condition of the neighborhood will decline. The police can't, and we think shouldn't, control who moves into the neighborhood. Migration patterns also stem from broad economic conditions. Put simply, people follow jobs. When people are moving into a neighborhood, they are pulled by economic opportunity. If they are moving out, they are being pushed by employment's absence. If people remain in an area in spite of an absence of jobs, then they are likely encountering racist barriers in education, housing, or employment that prevent them from migrating to more prosperous areas. Finally, research suggests that the public probably doesn't want the police to intervene in public-order problems on any significant scale. As Glazer (1988) observed, there are limits to which the public tolerates governmental intervention.

## *(3) The Role of the Police in the Preservation of Order*

What is the proper public-order role of the police? Wilson and Kelling (1982) described **order maintenance policing** as follows:

> The essence of the police role in maintaining order is to reinforce the informal control mechanisms in the community itself.
>
> (1982:431)

This colorful phrase suggests to us that the police should assess the kinds and levels of order that local residents find tolerable. With this information in hand, police should then act in an official capacity to preserve or reassert that idea of order. Put simply, police public-order activity should be shaped by the standards of the neighborhood. They suggested that a model taken from America's past, the "watchman," provided a way to model police behavior. Under the watchful surveillance of the "watchman," communities kept public order, thus preventing a downward spiral of physical decay that began with uncivil behavior and ended in criminal activity.

The idea that there is a common notion of public order simply does not fit many neighborhoods very well. The places most likely to develop public-order problems, our inner cities and their proximate environments, are zones of high mobility. There is rarely enough long-term residential stability to develop a publicly shared idea of order. Residents' notions of disorder management may be no more than a vague hope that the police will fix problems that get out of hand. What, then, can the police contribute to public order?

This may be our most far-reaching recommendation, and it is philosophical as well as practical in its implications. It is that, in the practice of the craft of public order, the responsibility of a police officer is emphatically not to reinforce the informal norms of communities and neighborhoods. Neighborhood residents infrequently share a common vision of orderly relations. This is especially the case in our hardest hit inner cities, areas characterized by high crime and high population mobility, where we see diverse groups seeking to improve their quality of life with scant resources and where life's problems are the most deeply entrenched.

Consider this. We ask officers to "reinforce a community's informal sense of order" or the "political will of the community" (Kelling, 1987). We then provide her or him with responsibility for maintaining law and order in a community that may be diversified by religion, age, income, culture, and ethnicity. We give that officer wide discretion to act on behalf of community order and to protect its traditions. But where's the order? The order is not in the neighborhoods—that's the problem. No, the order is in the officer's sense of morality. Officers will use public order as a justification for value-based decision-making and for carrying out the noble cause.

## *(4) The Police as Peacemakers*

We believe that the police should view themselves as peacemakers. They shouldn't distribute morality in the name of public order or law enforcement, as we've argued that they do today. How can the police assert or enforce a shared vision of order where none exists? They can't. They can, however, facilitate the ability of people to work together, to get along, to negotiate problems. This role is called **order negotiation,** which means that they can provide a constructive environment and practical people-skills to negotiate solutions to commonly occurring people problems—relations between landlords and tenants, between youth and oldsters, different ethnic and religious groups, the homeless and business, and traditional locals and recent arrivals.

The promise and danger of negotiating order can be seen in Kelling and Coles's (1996; See also Kelling, 1998) recommendations for fixing "Broken Windows" (also the title of their book). The authors recognize the critical role that the police play in negotiating order among diverse community groups. The role is briefly described in Box 9.8.

Box 9.8

**Fixing Broken Windows and Negotiating Order**

Kelling and Coles (1996) recommended that the preservation or restoration of order require an integrated effort involving many agencies and social service providers. The role of the police was integral to this effort. They noted:

> A real police presence in neighborhoods, one that persists over time and is intimately familiar with the community and its strengths and problems, would be crucial to this consensus-building process, for good policing will help shape, identify, and give legitimacy to neighborhood standards. Newark police officers negotiated informally with local residents during the 1970s over neighborhood standards; the same informal process took place in Somerville, Massachusetts, when officers negotiated with youths and neighborhood residents over how parks could be used on warm summer nights. Negotiation of standards could also be highly structured and formal, as they were in Dayton in the late 1970s and in New York's subways during the early 1990s.

The key to restoring order, they argued, was a "problem-solving process" in which the authority of the police and community resources are brought to bear on problems and in which the police use their authority to maintain order once established.

Source: George Kelling and Catherine Coles (1996). "Fixing Broken Windows," p. 249. New York, NY: The Free Press.

Kelling and Coles provide a conception of the police as negotiators of order. In it, we see the promise; problems confronted by local neighborhoods can, under some circumstances, be mediated by the police. What we consider to be the danger in negotiation of order lies in how order is maintained after it is negotiated. Kelling and Coles, for example, suggest that "Those who absolutely refuse to cooperate and violate both the informal standards and the law may be arrested" (Kelling and Coles, 1996:250). We are troubled by aspects of this statement. Police should not use the power of coercion, as Muir (1977) so aptly described it, to enforce informal notions of order. The coercive authority of the police ends at the boundaries of the criminal law. This is how it must be if democracy is to prevail. In the realm of order under democracy, the authority of the police lies in the powers of voice, of self, and of the purse. Through the power of voice, they exhort for the ends they seek. Through the power of the purse, they connect people who have problems with social services or other means that can help them. Through the power of self, they lead by example. These skills will be essential if the police are to assist us in the complex and troubling public-order problems that we will confront in the twenty-first century. But the circumstances permitting the use of coercive force must be defined by a criminal code and never by informal notions of community order.

Kelling's work on the dilemmas confronting police who seek to maintain public order in a democratic environment is increasingly nuanced and reflects a long scholarly career working with the police. He has more recently suggested that the police must focus on their law enforcement role and in the provision of support for citizen groups that have mobilized in the name of crime prevention. It is a vision based in the development of a practical understanding of crime problems—regardless of where that inquiry leads—and acting in a lawful way to resolve those problems. As he noted (1998:18), "Policing and criminal justice practice must be legal and constitutional." Nor is his vision a call for hard-nosed policing: Kelling suggested that order is a negotiated outcome. He observed:

> The old role of police as discussed in "Broken Windows"—roughing up "undesirables"—is now unacceptable to police as well as to citizens. The new role of police and other criminal justice agencies is to back up the activities of citizens and social institutions.
>
> (Kelling, 1998:16)

Kelling's more recent work is practically grounded in the enforcement of the law and the thoughtful solution of problems, and it recognizes the central role of democratic traditions in peacekeeping.

Perhaps it is in the police-immigrant relationship that we can see the central flaw in the "Broken Windows" idea of police and public order.

The Broken Windows perspective is too often interpreted as a need to enforce local customs against outsiders with a different idea of public order. In the current age, the avoidance of outsider influence is not an option that we have. When we look at the history of police in the United States, we find that they have been intertwined in profound ways with immigrant populations. The true lesson of our immigrant past lies not in thinking we can protect ourselves from the world around us but in the importance of engaging the citizenry of the world in which we live. We need to learn the right lesson from the past: that we are an international people, and we must embrace—not fight—our diversity. In the following section, we will more closely look at the new demographics of the United States and its implications for public-order policing.

## *Order Negotiated*

Guyot expressed the spirit of negotiating order in her 1991 book titled *Policing as Though People Matter*, and we will conclude this section with one of her quotes (see Box 9.9).

Box 9.9

**To Keep Different Moral Worlds from Colliding**

To "keep different moral worlds from colliding" is the phrase of Police Chief David Couper of Madison, Wisconsin (Couper, 1979). The larger the city, the more likely it is to be the home of people with diverse life-styles, some of whom will take offense at the life-styles of their neighbors. For the most part, Americans accommodate each other's diverse ways, but when tolerance wears thin, police have a crucial role in building bridges between citizens.

Source: Dorothy Guyot (1991). *Policing as Though People Matter*, Philadelphia: Temple University Press. p. 281.

The United States is becoming an inter-ethnic, international nation-state, diversifying on religious, ethnic, and status fault lines. If police continue to be drawn from the ranks of the ideologically pure, we will encounter increasing friction between them and the public in our changing society. An ends-based police ethic will increasingly be at odds with the problems confronted by American society.

Many police departments today share a common path. They recruit individuals with a fixed, narrow moral view of their world, individuals who believe that it is right to impose their definition of morality on the rest of us. They encourage that narrow view in training practices. These departments will be morally underequipped to deal with America's future. This path will only contribute to division and confrontation. A wider vision is needed. Adaptation of the police to tomorrow's world will be facilitated by a peacekeeping philosophy, based in the negotiation of order and enforcement of law, by cultivating the skills of voice and of self, to lead through reason and by example.

## Into the Future

Community policing appears to have run its course as a movement in American policing. Heavily sponsored by the National Institute of Justice through the 1990s through the provision of grants monies for community policing research and applications and by President Clinton's program aimed at hiring 100,000 police officers, called COPS, the movement is today largely absent funding. The administration in 2000, under President Bush, began to disable these programs. Funding for the research component for the National Institute of Justice community policing disappeared. And the funding program for the COPS program was cut drastically, as officer hiring was shifted to other venues, particularly school resource officers.

Federal processes of disinvestment in community policing were already under way when the terrorist attacks of 9/11 occurred. These attacks have furthered the diversion of monies away from community policing and into homeland security. Homeland security policing is likely to be a part of the future of policing. Oliver (2004) described this process and its implications for community policing in Box 9.10. At the present time, all signs suggest that Oliver's pessimistic view of the future of community policing was accurate.

Box 9.10

**Homeland Security and the Future of Community Policing**

In a paper for the magazine *Crime and Justice*, Oliver (2004) suggested that the community policing era might be approaching its end. The events of 9/11 had led to a dramatic shift in expenditures for policing by the federal government. By 2002, the Office of Community Policing Services had shifted to Homeland Security through Community Policing (HSCP). This office came about from a conference held in 2002 by the COPS Office. At the conference, several ways that the Office of Homeland Security could be enhanced by community policing were advanced:

1. Local police could play an important role in gathering information on suspects. Many police officers know their community well, and citizens often feel more comfortable talking with local officers than federal agents. And local police have more detailed knowledge of their communities than federal agencies.

2. Police and citizens could make use of community policing initiatives on how to be better prepared to respond to terrorist attacks. This would "tap into the Community Policing framework for the creation of a modern World War II civil defense committee that would be trained on what to do in an emergency" (Oliver, 2004:9).

Box 9.10, *continued*

Oliver expressed the concern that the purpose of HSCP was not so much the application of community policing principles and philosophy to counter-terrorism practices but about shifting funds from COPS to homeland security. He noted that President Bush's administration had started to shift funds in 2001 from the COPS Office to the hiring of school resource officers. The HSCP provided a justification for shifting additional funds out of community policing and into counter-terrorism vis-à-vis the Department of Homeland Security.

Oliver concluded that the shift of emphasis toward homeland security would not further community policing efforts. The two strategies used by the police were incompatible: using local police to "ferret out" terrorists living in local communities "is not a goal nor supportive of the Community Policing philosophy."

Homeland security would have the neighborhoods provide intelligence to the police on suspicious activities and suspicious persons to be channeled up to Federal agencies in order to create an intelligence network regarding this activity . . . this type of intelligence network could actually serve to destroy the relationship between the police and community partners as the emphasis would shift to fighting an unseen enemy, rather than the prevalent and highly visible problems of street crime and disorder (Oliver, 2004:10). Oliver correctly concluded that the future of community policing was bleak; only those departments with fully integrated and developed community policing programs would be likely to survive, and these would be isolated cases. Speaking of policing in general, "whether we like it or not, it is time to brace for a new era of policing, the era of Homeland Security" (2004:10).

Source: W. Oliver (2004). "The Homeland Security Juggernaut: The End of the Community Policing Era?" *Crime and Justice International, 20* (*79* March/April): 4–10.

Our larger concern is whether the twenty-first century will herald in a state-based notion of internal security that replaces the citizen-based notion of policing that drove many of the twentieth-century reforms, including community policing. Police departments are more technologically savvy, more involved in intelligence and surveillance activities, larger, more involved in a wide range of community activities through third party policing practices, and more interlinked with the federal government than ever before. As witnesses to the birth of a new age of policing, we are hopeful and fearful. With the enormous support the American public has of the police, we are hopeful they continue as a pillar of democratic support.

Put differently, we do not want any officer to hear a citizen say, "You don't represent us." Fearfully, we see that policing is a growing leviathan in American life. Used the wrong way, this force becomes an actor for states interests, even when those interests conflict with citizen rights. Used the right way, police can help us reach across the social divides that breed conflicts.

As we confront a new kind of crime and security environment in the post-9/11 world, we should remember that community policing has done much to help citizens reclaim a voice in the affairs of their municipal governments in matters of policing. Community policing gradually emerged in response to the riots of the 1960s, their subsequent loss of life, the breakdown of social order in many cities, and inability of police to carry out basic police services. As we move forward to a new era, let us not forget that community policing has also a contribution—perhaps not as broad as originally envisioned but important nevertheless—to the security of our cities and the citizens therein.

# The Stakes

# 10

## Key Terms

- ticking time bomb
- torture memo
- Intelligence-Led Policing
- Criminal Intelligence Model
- crime mapping
- police militarization
- lever pulling
- Broken Windows
- hot spot policing
- fear justification
- neo-professionalism
- intelligence function
- Compstat
- third-party policing
- zero-tolerance
- crackdown

## Introduction

Chapter 10 explores the transformation of modern policing through the lens of the noble cause and its implications for democratic society. It critically examines the rise of neo-professionalism, a model emphasizing aggressive law enforcement, intelligence collection, and state-centered policing. Strategies such as Broken Windows, zero tolerance, and hot spot policing are analyzed for their role in reshaping community engagement, often replacing traditional community policing with surveillance and suppression. Tools like Compstat and crime mapping enhance operational efficiency but risk reducing citizens to data points. The chapter critiques Homeland Security policing, Criminal Intelligence, and Intelligence-Led Policing for expanding police authority under the guise of national security, often justified by the fear explanation. The ticking time bomb scenario and the infamous torture memo are used to illustrate how fear can erode legal and ethical boundaries.

DOI: 10.4324/9781003626916-14

> Mike. *No matter what you say, there are times when you will choose the good end over legal means. It all depends on the stakes. Consider this. Two men are driving by. They look a bit rough. You have no basis for a stop, not even a profile. The vehicle is street legal. But you have an uneasy feeling. So you follow them for a while. You call in the plates, and they're fine. Vehicle looks fine. They could be a couple of scruffy criminal justice college teachers, for all you know. Are you going to stop them? Are you going to search the car, with no basis, or try to impound it and get an administration search? I don't think so. Police work is full of uneasy feelings. But you might.*
>
> Let's raise the stakes. A child, a 4-year-old girl, went missing about an hour ago. An amber alert went out. No one has any idea what happened to her. Your discomfort is higher. Could she be in the trunk? You are really going to want to see what is in that trunk. You called the vehicle in, it's clean. Are you going to stop and search, even if it would be a bogus stop and illegal search? I think you will find a way.
>
> Mike pauses for a minute. *Let's raise the stakes again. You're on alert for suspected terrorist activity. Your department received an alert from the FBI saying that intelligence chatter was intense, and they were deeply concerned that there would be a major action with potentially significant loss of life. If you don't make the stop, and they're terrorists, 1,000 people could die. You make the stop, they are terrorists; you're a hero. The driver? Hmmm. He looks kind of Mediterranean, with dark hair and swarthy skin, though it could be the shadows across the visor. You really want to know who they are and what's in the trunk. Are you going to make the stop? Search the car? I bet you'll find a reason.*
>
> This is the point with the noble cause. Where do the stakes get high enough that you'll risk a promotion, maybe a lawsuit, and possibly your job? Just to make sure that whatever is in the trunk is not the worst thing it could be? Because maybe, just maybe, it really is the worst thing it could be.

Anyone in counter-terrorism can recognize the final scenario Mike presented. It's called the **ticking time bomb.** It's often used in discussions about the limits of coercive interrogation. The question—also a form of the noble cause—is this: If you knew that a terrorist had information about a ticking time bomb, and that many people would be killed if you don't get the information rapidly, would you use torture to extract information from the terrorist?

The ticking time bomb scenario, unfortunately, is an illusion wrapped in a noble cause fantasy. It is often used to justify ends that would ordinarily be unacceptable in civilized society. Often pled as an excuse for torture, it is never proven, at least as far as we know, and evidence is not provided but claimed to be a state secret, justified by vague policy prescriptions such as *we don't want the terrorists to know our strategy so we can't talk about specific cases and techniques*. Critics suspect that evidence is not forthcoming because there isn't any. Critics are likely right. The CIA used SERE[1] groups to carry out coercive interrogations at Guantanamo and later at Abu Ghraib, stemming from the belief that the prisoners had information and were too mean and cunning to give it up. The teams were trained in all forms of torture—though the original purpose was for training U.S. soldiers to resist torture—and have been accused of using their expansive knowledge of pain inducement in the brutal mistreatment of prisoners. We now know that the majority of prisoners who were tortured did not provide information not because they were savvy tough terrorists but because they didn't know anything (Mayer, 2008).

The noble cause is a powerful force; we all want to believe in the rightness of something that is beyond and greater than us. Few are so cynical that they really believe that good cannot possibly win out, though sometimes cops end up that way (see Niederhoffer, 1967; see also the substantial body of scholarship carried out on the topic of cynicism by Robert Regoli). And in an age of terrorism, the noble cause is even stronger. When we fail to check the trunk, we are not talking about a single life anymore, as important as that is and as committed to the smell of a victim's blood as cops are. The noble cause has shifted from local focus to international recognition and is ascendant in politics today. The ascendancy of noble cause is our next topic.

## The Noble Cause Ascendant

Mike. *What would you think if all the laws were written so that you could always look in the trunk? Imagine this. All the legal doors are open, if you act in good faith on behalf of the public interest. If by chance some due process laws seems to conflict with your desire to act against some threat or to find out some bit of information, you have legal protection. You have a blanket legal opinion signed by a judge stating that as long as you are acting on what you believe to be the public interest, due process laws did not apply to you? Moreover, the criminal statutes do not apply to you, either, because you are acting in good faith. That you could never be prosecuted for protecting the public? What do you think of that?*

"We already have good faith," says one officer.

MIKE: *You have good faith protection that you acted or sought to act in a way that was legal. Good faith protects you from reasonable errors, so that a technical violation of a warrant cannot be used to suppress evidence. I'm talking about something different—good faith that you acted in the best interests of the public.*

"Open season on criminals," commented an officer to subdued laughter.

"That would cover everything we do. That will never happen in this country," responded another.

> Mike acts surprised. *Oh it's not? This is exactly* (Mike emphasizes the word exactly) *how our government is carrying out the war on terror. I want to talk about this, because there is a message in this for the police. I'm here to tell you that it's a dangerous power to have. It's one of those wishes that falls into everybody's favorite category called "be careful what you ask for."*

The "War on Terror" has been fought with an arsenal of powerful entities, including the U.S. military, the CIA, and the FBI. Not least among these are legal opinions crafted by the Office of Legal Counsel (OLC), aimed at protecting the President, administration officials, and the CIA from prosecution related to their conduct during the war. These legal opinions are of immense aid because it is virtually impossible to prosecute an administration official who acts in good faith that they are acting within the guidelines of the law. Because the OLC is a branch of the Justice Department, the department is inherently unlikely to prosecute someone for following its own advice (Goldsmith, 2008). Many of the "War on Terror" opinions have also been kept secret so that terrorists will not know what the U.S. authorizes itself to do and what it won't authorize. Among the most famous is the "Torture Memo."

In August 2002, the Office of Legal Counsel, responsible for providing the administration with legal advice regarding its activities, issued the infamous **Torture Memo.** The full wording of the memo remains a closely guarded secret. However, a former head of the OLC, Jack Goldsmith (2008:144), noted the extent to which it seemed to justify torture:

> Violent acts aren't necessarily torture; if you do torture, you probably have a defense; and even if you don't have a defense, the torture law doesn't apply if you act under color of presidential authority. CIA interrogators and their supervisors, under pressure to get information about the next attack, viewed the opinion as a "golden shield" as one CIA official later called it, that provided enormous comfort.

The torture memo was written by the Office of Legal Counsel. It carried a great deal of weight in terms of presidential decision-making. As Goldsmith (2008:96) further noted, "It is practically impossible to prosecute someone who relied in good faith on an OLC memo." This is because the OLC acts on behalf of the Justice Department, and it is the Justice Department that prosecutes violations of the criminal law. Consequently, an OLC opinion acts to provide an "advance pardon" for actions taken on the edges of the law,

> The question Goldsmith—who has been a staunch supporter of Presidential authority to conduct the War on Terror and a past director of the OLC—asked was this: How could the Office of Legal Counsel write an opinion that "reflected such bad judgment, be so poorly reasoned, and have such a terrible tone?"

The main explanation, he argued, was fear. The fear explanation is this:

When the original opinion was written in the weeks before the first anniversary of 9/11, threat reports were pulsing as they hadn't since 9/11. . . . Inside the administration the "end of summer" threat seemed much worse. "We were sure there would be bodies in the streets" on September 11, 2002, a high-level Justice Department official later told me. . . . The president believed that "the security of our nation and the lives of our citizens" depended on our ability to get this [plans for new attacks] from [Abu] Zubaydah [a senior terrorist leader in custody]. . . . "I've got reports of nuclear weapons in New York City, apartment buildings that are gonna be blown up, planes that are gonna fly into airports all over again . . . Plot lines I don't know—I don't know what's going on inside the United States," (George) Tenet (CIA Director) later said of the context in which the initial aggressive interrogations took place.

The fear explanation was an amplification of the noble cause; not only was the cause great—a potential second attack on U.S. soil—but the failure to recognize and stop the attack could harm the country in fearful ways, as Tenet noted in the previous paragraph. The administration "smelled the blood of the victims," the many thousands who were killed in the World Trade Center. And they were tower runners; they took the fight to Afghanistan, at that time the home of Al Qaeda.

The fear explanation was also flawed. If the administration was terrified of a second Al Qaeda attack, as they claimed, then why did they take their military sights off Bin Laden and deploy a second and more robust front to Iraq, a country that, at the start of the war, was hostile to Al Qaeda and perhaps could have been a powerful ally of the U.S. in anti-Qaeda actions? What national security interest made Iraq worth the lives of more than 4,000 soldiers? Why didn't we pursue Bin Laden into Pakistan? At this point, many years after the 9/11 attacks, Osama bin Laden has been killed, and Al Qaeda has morphed from a small terrorist band into an international movement. There remain many accounts to settle for the way in which the U.S. conducted the War on Terror. However, Goldsmith argues persuasively for the role of fear, a role that is also echoed to a lesser degree by Mayer (2008). In the U.S. today, the war is intensely politicized by both major political parties. It is unlikely that a consensus opinion of the war will be achieved either in the short or long term (see Crank et al., 2007a).

The noble cause achieved legal ascendancy in the war on terror, providing a broad blanket of protection for CIA, contractor, and administration officials to avoid existing U.S. and international law and treaty obligations in the conduct of the war. Yet there is a significant price for their actions.

Here is a thought experiment: Imagine that you were involved in the legal justification for torture. Now the conflict is winding down, but you ended up finding no lurking terrorists with useful information, and now the world knows you were instrumental in either writing the torture policy, complicit in torture through the chain of command, or were involved in carrying out torture at Abu Ghraib. Here are some possible outcomes that you might face.

1. Ongoing preoccupation with law. (Imagine going to bed every night wondering if your legal documents for justifying torture—which you now know was widespread—will hold up in U.S. courts. Even if they do, will you face prosecution and all the negative publicity that attends such prosecution? Will you face civil suits in the U.S. or internationally? Will the government support you in an international civil suit?)
2. Continued concerns about international prosecution. (You cannot fly internationally because you might be arrested on an international warrant when you land in some country friendly to war crimes prosecution against the U.S.).
3. A failure to find anything. (You debated endlessly before going ahead with torturous interrogations and decided to act on behalf of the country. And torture was carried out, and now you know that many people, in fact, died under coercive interrogation. And nothing was found. Now you know many of your victims were innocent.)
4. Loss of public moral standing. (Your employability is tainted and your reputation suspect. You continue to come across articles in the newspaper about what you justified. You stopped going to church because you worried that the pastor would lecture against your actions. Maybe it's time to move to the mountains.)
5. Loss of self. (Suppose you are Christian. Do you worry about your soul? Did you cross a bridge you cannot walk back over? How do you explain your actions to family and children? What if they find out?)

Mike. *These have been difficult times, and a lot of us have friends and family who were deployed to Iraq. I am here to think about the noble cause and its consequences. In the second Bush administration the noble cause achieved a moral and legal ascendancy. It was awesome power to wage war. No laws, no branch of government, could interfere with what they wanted to do. They were protected by the legal opinions of the OLC [Office of Legal Counsel]. But at what cost?*

*Do you want that kind of authority? You can see what is happening to the U.S. today. We've lost moral standing in the world. Administration officials are preoccupied about constant ongoing and future investigations. Officials are beginning to spill their guts about how decisions were (and are) made in the White House. You know, in this day and age, it all comes out. There are no secrets any more. Abu Ghraib became a testament to the power to conduct war without moral constraints, witnessed in released photos by our enemies. And it was all for nothing. We talked about that this morning; remember the central problem with the noble cause? You can never know for sure how things will work out. They, the administration officials and the SERE teams who carried out enhanced interrogations, they sold their souls for dross.*[2] *They justified torture, and used it to torture people who knew nothing. The public does not trust them. And, you know, Pinochet, the President of Argentina, was protected by law too. But in the end he was prosecuted and died publicly humiliated. Is that the way you want to do this thing you call policing? Do you still want open season on criminals?*

## Into the Twenty-First Century: Policing as a State-Centered Activity

After a pause, Mike starts a discussion of policing trends at the beginning of the twenty-first century and their implications for the noble cause.

*Let's go back to community policing. How's community policing in your department?* Mike smiles, giving away no information.

"In our department?" Cops always reference policing to their own department. At the level of practice, they are finely tuned to the differences between themselves and other police agencies in their region.

*In your department.* Still no information.

"We do a lot of community policing here. It works for us, and we believe in it."

*Oh.* Mike smiles, a stone's smile. Still no information. Pause. In some ways Mike will always be a cop—the style is imprinted.

"Look," another officer says, slightly chafed. "We are doing a lot of things. We have been doing zero-tolerance policing, taking care of the broken windows in our community. We are starting to use crime mapping, and it is helping us push up our arrest stats. We have a gang unit that is meeting with neighborhood kids regularly to find out more about gangs and we are beginning to try to get the kids into after school programs or into our PAL program. We arrest now for any outstanding warrant no matter how small, if it's a gang member. We work with the prosecutor to bring the hammer down on gun crimes. We've done some weed and seed, and we did our part by some very effective weeding, taking care of neighborhood nuisance problems. We solved several felonies by arresting for misdemeanors. We've done some problem-oriented policing—we have identified a lot of patterns and were able to use crime mapping to make arrests. We've moved officers into areas where we can do aggressive patrol in the roughest neighborhoods, and we added hot spot policing to it by pushing up the number of patrols in an area, and we think it is generating a significant deterrent to criminal activity. This department has taken community policing seriously, and we think it makes a significant contribution to the community."

These are good. These all sound like good police programs. I'm not taking anything away from them. But I'm curious. All these things you call community policing. How are they designed to bring the police and the community together? To make the police and the community, as one person said, co-authors of crime prevention? You know, all that stuff that is supposed to make police more tuned into the broad needs of the community? These programs are all hammers.

An officer starts to talk and then hesitates. She senses where Mike is going and does not want to be the one remembered as being used by Mike to make a point. No command points for that. Silence, as she mulls it over. After a moment she speaks out.

"Our programs aren't community policing in that sense. We do community policing in that we give a damn for the community and we're willing to take some risks for the community. We're probably closer to problem-oriented policing, though only up to a point. We saw New York have a lot of success with Compstat and crime mapping, and we took that up two years ago. Now we have real time intelligence. We can use it to do hot spot policing, which makes natural sense. We've also got to deal with a massive influx of felons being released and moving back into the community. We can't keep up with that—it is really feeding the gang-bangers. If community policing is hand holding citizens, then I guess we are into tough love. We're busting our collective asses to help the community in the way we do best—try to get bad people off the streets."

Mike hesitates a moment. *That's good.* He won't overstate the point and embarrass her, but she was on point. *OK, let's work with that. You are doing aggressive order maintenance policing, and you call it community policing. You are doing heavy-duty surveillance of at-risk groups and you are calling it community policing. You think about it in terms of getting rid of the broken windows, so you are hard on both misdemeanants and felons alike. You are not alone. If you look around the country, you find that the nature of policing is changing, and what you're doing is the new face of policing. What we called community policing back in the 1970s is pretty much history. A much more aggressive policing is out there today. We still use the words, but the work is different. Today it's about hard law enforcement.*

## Police at the Beginning of the Twenty-First Century: The Neo-Professionalism Movement

We think that the police are in a transition to neo-professionalism. It is **neo-professionalism** in that, like the professionalism movement, it refocuses the police toward law enforcement, as did the professionalism movement. It also emphasizes the moral commitments of officers to their work, as did the professionalism movement under Vollmer's influence. And it re-invigorates the notion of private policing, according to which police decide what constitutes good policing, and then act on that definition.

It is new in several ways—hence, the "neo" in "neo-professionalism." The police function is broadly expanded today through third-party practices, the use of technology for data-mining purposes, surveillance of risk populations, and the control of hot spot geographies. It also shifts from reactive activity to "real-time" or proactive tactics and strategies. And it increasingly incorporates assessments of operational effectiveness through crime mapping and other real-time outcome measures. Through these changes, police increasingly represent the interests of the state, and their non-coercive ties to citizens are diminishing. The following is a discussion of specific characteristics of the transition toward neo-professionalism.

## *Community Policing: A Bright, Shining Idea Dims*

Police history is dense in reform efforts, typically tied to two kinds of events: public perceptions of widespread corruption and efforts to make the police more responsive to citizen oversight. The former, focusing on economic corruption, were common in the U.S. through the early and mid-twentieth centuries. Community policing is an example of the latter kind of police reform in the U.S. and was historically tied to lack of police responsiveness to urban, and especially urban African American, social dislocations in the 1960s (Crank and Langworthy, 1992; Scrivner, 2004). Over its life-course, the community policing was extended to organizations across the urban and rural landscape and was associated with all efforts to build better relations between citizens and police.

By the end of the twentieth century, scholars noted that the implementation of community policing (COP) was slowing (Myers, 2004). In spite of its popularity among reform advocates, police departments did not implement many of the supportive structural changes necessary for institutionalizing behavioral change (Maguire and King, 2007; Walker, 1993; Zhao et al., 2000). Further, the early 2000s marked the loss of grant funding previously offered by the Office of Community-Oriented Policing Services (Bohrer, 2004).

In 2001, the terrorist attacks, popularly referred to as "9/11," marked a sharp deceleration in community policing. Much of this deceleration stemmed from the collapse of government funding; aside from some continuation funding for crime prevention, community policing monies generally disappeared. The two questions for community policing after 9/11 were (1) whether community policing could actually do anything about crime (for which there was a growing body of evidence that it could not) and (2) whether it could facilitate post-9/11 homeland security efforts.

By research indicators, community policing showed mixed effectiveness. For example, from 1995 to 1999, funding from the COPS Office showed significant reductions in both violent and nonviolent crime in cities with populations greater than 10,000 (Zhao et al., 2002; Scrivner, 2004). Furthermore, a 2002 survey by the Police Executive Research

Forum (PERF) noted significant reductions in crime against property and persons (Fridell, 2004). These findings could not be directly attributed to community policing, however, and Zhao (2004) has asserted that, to date, there exists "no irrefutable evidence that [community policing] significantly reduces crime within a community" (2004:371).

In the current era, community policing is clearly waning. It had always suffered three problems. First, community policing, in its early form, was about policing minority communities in a way that involved the police working with minority citizens. It rapidly spread beyond that base, spurred in part by academic research carried out by researchers concerned about minorities in the U.S. Second, it was largely carried through federal programs that rewarded local agencies for particular programs. When the money ended, so did the programs. Third, it never was effectively integrated into the line officer function. In many places where it was implemented, line personnel did not understand nor were effectively prepared for tasks that did not seem to have much to do with getting rough customers off the streets. Our view is that it is likely to survive, though as a set of localized programs aimed at community groups and middle-ground institutions. And it may coexist with much more aggressive police interdiction and Homeland Security–related programs.

Under the Homeland Security aspect of policing, there will be more of a focus on crime control, which incorporates increased security and counter-terrorism. This will include identifying potential threats, gathering intelligence, and disrupting criminal networks. The police will also work closely with law enforcement partners at every level to ensure public safety and form the nation's primary domestic shield against terrorism. Much of this will be done using local threat assessments and practical intelligence gathering, something which the police have been doing effectively as part of their primary job for a long time.

## *Problem-Oriented Policing: Still Seeking a Foothold*

Problem-Oriented Policing (POP), a strategic police development in the late 1970s, is also not catching on to the extent its supporters had hoped. First introduced by Herman Goldstein in his seminal 1979 article, "Improving Policing: A Problem-Oriented Approach," the notion that police could become more effective by focusing on underlying problems has kindled a great deal of research (Scott, 2000). Moreover, research has consistently shown that POP can be effective in reducing crime, disorder, and fear of crime (Weisburd and Eck, 2004). POP works. Yet as Boba and Crank noted (2007; see Scott, 2000):

> The core ideas of POP have not become routinized into the police mission of most departments and its central element—the distinction

> between an incident and a problem—has been underdeveloped and often misunderstood. The promise of POP, as a mainstay of police practice, remains unfulfilled.

Programs that are catching on in the current era can be loosely fit under a "neo-professionalism/Homeland Security" umbrella.[3] They are discussed next.

## *Intelligence-Led Policing*

Intelligence-Led Policing (ILP) has been heralded both for its ability to make use of community policing endeavors and as a police strategy adept in the use of intelligence. It is increasingly in use in the United States.

**Intelligence-Led Policing (ILP)** is a relatively recent development that can be traced to the Kent and Northumbria Constabularies of the United Kingdom (Ratcliffe, 2016; McGarrell et al., 2007). In general, ILP "provides strategic integration of intelligence into the overall mission of the [police] organization" (Carter, 2004:41). The delicate social climate that existed post-9/11, proponents argue, necessitated an even greater emphasis on interactive dialogue between the police and society than in the past (Carter, 2004; McGarrell et al., 2007). In this way, ILP and community policing might piggy-back off each other to strengthen local community security. ILP, critics suggest, is an umbrella term for questionable police practices in the gathering of information about groups and individuals.

A review of functions of ILP includes the following: multi-jurisdiction oriented, threat driven, and assessment of threats from different areas of the economy and polity; focus on criminal enterprises and terrorism; assessments of commodity flow, trafficking, and transit characteristics; concerned with disrupting ongoing enterprises; coordinates and drives operations related to joint terrorism task forces, organized crime, and other task forces; and analyzes enterprise MOs (Ratcliffe, 2016).[4]

New Jersey has instituted a broad information awareness agenda aimed at policy and planning, organized around the development of intelligence. They define the **intelligence function** as a "management philosophy supporting optimal resource allocation based on fully understanding the operating environment." In turn, intelligence is differentiated from raw data or information. It is defined as "the synthesis of known data/information and analytic reasoning to create a determination about the overall operating environment" (New Jersey State Police, 2006:3). Three kinds of intelligence are collected. Tactical intelligence aims at specific targets, such as the leadership of a specific gang. Operational intelligence is for planning at the unit level. Strategic intelligence is for planning and policy formulation. Their Regional Operations and Intelligence Center (ROIC) in turn assesses and organizes intelligence for use across the agency. Reports produced by ROIC are called intelligence reports, and "the aim of intelligence reports is to provide lead information necessary for preventing crime, identifying and interdicting targets, influencing future operations, and policy decisions, and guiding resource allocation." Put in more conventional terms, these purposes are generally the management and tactical deployment of crime suppression and prevention practices.

## Criminal Intelligence Model

The Criminal Intelligence Model represents a significant shift in modern law enforcement, emphasizing the proactive use of information to prevent and disrupt criminal activity. The model uses a modern approach to crime prevention by focusing on patterns and trends rather than simply reacting to individual events. The model is based on three types of information: geographical analysis, data relating to relationships between offenders and groups of offenders, and crime pattern analysis (Peterson et al., 2017). Prior to the modern criminal pandemic of cybercrime, in which the perpetrator or perpetrators can be anywhere in the world, the victim of a crime and the person or persons who caused or committed it were usually geographically co-located and normally in the same jurisdiction. In the era prior to crimes via computers (and in today's world, for non-cybercrimes), the closer the alleged perp lived (or lives) to the victim, the more likely that person was to have committed the crime. Geographic criminal analysis was derived from and is based on several factors, including demographic composition, sociocultural and economic context, degree of urbanization, population density, etc. The basis of focusing on the relationships between offenders and groups of offenders is Ratcliffe's assertion that about 6 percent of the population is responsible for 60 percent of the crimes (2002). Non-cyber crime uses networks to facilitate disposing of stolen goods, among other things, and is a reality in the criminal world. According to crime pattern analysis, usual crime is not randomly distributed but occurs in relatively predictable patterns linked to an offender's routine activities and spatial awareness. In terms of routine activities, the activity spaces are the specific locations and routes the individual regularly uses. Nodes are locations integral to his or her routine, and paths are the routes between nodes the offender uses. Spatial awareness in terms of crime are the areas the offender knows and is comfortable traveling within, which influences decision-making and target selection.

Intelligence gathering in this context involves the systematic collection, analysis, and dissemination of information related to criminal enterprises, terrorist threats, and other public safety concerns. This process enables law enforcement to identify patterns, assess risks, and allocate resources more effectively.

## *Compstat and Crime Mapping*

Two interlinked innovations, one organizational and the other technical, have been of substantial and growing interest in police work. Compstat and crime mapping share in common that they tend to be viewed as essentially interlinked strategies by police departments, even though each is quite different.

**Crime mapping** is the visual representation of crime information on a screen. It is tied to a variety of algorithms that permit the collation of crime patterns by type, area, time, and any of a wide assortment of variables. Hence, it provides immediate utility for commanders who want to know about crime patterns (Boba, 2005). Crime mapping also has become popular, in part because of its focus on crime—a focus never adequately addressed by community policing—and in part for its visual appeal to commanders who rely on it to make operational action. It is a metaphorical device allowing images of crime. It does not provide either explanation or problem identification. Commanders who rely on it have been criticized for confusing problem-solution à la POP for computer-driven incident management.

**Compstat** (Comparative Statistics) is widely popular among police departments. Initially created by the New York City Police Department to formalize a structure of management accountability for strategic problem-solving, Compstat combines meetings in which commanders are held accountable for the improvement of crime statistics in their area with crime mapping, the technique which allows for the visual inspection and systematic clustering of crime incidents (Weisburd et al., 2003; Henry, 2002). Compstat is seen in most law enforcement agencies as problem-oriented policing, though it does not deal with underlying problems, a POP mainstay (Willis et al., 2007). Compstat is aggressive incident management through the identification and mitigation of visual incident clusters. Both of these practices are quite popular today and reflect a likely technology-command mix that will infuse police administration with energetic visual/tactical applications and public support for the near-term future.

## *Police Militarization*

Police militarization has been described as "the process whereby civilian police are increasingly drawn from, and pattern themselves around, the tenets of militarism and the military model" (Kraska and Cubellis, 1997). PPUs, or police paramilitary units, are more commonly called SWAT units and were initially established for real-time hostage scenarios needing a specialized response that included tactical firefighting and sniper skills. They rapidly became normalized and, by the end of the century, were in 90 percent of American police departments (cf. Haggerty and Ericson, 1999; Kraska and Cubellis, 1997; Kraska and Kappeler, 1997; Meeks, 2006). These units resonate with the war symbolisms widely used in the post-9/11 era, adding the "War on Terror" to the "war on crime."

The rise in specialized police paramilitary units represent a militaristic *esprit de corps* in police organizations, and the militaristic symbolisms they use generate both support and criticism. The units are characterized by popularity in departments as elite police. Their use of innovative technology, their sophisticated fire-fight weaponry, and their hours of specialized training contribute to their internal popularity (Haggerty and Ericson, 1999; Kraska and Cubellis, 1997; Polk and MacKenna, 2005). As a militaristic entity, they are a visible public symbol of a "war on crime" that, advocates argue, resonates positively with victims of crime and their constituencies. Critics have expressed concerns that increases in military-style policing units in urban communities have taken on the tone of an indeterminate economic and social war against the urban underclass (Meeks, 2006). In the post-9/11 era, these practices run the risk of furthering the rift between inner-city residents and law enforcement agencies.

## *Third-Party Policing*

Policing through third parties refers to police efforts to persuade or coerce third parties, such as landlords, parents, local governments and other regulators, and business owners, to take responsibility for crime control and prevention. In **third-party policing,** the police create crime control guardians through efforts to exert control over offenders in situations historically problematic. This can be through "cooperative consultation" with community members or through coercive threats backed up by civil and regulatory laws. The distinguishing feature of third-party policing is the use of a third, non-offending population to enact the law: As noted by Buerger and Mazerolle (1998:301):

> Though the ultimate target of police action remains the population of actual and potential offenders, the proximate target of third party policing is an intermediate class of non-offending persons who are thought to have some power over the offender's primary environment.

Third-party policing, Mazerolle and Ransley (2005, 2006) noted, is a relatively unknown phrase and has not yet entered the police lexicon of strategic crime control interventions. Consequently, its extent and efficacy are still relatively unresearched. Yet the authors argued that it appeared to be both widespread and effective. This means, for the police, that they are no longer limited to their understanding of the criminal law within a due process legal environment in order to carry out crime control. They can use the much more flexible body of civil law to generate or threaten sanctions on business entrepreneurs to assist in the crime control and prevention effort. Civil sanctions, as Mazerolle and Ransley (2005, 2006) noted, have an extended range of sanctions, lower standards of proof, and fewer rights-based legal obligations. However, it also is associated with negative side effects. These might be unanticipated costly repairs to a business, retaliation on a business owner for working with the police, and a feeling that the police are manipulating business owners and are to be themselves feared.

Third-party policing tends to accompany other police tactical interventions. It is closely tied to "lever pulling" in that it is used to develop civil remedies as one of the coercive levers used to control risk group behavior. It might be linked to drug crackdowns, in which a property owner is forced to renovate property or have it condemned by the city.

Broad social changes, Mazerolle and Ransley (2005) suggested, facilitate the use of third party policing. It is a part of a general transformation of the police to the regulation of risk populations in a neoliberal environment that increasingly focuses on business rather than governmental solutions to problems. It also reflects the fragmentation of interests in broader society. This means that specific crime control and prevention activities tie the police to other groups in what can be called "nodal" policing, in which policing is the product of several different groups acting in concert on a particular kind of problem.

## *Lever Pulling*

The concept and terminology of "lever pulling" emerged from Operation Cease-Fire in Boston carried out in 1996 and 1997, a program aimed at gun crimes. **Lever pulling** is based on deterrence and is enacted through meetings with a target population followed by prosecution if those meetings fail to deter. A multi-agency working group made up of parole and probation officers, the police, prosecutor—sometimes also including social workers—is assembled to meet with and, through explicit warnings, deter the future violent behavior of chronic offenders. The target group, gang members or parolees and probationers, are warned that violence will no longer be tolerated and will be met with a certain and severe criminal justice response. "Pulling levers" is considered a focused deterrent strategy in which potential offenders are brought into a general meeting of justice practitioners and warned that future misbehavior would be met with all possible sanctions (levers) and that they were being watched. Lever pulling consequently focuses on high-risk targets.

The key elements of this strategy (cited from Chermak, 2008)[5] are as follows:

1. It applies a problem-solving approach, where a specific problem is selected and then quantitative and qualitative data are collected to achieve a deep understanding of the nature of the problem. The qualitative data is the record of front-line intelligence related to understanding the network of offenders involved in gang-related violence.
2. The effort is coordinated by an interagency working group involving federal and local police, probation, prosecutors, and community resource personnel. For example, the interagency working group in Boston coordinated the activities of the Boston Youth Violence Strike Force—a unit with 40 detectives or officers (Braga and Winship, 2006).
3. There is an effort to communicate directly and persuasively to the offending population that the "rules of the game" have changed and that there is an intensive effort ongoing to disrupt specific problem area activities. In general, this communication occurs at a "call-in" meeting between probationers and members of the working group.
4. The message delivered includes a summary of the changing nature of the criminal justice response (sticks) and available opportunities for program participation (carrots). Finally, follow-up includes applying "levers" where appropriate. A response is specifically tied to behavior and includes exploring all possible sanctions for individuals involved in the offending group.

How successful is lever pulling? The Boston project appeared quite successful. As Braga et al. (2001) noted:

> Youth homicides in Boston decreased dramatically following the first gang forum in May 1996 and has remained low to the present. The implementation of Operation Ceasefire was associated with a 63 percent decrease in youth homicides per month, a 32-percent decrease in shots-fired calls for service per month, a 25-percent decrease in gun assaults per month, and a 44-percent decrease in the number of youth gun assaults per month in the highest risk district.

Chermak noted in a follow-up 2008 lever-pulling program in Indianapolis that lever pulling did not demonstrate the same level of successes as did Boston. He attributed the lack of success in Indianapolis to inadequate justice system follow-through; levers were threatened but not invoked for failures. Follow through was related to a failure of communication across the various elements of the criminal justice system involved in the initial lever-pulling meetings. However, some successes were noted: the meetings were an effective communications forum, and law enforcement-oriented meetings tended to result in recidivism "downwards," that is, toward less serious offenses.

## *Zero-Tolerance/Broken Windows*

Zero-tolerance and Broken Windows are interrelated policing strategies that emerged in the late twentieth century that resonate with police today.[6] **Broken Windows** is a policing strategy organized around the metaphor that a broken window on a house, unrepaired, invites vandalism. The metaphor is extended to communities, according to which incivilities and public order problems, if not handled aggressively by the police, will lead to neighborhood breaks and criminal invasion. **Zero-tolerance** policing refers to non-discretionary police work, or the blanket enforcement of all law, however minor.

Broken Windows is widely popular among police organizations and personnel, even though supporting research evidence is sparse and at best mixed. Research has consistently shown that crime does not increase in neighborhoods because of disorder problems introduced from the outside at an earlier point in time. Instead, the best predictor of neighborhood crime seems to be the economic health of a neighborhood—a social problem that it unsatisfactory for police because it suggests that crime cannot be adequately addressed on any kind of permanent basis with police intervention. One is hard pressed to talk to police today without someone emphasizing the importance of fixing neighborhood "Broken Windows."

The tactical work sometimes used to fix Broken Windows is frequently described as zero-tolerance policing. **Zero-tolerance** has three interrelated elements:

- Being tough on crime. All laws enforced, all crimes punished, criminals will not get away.
- Strict, non-discretionary law enforcement.
- Police action against minor offenses and disorder. Quality of life offenses will be enforced. Heavy focus on alcohol, drugs.

Hence, the way in which neighborhoods are fixed is through frequent interdictions of minor offenders, close questioning, and arrest if circumstances are favorable.

It should be emphasized that zero-tolerance and Broken Windows are not closely linked by all scholars. Kelling and Sousa, in their assessment of what they called "Broken Windows policing" in New York, stated:

> As implemented by the NYPD, "Broken Windows" policing is not the rote and mindless "zero-tolerance" approach that critics often contend it is. Case studies show that police vary their approach to quality-of-life crimes, from citation and arrest on one extreme to warnings and reminders on the other, depending upon the circumstances of the offense.
>
> (Kelling and Sousa, 2001)

Kelling and Souza's argument is important because it suggests that the more flexible and arguably discretionary style of policing historically associated with order maintenance policing in the twentieth century continues in some places to be the case. Yet numerous other cases show that zero-tolerance, advanced as an aggressive form of order maintenance policing focusing on arrest for even minor fractions, is often associated, at least in the minds of officers, with "fixing Broken Windows."

## *Crackdowns*

Crackdowns are a popular idea in contemporary policing and have been throughout the latter twentieth century. Scott (2003:1) defined a **crackdown** as "sudden and dramatic increase in police officer presence, sanctions, or threats of apprehension either for specific offenses or for all offenses in specific places." The purpose of a crackdown is to both increase the certainty that offenders will be caught (a specific deterrent strategy) and increase their perception that they will be caught (a general deterrent). Hence, advertising that there will be a crackdown may itself be a deterrent to some crime.

Crackdowns appear limitedly effective. Research consistently shows that the lifetime of a post-crackdown deterrent effect is short, often measured in hours. They are also associated with some negative effects. They are manpower intensive and consequently expensive. They also are capable of generating public hostility. As Scott noted, when they are carried out against street activity, police are criticized for disproportionate response to minority communities, where drugs are most likely to be sold on the street. Researchers at one time expressed the concern that crackdowns, to the extent they suppressed crime, might push it into other areas. In the current era, however, research indicates a "diffusion of benefits," where crime, when it is curtailed in one area, also tends to diminish in surrounding ones.

There are many different kinds of crackdowns. Scott sought to organize crackdowns along four dimensions.

1. Visibility and enforcement action. This means that sometimes a crackdown is only a sharp increase in visibility and may or may not be associated with enforcements. The Kansas City Patrol Experiment is an example of a change in visibility of patrol and suggested that visibility in itself is not particularly helpful. Visibility in conjunction with crackdowns tends to be effective, however.
2. Kind of action carried out. What is it that the police actually do to crack down? These can include arresting offenders, issuing citations, conducting knock and talk operations, serving search and/or arrest warrants, and taking juvenile offenders into custody.
3. Geographic target. Is the practice focused on a specific structure, such as a high-rise, a neighborhood, or is it sector wide?

4. Type of offense targeted. Crackdowns often focus on specific violations—drunk driving, drugs, robbery, speeding, and the like. Some may be more widely aimed, seeking to crack down on all crime in a specific area.

Crackdowns are consistent with the widely held belief that policing, done right, can deter. They represent a "logic of good faith"—that the police are doing something that works and that it has an impact on crime regardless of whether that impact can be measured.

## *Hot Spot Policing*

**Hot spot policing** can be defined as the "concentration of police resources in small discrete areas such as addresses, street blocks, or clusters of addresses or street blocks" (Weisburd, 2005:221). Weisburd argued that hot spot policing has become a central police tactic across the country at the end of the twentieth century and can be traced directly to research emphasizing the importance of place in understanding crime. He noted:

> There were often discrete places free of crime in neighborhoods that were considered troubled and crime hot spots in neighborhoods that were seen generally as advantaged and not crime prone. [Such findings] redirected the attention of crime prevention scholars to small areas often encompassing only one or a few city blocks that could be defined as hot spots of crime.
>
> (Weisburd, 2005:226)

Hot spots has been one of the few areas in police work where experimentation has become routine (see Braga, 1997).[7] Its research popularity can be traced to the Minneapolis Experiment in hot spots policing (Sherman and Weisburd, 1995). As Weisburd and Braga noted, this experiment sought to challenge the null findings of the widely cited Kansas City Patrol Experiment in the early 1970s. This experiment differed in an important dimension; it focused on specific, identifiable "hot spots" rather than larger beat areas used in Kansas City. They justified this approach with the recognition that around 3 percent of the areas in Minneapolis accounted for more than one-half of all the police calls for service. Findings indicated that significantly lower levels of crime were found in the areas where the interventions took place. Weisburd and Braga (2006:239) concluded with the observation:

> Hot spots policing is as model for the integration of research in the world of policing, and this integration has produced what is, according to empirical evidence, the most effective police innovation of the last decade.[8]

Concerns have been raised as to the extent to which hot spots policing actually solves crime problems. Rosenbaum (2006) noted that, while hot spot policing has short-term deterrent effects, it does not, in any way, actually do something about crime in areas. It is not a solution, he suggested, but a temporary deterrent.[9] It is consequently an expensive use of police resources for a limited overall effect. Moreover, violence and illicit activity that are hot spot targets are most likely to be found in minority communities, increasing the extent to which police work is perceived to be biased again minorities. Rosenbaum noted that the number of police-initiated contacts increases substantially with little overall success, while at the same time producing hostility in the community.

## *Neo-Professionalism and Higher Education*

One sees in hot spot policing some of the fruition of the overlap of academics and policing, a process of institutional convergence that began with the LEAA programs in 1972. Academic focus on outcomes has led police to increasingly assess the effectiveness of their programs. In problem-oriented policing, we find academic legitimation of an aggressive order maintenance style of policing focusing on zero-tolerance and wide use of arrest. The academic language of problem-solving infuses Compstat and crime mapping, though there are important differences. And police practices aimed at the suppression of crime at hot spots is closely tied to academic efforts, through research, to better understand crime prevention. Moreover, many of the frustrations and failures of measurable benefits from community policing are a direct product of grants carried out in academe through funding from the National Institute of Justice. In a word, academic research is closely tied and, in significant part, responsible for the emergence of neo-professionalism and state-centered policing in the current era.

## *The Facilitations of Technology*

All of the changes described herein are facilitated by advanced technologies. These technologies have fired the expansion of the police function in significant ways. In the post-9/11 Homeland Security era of policing, the gathering of intelligence for counter-terrorism purposes has become a technological priority. Unmanned aerial vehicles (UAVs), for instance, are slowly becoming crime scene mapping, traffic control, and U.S. border-monitoring devices. Global positioning systems (GPS) and high-tech video surveillance equipment with infrared and heat-seeking capabilities are becoming mainstream methods for tracking criminal suspects as well as suspected terrorists, and public video monitoring devices are increasingly popular. Fourth Amendment challenges have received mixed messages from state and federal courts on the stipulations regarding their use (Caerula, 2004), but generally, the courts have not impeded the use of new information-gathering technologies. The USA PATRIOT Act has given the government unprecedented authority to tap phones and computers with cursory FISA court oversight. Surveillance extends to libraries and Internet service providers, who may be required to report to the government and forbidden to inform suspects of the surveillance. For police, one of the most significant issues today is in the processing of massive amounts of information acquired by the new surveillance technologies.

Maguire (P.C.), cited in a paper by Crank et al. (2009), noted:

> As a consequence, the occupation of the police is becoming . . . an industry that each passing year is more and more omnipresent in our lives. In American policing, we are facing a future of larger, more complex, more formal, more militaristic agencies with greater surveillance capacity. . . . These agencies will be enmeshed in powerful networks of agencies and institutions responsible for the "governance of security". . . . Since 9/11, powerful social forces are accelerating these trends. There appears to be little recognition among the populace that formal social control mechanisms are increasing so rapidly. Moreover, the forces that would serve to counter the growth of these mechanisms are weak.

In the same paper, the implication of these changes was noted by Haberfeld (P.C.), who argued that the veneer of citizen-based policing was slipping away. With the Homeland Security era accelerating pro-militaristic changes among the police, U.S. police were increasingly becoming a force that conceptualizes its responsibilities in terms of the protection of the state or its corresponding political unit, not just citizen-based to the extent that it was in the twentieth century.

> Mike knew the conversation was going to be uncomfortable. Police don't know who they are today. Too many powerful toys. Well, here goes. *What's going to be the role of citizens in all of these strategies?*
>
> THE RESPONSE WAS QUICK: "We need citizens to help collect information, so we can be more effective. They are our eyes and ears. Without them we can't adequately address threats."
>
> Mike. *Oh. You need citizens to spy on each other.*
>
> THE ROOM WAS STONY. AFTER A PAUSE AN OFFICER RESPONDS: "Your implication is unfair. We have always relied on citizens for minor crimes. Citizens are essential for the enforcement of misdemeanors, which are central to public order. They have always already been our eyes and ears. How else could we police? Of course we police for citizens."
>
> Mike. *I want you to think about this. An officer on the beat gets dispatched to deal with a noisy neighbor. The complaining neighbor won't sign a complaint. He's afraid of conflict with the bad neighbor. The officer goes next door, talks to the neighbor for a while, and the stereo is turned down for about 15 minutes. Maybe the complaining neighbor*

*calls the police again, maybe he doesn't. If he does, then he still will have to sign a complaint, or it is very unlikely that something will be done. If he does sign a complaint, then at most a citation will be issued. That's your basic reactive policing. That's what you are talking about.*

Let's shift. The department is collectively gathering intelligence from a wide variety of citizens, and loading it into the intelligence center. They call it the evaluation of threat. It's fed into a threat matrix that you developed with the JTTFs [joint terrorism task forces]. They identify particular groups they want to track, for gang activity, for the JTTFs, for post-release, you get the picture. It is being collated for buzz phrases, cross-tabulated with known gang and ex-offender names and addresses, and organized crime rosters, and tied to crime mapping geographies. Investigation is in some cases secret, protected by JTTF requirements that citizens cannot oversee federal investigations. Citizen information becomes real time intelligence with which to act. Potential risks are identified and watched.

You see, the fundamental nature of your work has changed. You are not doing reactive policing in any of these. All of these move police out of a reactive into either a "real time" or proactive stance. And you're not doing this to enforce misdemeanors. You're doing it to throw the book at criminals. Huh? Huh? Get the trash off the streets? This is heavy-duty felony stuff you are doing. How could this be more different than reactive responses to misdemeanor problems? Not waiting for the public, you are going out there and getting what you need. This is policing stripped of all but crime control and law enforcement. You're managers of groups you think are a risk to society, and you manage them by trying to find out if there're in actual criminal activity, in potentially criminal activity, if they're connected to criminal activity in some articulable way that allows prosecution, and then you bring down the hammer if you can.

What you need to recognize is that your connection to citizens is slipping away. You don't work with them nearly as close as community policing. You like this. It feeds the noble cause. You need to think about what you've lost.

OFFICER: "That was inefficient police work. It sucked always being a step behind crime. We have always wanted to get ahead of crime. Now, with these tools like Comp Stat, real time analysis, and our proactive gang and drug activity, we can do that."

MIKE: *Who are you working for?*

OFFICER: "What do you mean?"

MIKE: *I'm here to tell you that, if you think about this stuff, you don't work with citizens. Not like before. You are defining your own threats; you identify your own risk groups. You are losing your non-coercive connections to citizens. It's starting to fade with all these changes. All over the country, it's fading; not just here. You are policing increasingly for the state, which, in day-to-day work, means that you decide what is good policing, who is dangerous, and what to do about it. Citizen input is only for the collection of intelligence. You protect the interests of government, as you see it.*

OFFICER: "We do not police for the government. We use our skills and strategies to determine who is dangerous, and we've developed some pretty good practices in recent years."

MIKE: *Ok, take a step back. Listen. You are the government. Who do you think the government is? And you're deciding who is dangerous and what to do about it. That is the definition of state policing. That's what you are doing.*

You define your work increasingly in terms of groups and kinds of people who are a risk or threat to the state—or in your day-to-day work, who are good targets for police tracking, surveillance, and crime suppression.

I'm not here to tell you that all these changes are wrong. But they're perilous. You are on the brink of losing your connection to citizens. Think about where you are going and you can see it. Look at your work—where is the community connection? Where is the citizen input? You talk about the changes you made, and I can tell you that you aren't working with communities, especially with minority communities; you're out there bringing the hammer down on them. Isn't that where all your risk groups are? Minority communities? Where are the gangs? Where are the druggies? Where are the excons? I bet you are starting to talk about putting up concrete barricades to control the flow of traffic in and out of these communities. We need to be very, very careful as we go down this road.

You are more powerful than ever. You are committed to the noble cause, and the government is giving you wide latitude. Your tools are better than ever. This is powerful stuff. But remember what I said earlier, about the "noble-cause ascendant." At the end of the day you go home to wonderful families and kids. They make your life worthwhile. Just don't forget—so do the people you police.

It's not about you, you know. Government's not about you. It's about them. These citizens, even the riff raff, the ones who struggle every day to find a buck for a bottle of booze. Life is tough, and you can make it a lot meaner, especially now that your friendly contacts with citizens are fading away. Don't forget that. That's my message. Don't lose that contact. It's too important.

## Notes

1 SERE refers to "survival, evasion, resistance, and escape." Mayer (2008:159) noted that "SERE was a repository of the world's knowledge about torture. . . . SERE was a defensive program, meant to protect American soldiers from torture. But in the CIA's hands after September 11, critics close to the program said, it was "reverse engineered" into a blueprint for abuse."

2 Steven Miles, in the opening of the book *Oath Betrayed* (2006), attributed the opening statement, "We are selling our souls for dross," to Craig Murray, who then was the British Ambassador to Uzbekistan. The comment was occasioned by intelligence he had received from Uzbek intelligence services that tortured "dupes" were being forced to sign confessions that showed the U.S. what they wanted to believe about the conduct of the War on Terror.
3 Neo-professionalism was a term Crank (1994) used in describing anticipated police futures in 2010. He argued that community policing would likely end and be replaced by a return to a law and order mandate. See "The Community Policing Movement of the Early 21st Century: What We Learned." Pp. 107–126 In J. Klofas and S. Stojkovic (eds.), *Crime and Justice in the Year 2010*. 1994. Macmillan.
4 Ratcliffe, J.H. (2016). *Intelligence-Led Policing*, Second Edition. Oxford: Routledge.
5 Chermak, Stephen (2008) Executive summary, in *Reducing Violent Crime and Firearms Violence: The Indianapolis Lever-Pulling Experiment*. www.ncjrs.gov/pdffiles1/nij/grants/221077.pdf.
6 Grabosky argued that zero-tolerance emerged in New York as a direct result of the Broken Windows narrative of community life, in which it was seen as the strategic expression of that narrative. Grabosky, P.N. (1998) *Zero-Tolerance Policing*. Australian Institute of Technology. www.aic.gov.au/publications/tandi/ti102.pdf.
7 Braga, Anthony (2008) *Crime Prevention Research Review No. 2: Police Enforcement Strategies to Prevent Crime in Hot Spot Areas*. Washington, DC: U.S. Department of Justice Office of Community Oriented Policing Services.
8 Weisburd, David and Anthony Braga (2006) "Hot Spots Policing as a Model." Pp. 225–244 in Weisburd, David and Braga, Anthony (eds.), *Police Innovation: Contrasting Perspectives*. Cambridge University Press: United Kingdom.
9 Rosenbaum, Dennis (2006) "The Limits of Hot Spot Policing." Pp. 245–263 in Weisburd, David and Braga, Anthony (eds.), *Police Innovation: Contrasting Perspectives*. Cambridge University Press: United Kingdom.

# Recommendations 11

## Key Terms

internal affairs units
feedback
importance/usefulness dilemma
complaints
transfer function
modeling ethics
performance evaluations
"Scared Straight" programs

## Introduction

Chapter 11 addresses the organizational and ethical reforms necessary to mitigate noble-cause corruption in policing. Central to the discussion is the concept of modeling ethics, emphasizing that ethical behavior must be demonstrated by leadership rather than merely taught. The chapter critiques ineffective strategies such as "Scared Straight" programs, which often backfire, and instead advocates for mentorship and example-setting by training officers and supervisors. Internal affairs units are reimagined not as punitive bodies but as proactive agents of ethical development, capable of providing guidance before misconduct occurs. The chapter also explores the importance/dilemma in performance evaluations—how their significance for promotions can undermine their usefulness as tools for constructive feedback. It recommends separating evaluations from disciplinary systems and using them instead to support officer growth and innovation.

MIKE: *Once we recognize that officers who are doing what we call noble-cause corruption are engaged in what they believe to be highly ethical*

DOI: 10.4324/9781003626916-15

> *behavior, we have to ask how do we change that behavior? That behavior is tied to a morality, which means that they are doing value-based decision-making. If they are acting morally—you guys are all with me, right?—and now we know that they are acting very morally, then we are dealing with the culture of the police. We're not dealing with individual rogue cops.*
>
> The commitment to the noble cause is the moral heart of police culture. How do we change that? If they are making value-based decisions, how do we change the values?
>
> I'm going to make some recommendations. Some of them are very important. Some of them may not work for you. They are about who you hire, about how you evaluate them, and about how you train them. Remember that we want to preserve the best about the noble cause, the commitment your officers have to the public and to good policing. I want you to take these recommendations in that spirit. And that's up to you.

Our recommendations are based on the idea that the behavior of the police should respect values across the due process/crime control continuum. The continuum characterizes the diversity of American political and moral life—a concern for victims and a need to do something about bad people and, at the same time, a commitment to ensure that fairness and due process are the cornerstones of public service. We want to take the best of the noble cause and blend it with a respect for all different kinds of people. It's not much more complicated than that.

We have focused on corruption of the noble-cause variety because noble-cause corruption is a problem in police departments today. We think it's a big problem. We believe in the noble cause, but in balance, because just means are also important. We need to remember that the pursuit of justice is not about making people more just but in helping everyone—with all their different and sometimes bizarre notions of justice—to simply get along. The blending of noble cause and just means represent what we believe is a balanced, thoughtful way to do this work called policing. The blend is also a good way for police to treat each other in the process, particularly across the administrative-line crevasse.

In this chapter, we present recommendations that are in line with this way of thinking. Some of the recommendations are practical, while others are more far-reaching. Yet all recommendations, in one way or another, serve the goal of ethical balance in the practice of police work.

## Preparing Recruits for Ethical Decisions

This book is about putting a notion of ethics to print. It is a notion that has been widely discussed in recent years but whose implications have not been explored. We believe that officers will benefit from studying this notion of ethics. In these conclusions, we print several recommendations, and these recommendations can become part of the body of ethics instruction and discussion for future police officers. This chapter provides recommendations that take seriously the issues raised regarding the noble cause. We want them discussed, weighted, taken seriously. The act of discussing the recommendations in itself broadens the ethical knowledge that officers bring to bear when they think about their work and their organization.

Ethics can be presented in a way that alienates and offends police officers. We recommend that any ethics discussion begin with an underlying assumption. This assumption is that police officers are already ethical, and they are ethical in a sophisticated way. They are, as Mike observes, tower-runners. They will put their lives on the line for the public. That is an ethical statement at the highest level—the willingness to place one's life on the line for a stranger. Unless ethics begins with that presumption, it will fail. Ethics should begin with that assumption and then aim at encouraging awareness of the full implications of their ethics.

The most important form of instruction does not occur in the classroom; it is education through modeling and example. This section is devoted to that spirit. Later, we will review our belief that ethics has to be modeled by commanders, and only then will it begin to take hold in organizations and provide a guild for lower-ranking officers.

## *Ethics Has to Be Modeled*

It is not enough to teach ethics. The central problem with in teaching ethics is that it may not be taken seriously. And if line officers are in an environment where they do not see their TOs or managers practicing the ethics that they are being taught, they will think ethics instruction is a joke. Ethics training will fall into that great reservoir of unapplied training knowledge that is shelved away into the cabinet called "forget everything you learned in training; this is how we do it on the street."

In studies of juveniles, we have learned the importance of mentoring and responsible adult supervision. In research on crime prevention, we have discovered that a central element of crime is the absence of capable guardianship. In other words, what we have learned is that people take far more seriously the actions of other people rather than what they say. This indicates the importance of **modeling ethics.**

Alternatively, we have learned in recent years that programs and training strategies based on exhortation or the manipulation of emotions do not work. After a great deal of research, we have found that DARE programs, which aim at motivating young people to "just say no," do not lower the likelihood that young people will use drugs. Similarly, **"Scared Straight" programs** aimed at curbing tendencies toward a life of crime by exposing young people to the horrors of a life behind bars not only don't work but also tend to backfire, desensitizing young people about prison life. This tells us that programs aimed at telling people what is morally right are likely to have little success in themselves.

Ethics education, if not supplemented by examples of correct and moral behavior on the part of executives and training officers, is a waste of time. What managers, TOs, and others in the criminal justice system must do is model appropriate behavior. To be just (and to be perceived as just), one must act justly. It is from the cues provided by responsible organizational actors that recruits will learn how to act justly.

What is important to recognize is that training supervisors are giving cues and that officers are following those cues. Consider the infamous Rodney King incident involving the Los Angeles Police Department in 1991. Training officers were present when Mr. King was beaten by several police officers, and the entire incident was captured on videotape. The implicit message provided by the TOs was clear—the beating of a suspect is appropriate under some circumstances—in that case, where the suspect did not display complete compliance to police requests. Did the officers believe that they were doing the right thing? Yes, they were applying their training to a suspect who they believed was not displaying adequate compliance. Were they acting ethically? They believed they were protecting the public from a crackhead menace. Did they get cues from their training officers that they were doing the right thing? You bet. Training officers were present who did nothing to stop them.

Was their behavior wrong? There's the rub. Certainly, the beating of Mr. King has been appropriately condemned by commissions, police professionals, prosecutors, and the public alike. The case has resulted in criminal convictions against the police. But many police officers and justice professionals look at the entire video of the incident and come to a different conclusion: that the beating was justified given the totality of circumstances. This tells us that the beating of Rodney King was morally complex and that quick and easy assignations of guilt and innocence in the King incident will only lead to taking sides and not contribute to the intellectual maturation of police officers. Would ethics education of those officers, in and of itself, have helped? Not a whit.

> *Recruits are being modeled at every turn. Their words, the way they look at other cops, the way they treat the public, the courts, it's all being modelled. You're the model.* Mike reminds the commanders.

> Recruits were in Los Angeles during the Rodney King incident, and they are in your department. Before you condemn those officers who beat up Rodney King, I want you to answer two questions. Do you see how they were engaged in moral behavior? And what would you have them do that was different from what they did? You may not like this. I didn't, and I really had to think hard about this. But we can understand the morality of the Rodney King incident better when we imagine ourselves there, standing next to one of the trainers, Stacey Kuhn. Don't

> just imagine standing there. Imagine talking to him. Imagine him talking back, answering your questions about what is going on. You can picture this. Then you will understand better. If you want do deal with that morality—and it is a morality, you have to provide a different morality. A different way to think through the problem.
>
> You can never forget that those officers believed they were acting out the morality of the department, just like yours are. If you want to deal with noble cause, you are talking about the organization. You are talking about yourselves first. Your officers are the front line for the public, but for them, you are the front line. Are you there for them? Are you the kind of model that they need?

If managers are serious about changing the ethics of their line officers, they will have to take a long, hard look at their own behavior and assess what they are cueing to recruits. It is our belief that many TOs and managers may be sending out signals regarding noble-cause corruption even when they don't intend to. Managers may be careless about who they send out in the field to act as a TO. Commanders may stay behind their desks, not going into the field to find out what is actually happening on the streets with their officers, only coming out when there is a high publicity incident—or to gasp in surprise in front of the cameras when they are told that their officers have done something wrong.

> Don't make the mistake of blaming your line officers here and thinking you can deal with the problem by punishing them. Your line officers are doing exactly what they have been set out by their administrators and supervisors to do—fight a war, defend the innocent, and win the war on crime. The problem therefore is not with the bottom but rather the top. It's an organizational problem, don't forget that. Change the top first.

Everyone falls into habits of behavior, and they often do not fully recognize what it is that they communicate with that behavior. As a commander once mentioned to one of the co-authors, all police officers are 90–10. Ninety percent of the time, they act and think on a very high level. However, all of them carry that 10 percent that is uncomfortable to be around or otherwise flawed or unpleasant for other people. That astute observation could be applied to most people. What we are asking is that commanders and training personnel reflect on that 10 percent, that part of ourselves that we don't tend to look at too closely, and try to assess what is happening there. It may be that we are giving cues that we don't recognize and that we are uncomfortable with.

What we all need to do—not only commanders but all of us—is to take a look at ourselves and try to assess what cues we give to other people. We may not want to be role models. Yet the nature of police work is that the police are received by the public as role models, and we communicate, by our simple presence and behavior, what we think is right and wrong. In important ways, that is our charge from society. And in the same way, that is the charge of commanders to their line officers as well. Officers are what commanders want them to be. And commanders, executives, and training officers communicate that information with their behavior.

If the goal is to change the behavior of line officers, to move their behavior toward the center of the continuum, then the work has to begin with those responsible for modeling appropriate behavior for line officers to follow. For this reason, police departments cannot be "fixed" by hiring new personnel. The fixing has to begin with executives and experienced personnel.

MIKE CONCLUDES THE DISCUSSION OF ETHICS TRAINING: *Ethics is not something that can simply be taught. This is where it gets tough. Ethics must be modeled, demonstrated, reinforced, evaluated for, promoted for, and cued. This means the organization has to be changed. Commanders must change themselves first. Then your line officers will follow.*

## *Add a Proactive Component to Internal Affairs*

MIKE: *What does internal affairs do?*

An officer neutrally responds "Internal affairs is how we police our organization."

Tell me about that.

"In our organization, internal affairs is separated from the other command functions so the Lieutenant in charge can act without worrying about pressure or retaliation from others in the chain of command. We use both an internal affairs officer and a civilian officer who is not sworn but works directly for the Chief. They work with the city attorney on significant cases. It's a small unit but it can carry out very thorough investigations."

Another officer adds, "The city also has a citizen review board, but IA works better. The people in IA know what they're doing. They know police. The citizen review board doesn't have the knowledge, and they have very limited resources for investigations. They can't subpoena us."

Mike thinks for a moment. *So you're telling me that the IA is in an adversarial relationship with officers, who are intimidated by it, which is what you want. That's what you want, right? So that you can claim to be more effective than the citizen review board?*

The officer considers Mike's comment. "It's not that we want IA to be in an adversarial relationship with our line officers. But we respond professionally when we have a situation that requires investigation, when we have a citizen complaint. We need someone who knows the police, who is trained in interrogation, and who knows the law as it relates to police behavior. That kind of person can get at the truth much better than an outsider."

Mike considers this. OK, *I understand that, but it's still an adversarial relationship. It's about a cop getting over another cop. It can contribute to secrecy and departmental distrust. You all know that IA officers walk a fine line between luke-warm acceptance and outright dislike. Let me suggest another dimension of IA that most departments don't think about. What if IA told officers ahead of time what they're concerned about? How about an ethically proactive internal investigation unit?*

**Internal Affairs units** in police organizations are designed for a focused purpose: controlling police behavior. Internal affairs may be only a single officer in a small organization or may be a unit comprised of a command staff and subordinates in larger organizations. Their primary purpose is to review **complaints** against officers. When reviewing complaints, units typically proceed with the following steps (Roberg et al., 2000):

1. Review the allegation and determine what laws or departmental standards were broken.
2. Interview witnesses. Interview complainant.
3. Collect evidence, including medical reports and police reports.
4. Acquire background information on the complainant, such as criminal history.
5. Interview all departmental members who may be involved.

Complaints are then classified in four ways. They may be sustained, which means that they are determined to be justified. They may be unsubstantiated, which means that there is no sustaining evidence so their truth or falsity cannot be substantiated. Complaints may be unfounded, which means that the IA review determines that events did not occur as stated by the complainant. Or the IA may exonerate the officer, which means that the behavior was as stated in by the complainant but that the officer's behavior was legal and within organizational policy (Roberg et al., 2000).

IA units are classified in a variety of ways. One of these is whether or not they are proactive or reactive. A reactive IA unit is one that waits for a complaint to be filed before carrying out an investigation. A reactive unit seeks out officers who might be involved in illegal behavior, for example, offering officers bribes. As Roberg et al. (2000) note, such units are often strongly resented by officers because of the climate of mistrust they create in the organization.

When Mike talks about ethical proactivity, he is not referring to the kind of proactive unit described by Roberg, Crank, and Kuykendall earlier. An ethically proactive unit meets with various units, carries out in-service training, and provides officers with discussions and examples of complex corruption cases.

> MIKE: *All officers know that it's wrong to steal. That's a no-brainer, cops know that. But books on police corruption still see problems in those economic terms. But how many officers have had someone in their organization tell them that sometimes it's not right to back up another officer? If you want to change the culture of the organization, use the IA unit for something other than punishing officers. It's no wonder officers don't trust the organization. Use the IA unit for training about complex real ethical problems that they have encountered. Let them be ethically proactive, describing how officers can get into trouble. Just make sure that your unit isn't training officers how to avoid the law in noble-cause situations.*
>
> The IA is central to Mike's ideas of reform. He continues the dialogue in a different direction. *I gotta question for the commanders in here. What do you do with complaints?*
>
> The room is filled with groans.
>
> Mike smiles, his head nodding up and down. *Exactly. Exactly. They take a small problem and turn it into a big one. Let's talk about complaints and evaluation.*
>
> Mike focuses on the significant and always troubling issue of line evaluation. *In most departments officer evaluation occurs once a year, sometimes twice, though that's a rarity. It's always a pain, because it is a zero sum game—someone wins and is happy, someone loses and is pissed. And they'll both probably be around for the next 20 years.*

Let's say that an officer does something really good. She makes an arrest that is popular with the media and with the chief. This is something the chief or sheriff has a current campaign against, such as gang bangers, drug dealers, child molesters, burglars, or robbers. She likely will receive a letter of commendation, commonly called an attaboy—or in this case, attagirl. These are good.

If an officer does not have a reprimand in their file—that is, if she's managed to stay out of trouble, and she has enough attagirls—she can look forward to a good "office recommendation." These will substantially improve her chances for promotion. Promotions and good recommendations can be measured by the pile of letters she has and the fact that she didn't get caught doing something that embarrassed the department. It used to be said that the predominant posture of officers was consequently to "lay low." Our take on this is different. "Laying low" is for public consumption, to create the image that police should not be expected to work without adequate public protections, retirement benefits, and pay. Inside, you do what you need to get promoted.

In most departments, working the edges of the law, which typically means engaging in noble cause corruption, is the fastest way to good recommendations and promotions—that is, as long as you don't get caught. A brutal cop, or even one that isn't brutal but gets regular complaints from the public for "attitude" problems, is only disciplined if he/she is "caught" by the brass. Caught means public exposure that the brass cannot avoid dealing with.

Why is this? Departments operate on a negative reward system. Recall our earlier discussion about the crevasse and the two cultures of policing. There are two informal organizations, one for the street and one for the administration, and their operations determine the outputs that the formal organization has to deal with.

Consider a hypothetical case of a young star in the police field. We'll call her Grace. Grace became a star because she figured out early how things worked. She learned quickly that she had to "forget what she learned in the academy," that everything she needed to know is learned on the street. The meaning of this was clear, and it wasn't what academics think, which is that cops are against book learning. It meant that she had better pay attention to department loyalties first to find out what she can get away with and who she has to suck up to. She performed the job, looked for opportunities and sometimes created them, and hoped she didn't get caught. She was good, got ahead fast, and had a pile of attagirls. Commanders smiled at her.

She went into the promotion pool, but there were other strong candidates in the pool. Only two slots and six candidates were in the pool. She needed to beef up her paper trail. So she took chances, and she sailed for a while. Looked good—made her sergeant look good, never complained about all the assholes in the department who put their hands all over her. Then it happened—she busted a felon, and she KNEW he was carrying drugs, so she shook him down and searched the car. No warrant, no permission. Nothing. He was guilty as hell, but there was no evidence. She should have skated. There was the damn video camera, son of a bitch.

What would our hypothetical "star" think? It's not hard to imagine.

> Game over, just like that. Full investigation, heavy degradation. Boy can administrators get even when they're publicly embarrassed! They put the IA on me. That's all it took. Permanent record. Newspapers called me racist 'cause the asshole was black. End of game. After that it was all FIDO (Fuck it Drive on). She knew that she could get away to Idaho, had some friends up there. It was quiet, no people, beautiful unlike this ugly street, she had to get away. Only twelve years to early retirement. It became her mantra . . . FIDO, Idaho, FIDO Idaho.

The description earlier is too common. It is of an agency in which traditional oversight, with administration using a punishment-oriented IA to carry out personnel assessments after complaints, is routine. Almost everything is wrong with the way the organization does its line oversight and internal review. And the underlying dynamics are noble-cause corruption, its close tie to race, and how integral the corruption of noble cause is to routine police work and getting ahead.

Mike suggests a different approach to IA, one he believes is a win/win scenario. It has the following elements.

1. The first and most important change is at the top. This book has emphasized throughout the importance of management leadership by example and emulation.
2. The bean-counting and letter-stacking system has to be replaced with evaluations that reflect what a "good" cop does. That is, it needs to shift from hostility production to positive reinforcement. For example, IA personnel can regularly review a police officer's arrest reports to see if a standard "fairy tale" has been utilized to establish the probable cause that resulted in an arrest. These are obvious because they are used repeatedly in a variety of different circumstances. If one is found the officer is "counseled" by the IA investigator. By counseled, Mike does not mean disciplined, with a letter that creates a permanent and career-ending paper trail. He means something like this.

   "Hey guy, I realize you mean well by catching all these bad guys but I think your good intentions are leading you astray. Now here is why I believe that, etc., etc., Now, if you want to improve your performance and increase you evaluations I suggest you do this: only make proper arrests no matter what the pressure, always follow Constitutional guidelines, understand that being a good cop doesn't always mean catching the bad guy, it instead means always doing the job the 'right way.'"

This approach to IA-officer oversight could be carried out in the form of coaching and mentoring rather than punitive discipline. After an appropriate number of follow-up contacts, an assessment is made. When the officer's new reports reflect not simply a new "fairly tale" but the true spirit of the job, the contact becomes a positive reinforcement. Officers who get too many citizen complaints, be it for bad attitude or physical brutality or everything in between, would be treated employees who need professional development, whether it is through training, additional counseling, or other methods. It is important that "professional development" doesn't become another buzz phrase for oversight and punishment. It should convey to the officer know the department gives a damn about the officer as a valued employee who can improve his or her chance at promotion and make a positive and valued contribution to the organization.

As things stand now, the only regular contact an officer receives is with other officers, that is, unless the department DECIDES to discipline the officer, as in the case of Grace earlier. It is often only under sanctions, then they see brass in action. It is certainly not a role for line officers to emulate. Too often, it becomes a role to hate.

The positive reinforcement approach can be expanded in many ways. For example, random interviews of arrestees might show if a pattern of abuse is present. Of course, this requires that police respect prisoners, who are people they don't much like. Unfortunately, there is rarely any other way to find out these kinds of problems, which is precisely why arrestees are so vulnerable to abuse. Citizens who call for service can also be interviewed just to see how the officer treated them. In this way, problems are headed off before they show up on *America's Funniest Home Videos* or are on view every half hour for three days on CNN 24-hour news. This way of thinking about working with outside groups can help locate negative racial attitudes before they are discovered differently—by videotaping or lawsuit. Officers who show special talents with certain groups—a cop on foot patrol who works well with the minority community, drug addicts, or the poor, for example. In the present system, cops who make mistakes are punished when they are caught, and those with special talents remain anonymous, their human and social skills unrewarded.

A commander listens to this discussion. He looks at Mike. Then in a slow voice. "Hmmm. Do you think we ought to hold their hands, too? Maybe have a group hug?"

Mike. *Yeah, I know. It sounds that way. But I bet you would hold someone's hand for five minutes, if it meant that you weren't up to your butt with lawyers and union actions for the next five years.*

Commander. "Well . . . I'd have to think about that."

Laughter.

Mike. *I'll tell you something else. If you look at the past 20 years, your organization has made some pretty major strides in IA, providing legal opportunities for line personnel when there are complaints, sometimes refocusing on training. You are doing some counseling. Your organization does management training, it seeks good officers. You do in-service training. I'm only talking one more step. You don't have to do everything at once. You take a look at IA, and I bet you could find a way to make it both positive and proactive.*

Internal Affairs recommendation. Reorient internal affairs toward positive strategies for dealing with problems.

## *Hire Toward the Policed*

One of the central issues facing police departments is hiring individuals with cultural skills that are similar to the populations policed. Among the most important cultural skill is the capacity for language or local linguistic skills spoken within a jurisdiction. Early on, many advocates of community policing argued that, by hiring individuals with cultural skills, police would maintain better community relations with community members. We argue for the importance of hiring individuals with local cultural and linguistic skills and agree that getting along with local populations is a widely sought goal of police agencies. However, linguistic skills serve other purposes as well. Linguistic skills enable officers to do better traditional police work of solving crimes. Consider the work carried out by Deputy Anthony Dalem in the Martin County, Florida Sheriff's Office in Box 11.1.

Box 11.1

**Crime Solving and Linguistic Skills**

Officer Dalem works in a county that is highly diverse and in which a variety of languages are spoken by residents. Because of this, Dalem is highly sought. He has a particular skill. He speaks five languages: Portuguese, English, French, Italian, and Spanish. He is particularly proud of his ability to work with victims. He described the following instance of his ability to assist someone in need:

> There was the case when he was called to a local hospital to translate for a young sexual assault victim. "It felt great I was able to help her," he said. His skills frequently come in handy when other officers are faced with people who speak foreign languages as well.

He finds that he is frequently called to assist other officers who are faced with people speaking other languages, a not uncommon occurrence in the ethnically diverse county. However, he also is able to use his skills for crime solving. He is often called to bars and hang-outs because many people know him. They often help him solve crimes; as he says, they help him "because they know they can talk to me." He also sometimes hears foreign-language conversations at crime scenes that contain critical information. He related the following instance.

On a stabbing call in Golden Gate, he arrived to find a group of Spanish speakers discussing the suspect's hiding place—but not sharing it with the English-speaking deputies already on the scene.

"They had no clue. When I walk up to somebody, they have no clue I speak the language," he said. "I heard the guy that did it was under the bed. Sure enough."

Source: Adapted from Gabriel Margasak (2004) "Victims Pleased Martin County Deputy Speaks their Language." *Port St. Lucie News*, February 8: B2, B7.

Many departments are already committed to hiring toward their local resident populations, particularly in the area of linguistic skills. To an extent, we are preaching to the choir. However, this is an area of hiring that is so significant that we want to emphasize its importance. Cultural and linguistic skills are not only about community relations, which many police officers take to be a soft aspect of community policing. They are also about helping victims and solving crimes. The following recommendation is included with the recognition that many departments are already doing this.

> Hiring recommendation: Hire those with specialized linguistic skills. Encourage officers to return to school to take language classes.

## *Hire Toward the Center of the Continuum*

We have argued throughout this book that police officers enter police work already committed to the noble cause, and their commitments are finely tuned through formal and informal training processes. They are hired with predispositions sharply to the crime control side of the due process crime control continuum. And there is precious little in the work, administration, or environments of the police that pull them back toward the center. Indeed, if one were to design a hiring process and work setting that emphasized the corruption of noble cause, it would be difficult to design a more effective system than American policing today. What is needed is a way to moderate the powerful influence of crime control over the work of police. Efforts to encourage a balanced perspective needs to be initiated in the hiring process.

We encourage departments to hire toward the center of the continuum. Recruits will tend to be ideologically committed to crime control. A commitment to crime control only becomes a problem when excessive crime control shades into noble-cause corruption. Departments can counter the tendency toward excessive crime control by emphasizing the importance of just means at each stage of the hiring process. This can be carried out in a way that does not undercut the importance of the noble cause (a doomed effort were it to be undertaken). It is unlikely that departments could be, or unclear that they should be, staffed with those whose sentiments aren't mobilized by noble-cause considerations. However, if just means are emphasized at each step of the hiring process, officers will learn that their parent organization encourages a balanced perspective, grounded in concern for fair play and democratic process as well as sympathetic to the plight of victims and determined to serve and protect.

The key to balanced hiring is for administrators to recognize that officers are easily corrupted by the current overemphasis on the noble cause and that administrators and trainers carry the responsibility for embedding balance into the hiring and training process. Administrators set the ethical tone of the department. They select trainers, who pass on to recruits what they think is good policing. Recognizing that recruits will likely be committed to the noble cause, the hiring process at every step should encourage officers to consider the ways in which just means are important to their work. Boxes 11.2 through 11.4 discuss the elements of the hiring process that bear on the noble cause, and each is followed by a recommendation.

Box 11.2

**Preemployment Knowledge Testing**

Police departments prefer to hire technically efficient officers—as long as they are not too intelligent. Some departments do not hire officers who test too highly on knowledge examinations. They fear that high-scoring officers will think about police work in too complicated a manner, will become too easily cynical about police work, or will be frustrated by the long wait for eligibility for promotion to sergeant, typically six years in most departments.

Hiring practices that reject the most intelligent applicants should end. Officers should be hired that are intelligent enough to think through the complex human issues confronting them. Ethical problems are the most complex that police face, and they are sometimes confronted on a daily basis. If recruits lack the intellectual capacity to make thoughtful decisions in the complex ethical environment inhabited by the police, either they should not be hired or detailed attention should be provided for their ethical training.

Pre-employment testing recommendation: We recommend that departments do not over-rely on broad-based intelligence tests and incorporate into their pre-employment testing jobs and skills-based tests that also include ethical decision-making as a component. Don't reject applicants because they score too high; IQ tests in any case are overrated and mostly register socialization and education. Recruits should be presented with non-solvable ethical dilemmas to see if they can recognize their complexities.

Box 11.3

**Oral Interview**

Commanders skilled in oral interview techniques will use the interview to probe for stress points. Can the recruit make reasoned decisions in conflicting situations? How do recruits respond when commanders make conflicting requests? We recommend that commanders expand their often considerable oral interview skills to include ethical problems. Ethical problems can be presented that are substantial. Officers should be pressured for their ability to think through ethical problems.

Oral interview recommendation: Provide a non-resolvable ethical question in the oral interview. This is already done in many departments.

Box 11.4

**POST Academy, TOs, and the Problem of War Stories**

Employers must recognize that anecdotal stories told by trainers, TOs, and seasoned officers to new recruits are more than simple war stories or "tales of the wild." All stories involving the department carry in them its traditions and values. Even a single story, told by a trainer in a class on topics such as "due process" or "officer safety," can undercut the importance of just means or encourage noble-cause corruption. The message conveyed in such stories is "don't pay attention to what the class is officially about. Here's what the organization really considers valuable."

One of the authors of this book attended a parole and probation training class. The opening day, one of the lead trainers said, "We don't tell war stories here," and immediately launched into a war story explaining why he didn't use war stories. Our position is that war stories are essential for passing on the traditions and practices of the department. Following Ford's (2003) lead and recognizing that stories have manifest and latent content (see Chapter 7), we recommend a "train the trainers" in-service day to discuss the power of stories and encouraging their use but cautioning against inadvertently using them to send messages that the trainers themselves may not even be aware they're sending.

POST training recommendation: Monitor the use of war stories for content; instructors may be unaware of some of the implications of their stories. Hold a training day to explain the power of such stories. Stories are powerful forces that convey the traditions of the department to recruits. Make sure that officers hear stories that reaffirm the importance of both substantive and due process law. Watch for "Black Swans" that undercut the importance of due process.

## *Make Pre-Service College Education of the Police a Priority*

The idea that police officers should be educated has been around for many years. College education has been available since Vollmer founded the first college program at Berkeley, California, in 1919

(Carte, 1986). Since then, college education in the areas of criminal justice has expanded dramatically. Today, there are more than 1,000 programs and departments of criminology or criminal justice in the United States.

Our needs are perhaps even greater in the current era than they were in the 1920s. The dramatic diversification of the American population has created a working police environment that requires intelligence, quick thinking, and breadth of human experience. As Garner (1999:91) noted, "Policing is an occupation that demands the education and skills of a teacher, lawyer, counselor, social worker, doctor, psychologist, and minister. Yet it is interesting that all of these professions long ago required a college degree." We need officers with the capacity to think through problems in a multi-ethnic, multi-religious society. We believe that a four-year college education is a minimal requirement for the complex ethical demands on police in the coming century (see Box 11.5).

Box 11.5

**The Value of the College Experience**

As Goldstein (1986) observed, the college experience not only provides substantive course content but college experience will also provide a better officer. Departments that recruit college-educated officers benefit. The following are ways in which the experience contributes to the police, independent of the specific content of particular courses:

1. A greater share of intelligent young people.
2. Individuals with a wider view of the people with which they must deal.
3. Degree-carrying officers will bring greater confidence to citizen interactions.
4. The field as a whole will gain in status and dignity.
5. Officers are older and more mature when they begin their police careers.
6. Highly motivated youth.

Carter et al. (1988) described eight ways in which college education can enhance decision-making skills. These ways are pertinent to ethical decision-making and are included here. They are reproduced from Palmiotto's (1999:73–74) discussion of police education in Box 11.6.

Box 11.6

**Advantages of College Education for Decision-Making Skills**

1. College education develops a broader base of information for decision-making.
2. Course requirements and achievements inculcate responsibility in the individual and a greater appreciation for constitutional rights, values, and the democratic form of government.
3. College education engenders the ability to flexibly handle difficult or ambiguous situations with greater creativity or innovation.
4. Higher education develops a greater empathy for diverse populations and their unique experiences.
5. The college-educated officer is assumed to be less rigid in decision-making and more readily accepts and adapts to organizational change.
6. The college experience will help officers better communicate and respond to crime and service needs of a diverse public in a competent manner with civility and humanity.
7. College-educated officers exhibit more "professional" demeanor and performance.
8. The college experience tends to make the officer less authoritarian and less cynical with respect to the milieu of policing.

Source: Carter et al. (1988). Reproduced in Palmiotto (1999). "Should a College Requirement Be Required for Police Officers." J. Sewell (ed.) *Controversial Issues in Policing*. Boston: Allyn & Bacon.

It is our belief that only college-educated officers will be able to grasp the social complexities of the working environment they will encounter in the twenty-first century. It is preposterous that we continue debating the merits of college education for the police. A four-year degree is the minimum intellectual capital needed to participate in public life.

As more and more middle-class jobs are outsourced to other countries, potential recruits will find themselves competing against some highly educated individuals for jobs.

Failure to educate the police is simply another mark of decline in the quality of public education in the United States. Officers with only a high school education will be psychologically unprepared and intellectually ill-equipped for all but the most parochial of police jobs—and probably even those.

Police without college degrees—uneducated by the world's standards—will be relegated to second-class citizen status in their own country.

> Education Recommendation 1: Hire only college-educated officers, and at the level of sergeant and above, promote only those who have attained four-year college degrees.

In the United States at the turn of the twenty-first century, there has been a decided effort to increase the educational requirements among police recruits. We are witnessing what may be the most dramatic growth in the history of college education for police (Crank, 2003). The bulk of this educational growth has been at two-year programs and has been spectacular. However, hidden in this growth is a new problem.

Most two-year programs offer an associate of arts and an associate of science. The associate of arts satisfies what is called the **"transfer function,"** which means that a student receiving the degree can transfer directly to a four-year program in their state. The associate of science degree satisfies the community college function, which means that its students are getting an education that will enable them to immediately enter the workforce locally. It tends to be more technically oriented, providing a greater variety of classes with practical application. However, it does not have the same degree requirements as the associate of arts and is not intended to provide the transfer function. That means that students receiving it cannot go to a four-year program until they acquire additional classes, which often means that they have to go back to the two-year program and take three to five more classes.

Criminal justice students are often attracted to the associate of science degree because they learn more practical police skills and because they can go to work quickly as police officers. In some places, the associate of science degree is coupled with POST training, so a student can acquire both the required pre-service training and the AS degree at the same time. It appears to offer the best of all worlds.

Sometimes, students find that the associate of science is a trap. They are able to go to work as police officers; however, they are not competitive at acquiring higher rank where they may have to compete against other line officers who have a bachelor's or master's degree. They cannot go back to school to get the four-year degree because they still need to take classes to gain upper-division admittance. And they may find that they cannot qualify for a loan to go back to the community college to complete the two-year associate of arts requirements because they are not in a degree-seeking status.

> Educational Recommendation 2: Build bridges between community colleges and institutions offering degrees at the four-year and graduate level. This is accompanied by three sub-recommendations:
>
> > 2A: One way to do this is to encourage all degree-seeking students in two-year programs to acquire the Associate of

Arts. We recognize that this will make many college administrators unhappy, because students will not be purchasing so many college credits that tend to accompany the Associate of Science degree.

2B: Secondly, build reasonable articulation agreements between nontransfer degree programs and four-year programs, with an emphasis on "reasonable." One of the authors works at an institution with an articulation agreement in place to community college students who have received an A.S. into a B.A. program at a sister institution, yet the sister institution offers none of the articulated requirements. This is an injustice to students who believe that they can acquire an A.S. and take a few classes to transfer after beginning employment in a police department, and then discover too late that classes they need do not exist.

2C: Third, recognize that police training should provide a certain amount of general elective college credit in a four-year program. We have heard academicians complain that police training lacks rigor, yet the institutions in which they work offer college credit for courses in weightlifting and similar courses.

## *Evaluate All Agency Tactical Practices*

Police departments do not have a good grasp of the consequences of their tactical practices, from routine patrol to detective work. They rarely know if what they do works. Consider Skolnick and Fyfe's (1993) comments:

> The incapacity of police departments to evaluate their own effectiveness is a . . . significant impediment to innovation. With hardly any exception, police departments don't know whether the innovations they are trying are preferable to the old ways. . . . Rarely have traditional practices been subjected to rigorous evaluation. When they have, they have usually been found wanting.

How does the evaluation of police tactics foster a balanced perspective? In public organizations, habitual practices take on a life of their own. If not periodically examined, they can become valued in themselves. In short, *they become institutionalized*, which means that they are seen as the right thing to do simply because they have been done for a long time. Through evaluations, taken-for-granted practices can be rationally examined and their consequences assessed in terms of organizational goals and strategies.

Lawrence Sherman and his colleagues (1997) published a comprehensive overview of what works, what doesn't, and evaluational criteria across a wide breadth of research in policing. It is beyond the scope of this book to review Sherman et al.'s findings. The document, however, may be the most important single academic contribution to criminal justice policy to date. Agencies are advised to continue its tradition: evaluate the effects of what they do. This applies equally to new and to taken-for-granted traditional practices.

Efforts to systematically evaluate programs may default to commanders, who are responsible for forecasting and budgeting in their respective areas of command. Most commanders are already busy, dealing daily with their unique blend of structured (long-term) and unpredictable (short-term) elements of command. The notion of expanding existing workload for commanders will be received as unfair and burdensome and may consequently be carried out haphazardly. Where possible, we recommend a reallocation of budget priorities so that evaluation can be carried out by a department's research and development unit.

Many departments and agencies today are adopting problem-solving practices as a component of their routine staff meetings. These practices tend to be called problem-solving and tend to be reviews of repeat calls for service and a quick scan of incident clustering over the previous month. This is not problem analysis. This is crime analysis. Problem-solving is analysis of these patterns over longer time spans. And problem analysis also involves looking for underlying problems, which is a great deal more than the response many agencies call problem analysis, which is the suppression activities in hot spots. Crime analysis reverts departments back into the collection of crime statistics as their primary measure of success and reinforces the sort of arrest efficiency way of thinking that encourages noble-cause corruption. Crime analysis can subvert problem analysis, which is not efficient and requires a detailed and lengthy consideration of underlying dynamics whose solution may not generate any arrests. Crime analysis can be good policing, but it is not problem analysis.

Finally, we suggest that police agencies contact local colleges to see if faculty in criminal justice departments can contribute. Although evaluations tend to be expensive, sometimes police departments can barter with local college programs. For a modest expense, college students can be hired to carry out much of the evaluation activity. Agencies can encourage the use of college-based interns for some of the work as well.

> Evaluation Recommendation 1: Evaluate tactical practices on an ongoing basis.
>
> Evaluation Recommendation 2: Use problem-solving analysis as your primary evaluation method. Do not confuse it with crime analysis, which is an efficiency strategy for crime management.
>
> Evaluation Recommendation 3: Contact the Chair or Head of the local college or university criminal justice department for assistance and to find out which faculty might be interested. Gently remind him or her that the criminal justice department is a part of the criminal justice community, and the community will benefit from the participation of

its faculty. They will also receive community legitimacy and agency credibility in the process.

## *Use Performance Evaluations to Provide Feedback for All Officers*

Police departments are increasingly using performance evaluations to assess the work of police officers. **Performance evaluations** are instruments that assess the nature of the work process, specific accomplishments of police officers, and public attitudes about the performance of the department in general. Thoughtful performance evaluations can provide suggestions for work improvement and direction in an unstructured environment. And they can be a managerial tool for directing officers how to adapt to innovation in their departments. They can also be used to punish officers who aren't performing like their superiors want them to perform.

The evaluation of individual-level performance in police departments is complicated for two reasons. First, managers can unintentionally turn evaluation into a hostile process. Personnel systems in police departments tend to be oriented toward punishment more than reward. Officers who are not performing up to some formal level of expectations may face reprimand or find that their chances of promotion are diminished. Consequently, poorly constructed or misused performance evaluations can have an alienating effect on line officers and encourage more secretive elements of line-level culture.

Second, performance evaluations confront an **importance/usefulness dilemma.** The dilemma can be stated as follows: The more important the performance evaluation is for a candidate's career, the greater the likelihood that evaluators are not going to provide useful distinctions among candidates. Chief executives often want to use performance evaluations for purposes important to line officers—promotion or salary, for example. Commanders who carry out the evaluations, and who have to work with both the promoted and the unpromoted, tend to give similar scores to the candidates competing for promotions. Even if they prefer a particular candidate, they may not want to hurt the feelings (or make enemies of) other candidates or offend colleagues that support other candidates. The problem is a genuine pickle.

We recommend that evaluations be used as "feedback" instruments rather than as tools to assess officer's competency or performance. By **feedback,** we mean that they provide useful and practical information to officers taking the evaluation, rather than turning the information over to commanders or to personnel units. First, evaluations can be used for constructive feedback for employees while abandoning their use for differentiating among employees (Oettmeier and Wycoff, 1997; Gabor, 1992). If the purpose of the evaluation is to provide constructive feedback to police officers, there is little gained by incorporating them into the department's promotional system. Secondly, evaluations should not become a part of an officer's permanent file. If they do, they will always be controversial. Third, evaluations can be conducted of officer teams as well as individuals. This further distances evaluations from the departmental reward system while at the same time integrates them more effectively with the team assignment nature of community policing.

Performance evaluations play an important role in organizational innovation in a police organization—precisely the kind of issue that departments undergoing transition to community policing face (Oettmeier and Wycoff, 1995). Evaluation can enhance the innovative process by providing line officers with job expectations consistent with sought changes. The adoption of innovative police procedures and tactics, to be successful, requires changes throughout the organization's infrastructure. A performance evaluation process can be a critical element of the adoptive process:

> a personnel performance measurement process designed to reflect and reinforce the functions that officers are expected to perform can provide structural support for a philosophy of policing and can be a valuable aid in the implementation of organizational change.
>
> (Oettmeier and Wycoff, 1995:136)

Performance measures should be tied to organizational purposes. This is particularly important for agencies adopting a community policing model of service delivery. It should be clear that evaluation is not to be used to punish but carries other organizational purposes. In this context, evaluation is not simply a process of discipline and punish but serves other important organizational objectives. It allows officers to assess their success in implementing community policing objectives. It provides commanders with an opportunity to see if their innovations are viable. It enables problem-solvers to reflect on their successes and failures (see Box 11.7).

Box 11.7

**Performance Evaluation in a Problem-Solving/Community Policing Environment**

The following purposes can be accomplished by performance evaluation in a problem-solving/community policing environment (Oettmeier and Wycoff, 1997):

1. **Socialization.** The evaluation should "convey expectations content and style of (an officer's) performance" and reinforce the mission and values of the department. In our recommendation,

Box 11.7, *continued*

officers should discuss this among themselves instead of turning the meeting into a departmental mission accomplishment assessment.

2. **Documentation.** Evaluations should record the types of problems and situations officers encounter in their neighborhoods and their approaches to them. This also allows for officers to have their efforts recognized.

   Here, we distinguish between performance evaluation and annual supervisor evaluations. Our recommendation is that officers keep performance evaluation information derived from this meeting to themselves since what commanders can use to reward, they can also use to punish. In this instance, the aphorism "no good deed shall go unpunished" applies. Only that information or those recommendations that officers would like to pass on to commanders should be passed on, and that should be conveyed by the person coordinating such staff meetings.

3. **System Improvement.** What organizational conditions impede improved line officer performance? We share with Oettmeier and Wycoff the belief that the best way to assess problem-solving is through staff meetings of those actively involved in carrying out such activities. What we seek is a subtly different end. Our "evaluation" is not an evaluation per se, as theirs is but an effort to separate efforts to improve community policing and problem-solving through departmental staff meetings from the annual evaluation process.

Source: T. Oettmeier and M.A. Wycoff (1997). *Personnel Performance Evaluations in the Community Policing Context: U.S. Department of Justice.* Washington, DC: Community Policing Consortium.

Finally, performance evaluation, we think, should be implemented throughout the organization. Put simply, what's good for the goose is good for the gander. Managers can demonstrate through example that evaluational procedures are not a punitive tool to extend autocratic control over line officers.

> Performance Evaluation Recommendation 1: Separate performance evaluation from annual job evaluations. Carry out periodic meetings to discuss the way in which officers are doing community policing and problem solving. Lead the meetings with someone outside the unit to provide neutrality.

Performance Evaluation Recommendation 2: Do not call them "performance evaluations," and don't use them to evaluate. Their purpose is to increase the range of options and ideas available to officers for carrying out problem solving and community policing projects. If they are used to evaluate officers will become reasonably defensive. Discuss ongoing projects and develop ideas for strategies to improve them. Take detailed notes, and then turn the notes over to the officers who will use them. Do not turn copies over to commanders. Do not keep records.

# 12

# Conclusion: The Noble Cause

## Introduction

Chapter 12 concludes the discussion on police ethics by reflecting on the enduring influence of the noble cause in shaping officer behavior. It warns that when officers prioritize outcomes over lawful procedure, they risk reversing justice itself—an inversion likened to the surreal logic of *Through the Looking Glass*. The chapter critiques the rise of Homeland Security policing, which emerged post-9/11 and emphasizes intelligence gathering, crime control, and militarized tactics. This shift has distanced officers from community engagement, reinforcing a warrior mindset that views citizens as potential threats rather than partners in public safety. The chapter argues that such a transformation may risk undermining democratic policing by replacing the power of voice and self with coercion and fear. Officers are reminded that their moral center must remain intact and that ethical policing requires treating people as ends in themselves, not as means to achieve order. The chapter calls for a return to procedural integrity, where justice is not sacrificed for efficiency or control.

The noble cause is the heart of police culture: it inspires the values that officers carry and animates their daily work routines. If police officers are so moved by the noble cause that they are willing to do anything to achieve so-called good ends, they have corrupted their craft. They have learned all the wrong things about policing and doing good things. They have become part of the problem, not the solution. There will be a price to pay, and they will pay it as surely as their department will, and as will the citizens they police.

> Mike tells a story about perspective. *You will be tempted to pop some asshole with your PR 24. It happens. It's a bad idea. What if you kill him? It happens. You can never control the outcome—don't forget that. You'll think you can—until something goes wrong. Then it's too late.*

DOI: 10.4324/9781003626916-16

> *Someone really gives you a hard time. You put a carotid choke-hold on him, to inflict a little extra punishment. That's wrong.*
>
> You have to learn to keep your moral center inside you. Never let someone take it from you. If someone is pushing your buttons, that's their problem. How you react is your problem. Don't let them direct the action. Never use somebody else as a justification for what you do. Don't blame the courts, the public, or some asshole for your behavior. It's your behavior. Never forget that. It's your moral center, and you can lose it. You can lose it forever.

A Hispanic song, popular in 1995, carried the theme "no somos verbos somos sustantivos." It translates as "we're not verbs, we're nouns." It's perhaps not the most elegant translation, but the meaning is important. The message it contains is that we should not use people to achieve material or ideological goals. We should focus our efforts on getting along with each other. The ends we seek are us, our ability to get along. And that is the end that justice should serve as well.

Kleinig captures the spirit of ethics that we share in this book. He observes:

> Morality is concerned essentially with humans in their relations with each other, whether those relations are interpersonal, collective, or structural. Aspirationally, the "we" of morality is first and foremost a human we—not an American or European or Black or capitalist or police "we." Morality is concerned with being and doing at the most basic level, with people's common standing as human beings. For that reason there can be no distinctive police ethic but only a human ethic applied to police situations.
>
> (Kleinig, 1990:2)

Sometimes we get it backwards. We use people to achieve ends personally meaningful to us. When people don't conform to our way of thinking, we might feel a need to punish them, to make them behave. There are real problems with thinking about people as means to an end, rather than as ends in themselves. Noble-cause corruption makes the cause the ultimate end, with people the means to achieve that end.

Consider Silberman's (1978) description of ends and means. His words, found in Box 12.1, were written about the courts, but they apply equally well to the police.

Box 12.1

**The Substantive Importance of Procedure**

If Watergate taught us anything, it is what the legal historian Willard Hurst calls the substantive importance of justice—the recognition that means shape ends, that how people do things may be as important as

Box 12.1, *continued*

> what they do. All the more so in criminal court, for the criminal law is an instrument of education as well as coercion, shaping behavior through its moral influence as well as through fear of punishment. When the law is educating effectively, people conform to it because they want to; law-abiding behavior becomes a matter of habit, of voluntary (if unconscious) choice, rather than a means of avoiding punishment. In a large and complex society such as ours, respect for law—the willingness to obey the law because it is the law—is a more effective instrument of social control than is fear of punishment.

Source: Charles Silberman (1978). *Criminal Justice, Criminal Violence*, pp. 345–346.

Mike continues. *I want to share something with you I recently came across, in Silberman's book on criminal justice (Silberman, 1978:418). It's from* Through the Looking Glass, *by Lewis Carroll. You remember this book? In this part of the book, everything is happening backwards. The quote goes as follows:*

"there's the King's messenger. He's in prison now, being punished; and the trial doesn't even begin till next Wednesday: and of course the crime comes last of all." "Suppose he never commits the crime?" said Alice. "That would be all the better, wouldn't it?" the Queen said.

*What's the problem here?* Mike asks.

One of the officers responds, "Well, punishment comes before the trial, and there's not even a crime yet."

Is it a good way to run a criminal justice system?

"It could be," one of the officers replies. The others chuckle. It's a normal response. Another hesitates and responds. "Oh, I get it. We have to put everyone in jail."

Mike smiles and holds his arms out, as if holding up the idea for all to see. *Exactly. We have to put everyone in jail. It's the only way we can really control the outcome. Why don't we want to do that?*

The commanders give him reserved looks.

OK. Good. Let's go back to the beginning. I've got this loud-mouthed asshole. He hangs with bad company, and I know he's selling drugs. I know it. I catch him drinking beer in the park. So I pat him down, all legal, and feel a small bag. Then, voilà, it just slips out of his pocket, onto the ground, a small bag containing a powdery white substance. I got him. I use my super-duper magic pencil, and he's got five years. I sleep better tonight, knowing another asshole is off the street. He knows the truth, but who's going to believe him?

Justice is reversed. I've arrested and booked this guy. Pure noble-cause corruption. He's already in jail serving time. There's no trial. I got him

> before he hurt someone. It's beautiful. But it's Alice in Wonderland justice.
>
> Mike pauses for a moment, to collect his words carefully. *And the crime this guy committed. What's the crime? What's the crime?*
>
> "Possession," one commander responded.
>
> What was the crime? Possession? Wasn't the crime created by the officer?
>
> "The guy was in possession of drugs."
>
> Mike turns to face the commander squarely. *Are you sure? Are you absolutely certain of that? You already know that the officer uses the law to act out his values on the street. You already know that the officer acted illegally. Can you be absolutely certain that the officer didn't take one more step?*

The commander blushes. It had not crossed his mind that the officer might have planted the drugs. The room is quiet.

This is the problem with confusing means and ends. Humans are the ends, not the means. Law and order are the means, not the ends. We have law and order in the service of humans. When we reverse them, we have *Alice in Wonderland* justice. For one commander, the lesson is learned.

A captain speaks out, miffed by the example, "I know that I did not carry drugs when I was a street officer. Run your example another way." Cops often ask questions by making direct statements.

> OK. Let's think about a partner you had. You had a pretty good idea how he thought about things. Sometimes he's your best friend, sometimes he's a real asshole. Right? Now how would you feel about having to do everything the way he wanted to do it?
>
> "When I was a patrol officer my partner was a female," the officer responds. Everyone laughs.
>
> I'll take that. Your partner was a woman. How would you feel about living in that world? Did she ever say anything about your diet? About how you drive? How you dress? Your drinking habits? Your range skills? You didn't have to listen to her, did you?
>
> "Sometimes." They laugh again. Nervously. Boisterous laughter is no longer permitted on this topic.
>
> But you didn't have to. But what happened when she was dealing with someone on the street? Did they have to listen to her? You didn't have to put up with her bullshit, but I bet they did. If they blew her off, then what happened to them?
>
> No comment.
>
> What happened?
>
> "COC." one commander replies.

> *Exactly. Contempt of cop. They went to jail. But that's Alice in Wonderland justice.* Mike smiles. *Now they understand. Finally, they've got it. Justice reversed, in the name of the noble cause. It seems normal, but it's not justice at all. It's just order.*
>
> If people are your means to achieve order, you don't have a society. You have a prison. It's the only way you can be sure. It's the only way you can control the outcome. You want to be a prison guard? Is that what you want?

Under the Homeland Security aspect of policing, which effectively began on September 11, 2001, there will be more of a focus on crime control, which incorporates increased security, intelligence gathering, and counter-terrorism. This will include identifying potential threats, gathering intelligence, and disrupting criminal networks. The police will also work closely with law enforcement partners at every level to ensure public safety and form the nation's primary domestic shield against terrorism. Much of this will be done using local threat assessments.

Today, officers are taught to think like warriors. They believe that they're in a "war" against crime and drugs. They are increasingly heavily armed, often with a minimum of a 9mm and shotgun, they wear body armor, and they carry a variety of sub-lethal weapons. They are the young Centurions, and they occupy the streets like warriors. They generate fear in bad guys. And they don't recognize the extent to which they cause fear in ordinary citizens. They are trained for battle, and they dream warrior dreams.

This is wrong. The police in America are not about making war. All the metaphors are cockeyed. Warriors search out and destroy the enemy. But this is not how the police can maintain order. How can they accomplish this important goal?

They can use the powers of voice and of self in the name of peace. Peace is, after all, the visible, social expression of our ability to get along. To ensure that we somehow, and against some pretty long odds, survive as a democratic people. For neighborhood groups in conflict, to negotiate order when we disagree, so that we don't settle our differences with violence and the politics of exclusion. To find the middle ground. For the disenfranchised and the poor, to help them reclaim the middle institutions of American life. For victims, to help them find critically needed community services to heal their minds, bodies, and souls so that they can move forward with their lives, not backward into despair and vengeance. These tasks are the burden of a democratic police, of a police force that leads by the power of self as well as authority of law. To return all citizens the station to which they rightfully belong—as the true ends of policing. And finally, as a police officer, to know that you are an inspiration to others and, for that, respected.

# Bibliography


Ahern, J. (1972). *Police in Trouble: Our Frightening Crisis in Law Enforcement.* New York, NY: Hawthorne Books.

Alexander, K., S. Rich and H. Thacker (2022). "The Hidden Billion-Dollar Cost of Repeated Police Misconduct." *Washington Post*, March 9, 2022.

Armstrong, K. and M. Possley (1999). "Break Rules, be Promoted." *Chicagotribune.com/news*, January 14.

Associated Press (2001). "Jury Pick Starts in Crime Lab Case." *The New York Times*, September 4.

Associated Press (2003). *Central Park Jogger Case was Handled Properly, N.Y.P.D. Says*, January 27. Retrieved from: www.nytimes.com.

Baker, J.N. and L. Wright (1991). "Los Angeles Aftershocks." *Newsweek*, April *1*: 18–19.

Baker, M. (1985). *Cops: Their Lives in their Own Words.* New York: Pocket Books.

Barker, T. (1996). *Police Ethics: Crisis in Law Enforcement.* Springfield, IL: Charles C Thomas.

Barker, T. and D.L. Carter (1994). "Police Lies and Perjury: A Motivation-Based Taxonomy." In T. Barker and D. Carter (eds.) *Police Deviance*, Third Edition, pp. 139–153. Cincinnati, OH: Anderson.

Barker, T. and D.L. Carter (1999). "Fluffing up the Evidence and Covering Your Ass: Some Conceptual Notes on Police Lying." In L.K. Gaines and G.W. Cordner (eds.) *Policing Perspectives: An Anthology*, pp. 342–350. Los Angeles, CA: Roxbury.

Barker, T., R. Friery and D. Carter (1994). "After L.A., Would Your Local Police Lie?" In T. Barker and L. Carter (eds.) *Police Deviance*, Third Edition, pp. 155–168. Cincinnati, OH: Anderson.

Baron, A.S. and M.R. Banaji (2006). "The Development of Implicit Attitudes: Evidence of Race Evaluations from Ages 6, 10 & Adulthood." *Psychological Science*, *17* (*1*): 53–58.

Batton, C. and C. Kadleck (2004). "Theoretical and Methodological Issues in Racial Profiling Research." *Police Quarterly*, *7* (*1*): 30–65.

Bayley, D.H. and C.D. Shearing (1998). "The Future of Policing." In G. Cole and M. Gertz (eds.) *The Criminal Justice System: Politics and Policies*, Seventh Edition, pp. 150–168. Belmont, CA: West/Wadsworth.

Bechara, A. (2005). "Decisionmaking, Impulse Control and Loss of Willpower to Resist Drugs: A Neurocognitive Perspective." *Nature Neuroscience*, *8*: 1458–1463.

Bechara, A. and A. Damasio (2005). "The Somatic Marker Hypothesis: A Neural Theory of Economic Decisionmaking." *Games and Economic Behavior*, *52*: 336–372.

Belluck, P. (1999). "Convict Freed After 16 Years on Death Row." *New York Times National Report*, Saturday, February 6.

Bennett, R.R. (1984). "Becoming Blue: A Longitudinal Study of Police Recruit Occupational Socialization." *Journal of Police Science and Administration*, *12* (*1*): 47–57.

Berman, J.S. (1987). *Police Administration and Progressive Reform: Theodore Roosevelt as Police Commissioner of New York*. New York, NY: Greenwood Press.

Bittner, E. (1970). *The Functions of Police in Modern Society*. Washington, DC: U.S. Government Printing Office.

Black, D. (1973). "The Mobilization of Law." *Journal of Legal Studies*, *2*: 125–144.

Black, D. (1980). *The Manners and Customs of the Police*. New York: Academic Press.

Blumstein, A. (1992). "Some Trends in U.S. Punishment." *Presidential Address, American Society of Criminology*. Fairmont Hotel, New Orleans (LA), November 4–7.

Boba, R. (2005). *Crime Analysis and Crime Mapping*. Thousand Oaks, CA: Sage.

Boba, R. and J. Crank (2007). "Toward an Integrated Model of Police Problem Solving." In D. Palmer, C. Shearing and D. Das (eds.) *Coping with the Global Challenges: How are the Police Responding to New Demand*. Thousand Oaks, CA: Sage.

Bohm, R.M. (1984). "The Politics of Law and Order." (Book Review). *Justice Quarterly*, *3* (*1*): 449–455.

Bohrer, B. (2002). "Montana Scientist Under Fire After DNA Clears Man of Rape." *The Idaho Statesman*, December 15: 18.

Bohrer, B. (2004). "Federal Grant Money Drying Up for Community Cops." *The Associated Press*, September 27. Retrieved November 2009 from: www.policeone.com/pc_print.asp?vid=92336.

Bordua, D. and A. Reiss (1986). "Command, Control and Charisma: Reflections on Police Bureaucracy." In M.R. Pogrebin and R.M. Regoli (eds.) *Police Administrative Issues; Techniques and Functions*, pp. 31–36. Millwood, NY: Associated Faculty Press.

Bouza, A. (1990). *The Police Mystique: An Insiders Look at Cops, Crime, and the Criminal Justice System*. New York, NY: Plenum Press.

Braga, A., D. Kennedy, D.M. Waring and A.M. Piehl (2001). "Problem-Oriented Policing, Deterrence, and Youth Violence." *Journal of Research and Criminal Development*, *38*: 195–225.

Braga, A., D. Kennedy, D.M. Waring and A.M. Piehl (2001). "Reducing Gun Violence: The Boston Gun Project's Operation Ceasefire." *National Institute of Justice*. Washington, DC: US Department of Justice.

Braga, A.A. (1997). "Pulling Levers: Focused Deterrence Strategies and the Prevention of Gun Homicide." *Journal of Criminal Justice*, *36* (*4*).

Braga, A.A. and C. Winship (2006). "Partnership, Accountability, and Innovation: Clarifying Boston's Experience with Pulling Levers." In D. Weisburd and A.A. Braga (eds.) *Police Innovation: Contrasting Perspectives*, pp. 171–190. Boston, MA: Cambridge University Press.

Brantingham, P.J., G. Mohler and J. MacDonald (2022). "Changes in Public-Police Cooperation Following the Murder of George Floyd." *Proceedings of the National Academy of Sciences (PNAS)*. Retrieved May 2025 from: www.ncbi.nlm.nih.gov/pmc/articles/PMC9802335/

Brinton, K. and K. Lieberman (1994). *Basics of DNA Fingerprinting*. Retrieved from: www.biology.washington.edu/fingerprint/dnaintro.html.

Brooks, P. (2000). *Troubling Confessions: Speaking Guilt in Law and Literature*. Chicago: University of Chicago Press.

Brown, H. (2004). "Final Report of the Independent Panel to Review Department of Defense Detention Operations." *Testimony before the Committee on Armed Services United States Senate*, Washington, DC.

Brown, J.A. and E.A. Campbell (1990). "Sources of Occupational Stress in the Police." *Work and Stress*, *4*: 305–318, cited in *Law Enforcement Ethics: Classic and Contemporary Issues*, B.D. Fitch (ed.) Thousand Oaks, CA: Sage.

Buerger, M. (1998). "Police Training as a Pentecost: Using Tools Singularly Ill-Suited to the Purpose of Reform." *Police Quarterly*, *1* (*1*): 27–63.

Buerger, M. and L. Mazerolle (1998). "Third-Party Policing: A Theoretical Analysis of an Emerging Trend." *Justice Quarterly*, *15* (2): 301–328.

Bureau of Justice Statistics (2016). *Office of Justice Programs, BJS*. Washington, DC: US Department of Justice.

Caerula, R. (2004). "GPS Tracking Devices and the Constitution." *The Police Chief*, *71* (*1*).

Caldero, M. (1997). "Value Consistency Within the Police: The Lack of a Gap." *Paper presented at the (March) 1997 Annual Meetings of the Academy of Criminal Justice Sciences*, Louisville, KY.

Camp, E. (2024). "5 Years of Chicago Police Misconduct Cost Taxpayers Almost $400 Million." *Reason*, August 12. Retrieved from: https://reason.com/2024/08/12/5-years-of-chicago-police-misconduct-cost-taxpayers-almost-400-million/.

Camus, A. (1974). *Resistance, Rebellion, and Death*, trans. Justin O'Brien. New York, NY: Vintage Books.

Cao, L., J. Frank and F.T. Cullen (1996). "Race, Social Context, and Confidence in the Police." *American Journal of Police*, *15* (*1*): 3–22.

Carpenter, S. (2008). "Buried Prejudice: Stereotypes on the Brain." *Scientific American Mind*, *19* (2): 32–39.

Carroll, J. (2007). "When the War Comes Back Home." *Christian Science Monitor*, July 11. Retrieved from: www.csmonitor.com/2008/0712/p02s01-usmi.html.

Carte, G. (1986). "August Vollmer and the Origins of Police Professionalism." In M. Pogrebin and R. Regoli (eds.) *Police Administrative Issues: Techniques and Functions*, pp. 3–9. Millwood, NY: Associated Faculty Press.

Carte, G. and E. Carte (1975). *Police Reform in the United States: The Era of August Vollmer, 1905–1932*. Berkeley, CA: University of California Press.

Carter, D., A. Sapp and D. Stephens (1988). "Higher Education as a Bona Fide Educational Qualification (BFQ) for Police: A Blueprint." *American Journal of Police*, *7* (2): 16–18.

Carter, D.L. (1999). "Drug Use and Drug-Related Corruption of Police Officers." In L.K. Gaines and G.W. Cordner (eds.) *Policing Perspectives: An Anthology*, pp. 311–323. Los Angeles, CA: Roxbury.

Carter, D.L. (2004). *Law Enforcement Intelligence: A Guide for State, Local, and Tribal Law Enforcement Agencies*. Washington, DC: U.S. Department of Justice, Office of Community-Oriented Policing Services.

Casey, R. (1996). "Cop Wins One Million in Whistleblower Appeal." *The Ethics Roll Call*, *4*: 6.

Chermak, S. (2008). "*Reducing Violent Crime and Firearms Violence: The Minneapolis Lever Pulling Experiment*." National Institute of Justice, U.S. Government Printing Office. Retrieved November 2009 from: www.ncjrs.gov/pdffiles1/nij/grants/221077.pdf.

Chishti, M., K. Bush-Joseph, C. Putzel-Kavanaugh and M. Greene (2024). "*Biden's Mixed Immigration Legacy: Border Challenges Overshadowed Modernization Advances*." Migration Policy Institute. Retrieved May 2025 from: https://migrationpolicy.org/article/biden-immigration-legacy.

Chishti, M., J. Gelatt, C. Putzel-Kavanaugh and M. Greene (2023). *New York and Other U.S. Cities Struggle with High Costs of Migrant Arrivals*. Migration Policy Institute. Retrieved May 2025.

Christopher, W. (1991). *Report of the Independent Commission on the Los Angeles Police Department*. Los Angeles, CA: City of Los Angeles.

Cohen, A. (2000). "Gangsta Cops." *Time Magazine*, March 6.

Cohen, H. (1986). "Exploiting Police Authority." *Criminal Justice Ethics*, *5* (*2*): 23–30.

Cohen, H. (1996). "Police Discretion and Police Objectivity." In J. Kleinig (ed.) *Handled with Discretion: Ethical Issues in Police Decisionmaking*, pp. 91–106. New York, NY: Rowman & Littlefield.

Connell, R. and R. Lopez (1999). "Abuse Claims Went Updates at 77th St. Station." *Los Angeles Times*, December 27. Retrieved from: www.latimes.com.

Coser, L. (1956). *The Functions of Social Conflict*. New York, NY: The Free Press.

Couper, D. (1979). "Police: Protectors of Peoples Rights." *Law Enforcement News*, *5* (March 12): 8.

Crank, J. (1994). "The Community Policing Movement of the Early 21st Century: What We Learned." In J. Klofas and S. Stojkovic (eds.) *Crime and Justice in the Year 2010*, pp. 107–126. Macmillan.

Crank, J. (2003). *Imagining Justice*. New York, NY: Routledge.

Crank, J. (2004a). *Understanding Police Culture*, Second Edition. New York, NY: Routledge.

Crank, J. (2004b). "Standpoints of Police Culture." In Q. Thurman and A. Giacomazzi (eds.) *Controversies in Policing*, pp. 53–75. New York, NY: Routledge.

Crank, J. and M. Caldero (1991). "The Production of Occupational Stress Among Police Officers: A Survey of Eight Municipal Police Organizations in Illinois." *Journal of Criminal Justice*, *19* (*4*): 339–350.

Crank, J., M. Conn and D. Hoffman (2007a). "The 'War on Terror' and Iraq: The Collapse of a Hegemonic Narrative." *Homeland Security Review*, *2* (*1*): 29–44.

Crank, J., D. Flaherty and A. Giacomazzi (2007b). "Noble Cause: An Empirical Analysis." *Journal of Criminal Justice, 35* (1).

Crank, J., C. Kadleck and C. Koski (2009). "The Next Big Thing." *Police Practice and Research: An International Journal, 11* (5): 405–422.

Crank, J. and R. Langworthy (1992). "An Institutional Perspective of Policing." *The Journal of Criminal Law and Criminology, 83*: 338–363.

Crank, J. and R. Langworthy (1996). "Fragmented Centralization and the Organization of the Police." *Policing and Society*, 6: 213–229.

Crank, J., B. Regoli, J. Hewitt and R. Culbertson (1993). "An Assessment of Work Stress Among Police Executives." *Journal of Criminal Justice, 21* (4): 313–324.

Crank, J. and L. Rehm (1994). "Reciprocity Between Organizations and Institutional Environments: A Study of Operation Valkyrie." *Journal of Criminal Justice*, 22 (5): 393–406.

Cullen, F., B. Link, N. Wolfe and J. Frank (1989). "The Social Dimensions of Police Officer Stress." *Justice Quarterly*, 2: 507–533.

Cunningham, W.A., M.K. Johnson, C.L. Raye, J.C. Gatenby, J.C. Gore and M.R. Banaji (2004). "Separable Neural Components in the Processing of Black and White Faces." *Psychological Science, 15*: 806–813.

Damasio, A.R. (1994). *Descartes' Error: Emotion, Reason and the Human Brain*. New York: Putman and Sons.

Daunt, T. (2001). "Consent Decree Gets Federal Judge's OK." *Los Angeles Times*, June 16. Retrieved from: www.latimes.com.

Decker, S. (1981). "Citizen Attitudes Toward the Police: A Review of Past Findings and Suggestions for Future Policy." *Journal of Police Science and Administration, 9*: 80–87.

Delattre, E.J. (1996). *Character and Cops: Ethics in Policing*, Third Edition. Washington, DC: American Enterprise Institute.

de Tocqueville, A. (1969). *Democracy in America*, trans. George Lawrence, ed. J.P. Mayer. New York, NY: Anchor, Doubleday.

Donziger, S. (1996). *The Real War on Crime: The Report of the National Criminal Justice Commission*. New York: HarperCollins.

Dovidio, J.F., M. Vergert, T.L. Stewart, S.L. Gaertner, J.D. Johnson, V.M. Esses, B.M. Riek and A.R. Pearson (2004). "Perspective and Prejudice: Antecedents and Mediating Mechanisms." *Personality and Social Psychology Bulletin, 30*: 1537–1549.

Dunham, Y., A.S. Baron and M.R. Banaji (2008). "The Development of Implicit Intergroup Cognition." *Trends in Cognitive Science, 12*: 248–253.

Dwyer, J. and K. Flynn (2002). "New Light on Jogger's Rape Calls Evidence into Question." *The New York Times*, December 1. Retrieved from: www.nytimes.com.

Dwyer, J. and S. Saulny (2002). "Judge Vacates Convictions in Central Park Jogger Case." *The New York Times*, December 19. Retrieved from: www.nytimes.com.

Elliott, K.A. and J.M. Pollack (2014). "The Ethics of Force: Duty, Principle, and Morality." In B. Fitch (ed.) Law Enforcement Ethics: Classic and Contemporary Issues, p. 243. Thousand Oaks, CA: Sage.

Engel, R., J. Calnon and T. Bernard (2002). "Theory and Racial Profiling: Shortcomings and Future Directions in Research." *Justice Quarterly, 19* (2): 249–274.

Felson, M. (1994). *Crime and Everyday Life*. Thousand Oaks, CA: Pine Forge Press.

Ferguson, K.E. (1987). "Male-Oriented Politics: Feminism and Political Science." In T. Ball (ed.) *Idioms of Inquiry: Critique and Renewal in Political Science*. New York, NY: State University of New York Press.

Festinger, L. (1957). *A Theory of Cognitive Dissonance*. Evanston, IL: Row, Peterson.

Fitch, B.D. (2014). *Law Enforcement Ethics: Classic and Contemporary Issues*. Thousand Oaks, CA: Sage.

Fitch, B.D., C.H. Jones and L.P. Pannell (2014). "Rhetoric Versus Reality." In B. Fitch (ed.) *Law Enforcement Ethics: Classic and Contemporary Issues*. Thousand Oaks, CA: Sage.

Fitch, B.D., R.B. Means and G. Seidel (2014). "The Role of Supervision in Motivating and Maintaining a Culture of Ethics." In B. Fitch (ed.) *Law Enforcement Ethics: Classic and Contemporary Issues*. Thousand Oaks, CA: Sage.

Fletcher, C. (1990). *What Cops Know*. New York, NY: Pocket Books.

Fletcher, C. (1991). *Pure Cop*. New York, NY: St. Martin's Paperbacks.

Flynn, K. (2003). "How to Sue the Police and Win." *The New York Times*, October 2, 1999: A11.

Fogelson, R. (1977). *Big-City Police*. Cambridge, MA: Harvard University Press.

Ford, R. (2003). "Saying One Thing, Meaning Another: The Role of Parables in Police Training." *Police Quarterly, 6 (1)*: 84–110.

Frank, J., S. Brandl, R. Worden and T.S. Bynum (1996). "Citizen Involvement in the Coproduction of Police Outputs." *Journal of Crime and Justice, 12* (2): 1–29.

Frazer, D.M. (1985). "Politics and Police Leadership: The View from City Hall." In W.A. Geller (ed.) *Police Leadership in America: Crisis and Opportunity*, pp. 41–47. New York, NY: Praeger.

Fridell, L. (2004). "The Results of Three National Surveys on Community Policing." In L. Fridell and M.A. Wycoff (eds.) *Community Policing: The Past, Present, and Future*. Washington, DC: Police Executive Research Forum.

Frontline (2004). *L.A.P.D. Blues: The Scandal: Rampart Scandal Timeline*. Retrieved from: www.pbs.org.wgbh/pages/frontline.shows/lapd/scandal/cron.html.

Gabor, A. (1992). "Take This Job and Love It." *The New York Times*, January 26.

Gamez, A.M. and G. Collins (2014). "Psychological Evaluations of Law Enforcement Applicants." In B. Fitch (ed.) *Law Enforcement Ethics: Classic and Contemporary Issues*, pp. 30–57. Thousand Oaks, CA: SAGE Publications.

Garner, R. (1999). "College-Educated Cops: Is the Time Now? Yes." In J. Sewell (ed.) *Controversial Issues in Policing*, pp. 89–97. Boston, MA: Allyn and Bacon.

Geller, W. (1985). *Police Leadership in America: Crisis and Opportunity*. New York, NY: Praeger.

Geller, W. and G. Swanger (1995). *Managing Innovation in Policing: The Untapped Potential of the Middle Manager*. Washington, DC: Police Executive Research Forum.

Getlin, J. (2002). "Five Convictions in the 1989 Rape of a Jogger in New York's Central Park a Question After DNA Tests and a Prisoner's Admission of Guilt." *Los Angeles Times*, October 21. Retrieved from: www.latimes.com.

Glazer, N. (1988). *The Limits of Social Policy*. Cambridge, MA: Harvard University Press.

Glimcher, P. (2003). *Decisions, Uncertainty, and the Brain: The Science of Neuroeconomics*. Cambridge, MA: Bradford Books.

Glover, S. and M. Lait (2000a). "Police in Secret Group Broke Laws Routinely, Transcripts Say." *Los Angeles Times*, February 10. Retrieved from: www.latime.com/news/state/updates/lat_rampart000210.htm.

Glover, S. and M. Lait (2000b). "Rampart Squad Framed Them." *Los Angeles Times*, April 27. Retrieved from: www.latime.com/news/state/reports/rampart/lat_rampart000427.htm.

Glover, S. and M. Lait (2000c). "DNA Evidence in 4 Drug Cases Refutes Officers." *Los Angeles Times*, April 26. Retrieved from: www.latime.com/news/state/reports/rampart/lat_rampart000426.htm.

Glover, S. and M. Lait (2000d). "Beatings Alleged to be Routine at Rampart." *Los Angeles Times*, February 14. Retrieved from: www.latime.com/news/state/updates/lat_rampart000214.htm.

Goffman, E. (1967). *Interaction Ritual*. Garden City, NY: Anchor Books.

Gold, M. and M. Landsberg (1999). "In Rampart, Support Strong." *Los Angeles Times*, September 23.

Goldsmith, J. (2008). *The Terror Presidency: Law and Judgment Inside the Bush Presidency*. New York: W.W. Norton & Co.

Goldstein, H. (1986). "Higher Education and the Police." In M. Pogrebin and R. Regoli (eds.) *Police Administrative Issues: Techniques and Functions*, pp. 243–256. Millkwood, NY: Associated Faculty Press.

Goleman, D. (1994). *Emotional Intelligence: Why it can Matter More than IQ*. New York: Bantam Books.

Goolkasian, G., R. Geddes and W. DeJong (1989). "Coping With Police Stress." In R. Dunham and G. Alpert (eds.) *Critical Issues in Policing*, pp. 498–507. Prospect Heights, IL: Waveland.

Grandani, A.R. (2014). "Ethics and Accountability." In B. Fitch (ed.) *Law Enforcement Ethics: Classic and Contemporary Issues*, pp. 84–105. Thousand Oaks, CA: Sage.

Greene, J.D., R.B. Sommerville, L.E. Nystrom, J.M. Darley and J.D. Cohen (2001). "An fMRI Investigation of Emotional Engagement in Moral Judgment." *Science*, *293*: 2105–2108.

Greene, J.R. and S.D. Mastrofski (1991). *Community Policing: Rhetoric or Reality?* New York, NY: Praeger.

Guyot, D. (1979). "Bending Granite: Attempts to Change the Rank Structure of American Police Departments." *Journal of Police Science and Administration*, *7*: 235–284.

Guyot, D. (1991). *Policing as Though People Matter*. Philadelphia, PA: Temple University Press.

Haggerty, K.D. and R.V. Ericson (1999). "The Militarization of Policing in the Information Age." *Journal of Political and Military Sociology, 27* (2): 233–255.

Harmon, M.M. (1995). *Responsibility as Paradox: A Critique of Rational Discourse on Government*. Advances in Public Administration Series. Thousand Oaks, CA: Sage.

Harris, D. (1999). *Profiles in Injustice: Why Racial Profiling Cannot Work*. New York, NY: The New Press.

Harris, R. (1973). *The Police Academy: An Inside View*. New York, NY: Wiley.

Haslam, A. and S. Reicher (2008). "Questioning the Banality of Evil." *The Psychologist, 21 (1)*.

Henry, V. (2002). *The COMPSTAT Paradigm*. Flushing, NY: Looseleaf Law.

Herald.com (2002). *The Miami Herald*. Retrieved December 22, http://www.miami.com/mld/hiamiherald/4791670.html.

Hersh, S. (2004). "Torture at Abu Ghraib." *The New Yorker*, May 10. Retrieved from: www.newyorker.com/archive/2004/05/10/040510fa_fact.

Higham, S., J. White and C. Davenport (2004). "A Prison on the Brink: Usual Military Checks and Balances Went Missing." *Washington Post*, May 9. Retrieved from: www.washingtonpost.com/wp-dyn/articles/A11413-2004May8.html.

History.com. (2009). *Alexis de Tocqueville*. A&E Television Network.

Hopkins, E. (1931). *Our Lawless Police*. New York, NY: Viking Press.

Horowitz, R. (1984). *Honor and the American Dream: Culture and Identity in a Chicago Community*. New Brunswick, NJ: Rutgers University Press.

Hudnut, W.H. III (1985). "The Police and the Polis: A Mayor's Perspective." In W. Geller (ed.) *Police Leadership in America: Crisis and Opportunity*, pp. 20–29. New York, NY: Praeger.

Hughes, T. (2001). "Police Officers and Civil Liability: The Ties that Bind? Policing: An International." *Journal of Police Strategies and Management, 24*: 240–262.

Human Rights Watch (1998). *Shielded From Justice: Police Brutality and Accountability in the United States*. New York, NY: Human Rights Watch.

Huntington, S. (1996). *The Clash of Civilizations and the Remaking of World Order*. New York, NY: Simon & Schuster.

Jefferson, T. (1987). "Beyond Paramilitarism." *British Journal of Criminology, 27*: 47–53.

Johnson, K. (1998). "New Breed of Bad Cop Sells Badge, Public Trust." *USA Today*, April 16. Internet.

Kania, R.R.E. (1988). "Should we Tell the Police to Say 'Yes' to Gratuities?" *Criminal Justice Ethics, Summer/Fall*: 38–48.

Kaplan, R. (1998). "Travels Into America's Future." *Atlantic Monthly*, August 1998.

Kappeler, V.E. (2001). *Critical Issues in Police Civil Liability*, Third Edition. Prospect Heights, IL: Waveland.

Kappeler, V.E. and P.B. Kraska (1998). "A Textual Critique of Community Policing: Police Adaptation to High Modernity." *Policing: An International Journal of Police Strategies and Management, 21* (2): 293–313.

Kappeler, V.E., R.D. Sluder and G.P. Alpert (1994). *Forces of Deviance: The Dark Side of Policing*. Prospect Heights, IL: Waveland.

Kelling, G. (1987). "Acquiring a Taste for Order: The Community and the Police." *Crime & Delinquency*, *33*: 90–102.

Kelling, G. (1998). "Crime Control, the Police, and Culture Wars: Culture Wars and Cultural Pluralism." In G. Kelling, R. Kennedy, D. Musto, J. Petersilia and P. Cook (eds.) *Perspectives on Crime and Justice:* 1997–1998 *Lecture Series*, pp. 1–19. Washington, DC: U.S. Department of Justice.

Kelling, G. and W.J. Bratton (1993). "Implementing Community Policing: The Administrative Problem." In *Perspectives on Policing*, Vol. *17*. Washington, DC: National Institute of Justice. Washington, DC: US Department of Justice.

Kelling, G. and C. Coles (1996). *Fixing Broken Windows: Restoring Order and Reducing Crime in Our Communities*. New York, NY: The Free Press.

Kelling, G. and W. Sousa (2001). "Do Police Matter? An Analysis of New York City's Police Reforms." *Civic Report*, 22.

Kennedy, D., A.M. Piehl and A. Braga (1996). "Youth Violence in Boston: Gun Markets, Serious Youthful Offenders, and a Use-Reduction Strategy." *Law and Contemporary Problems*, *59*: 147–196.

Kennedy, R. (1997). *Race, Crime, and the Law*. New York: Pantheon.

Kerner, O. and the National Advisory Commission on Civil Disorders (1968). *Report of the National Advisory Commission on Civil Disorders*. Washington, DC: U.S. Government Printing Office.

Kilborn, P.T. (1994). "Police Profile Stays Much the Same: A Try for Diversity Meets Old Patterns." *The New York Times*, *B1*, *B3*, October 10.

Klaver, J.J. (2014). "Law Enforcement Ethics and Misconduct: An Introduction." In B. Fitch (ed.) *Law Enforcement Ethics: Classic and Contemporary Issues*, pp. 8–30. Thousand Oaks, CA: Sage.

Klein, N. (1999). "A Free Woman, Finally." *ABCNEWS.com*, February 8.

Kleinig, J. (1990). "Teaching and Learning Police Ethics." *Journal of Criminal Justice*, *18* (*1*): 1–18.

Kleinig, J. (1996). "Handling Discretion with Discretion." In J. Kleinig (ed.) *Handled with Discretion: Ethical Issues in Police Decisionmaking*, pp. 1–12. New York, NY: Rowman & Littlefield.

Klockars, C. (1983). "The Dirty Harry Problem." In C. Klockars (ed.) *Thinking about Police: Contemporary Readings*, pp. 428–438. New York, NY: McGraw Hill.

Klockars, C. (1985). *Law and Criminal Justice Studies*, Vol. *3*. Beverly Hills, CA: Sage.

Klockars, C. (1991). "The Rhetoric of Community Policing." In C. Klockars and S. Mastrofski (eds.) *Thinking About Policing*, Second Edition, pp. 530–542. New York, NY: McGraw Hill.

Klockars, C. (1995). "The Legacy of Conservative Ideology and Police." In V. Kappeler (ed.) *The Police and Society: Touchstone Readings*, pp. 349–356. Prospect Heights, IL: Waveland.

Knapp Commission (1972). *Report on Police Corruption*. New York, NY: George Braziller.

Kop, N. and M.C. Euwema (2001). "Occupational Stress and the Use of Force by Dutch Police Officers." *Criminal Justice and Behavior*, *28* (*5*): 631–632, cited in *Law Enforcement Ethics: Classic and Contemporary Issues*, B.D. Fitch (ed.) Thousand Oaks, CA: Sage.

Kraska, P. and V.E. Kappeler (1997). "Militarizing American Policing: The Rise and Normalization of Paramilitary Units." *Social Problems*, *44* (*1*): 1–18.

Kraska, P.B. and L.J. Cubellis (1997). "Militarizing Mayberry and Beyond: Making Sense of American Paramilitary Policing." *Justice Quarterly*, *14* (*4*): 607–629.

Kraska, P.B. and D. Paulsen (1996). "Forging the Iron Fist Inside the Velvet Glove: A Case Study of the Rise of U.S. Paramilitary Units." *Paper presented at the Annual Meeting of the Academy of Criminal Justice Sciences*, Las Vegas, NV.

Krimmel, J. and C. Tartaro (1999). "Career Choice and Characteristics of Criminal Justice Undergraduates." *Journal of Criminal Justice Education*, *10* (*2*): 277–289.

LA Times (2008). *Latinos will be Part of a New U.S. Majority Sooner than Predicted.* Retrieved from: http://latimesblogs.latimes.com/laplaza/2008/08/latinos-will-be.html.

Launay, G. and P. Fielding (1989). "Stress Among Prison Officers: Some Empirical Evidence Based on Self Reports." *Howard Journal of Criminal Justice*, *28* (*1*): 38–47.

Lersch, K.M. (2002). "All Is Fair in Love and War." In K. Lersch (ed.) *Policing and Misconduct*, pp. 55–83. Upper Saddle River, NJ: Prentice Hall.

Lewis, D. and G. Salem (1986). *Fear of Crime: Incivility and the Production of a Social Problem.* New York, NY: Routledge.

Ludden, J. (2024). "100-Plus Cities in the U.S. Banned Homeless Camping This Year, But Will it Work?" *NPR*. Retrieved May 2025 from: www.npr.org/2024/12/26/nx-s1-5199103/homeless-camping-bans-grants-pass.

Luft, D. (1991). "When Amateurs Go After the News." *Columbia Journalism Review*. Retrieved from September/October. http://archives.cjr.org/year/91/5/camcorders.asp.

Lyng, S. (1990). "Edgework: A Social Psychological Analysis of Voluntary Risk Taking." *American Journal of Sociology*, *95* (*4*): 851–886.

Maguire, E. and W. King (2007). "The Changing Landscape of American Policing." In J. Schafer (ed.) Policing 2020*: Exploring the Future of Crime, Communities, and Policing*, pp. 337–371. Washington, DC: Police Futurists International.

Maguire, K. and A. Pastore (eds.) (1995). *Sourcebook of Criminal Justice Statistics.* Washington, DC: U.S. Government Printing Office.

Manning, P.K. (1979). "Metaphors of the Field: Varieties of Organizational Discourse." *Administrative Science Quarterly*, *24*: 660–671.

Manning, P.K. (1989). "The Police Occupational Culture in Anglo-American Societies." In L. Hoover and J. Dowling (eds.) *Encyclopaedia of Police Science*. New York, NY: Garland.

Manning, P.K. (1997). *Police Work: The Social Organization of Policing*, Second Edition. Prospect Heights, IL: Waveland.

Manning, P.K. and L. Redlinger (1977). "Invitational Edges of Corruption: Some Consequences of Narcotic Law Enforcement." In P. Rock (ed.) *Drugs and Politics*, pp. 279–310. New York: Routledge.

Margasak, G. (2004). "Victims Pleased Martin County Deputy Speaks their Language." *Port St. Lucie News*, February 8: B2, B7.

Mastrofski, S. (1991). "Community Policing as Reform: A Cautionary Tale." In C. Klockars and S. Mastrofski (eds.) *Thinking about Police: Contemporary Readings*, Second Edition, pp. 515–529. New York, NY: McGraw Hill.

Mayer, J. (2008). *The Dark Side: The Inside Story of How the War on Terror Turned into a War on American Ideals*. New York: Doubleday.

Mazerolle, L. and J. Ransley (2005). *Third Party Policing*. Cambridge: Cambridge University Press.

Mazerolle, L. and J. Ransley (2006). "Third-Party Policing." In D. Weisburd and A.A. Braga (eds.) *Police Innovation: Contrasting Perspectives*, pp. 191–206. Cambridge: Cambridge University Press.

McCoy, C. (1987). "Police Legal Liability is Not a Crisis." *Crime Control Digest, January*: 1.

McDonald, C.P. (1991). *Blue Truth*. New York, NY: St. Martin's Paperbacks.

McGarrell, E.F., J.D. Freilich and S. Chermak (2007). "Intelligence-Led Policing as a Framework for Responding to Terrorism." *Journal of Contemporary Criminal Justice*, *23* (2): 142–158.

McGuire, W. and C. McGuire (1988). "Content and Process in the Experience of Self." *Advances in Experimental Social Psychology*, *21*: 102.

McLeod, S. (2025). "*Stanford Prison Experiment: Zimbardo's Famous Study*." Simply Psychology. Retrieved May 30, 2025, from: www.simplypsychology.org/zimbardo.html.

Meadows, R.J. (1996). "Legal Issues in Policing." In R. Muraskin and A. Roberts (eds.) *Visions for Change: Crime and Justice in the Twenty-First Century*, pp. 96–115. Upper Saddle River, NJ: Prentice Hall.

Meagher, S.M. and N. Yentes (1986). "Choosing a Career in Policing: A Comparison of Male and Female Perceptions." *Journal of Police Science and Administration*, *14* (4): 320–327.

Meehan, A. and M. Ponder (2002). "Race and Place: The Ecology of Racial Profiling African American Motorists." *Justice Quarterly*, *19* (3): 399–430.

Meeks, D. (2006). "Police Militarization in Urban Areas: The Obscure War Against the Underclass." *Black Scholar*, *35* (4): 33–41.

Meyer, J.W. and B. Rowan (1992). "Institutionalized Organizations: Formal Structure as Myth and Ceremony." Updated Version. In J. Meyer and W. Richard Scott (eds.) *Organizational Environments: Ritual and Rationality*, pp. 13–21. Newbury Park, CA: Sage.

Miles, S. (2006). *Oath Betrayed: Torture, Medical Complicity, and the War on Terror*. New York: Random House.

Miller, M.R. (1995). *Police Patrol Operations*. Placerville, CA: Copperhouse.

Morris, P. and K. Heal (1981). *Crime Control and the Police*. London: Her Majesty's Stationery Office. Home Office Research Study #67.

Muir, W.K. Jr. (1977). *Police: Streetcorner Politicians*. Chicago, IL: University of Chicago Press.

Murphy, P. (1985). "The Prospective Chief's Negotiation of Authority with the Mayor." In W. Geller (ed.) Police Leadership in America: Crisis and Opportunity, p. 40. New York, NY: Praeger.

Myers, R.W. (2004). "What Future(s) do we want for Community Policing?" In L. Fridell and W.A. Wycoff (eds.), *Community Policing: The Past, Present and Future*. Washington, DC: Police Executive Research Forum.

Naqvi, N., B. Shiv and A. Bechara (2006). "The Role of Emotion in Decisionmaking: A Cognitive Neuroscience Perspective." *Current Directions in Psychological Science, 15* (*5*): 260–263.

New Jersey State Police (2006). *Practical Guide to Intelligence-Led Policing*, September. Retrieved from: www.state.nj.us/njsp/divorg/invest/pdf/njsp_ilpguide_010907.pdf.

Newton, J., M. Lait and S. Glover (2000). "LAPD Condemned by Its Own Inquiry into Rampart Scandal." *Los Angeles Times*, March 1. Retrieved from: www.latimes.com.

Niederhoffer, A. (1967). *Behind the Shield*. New York, NY: Doubleday.

Nosek, B.A., F.L. Smyth, T. Hansen, N.M. Lindner, K.A. Ranganath, C.T. Smith, K.R. Olson, D. Chugh, A.G. Greenwald and M.R. Banaji (2007). "Pervasiveness and Correlates of Implicit Attitudes and Stereotypes." *European Review of Social Psychology, 18*: 36–88.

O'Conner, A.-M. (2000). "Rampart Set up Latinos to be Deported, INS Says." *Los Angeles Times*, February 24. Retrieved from: www.latimes.com.

Oettmeier, T. and M.A. Wycoff (1995). "Police Performance in the Nineties: Practitioner Perspectives." In G.W. Cordner and D.J. Kennedy (eds.) *Managing Police Organizations*, pp. 131–156. Cincinnati, OH: Anderson.

Oettmeier, T. and M.A. Wycoff (1997). *Personnel Performance Evaluations in the Community Policing Context: U.S. Department of Justice*. Washington, DC: Community Policing Consortium.

Oliver, W. (2004). "The Homeland Security Juggernaut: The End of the Community Policing Era?" *Crime and Justice International, 20* (*79* March/April): 4–10.

Packer, H. (1968). *The Limits of the Criminal Sanction*. Stanford, CA: Stanford University Press.

Palmiotto, M.J. (1999). "Should a College Degree be Required for Today's Police Officer? Yes." In J. Sewell (ed.) *Controversial Issues in Policing*, pp. 70–75. Boston, MA: Allyn & Bacon.

Peterson, M., P. Carter and J. Johnston (eds.) (2017). *Applications in Intelligence-Led Policing: Where Theory Meets Reality*, pp. 24–30. Richmond, VA: International Association of Law Enforcement Intelligence Analysts (IALEIA).

Pollock, J.M. (1998). *Ethics in Crime and Justice: Dilemmas and Decisions*, Third Edition. New York, NY: West/Wadsworth.

Polk, O.E. and D.W. MacKenna (2005). "Dilemmas of the New Millennium: Policing in the 21st Century." *ACJS Today, 30* (*3*): *1*, 4–9.

Pomeroy, W.A.C. (1985). "The Sources of Police Legitimacy and a Model for Police Misconduct Review: A Response to Wayne Kerstetter." In W. Geller (ed.) *Police Leadership in America: Crisis and Opportunity*, pp. 183–186. New York, NY: Praeger.

Powers, M.D. (1995). "Civilian Oversight Is Necessary to Prevent Police Brutality." In P.A. Winters (ed.) *Policing the Police*, pp. 56–60. San Diego, CA: Greenhaven Press.

Quinones, M. (2013). *Factors that Influence Perceptions of Racial Profiling During Police/Motorist Interactions* (Doctoral dissertation). Alkek Library, Texas State University (Accession number AS36.T49 Q636).

Ramirez, D., J. McDevitt and A. Farrell (2000). "A Resource Guide on Racial Profiling Data Collection Systems: Promising Practices and Lessons Learned." *Monograph, Northeastern University.*

Ratcliffe, J.H. (2002). "Intelligence-Led Policing and the Problems of Turning Rhetoric into Practice." *Policing and Society, 12 (1)*: 53–66.

Ratcliffe, J.H. (2016). *Intelligence-Led Policing*, Second Edition. Oxford: Routledge.

Reaves, B.A. (2012). *Hiring and Retention of State and Local Law Enforcement Officers, 2008-Statistical Tables*. U.S. Department of Justice, Office of Justice Programs, Bureau of Justice Statistics.

Regoli, R. and J. Hewitt (1996). *Criminal Justice*. Englewood Cliffs, NJ: Prentice Hall.

Regoli, R. and E. Poole (1978). "Specifying Police Cynicism." *Journal of Police Science and Administration*, *6*: 98–104.

Reicher, S.D. and S.A. Haslam (2006). "Rethinking the Psychology of Tyranny: The BBC Prison Study." *British Journal of Social Psychology*, *45*: 1–40.

Reiner, R. (1992). *Politics of the Police*, Second Edition. London: Wheatsheaf.

Reuss-Ianni, E. (1983). *Two Cultures of Policing: Street Cops and Management Cops*. New York, NY: Routledge.

Reynolds, B. (2015). "3 Advantages of Becoming a Value-Based Police Agency." *PoliceOne.ComNews*, July 2. Retrieved from: www.policeone.com/chiefs-sheriffs/articles/8640838-3-advantages-of-becoming-a-values-based-police-agency/.

Rich, R. (1986). "Neighborhood-Based Participation in the Planning Process: Promise and Reality." In R. Taylor (ed.) *Urban Neighborhoods: Research and Policy*, pp. 41–73. New York, NY: Praeger.

Richeson, J.A. and S. Trawalter (2008). "The Threat of Appearing Prejudiced and Race-Based Attentional Biases." *Psychological Science*, *19*: 98–102.

Rieder, J. (1985). *Canarsie: The Jews and Italians of Brooklyn against Liberalism*. Cambridge, MA: Harvard University Press.

Roberg, R., J. Crank and J. Kuykendall (2000). *Police in Society*, Second Edition. Prospect Heights, IL: Waveland.

Roberg, R., K. Novak and G. Cordner (2005). *Police in Society*, Third Edition. Prospect Heights, IL: Waveland.

Roberg, R.R. and J. Kuykendall (1993). *Police & Society*. Belmont, CA: Wadsworth.

Roberts, S. (1994). *Who we are: A Portrait of America Based on the Latest U.S. Census*. New York, NY: Random House/Times Books.

Robertson, R. (1987). "Globalization Theory and Civilizational Analysis." *Comparative Civilizations Review*, *17*: 22.

Rohrlich, T. (1999). "Scandal Shows Why Innocent Plead Guilty." *Los Angeles Times*, December 31. Retrieved from: www.latimes.com.

Rokeach, M. (1973). *The Nature of Human Values*. New York, NY: The Free Press.

Rokeach, M., M. Miller and J. Snyder (1971). "The Value Gap Between Police and Policed." *Journal of Social Issues*, *27* (2): 155–171.

Rosenbaum, D. (2006). "The Limits of Hot Spot Policing." In D. Weisburd and A. Braga (eds.) *Police Innovation: Contrasting Perspectives*, pp. 245–266. New York: Cambridge University Press.

Russell, K. (1998). *The Color of Crime*. New York: New York University Press.

Sachs, S. (1998). "2nd Trial in Killing of Officer Ends with Acquittal." *The New York Times* on the Web, July 28, 1998.

Scott, M. (2000). *Problem-Oriented Policing: Reflections on the First 20 Years*. Washington, DC: U.S. Department of Justice, Office of Community Oriented Policing Services.

Scott, M.S. (2003). "The Benefits and Consequences of Police Crackdowns." *Problem Oriented Guides for Police Response Guides Series No. 1*, U.S. Department of Justice.

Scrivner, E. (2004). "The Impact of September 11 on Community Policing." In L. Fridell and M.A. Wycoff (eds.) *Community Policing: The Past, Present, and Future*. Washington, DC: PERF.

Shearing, C. and R.V. Ericson (1991). "Culture as Figurative Action." *British Journal of Sociology*, *42*: 481–506.

Sherman, L. (1985). "Becoming Bent: Moral Careers of Corrupt Policemen." In F. Elliston and M. Feldberg (eds.) *Moral Issues in Police Work*, pp. 253–265. Totowa, NJ: Rowman & Littlefield.

Sherman, L., D. Gottfredson, D. MacKenzie, J. Eck, P. Reuter and S. Bushway, in collaboration with members of the Graduate Program (1997). *Preventing Crime: What Works, What Doesn't, and What's Promising*. Washington, DC: U.S. Department of Justice.

Sherman, L. and D. Weisburd (1995). "General Deterrent Effects of Police Patrol in 'Hot Spots': A Randomized Controlled Trial." *Justice Quarterly*, *12*: 626–648.

Silberman, C.E. (1978). *Criminal Violence, Criminal Justice*. New York, NY: Vintage Books.

Skogan, W. (1990). *Disorder and Decline: Crime and the Spiral of Decay in American Cities*. New York, NY: The Free Press.

Skolnick, J. (1988). "Deception by Police." In F. Elliston and M. Feldberg (eds.) *Moral Issues in Police Work*, pp. 75–98. Totowa, NJ: Rowman & Littlefield.

Skolnick, J. (1994). "A Sketch of the Policeman's Working Personality." In *Justice Without Trial: Law Enforcement in Democratic Society*, Third Edition, pp. 41–68. New York, NY: Wiley.

Skolnick, J. and D. Bayley (1986). *The New Blue Line: Police Innovation in Six American Cities*. New York, NY: The Free Press.

Skolnick, J. and D. Bayley (1991). "The New Blue Line." In C. Klockars and S. Mastrofski (eds.) *Thinking about Police: Contemporary Readings*, Second Edition, pp. 494–503. New York, NY: McGraw Hill.

Skolnick, J. and J. Fyfe (1993). *Above the Law: Police and the Excessive Use of Force*. New York, NY: The Free Press.

Stinchcomb, J. (2004). "Police Stress: Could Organizational Culture be the Culprit?" *Law Enforcement Executive Forum*, *4* (3): 151–163.

Stutzman, R. (2002). "Crime Lab Worker Puts Case in Doubt." *Orlando Sentinel*, July 19.

Suburbanstats.org (2020). *Statistics of Asians in Minnesota.*

Sullivan, P.S. (1989). "Minority Officers: Current Issues." In R.G. Dunham and G.P. Alpert (eds.) *Critical Issues in Policing: Contemporary Readings*. Prospect Heights, IL: Waveland.

Sykes, G. (1989). "The Functional Nature of Police Reform: The 'Myth' of Controlling the Police." In R. Dunham and G. Alpert (eds.) *Critical Issues in Policing*, pp. 197–286. Prospect Heights, IL: Waveland.

Taguba, A. (2004). "Iraq Prisoner Abuse Investigation of the U.S. 800th Military Police Brigade." *Taguba Report*, May 2.

Teeter, B. (2003). "Houston Crime Lab Work in Doubt." *DFW.com*, March 11.

Terry, W. (1985). "Police Stress: The Empirical Evidence." In A. Niederhoffer (ed.) *The Ambivalent Force*, Third Edition, pp. 357–368. New York, NY: Holt, Rinehart and Winston.

Thomas, R. (1988). "Stress Perception Among Select Federal Probation and Pretrial Services Officers and Their Supervisors." *Federal Probation*, *52*: 48–58.

Trojanowicz, R., V.E. Kappeler, L.K. Gaines and B. Bucqueroux (1990). *Community Policing: A Contemporary Perspective*, Second Edition. Cincinnati, OH: Anderson.

USAFACTS (2024). *Statistics on Unauthorized U.S. Immigration and U.S. Border Crossings by Year*. Retrieved May 2025 from: https://usafacts.org/articles/what-can-the-data-tell-us-about-unauthorized-immigration/.

U.S. Department of Justice, Civil Rights Division (2000). *Letter From the U.S. Department of Justice*, May 8. Retrieved from: www.latimes.com.

U.S. Department of Justice, U.S. Attorney's Office, Northern District of California (2023a). *Antioch and Pittsburgh Police Officers and Employee Charged with Various Crimes Ranging from Using Excessive Force to Defrauding Their Employers*, August 18, 2023.

U.S. Department of Justice, U.S. Attorney's Office, Northern District of Illinois (2023b). *Two Suburban Chicago Police Officers Indicted on Federal Corruption Charges*, January 17, 2023.

U.S. Department of Justice, U.S. Attorney's Office, deviance Southern District of Texas (2019). *Goines Indicted on Federal Civil Rights Charge*, November 20. Retrieved from: www.justice.gov/usao-sdtx/pr/goines-indicted-federal-civil-rights-charge.

Van Maanen, J. (1978a). "The Asshole." In P.K. Manning and J. Van Maanen (eds.) *Policing: A View from the Street*, pp. 221–238. Santa Monica, CA: Goodyear.

Van Maanen, J. (1978b). "Observations on the Making of Policemen." In P.K. Manning and J. Van Maanen (eds.) *Policing: A View from the Street*, pp. 292–308. Santa Monica, CA: Goodyear.

Van Maanen, J. (1997). "Making Rank: Becoming an American Police Sergeant." In R. Dunham and G. Alpert (eds.) *Critical Issues in Policing: Contemporary Readings*, Third Edition, pp. 167–183. Prospect Heights, IL: Waveland.

Waddington, P. (1999). "Police (Canteen) Culture: An Appreciation." *British Journal of Criminology*, *39* (2): 287–309.

Wagner, A. and S. Decker (1997). "Evaluating Citizen Complaints Against the Police." In R. Dunham and G. Alpert (eds.) *Critical Issues in Policing*, Third Edition, pp. 302–318. Prospect Heights, IL: Waveland.

Walker, S. (1977). *A Critical History of Police Reform*. Lexington, MA: Lexington Books.

Walker, S. (1984). "Broken Windows and Fractured History: The Use and Misuse of History in Recent Police Patrol Analysis." *Justice Quarterly*, *1*: 57–90.

Walker, S. (1993). *Taming the System: The Control of Discretion in Criminal Justice, 1950–1990*. New York, NY: Oxford University Press.

Walker, S. (1994). *Sense and Nonsense about Crime and Drugs: A Policy Guide*, Third Edition. New York, NY: McGraw Hill.

Walker, S. (2005). *The New World of Police Accountability*. Thousand Oaks, CA: Sage.

Walsh, B. (2003). "The Camcorder Revolution." *Media Literacy Review*. http://www.interact.uoregon.edu/Medialit/JPC/articles.mlr

Weber, M. (1981). "Politics as a Vocation." In M. Curtis (ed.) *The Great Political Theories*, Vol. 2, pp. 426–436. New York, NY: Avon Books.

Weisburd, D. (2005). "Hot Spots Policing Experiments and Criminal Justice Research: Lessons from the Field." *Annals of the American Academy of Political and Social Science*, *599*: 220–245.

Weisburd, D. and A. Braga (2006). "Hot Spots Policing as a Model for Innovation." In D. Weisburd and A. Braga (eds.) *Police Innovation: Contrasting Perspectives*, pp. 225–244. Cambridge: Cambridge University Press.

Weisburd, D.L. and J. Eck (2004). "What Can Police Do to Reduce Crime, Disorder, and Fear?" *The Annals of the American Academy of Political and Social Science*, *593*: 42–65.

Weisburd, D.L., S.D. Mastrofski, A. McNally, R. Greenspan and J. Willis (2003). "Reforming to Preserve: COMPSTAT and Strategic Problem Solving in American Policing." *Criminology and Public Policy*, 2: 421–456.

Westley, W. (1970). *Violence and the Police*. Cambridge, MA: The MIT Press.

White, S.O. (1986). "A Perspective on Police Professionalism." In M. Pogrebin and R. Regoli (eds.) *Police Administrative Issues: Techniques and Functions*, pp. 221–232. Millwood, NY: Associated Faculty Press.

Wicklund, R. and J. Brehm (1976). *Perspectives on Cognitive Dissonance*. Hillsdale, NJ: Lawrence Erlbaum.

Williams, H. and P.V. Murphy (1995). "The Evolving Strategy of the Police: A Minority View." In V. Kappeler (ed.) *The Police and Society*, pp. 29–52. Touchstone Readings. Prospect Heights, IL: Waveland.

Willis, J., S. Mastrofski and D. Weisburd (2007). "Making Sense of COMPSTAT: A Theory-Based Analysis of Organizational Change in Three Police Departments." *Law and Society Review*, *41*: 147.

Wilson, J.Q. (1968). *Varieties of Police Behavior: The Management of Law and Order in Eight Communities*. Cambridge, MA: Harvard University Press.

Wilson, J.Q. and G. Kelling (1982). "The Police and Neighborhood Safety: Broken Windows." *Atlantic Monthly*, *249* (March): 29–38.

Witt, A. (2001). "Talked Into a Murder Charge: Marathon Interrogations, Abuse Allegations Mar Case." *Washington Post*, June 3: A01.

Wycoff, M.A. and W. Skogan (1994). "The Effect of Community Policing Management Style on Officers' Attitudes." *Crime & Delinquency*, *40*: 371–383.

Yardley, J. (2001). "Inquiry Focuses on Scientist Used by Prosecutors." *The New York Times*, National, May 2001.

Zhao, J.S. (2004). "The Future of Policing in a Community Era". In Q.C. Thurman and J. Zhao (eds.) Contemporary Policing: Controversies, Challenges, and Solutions, pp. 370–381. Los Angeles, CA: Roxbury.

Zhao, J.S., N. He and N.P. Lovrich (1998). "Individual Value Preferences Among American Police Officers: The Rokeach Theory of Human Values Revisited." *Policing: An International Journal of Police Strategies and Management*, *21*: 22–36.

Zhao, J.S., M.C. Schneider and Q. Thurman (2002). "Funding Community Policing to Reduce Crime: Have COPS Grants Made a Difference?" *Criminology & Public Policy*, *2* (*1*): 7–32.

Zhao, J.S., Q.C. Thurman and N.P. Lovrich (2000). "Community-Oriented Policing Across the U.S.: Facilitators and Impediments to Implementation." In R.W. Glensor, M.E. Correia and K.J. Peak (eds.) *Policing Communities: Understanding Crime and Solving Problems*, pp. 229–238. Los Angeles, CA: Roxbury.

Zimbardo, P. (2008). *The Lucifer Effect: Understanding How Good People Turn Evil.* New York, NY: Random House.

# Name Index

Ahern, J. 89, 208
Alexander, K. 172
Alpert, G.P. 58, 103, 213, 250
*Arizona v. Fulminante* (1991) 3
Armstrong, K. 190

Baker, J.N. 102
Baker, M. 25
Banaji, M.R. 101, 115
Barker, T. 2, 138, 181, 188, 222–224
Baron, A.S. 101
Batton, C. 219
Bayley, D. 6, 247, 251, 254–255, 257
Bechara, A. 98, 99
Bennett, R.R. 98
Berman, J.S. 122
Bernard, T. 218
Bittner, E. 220
Black, D. 245
Blumstein, A. 218
Boba, R. 286, 289
Bohm, R.M. 263
Bohrer, B. 195, 285
Bordua, D. 76, 159
Bouza, A. 57, 250–251, 254, 258
Braga, A.A. 292, 295
Brandl, S. 256
Brantingham, P.J. 245
Bratton, W.J. 78
Brehm, J. 253
Brinton, K. 194
Brooks, P. 231
Brown, H. 51
Brown, J.A. 154
Bucqueroux, B. 256
Buerger, M. 62, 85–86, 290
Bushway, S. 319
Bynum, T.S. 256

Caerula, R. 297
Caldero, M. 1, 6, 7, 17, 20, 63, 65, 68, 110, 111–113, 124, 153, 211
Calnon, J. 218
Camp, E. 172
Campbell, E.A. 154
Camus, A. 42
Cao, L. 250
Carpenter, S. 101, 115
Carroll, J. 36
Carte, E. 124
Carte, G. 123–124, 316
Carter, D.L. 2, 181, 188, 224, 226, 228, 230, 287, 316, 317
Carter, P. 288
Casey, R. 68
Chermak, S. 287, 292
Chishti, M. 259
Christopher, W. 78–79, 102–103
Chugh, D. 115
Cohen, A. 140
Cohen, H. 70, 132
Cohen, J.D. 99
Coles, C. 271, 272
Collins, G. 77, 83, 85, 89, 97
Conn, M. 281
Connell, R. 143
Cordner, G. 171
Coser, L. 210
Couper, D. 273
Crank, J. 20, 22, 54, 55, 58, 72, 84, 86–87, 89, 112, 153, 156, 159, 162, 166, 171, 210–211, 215–217, 222–223, 246–247, 254, 281, 285–286, 297, 300, 307, 318
Cubellis, L.J. 289–290
Culbertson, R. 156
Cullen, F.T. 154, 250
Cunningham, W.A. 115

Dailey, J.D. 136
Damasio, A.R. 95, 98–99
Darley, J.M. 99
Daunt, T. 166
Davenport, C. 36–37

de Tocqueville, A. 257
Decker, S. 79, 219
DeJong, W. 154
Delattre, E.J. 27, 41–43
Diallo, A. 102
Donziger, S. 219
Dovidio, J.F. 101
Dunham, Y. 101
Dwyer, J. 231, 232

Eck, J. 286, 319
Elliott, K.A. 208
Engel, R. 218
Ericson, R.V. 72, 290
Esses, V.M. 101
Euwema, M.C. 154

Farrell, A. 217
Felson, M. 258
Ferguson, K.E. 245, 257
Festinger, L. 252
Fielding, P. 154
Fitch, B.D. 59, 77, 83–84, 97, 208
Flaherty, D. 112, 281
Fletcher, C. 84, 126
Floyd, G. 165, 221, 245, 247, 266, 267
Flynn, K. 92, 93, 231–232
Fogelson, R. 88, 122–125
Ford, R. 60–62, 264, 315
Frank, J. 154, 250, 256
Frazer, D.M. 163
Freilich, J.D. 287
Fridell, L. 286
Friery, R. 224
Fyfe, J. 3, 102, 198, 236, 237

Gabor, A. 321
Gaertner, S.L. 101
Gaines, L.K. 256
Gamez, A.M. 77, 83, 85, 89, 97
Garner, R. 316
Gatenby, J.C. 115
Geddes, R. 154
Gelatt, J. 259
Geller, W. 159, 160, 255
Getlin, J. 231
Gettmeier, T. 321–323
Giacomazzi, A. 112, 281
Glazer, N. 269
Glimcher, P. 99
Glover, S. 141–145, 166
Goffman, E. 167
Gold, M. 142
Goldsmith, J. 280–281
Goldstein, H. 286, 316
Goleman, D. 97
Goolkasian, G. 154
Gore, J.C. 115
Gottfredson, D. 319
Grandani, A.R. 86
Greene, J.D. 99
Greene, J.R. 256
Greene, M. 259
Greenspan, R. 289
Greenwald, A.G. 115
Guyot, D. 25, 26, 89, 251–252, 273

Haggerty, K.D. 290
Hansen, T. 115
Harmon, M.M. 83, 87
Harris, D. 93, 216
Harris, R. 58
Haslam, S.A. 39–40
He, N. 20, 111–113
Heal, K. 264
Henry, V. 289
Hersh, S. 35
Hewitt, J. 156, 244
Higham, S. 36–37
Hoffman, D. 281
Hopkins, E. 79
Horowitz, R. 262
Hudnut, W.H. III, 164
Hughes, T. 171
Huntington, S. 261

Jefferson, T. 124
Johnson, J.D. 101
Johnson, K. 230
Johnson, M.K. 115
Johnston, J. 288
Jones, C.H. 77, 83–84, 97

Kadleck, C. 219, 297
Kania, R.R.E. 132, 137
Kaplan, R. 259–260
Kappeler, V.E. 2, 58, 103, 171, 213, 250, 256, 290
Kelling, G. 3, 78, 240, 247–248, 267–269, 270–272, 293–94
Kennedy, D. 292
Kennedy, R. 219
Kerner, O. 246, 250
Kilborn, P.T. 86
King, W. 285
Klaver, J.J. 59, 72
Kleinig, J. 69, 326

Klockars, C. 3, 43–44, 46, 162, 220, 231, 257
Kop, N. 154
Koski, C. 297
Kraska, P.B. 2, 246, 256, 289–290
Krimmel, J. 192
Kuykendall, J. 54, 55, 79, 171, 217, 307

Lait, M. 141–145, 166
Landsberg, M. 142
Langworthy, R. 89, 159, 166, 247, 285
Launay, G. 154
Lersch, K.M. 215–217
Lewis, D. 268, 269
Lieberman, K. 194
Lindner, N.M. 115
Link, B. 154
Lopez, R. 143
Lovrich, N.P. 20, 111–113, 285
Luft, D. 93
Lyng, S. 210

MacDonald, J. 245
MacKenna, D.W. 290
MacKenzie, D. 319
Maguire, E. 285
Maguire, K. 187
Manning, P.K. 22, 58, 72, 84, 207, 209, 225–227, 230
Margasak, G. 312
Mastrofski, S.D. 256, 262, 289
Mayer, J. 279, 281, 299
Mazerolle, L. 290–291
McCoy, C. 171
McDevitt, J. 217
McGarrell, E.F. 287
McGuire, C. 261
McGuire, W. 261
McLeod, S. 33
McNally, A. 289
Meadows, R.J. 169–171
Meagher, S.M. 103
Means, R.B. 77, 83–84, 97
Meehan, A. 217
Meeks, D. 290
Meyer, J.W. 167–168
Miles, S. 35, 51, 300
Miller, M. 66, 105, 107–108, 111–112, 250
Mohler, G. 245
Morris, P. 264
Muir, W.K. Jr. 46–49, 272
Murphy, P.V. 163–164, 250
Myers, R.W. 285

Naqvi, N. 99
Newton, J. 166
Niederhoffer, A. 279
Nosek, B.A. 115
Novak, K. 171
Nystrom, L.E. 99

O'Conner, A.-M. 143–144
Oettmeier, T. 321–323
Oliver, W. 274–275
Olson, K.R. 115

Packer, H. 10, 183–185
Palmiotto, M.J. 316–317
Pannell, L.P. 77, 83, 84, 97
Pastore, A. 187
Paulsen, D. 246
Pearson, A.R. 101
Peterson, M. 288
Piehl, A.M. 292
Polk, O.E. 290
Pollack, J.M. 208
Pollock, J.M. 46, 59, 67, 176–177
Pomeroy, W.A.C. 139, 148
Ponder, M. 217
Possley, M. 190
Powers, M.D. 250
Putzel-Kavanaugh, C. 259

Quinones, M. 220

Ramirez, D. 217
Ranganath, K.A. 115
Ransley, J. 290–291
Ratcliffe, J.H. 287–288
Raye, C.L. 115
Reaves, B.A. 98
Redlinger, L. 58, 225–227, 230
Regoli, B. 156
Regoli, R. 156, 244
Rehm, L. 215, 216, 217
Reicher, S.D. 39–40
Reiner, R. 21
Reiss, A. 76, 159
Reuss-Ianni, E. 72, 205–207, 213
Reuter, P. 319
Reynolds, B. 54, 196
Rich, R. 263
Rich, S. 172
Richeson, J.A. 101
Rieder, J. 262
Riek, B.M. 101
Roberg, R.R. 54, 55, 79, 171, 217, 307
Roberts, S. 259

Robertson, R. 261
Rohrlich, T. 145, 146
Rokeach, M. 95–96, 105–113, 250
Rosenbaum, D. 295–296
Rowan, B. 167, 168
Russell, K. 217

Sachs, S. 127
Salem, G. 268–269
Sapp, A. 316–317
Saulny, S. 232
Schneider, M.C. 285
Scott, M. 286, 294
Scrivner, E. 285
Seidel, G. 77, 83–84, 97
Sewell, J. 317
Shearing, C.D. 72, 247
Sherman, L. 121, 129, 131, 224, 295, 319
Shiv, B. 99
Silberman, C.E. 326–327
Skogan, W. 114, 263–265
Skolnick, J. 3, 6, 58, 98, 100, 102, 198, 223, 236, 237, 251, 254–255, 257
Sluder, R.D. 58, 103, 213, 250
Smith, C.T. 115
Smyth, F.L. 115
Snyder, J. 105, 107–108, 111–112, 250
Sommerville, R.B. 99
Sousa, W. 293, 294
Stephens, D. 316–317
Stewart, T.L. 101
Stinchcomb, J. 151, 154–156
Stutzman, R. 196
Sullivan, P.S. 98
Swanger, G. 160, 255
Sykes, G. 124

Taguba, A. 35, 37
Tartaro, C. 192
Teeter, B. 194
*Terry v. Ohio* (1968) 63
Terry, W. 154
Thacker, H. 172
Thomas, R. 154
Thurman, Q.C. 285
Trawalter, S. 101
Trojanowicz, R. 256

Van Maanen, J. 40–41, 57, 58, 60, 62, 66, 67, 72, 197–198, 209, 221–222
Vergert, M. 101
Vollmer, A. 123–124

Waddington, P. 21
Wagner, A. 79
Walker, S. 69, 77, 80, 88, 122–123, 187–188, 285
Walsh, B. 93
Weber, M. 47–49
Weisburd, D.L. 286, 289, 295
Westley, W. 220
White, J. 36, 37
White, S.O. 122
Wicklund, R. 253
Williams, H. 250
Willis, J. 289
Wilson, J.Q. 3, 81, 90, 124, 240, 244–245, 247–248, 267–269
Winship, C. 292
Withrow, B.L. 136
Witt, A. 234
Wolfe, N. 154
Worden, R. 256
Wright, L. 102
Wycoff, M.A. 114, 321–323

Yardley, J. 195
Yentes, N. 103

Zhao, J.S. 20, 111–113, 285–286
Zimbardo, P. 29–33, 39

# Subject Index

Note: Page numbers in *italics* indicate figures, and references following "n" refer to the notes.


372nd reserve unit, Abu Ghraib 36–37

ABF (American Bar Foundation) survey of 1956 69
Abu Ghraib 27, 35–40, 51n2, 148, 221, 245, 282; 372nd reserve unit 36–37; Final Report of the Independent Panel to Review Department of Defense Detention Operations 51n3; Taguba Report 37; *see also* Stanford Prison Experiment
acceptance of gratuities, policy regarding 131
acceptor, role of the receiver 134
accountability: external accountability mechanisms 76, 80; internal accountability mechanisms 80; internal solution to ethical accountability 83; of police 77, 80; procedures and police 80; scandal and accountability cycles 76–78; *see also* administrative accountability
Accountability Dilemma 1 75, 83–85
Accountability Dilemma 2 75, 85–86
acquittals 171, 245
administrative accountability 75–94; ethics as accountability 80–86; line officers 91–94; managerial limitations 80–86; police and accountability procedures 80; police as value-based decision-makers 91; police commissions and police brutality 79; police reform and controlling police officers 78; scandal and accountability cycles 76–78; upside-down bureaucracies 87–91; *see also* accountability
administrative protocols 17, 33, 83, 86
administrators: central ethical dilemma of 81; and political needs of chiefs 160
advocacy groups, Mothers Against Drunk Driving 16
agility, physical agility testing 55
Al Qaeda 281
American Bar Foundation (ABF) survey of 1956 69
American population, internationalization of 260
anthropological notion of culture 22
anticipation of danger 209
application process 55
*Arizona v. Fulminante* (1991) 3
arrests, bogus drug arrests 144
"The Asshole" 40–41, 221
"assholes" 41, 209, 221, 309
Association of Crime Scene Reconstruction 195
assumption of guilt 44, 203, 230–237
Austin 7 228–229
authoritarian leadership 39
authority, limits of police authority 263–265
avenging angel syndrome 222

backfiring effect of control-oriented police chiefs 90
background checks 55, 56, 165, 166, 218
beat officers: boomerang effect 211; culture 23; layers of street cop culture 203, 205; legitimacy and 162–163; solidarity 21, 25, 203, 210–211, 264; street environment 208

behavior: discretionary police behavior 68; formal ethical codes 76, 82; line officer behavior 81; line officers 205–206; nonverbal behavior 101; police officers, controlling 78; policy implications of emotional decision-making 104–105; qualified immunity 92, 152, 171; racial profiling 98, 213–220; "rational" notions of 20; scandal cycles 76–78; *see also* emotions
bending the law 8, 182
biases 32, 57, 95, 99–100; explicit 104; implicit 104, 105, 115n3; racial/ethnic 101, 102, 103, 105; weapon 101
Black Lives Matter (BLM) 245, 258, 267
Black Swans 53, 62
bogus drug arrests 144
bogus testimony 145
bond between police officers and victims 25–26
boomerang effect 211
bosses, rules relating to street cops 206
Boston detective 181–182
boundary spanner 152, 159
bounded rationality 20, 21
the brain, reasoning structures of 99
bribes 120, 122, 135, 227; material-reward corruption 119, 138–140
British Broadcasting Company (BBC) Prison Study 40–41
"Broken Windows" 240, 243, 267–268, 271, 272, 293–294, 300n6
brutality: Abu Ghraib 35; physical 104, 310; police brutality 27, 148, 221, 245; police commissions and 79; *see also* police brutality
bureaucracy 17–20, 24; departments as upside-down bureaucracies 54, 87–91; line officer accountability 85

California Highway Patrol Statement of Professional Values 66
camcorders 93
capitulator, role of the giver 134
celebrated cases 132, 175, 188
central ethical dilemma of administrators 75, 81
Central Park Jogger Case 231–233
CEO (chief executive officer) 87
ceremony of legitimacy 165–166
change and conflict 260–262
Christopher Commission 78, 79, 102
chronic stress 151, 155
CIA (group) 279, 280, 281
circumstantial corruptibility, model of 120, 131–138; application of 136–138; elements of 133; role of the giver 133–134; role of the receiver 134, *136*
citizen-centered policing 244–246, 258
civil liability 171, 79
classifying complaints 307
Code of Professional Conduct and Responsibility for Peace Officers 66
code of silence 199–201
coercion: authority of police 272; of confessions 3;threatened physical coercion 49
cognition 253
cognitive dissonance 243, 252–255; elements of 253
college education: for decision-making 317; morality of 190–191
college experience, values of 316
command control 90, 159
commanders 160–162, 255; crevasse 204–208
commissions 79
commitments: to crime control 124; Mama Rosa's test 127–128, 130; to the noble-cause 42; of police officers to their beats 17; slippery-slope model of noble-cause corruption 129–131; to social good 22; Vollmerian vision of police work 124
common good 257–258
common humanity 252
"common sense" 22, 154, 188, 210
communities 246–258; policing communities in conflict 262–267
Community Era (1980s to 2001) of policing 266
community policing (COP) 3, 285; cognitive dissonance and 252–255; demographics 269; disorder, causes of 263; expansion of state power and 247; future of 274–276; informal community norms 248–249; iron fist 246–258; neo-professionalism 285–286; order maintenance policing 244, 269–270, 284, 294; order negotiation 271, 273; reduction of social distance 250–252; shared order 262–263, 268–269; velvet glove 240, 243
complaining 153

complaints 307
complier, role of the giver 134
compstat (comparative statistics) 289, 296
concern for victims 302
conduct: formal ethical codes 76, 82; qualified immunity 92, 152, 171
confessions 230–236
conflict: and change 260–262; policing communities in 262–267
conqueror, role of the receiver 134
consent decree, between Department of Justice and city of Pittsburgh 148
content in war stories 315
contingency 121, 131
continuum of value-based decisions 183, *183*
contributor, role of the giver 133
controlling: line officer behavior 81; police officers 78
control-oriented chiefs, backfiring effects of 90; *see also* police chiefs
*Cool Hand Luke* (movie) 30
cops code 206
corroborative research 111–113
corruptibility 133; *see also* circumstantial corruptibility, model of
corruptible exchange 120, 133
corruption 5, 77, 128, 129, 167, 168; circumstantial corruptibility, model of 131–138; economic 5, 12, 117, 119–126, 128, 131, 285; economic corruption and police reform 122–125; "I am the law" perspective 130, 148–149; individual-level 120–122; material-reward corruption 119, 138–140; noble cause 2, 5–6, 12, 119–120, 122, 125–127, 129–131, 138–140, 213, 225; patterns of 143–147, 227; and peer pressure 131, 132; "Politics as a Vocation" 47; racial corruption of the noble cause 103–104; racial profiling 98, 213–220; slippery-slope model of economic corruption 120, 122, 127–128, 130; slippery-slope model of noble-cause 129–131; stages of moral career 121; Type 2 drug corruption 228; *see also* patterns of corruption
counter-terrorism, ticking time bomb 277, 278
court cases: acquittals 171, 245; *Monell v. Dept. of Social and Health Services of New York* (1978) 152, 170; murder cases, false confessions 233–234; prosecutors 187–190; *Terry v. Ohio* 63
cover your ass (CYA) 205
crackdowns 294–295
CRASH (Community Resources against Street Hoodlums): Rampart CRASH unit 119, 130, 140, 141, 142; socialization 142–143
crevasse 204; noble-cause corruption and 213–230; police culture and 204–208
crime: gambling 121; grafting subcultures 121, 128; regulative crimes 121; victimless crime 226; war theory of crime control 62, 79; zero-tolerance approach 257, 296, 300n6
Crime Commission 79
crime controls 85; chiefs 90; and due process 183–201; model 175, 184; war theory of 79
crime mapping 289, 296
crime solving 312
criminal intelligence model 288–299; "Broken Windows" 240, 243, 267–268, 271, 272, 293–294; compstat (comparative statistics) 289; crackdowns 294–295; crime mapping 289; facilitation of technologies 296–299; hot spot policing 295–296; lever pulling 291–292; neo-professionalism and higher education 296; police militarization 289–290; third-party policing 290–291; zero-tolerance 293–294
culture: anthropological notion of 22; aspects of 22–23; elements of police culture predisposing guilt 44; informal organization 21; Mama Rosa's test 127–128, 130; material elements of 22; moral environment of value-based decision-making 29; negative concept of police culture 21; police officers as cultural carriers 21–23; of policing 58, 205; and secrecy 211–213; "social structural" component of 22, 24; "somatic net" and police organizational culture 102–103; values and 20–21
CYA (cover your ass) 205
cycles of scandal 76–78

danger, anticipation of 209
deceptive legal practices 203, 236–238

decision-making: college education for 317; ethics reform and value-based 71–73; "just the facts" 69; moral 71; moral decision-making 71; moral environment of value-based 29; of police officers 48, 54; policy implications of emotional decision-making 104–105; rational decision-making 95, 97; reasoning structures of the brain 99; value-based 17–21 (*see also* value-based decision-making)
degradation, in Stanford Prison Experiment 30
demander, role of the receiver 134
democracy 4, 49, 272; Christianity and 176; police and 11, 261
demographics 269
deontological (means-oriented) ethics 175, 176–177, 183, *183*
departmental policy 82
Department of Homeland Security 274–275, 286, 296, 297, 325, 329
de-policing 152, 171
dilemma of ends-oriented ethics 177–182
dilemmas faced by police officers: Accountability Dilemma 1 75, 83–85; Accountability Dilemma 2 75, 85–86; "The Asshole" 40–41, 221; central ethical dilemma of administrators 75, 81; "Dirty Harry" problem 43–51; implications of the noble cause 41–43
*Dirty Harry* (movie) 43
"Dirty Harry" problem 43–51
discretion: American Bar Foundation and 69; police behavior 68; and values 70–71
disorder 263
distinctiveness theory 243, 261
DNA (deoxyribonucleic acid) 194–196, 232
documentation, performance evaluation 323
down-side to ethics education 54
drugs 224–230, 329; reintroduction 229; Type 2 drug corruption 228; usage 227
due process 17, 40, 42; code of silence 199–201; continuum of value-based decisions 183, *183*; courts and prosecutor 187–190; and crime control 183–201; forensic labs 193–197; local agency instructors 191–192; means-ends as crime control *versus* 183–186; model 175, 183, 184–185; morality of college education 190–191; moral predispositions of police students 192–193; numerology of authority 198; officers ending control 199–201; officers getting leads 186–187; research and service in local agencies 193; sergeants 197–198

early organizational experiences, influence on recruits 60, 66–68
early retirement programs 77, 89
edge control 210
education: performance evaluations 321–324; prioritizing pre-service college education of police 315–319; up-side and a down-side to ethics education 54
elements: of circumstantial corruptibility, model of 133; of cognitive dissonance 253; material elements of culture 22; of police culture predisposing guilt 44
emotions 114n1; ethics and 72; and implicit bias 105; and morality 99–100; policy implications of emotional decision-making 104–105; social psychology of 96–98; and somatic markers 96, 98–99
emulation 105
ends-oriented ethics: code of silence 199–201; deceptive legal practices 203, 236–238; dilemma of 177–182; tension between means and 46–48
enforcing narcotics laws 223–225; commitment of drug enforcement officers 230; zero-tolerance approach 257, 293–294, 296, 300n6
episodic stress 151, 155
ethics: as accountability 80–86; dilemma of ends-oriented 177–182; emotion and 72; formal ethical codes 76, 82; internal 75, 83; modeling 303–306; of police power 2; power of self 49–51; reform and value-based decision-making 71–73; training 86; up-side and a down-side to ethics education 54; wrong kind of morality 54
ethical decisions, preparing recruits for 302–324
ethical systems 176–177
evidence: deceptive legal practices 203, 236–238; means-ends conflicts 46, 47
excessive force 46; "rotten apple" theory 221

exchange 133–136, 141, 145; corruptible 120, 133; expansion of state power, impact on community policing 247; functions of model of circumstantial corruptibility 134–136
expector, role of the receiver 134
experience: early organizational experiences, influence on recruits 60, 66–68; "hands-on" 193
experiments: British Broadcasting Company (BBC) Prison Study 40–41; jealousy and uncertainty 237; Kansas City Patrol Experiment 285; Stanford Prison Experiment 29–35, 38
exploitation 135
external accountability mechanisms 76, 80
extortion 135

"face work" 167
facilitations of technology 296–299
false confessions, murder cases 233–234
fear of disorder 268
feedback, providing through performance evaluations 301, 321–324
Final Report of the Independent Panel to Review Department of Defense Detention Operations 51n3
firing of police chiefs, restoring legitimacy through 166
Floyd, George, death of 165, 221, 245, 247, 266–267
FOP (Fraternal Order of Police) 149
force: coercion 48; excessive use of force 46, 221
forensic labs 193–197
formal ethical codes 76, 82
Fraternal Order of Police (FOP) 149
friendliness, reduction of social distance through community policing 250–252
functions of model of circumstantial corruptibility 134–136

gambling crimes 121
gang members, deportation of 143
Garcetti, Gil 165
George Floyd Case 165, 221, 245, 247, 266–267
givers: role of in model of circumstantial corruptibility 133–134
giving 135
globalization theory 243, 261
global positioning systems (GPS) 296
goals: of IACP 123; teleological (ends-oriented) ethics 176–177
golden apples 10, 12, 119, 128–129
good cops 19, 58, 70, 73, 147, 310
gospel of professionalism 119, 123
grafting subcultures 121, 128; grass-eaters 124
grass-eaters 124
gratuities: giver, role of in model of circumstantial corruptibility 133–134; material-reward corruption 119, 138–140
great guilty place assumption 44
group behavior, in Stanford Prison Experiment 38–39
guilt: operative assumption of 230–236; suspicion of, "Dirty Harry" problem 44, 47

hierarchy of wickedness 135
higher education: local agency instructors 191–192; moral disposition of criminal justice students 191; and neo-professionalism 296; pre-service college education, prioritizing 315–319
hiring: of recruits 54–56; as value-based process 56
hiring practices: early organizational experiences, influence on recruits 60, 66–68; hiring toward the center of the continuum 313–315; hiring toward the policed 311–313; pre-hiring procedures 54–56; value-neutral hiring 54; values-learned-on-the-job perspective 53, 58
Homeland Security through Community Policing (HSCP) 274–275
homicide, police perjury in homicide cases 45
hopeful, role of the receiver 134
hot spot policing 295–296
Human Rights Watch 79
hypothesis 108; defined 107; somatic marker 98

IACP (International Association of Chiefs of Police) 78, 88, 123
"I am the law" perspective 130, 148–149
ignoble consequences 173
illegal searches 5, 11, 61, 64, 126, 130, 180, 220, 227
immigrant: distinctiveness theory 243, 261; dynamism 260; melting pot (metaphor) 261
"implausible performance by an actor" 167

implicit bias 104, 105, 115n3
importance of values 106
importance/usefulness dilemma 321
incivility 243, 267; shared order and 268–269
Independent Commission on the Los Angeles Police Department 79
individual-level corruption 120–122
individual rights 257–258
informal community norms 248–249
informal organization 21, 228, 309
informants 227
inmates, Stanford Prison Experiment 30–33
instrumental values 95, 107–108
intelligence function 287
intelligence-led policing (ILP) 287–288
intentional tort 170
internal accountability mechanisms 80
internal affairs: proactive component to 306–311; units 301, 307
internal ethics 75, 83
internal solution to ethical accountability 83
International Association of Chiefs of Police (IACP) 78, 88, 123
internationalization: of American population 260
international prosecution 282
interrogation, ticking time bomb 277, 278
iron fist tactics 246–258

jealousy and uncertainty, thought experiment 237
job-learned values, screening for 57–59
justice: avenging angel syndrome 222; due process model 175, 183, 184–185; means-ends conflicts 46, 47; police perjury in homicide cases 45; prosecutor 187–190; "rough justice" 16, 41
"just means" 42, 47, 302, 313–315

Kansas City Patrol Experiment 285
Knapp Commission 167–168
knowledge testing 55, 314; cognition 253
Ku Klux Klan Act of 1871 170

latent content analysis 61
Law Enforcement Code of Ethics 66
laws: bending 8, 182; deceptive legal practices 203, 236–238; enforcing narcotics laws 223–225, 230; legitimacy of the legal process 34; means-ends conflicts 46, 47; prosecutor 187–190
lawsuits, police 172
leadership: authoritarian 39; police chiefs 76
leads, sources of 186–187
legal coercion 48, 49
legitimacy 159; of legal process 34; mid-level executives 160–162; operative principles 163–168; organizational accountability 158–168; patrol officers and 162–163; stages of lost 168
lever pulling 291–292
liability: organizational accountability 168–172; police 172
limbic system 97
line officers 91–94, 169; Accountability Dilemma 1 75, 83–85; Accountability Dilemma 2 75, 85–86; behavior 205–206; behavior, controlling 81; boomerang effect 211; code of silence 199–201; layers of street cop culture 203, 205; Pascal's wager 92; quotas 88, 197; solidarity 21, 25, 203, 210–211, 264; uncertainty 87–88; unpredictability and discretionary nature of work 81
linguistic skills, effect on crime solving 312
local agency instructors 191–192
logic of confidence 167
logic of good faith 152, 167, 173, 185, 212., 295
loss of public moral 282
loss of self 282
loyalty: Mama Rosa's test 127–128, 130; peer pressure 121, 131–132; slippery-slope model of noble-cause corruption 129–131
loyalty back-up 130
lying, testilying 145

magic pencil 125–127, 130, 182
Mama Rosa's test 127–128, 130
management cop culture 203, 205, 207
managerial limitations 80–86
managing, noble cause 42–43
manifest content 61, 62
*Mapp* decision 223
matched groups 95, 109
material corruption, stages of 131
material elements of culture 22
material-reward corruption 119, 138–140
maturity 49
mayors, and police chiefs 163
meaning, search for 23

means-ends conflicts 46, 47
means-ends continuum 183–186
means-ends dilemma 40; "The Asshole" 40–41, 221; coercion 49; continuum of value-based decisions 183–186; deontological (means-oriented) ethics 175, 176–177, 183, *183*; "Dirty Harry" problem 43–51; "just means" 42, 47, 302, 313–315; tension between means and ends 46–48
medical model of stress management 151, 155
melting pot (metaphor) 261
middle-ground institutions 256
mid-level executives 160–162
Minnesota Multiphasic Personality Inventory (MMPI) 56
minority-police relationships: social stereotypes 100–102; "somatic net" and police organizational culture 102–103
Mobile Data Terminals (MDT) 218
modeling ethics 303–306; *see also* ethics
*Monell v. Dept. of Social and Health Services of New York* (1978) 152, 170
moral career, stages of corrupt 121
moral decision-making 71
moral environment of value-based decision-making 29
morality: Accountability Dilemma 2 75, 85–86; citizen-centered policing 244; of college education 190–191; and emotions 99–100; loss of public moral 282; noble-cause 71; police morality 41, 49; of the state 15–16; wrong kind of morality 54
moral worlds 273
Mothers Against Drunk Driving (MADD) 159, 161; advocacy groups 16
municipal system 152, 158, 163–164
murder cases, false confessions 233–234
myth of police discretion 68–69

narcotics 121, 142, 223–225, 227; *see also* enforcing narcotics laws
National Commission on Law Observance 79
National Institute of Justice 193, 244, 274, 296
National Opinion Research Center 108
negative concept of police culture 21
negligent tort 152, 170
negotiable issues 164
negotiating order 271, 273
neo-professionalism 284–288, 300n3; community policing 285–286; and higher education 296; intelligence-led policing (ILP) 287–288; problem-oriented policing (POP) 286–287
New York City Police Department (NYCPD) 86
noble cause 25–29; ascendant 279–283; commitment to 42; corroborative research 111–113; "Dirty Harry" problem 43–51; managing 42–43; Pascal's wager 92, 180; Peace Officer Standards and Training (POST) 25, 40; police perjury in homicide cases 45; racial corruption of 103–104; routine actions against citizens 130; slippery-slope model of corruption 129–131; and social psychology of emotions 96–98; and stress 152–154; tension between means and ends 46–48; and victims 26
noble-cause corruption 2, 5–6, 12, 120, 122, 225; avenging angel syndrome 222; crevasse and 213–230; excessive force 46, 221; golden apples 119, 128–129; "I am the law" perspective 130; the magic pencil 125–127, 130, 182; Mama Rosa's test 127–128, 130; material-reward corruption 119, 138–140; slippery-slope model of noble-cause corruption 129–131; Type 2 drug corruption 228
noble-cause violence 221–222
non-cyber crime 288
non-negotiable issues 164
nonverbal behavior 101; *see also* behavior
numerology of authority 198

objectification of police work 198
obstruction of justice 225
occupational socialization 95, 108, 109
Office of Legal Counsel (OLC) 280
Operation Valkyrie 215, 218
operative assumption of guilt 44, 203, 230–236
oral interview 55, 314
order maintenance policing 244, 269–270, 284, 294
order negotiation 271, 273
organization: early organizational experiences, influence on recruits 60, 66–68; informal organization 21, 228, 309
organizational accountability 72; chiefs and legitimacy 159–160;

commanders 160–162; legitimacy and patrol officers 158–159, 160–168; liability issues 168–172; mid-level executives 160–162
organizational stress 154–158
*Our Lawless Police* (Hopkins) 79
oversight: Accountability Dilemma 1 75, 83–85; strategies for protection from external oversight 210

Pascal's wager 92, 180
passion 47
patrol officers: legitimacy and 162–163; organizational accountability 162–168
patterns of corruption 143–147, 227; bogus drug arrests 144; bogus testimony 145; gang members, deportation of 143; violence against suspects 144–145
peacemakers, police as 270–273
Peace Officer Standards and Training (POST) 25, 40, 59, 66, 72, 205, 212, 315
peer pressure 121, 131–132
"The Perfect Storm" 140–147
performance evaluations 321–324
perjury 223–224; police perjury in homicide cases 45; "testilying" 145; wall of silence and 199–200
"perks" 121, 128
perspective 47; "I am the law" 130, 148–149; value-based perspective on hiring 57; value-neutral 56; value-neutral hiring 54; values-learned-on-the-job perspective 53, 58
physical agility testing 55
Pittsburgh Fraternal Order of Police (FOP) 149
platform of IACP 88
plea bargaining 189
plundering 135
police: and accountability procedures 80; authority, limits of 263–265; citizen-centered policing 244; commissions 79; corruption, re-thinking the bases of 125–127; democracy and 11, 261; discretionary behavior 68; emotional predisposition 100; history 285; lawsuits 172; liability 172; militarization 289–290; organizational culture 102–103; as peacemakers 270–273; perjury, in homicide cases 45; perspective 57; practices 250–251; professionalism movement 23, 123–125; stress 154; students, moral predispositions of 192–193; surveillance 92; as value-based decision-makers 91; values 248–249; violence 220–223
police accountability 77, 80; *see also* accountability
police brutality 221; and police commissions 79; *see also* brutality
police chiefs 267; average tenure of 89; citywide policymaker 164; control-oriented chiefs, backfiring effects of 90; emulation 105; International Association of Chiefs of Police 78, 88, 123; leadership 76; limits on the power of 88; maintaining legitimacy 159–160; mayors and 163; organizational accountability 159–160; political needs of 160; scandal cycles 76–78; stress of 156
police-community reciprocity 251
police culture: crevasse and 204–208; negative concept of 21
police departments: accountability mechanisms 80; the gospel of professionalism 119, 123; Independent Commission on the Los Angeles Police Department 79; matched groups 95, 109; as upside-down bureaucracies 87–91
police discretion: myth of 68–69; value-neutral model of 70
Police Executive Research Forum (PERF) 285–286
police officers: bounded rationality 20, 21; complainers 18; controlling 78; crime-control values 187; cultural predispositions 20–21; ending control 199–201; ethical dilemmas faced by 16, 65; getting leads 186–187; golden apples 128–129; police morality 41, 49; police perjury in homicide cases 45; reform and controlling 78; self-responsibility of 18, 255; street-level officers 75, 76, 80, 81; view of culture 22
police paramilitary units (PPUs) 289
police reform 75, 122–125; and controlling police officers 78; and economic corruption 122–125
policies: implications of emotional decision-making 104–105; written policies 81, 86

policing: on behalf of citizens empowering police and policed alike 256–257; communities in conflict 262–267; Community Era of 266–267; defined 316; disorder 264–265; hot spot policing 295–296; intelligence-led policing (ILP) 287–288; problem-oriented policing (POP) 286–287; reducing social distance for citizens 250–252; Reform Era of 266; "sixth sense policing" 22; as state-centered activity 283–284; third-party policing 290–291
policing in transition 258–262
"Politics as a Vocation" 47
polygraph testing 55
POST (Peace Officer Standards and Training) 25, 40, 59, 66, 72, 205, 212, 315
power: coercion 47, 49; and wickedness 47
power of self 49–51, 272, 329
predispose guilt 44
predisposition of guilt, elements of 44
preemployment knowledge testing 314
pre-hiring procedures 54–56; application process 55; background checks 55, 56; knowledge testing 55, 314; oral interview 55; physical agility testing 55; polygraph testing 55; psychological testing 55
prejudice: implicit bias 104, 105, 115n3; social stereotypes 100–102; "somatic net" and police organizational culture 102–103
preoccupation with law 282
presenter, role of the giver 133
preservation of order: and demography 269; role of police in 269–270
pre-service college education of police 315–319
pre-service training 60–68
President's Commission on Civil Rights 79
prison: Abu Ghraib 35–40; British Broadcasting Company (BBC) Prison Study 40–41; Stanford Prison Experiment 29–35, 38
prisoners, death 51n1
probable cause (PC) 63–65
professionalism, police professionalism movement 23, 123–125
progressive movement 122
prosecution, international 282
prosecutor 187–190
prostitution 121, 122
psychological tactics used in, the Stanford Prison Experiment 31
psychological testing 55; *see also* emotions
pulling levers 291–292

qualified immunity 92, 152, 171
quality of life 243, 245–247, 256, 268, 270, 293
questionnaires, Caldero's re-analysis of police values 110
quotas 88, 197

race: racial corruption of the noble cause 103–104; social stereotypes 100–102; "somatic net" and police organizational culture 102–103
racial animus 220
racial profiling 98, 213–220; police practices 250–251; as slippery slope 219
racial stereotyping 250–251
Rampart Corruption Task Force 141
Rampart CRASH unit 119, 130, 140, 141, 142
rational decision-making 95, 97
"rational" notions of behavior 20
reasonable suspicion standard 63
reasoning, role of emotions in 99
reasoning structures of the brain 99
recruits 72; early organizational experiences, influence on recruits 60, 66–68; ethical predisposition of 86; evaluating agency tactical practices 319–321; hiring of 54–56; modeling ethics 303–306; performance evaluations 321–324; pre-hiring procedures 54–56; preparing for ethical decisions 302–324; prioritizing pre-service college education of police 315–319; proactive component to internal affairs 306–311; stages in moral career 121; towards the policed 311–313; toward the center of continuum 313–315; value-based perspective on hiring 57
recruits preparing for ethical decisions 302–324
Red Green 104
reform: economic corruption and police reform 122–125; ethics reform and value-based decision-making 71–73; and values 113–114

Reform Era (1930s–1980s) 266
Regional Operations and Intelligence Center (ROIC) 287
regulative crimes 121
representativeness 112
research: corroborative research 111–113; noble cause, corroborative research 111–113; on police stress 154; Rokeach's values survey 105–109; and service in local agencies 193
responsibility 122, 154–156, 158
retaliation 67–68
"ride-alongs" 82
"Rodney King" beating 93, 102, 104, 164, 171, 304
Rokeach's values survey 105–109; Caldero's re-analysis of police values 109–111
role of the acceptor 134
roles of the giver 120, 135, *136*
role stress 154
"rotten apple" theory 5, 77, 128, 129, 167, 168, 221
"rough justice" 16, 41
routine NC (noble cause) actions against citizens 130
rules: due process 17, 40, 42; informal community norms 248–249; Stanford Prison Experiment 30–31

scandals: and accountability cycles 76–78; and accountability failures 165; Rampart police station 140
"Scared Straight" programs 301, 303
scientific management, management cop culture 205
screening: background checks 55, 56; MMPI 56; oral interview 55; psychological testing 55; value-based perspective on hiring 57; values-learned-on-the-job perspective 57–59
searches, illegal 5, 11, 61, 64, 126, 130, 180, 220, 227
search for meaning 23
secrecy, and culture 211–213
seduction 210
seized property 227
seizures 227
self-responsibility: of police officers 18, 255; power of self 49–51, 272, 329
sensibility 22–23
SERE (survival, evasion, resistance, and escape) 279, 283, 299n1
sergeants 197–198; station-house 175, 197, 198; street 175, 197–198
shared order 262–263; incivility and 268–269
simulation 226
situational uncertainty 209–210
situation ethics, Accountability Dilemma 1 75, 83–85
"sixth sense policing" 22
slave, role of the giver 134
slippery-slope model of economic corruption 120, 122; Mama Rosa's test 127–128, 130
slippery-slope model of noble-cause corruption 129–131
"smell of the victim's blood" 13, 24, 25–27
social distance 250–252
socialization: in CRASH 142–143; grafting subcultures 121, 128; occupational 95, 108, 109; performance evaluation 322–323
social psychology of emotions 96–98
social stereotypes 100–102
"social structural" component of culture 22, 24
solidarity 21, 25, 203, 210–211, 264
somatic markers 72; biasing 100; and emotions 96, 98–99; negative 101; racist 104
"somatic net" 95, 100–104; and police organizational culture 102–103
Special Emphasis Team (SET) 216
stages of material corruption 131
stages of moral career 121
standard operating procedures (SOP) 72
Stanford Prison Experiment 29–35, 38; degradation in 30; group behavior in 38–39; inmates 30–33; psychological tactics used in 31; rules 30–31
the state: expansion of power, impact on community policing 247; morality of 15–16; policing as state-centered activity 283–284
station-house sergeants 175, 197, 198; *see also* sergeants
stealth driving 82
stereotypes 100–102, 115n3; *see also* race
Stinchcomb's model of organizational stress 154–158
stories: Black Swans 62; war stories 315
strangers, "the tower" 27–28
strategies for protection from external oversight 210

street cop culture 203, 205
street culture, layers of 208–211
street environment 208
street-level officers 75, 76, 80, 81
street sergeants 175, 197–198; *see also* sergeants
street skills 61
street sweeps 143, 246, 258
stress: chronic stress 151, 155; episodic stress 151, 155; ignoble consequences 173; medical model of stress management 151, 155; and noble cause 152–154; organizational stress 154–158; research on police stress 154; role stress 154; source of 153; Stinchcomb's model of organizational stress 154–158
success of commissions in controlling police officers behavior 78
surveillance 92
surveys: ABF (American Bar Foundation) survey of 1956 69; Rokeach's values survey 105–109
suspicion 209
suspicion of guilt: "Dirty Harry" problem 43–51; operative assumption of guilt 44, 203, 230–236
"symbolic assailant" 98, 100
system improvement 323

Tacoma survey 112, 113
tactical practices, evaluating 319–321
Taguba Report 37
task environment 87, 161
teaching, local agency instructors 191–192
technology: facilitation of 296–299; forensic labs 193–197
teleological (ends-oriented) ethics 175, 176–177, 178; continuum of value-based decisions 183, *183*; dilemma of ends-oriented ethics 177–182
tension between means and ends 46–48
tenure, of police chiefs 89
terminal values 95, 107–108, 111
terrorism: Abu Ghraib 35–40; ticking time bomb 277, 278; torture memo 277, 280; "War on Terror" 280, 281, 290, 300n2
*Terry v. Ohio* 63
testilying 145
testimonial deception 223–224
testing: knowledge testing 55, 314; MMPI 56; physical agility testing 55; polygraph testing 55; psychological testing 55
third-party policing 290–291
threatened physical coercion 49
ticking time bomb 277, 278
Title 42, Section 1983 152, 169–170
torture memo 277, 280
TOs (training officers) 22, 33, 34, 66–67, 105, 130, 204, 255, 305
"the tower" 27–29
training: ethics instruction 72, 86; Peace Officer Standards and Training (POST) 25, 40, 59, 66, 72, 205, 212, 315; performance evaluations 321–324; up-side ad down-side to ethics education 54
training films 67–68; the magic pencil 125
training officers (TOs) 22, 33, 34, 66–67, 105, 130, 204, 255, 305
transfer function 318
troublemakers: "The Asshole" 40–41; assholes 41, 209, 221, 309
truth: bogus testimony 145; testilying 145
turbulence 210
*Two Cultures of Policing* (Reuss-Ianni) 205
Type 2 drug corruption 228

uncertainty: jealousy and uncertainty thought experiment 237; in police work 87–88; street cop culture 203, 205
unmanned aerial vehicles (UAVs) 296
unpredictability 209–210; Accountability Dilemma 1 75, 83–85; nature of police discretion 68–69; situational uncertainty 209–210
upside-down bureaucracies, police departments as 54, 87–91
up-side to ethics education 54
USA PATRIOT Act 297
U.S. Civil Rights Commission 79
use of force: excessive force 46, 221
utilitarianism 176

value-based decision-making 17–21, 177; "The Asshole" 40–41, 221; culture and 24; "Dirty Harry" problem 43–51; and limits of ethics reform 71–73; means-ends dilemma 40; moral environment of 29; noble cause 25–29, 41–43; Pascal's wager 92; police officers as cultural carriers 21–23; police perjury in homicide

cases 45; power of self 49–51, 272, 329; "smell of the victim's blood" 25–27; Stanford Prison Experiment 29–35; tension between means and ends 46–48; "the tower" 27–29; values and culture 20–21
value-based perspective on hiring 57
value-neutral: hiring 54; model of police discretion 70
value-predisposition perspective 58
values: Caldero's re-analysis of police values 109–111; of college experience 316; culture and 20–21; defined 106; and discretion 70–71; instrumental values 95, 107–108; noble cause, corroborative research 111–113; and pre-service training 60–68; probable cause (PC) and 63–65; and reform 113–114; Rokeach's values survey 105–109; "smell of the victim's blood" 25–27; stability of 110; terminal values 95, 107–108; training officers (TOs) 65–66
values-learned-on-the-job perspective 53, 58
value systems 70, 85, 95, 98, 107, 110, 112, 205
value transmission 53, 59
velvet glove 240, 243, 246–258
ventromedial prefrontal cortex 99
victimless crime 226
victims 25–26; concern for 302; and noble cause 26; "smell of the victim's blood" 13, 24, 25–27
view of culture, dependence on standpoint 22
violence: code of silence 199–201; excessive force 46, 221; means-end dilemma 46–48; noble-cause 221–222; physical coercion 49; police 220–223; "Rodney King" beating 93, 102, 104, 164, 171, 304; rotten apple theory 5, 77, 128, 129, 167, 168, 221; "smell of the victim's blood" 13, 24, 25–27; against suspects 144–145
Vollmerian vision of police work 124
voluntarily offering/giving 135

wall of silence 199–200
war against drugs 216, 218
"war on crime" mentality 70, 290
"War on Terror" ascendancy of noble cause 280, 281, 290, 300n2
warping effect 211
war stories 315; Black Swans 62
war theory of crime control 62, 79
well-being: quality of life 243, 245–247, 256, 268, 270, 293; research on police stress 154
whistleblowers 67–68
wickedness 47, 135
Wickersham Commission 78, 79
worst of all possible guilt 44
written policies 81, 86
wrong kind of morality 54

zero-tolerance approach 257, 293–294, 296, 300n6

For Product Safety Concerns and Information please contact our EU representative GPSR@taylorandfrancis.com Taylor & Francis Verlag GmbH, Kaufingerstraße 24, 80331 München, Germany